Managing the]

The reflection on university management is based on the question about the shape of universities of the future. Civic, responsible, sustainable, virtual, digital, and many other universities can be mentioned among the concepts present in the literature. All these names describe an important distinctive feature of a university, which will gain more and more importance in the future. However, given the fundamental importance of the radical change taking place, it seems that the most appropriate name, reflecting the essence of the emerging new formation, is "digital university." This is because of the importance of digital transformation, which has been developing for several decades, bringing deep and multidirectional changes in the areas of technology, economy, society, and culture. It is a disruptive civilizational transition and, although stretched over many decades, it is revolutionary in nature, significantly changing our lives in the Anthropocene.

The book has three cognitive and pragmatic objectives: to provide a new perspective on the changing academic organization and management; to reflect on higher education management concepts and methods; and to present an overview of university management, governance, and leadership, useful from the perspective of academic managers, and other stakeholders.

Lukasz Sulkowski is a Professor of Economics and Humanities and the Chair of HEI's Management Department of the Jagiellonian University, Poland. He serves as the President of PCG Polska Ltd. and the Vice-Rector of Academy WSB in Dabrowa Gornicza, Poland.

Routledge Studies in Organizational Change & Development

Series Editor: Bernard Burnes

For more information about this series, please visit: https://www.routledge.com/ Routledge-Studies-in-Organizational-Change--Development/book-series/SE0690

Managing the Digital University

Paradigms, Leadership, and Organization

Lukasz Sulkowski

Routledge
Taylor & Francis Group

NEW YORK AND LONDON

First published 2023
by Routledge
605 Third Avenue, New York, NY 10158

and by Routledge
4 Park Square, Milton Park, Abingdon, Oxon, OX14 4RN

Routledge is an imprint of the Taylor & Francis Group, an informa business

Library of Congress Cataloguing-in-Publication Data
Names: Sulkowski, Lukasz, 1972- author.
Title: Managing the digital university : paradigms, leadership, and organization / Lukasz Sulkowski.
Description: New York : Routledge, 2023. | Series: Routledge studies in organizational change & development | Includes bibliographical references and index.
Identifiers: LCCN 2022055580 | ISBN 9781032432472 (hardback) | ISBN 9781032432519 (paperback) | ISBN 9781003366409 (ebook)
Subjects: LCSH: Universities and colleges--Management. | Educational change. | Internet in higher education. | Distance education.
Classification: LCC LB2324 .S85 2023 | DDC 378.1--dc23/eng/ 20230203
LC record available at https://lccn.loc.gov/2022055580

ISBN: 978-1-032-43247-2 (hbk)
ISBN: 978-1-032-43251-9 (pbk)
ISBN: 978-1-003-36640-9 (ebk)

DOI: 10.4324/9781003366409

Typeset in Bembo
by MPS Limited, Dehradun

Dedicated to My Dearest

Contents

Figure

Tables

Introduction

The reflection on university management is based on the question about the shape of universities in the future. Civic, responsible, sustainable, virtual, digital, and many other universities can be mentioned among the concepts present in the literature. All these names describe an essential distinctive feature of a university, which will probably gain more and more meaning in the future. However, given the fundamental importance of radical change, the most appropriate name, reflecting the essence of the emerging new formation, is "digital university." The latter term emphasizes the importance of digital transformation, which has been developing for several decades, bringing significant and multidirectional changes in the areas of technology, economy, society, and culture. It is a disruptive civilizational transition and, although stretched over many decades, is revolutionary, changing human lives in the Anthropocene (Bond et al., 2018; Grosseck et al., 2020).

Academic management is a complex area of organizational activity in which different interpretations of how universities function intersect. This diversity of perspectives is due to many factors. Although changing dynamically in recent decades, universities are organizations with centuries of tradition, a strong identity, and professional ethos. Along with social and cultural transformations, the mission of universities is evolving, leading to a diversification of higher education institutions (HEIs), which, although referring to the same root of values, take very different organizational forms. These are reflected in the management of HEIs at all levels, from strategy and mission to functional areas and operational activities. Therefore, the question of whether we can observe any universal transformational trends in academic management arises.

Management in universities sails between the Scylla of academic freedom and creativity and the Charybdis of executive power and control. Freedom and creativity are inscribed in the implementation of all three missions of universities. Science is a collective cognitive endeavor based on creativity and leads to discovering unknown areas. Over the centuries, universities have established themselves as centers of thought that broaden the horizons of humanity. Creativity has become an imperative for research activities

DOI: 10.4324/9781003366409-1

based on curiosity about the world and the quest to understand reality. Scholarly activity, especially in the social sciences, is also creativity in the performative sense, shaping a better world. The Enlightenment archetype of the researcher refers to creating originality and striving to use reason to know and improve the world and people. The scholar is a figure inseparable from Western civilization and the formation of medieval universities and later Humboldtian universities. Today, the diversification of post-Humboldtian university models and the entrepreneurial university leads to questioning this utopian value of creative science. Depending on their mission, universities tend to be "quasi-businesses" oriented towards economic goals or could focus exclusively on teaching. Freedom and creativity also play a fundamental role in the education of students. The classical educational mission, appealing to intellectual liberty reflexivity and the courage to explore and change the world for the better, was realized through master–student relationships. The second half of the 20th century brought the massification of education at the higher level, which lost its role of shaping intellectual elites and focused more on imparting packages of professional competencies needed in the labor market. However, in the axiological sphere, academic culture and university employees still orientate toward freedom of learning and creativity as part of the academic ethos. The essence of management is the exercise of managerial power and control. Of course, this does not exclude freedom and creativity but shifts the most important value from the creative endeavor to organizational activity. Mainstream management offers us a reified vision of reality. According to classic, essential managerial functions, we can shape reality to achieve organizational goals by planning, coordinating work, directing, and controlling. Administrative control over the organization is supposed to be the result of the development of management as a science and, above all, of its application in practice. In such a neo-positivist ideal, the manager implements science's proven achievements according to his competencies in a specific organizational context. He uses the power of science for instrumental purposes of practice, which is both a craft and an art. It is worth looking at the characteristics of academic management, a hybrid of the Humboldtian organization's tradition with contemporary management knowledge and practice.

The belief in the academy's mission, combining learning with teaching and serving the environment, is the core of the identity of the university and the academic staff. Still, at the same time, it is changing radically with the transformations of the modern world. The shift toward managerial power was the driving force behind the transformation of the entrepreneurial university. The transition toward networking and computerization is driving the revolution toward the next level formation of the digital university.

The year 2088 will mark the millennium of the founding of the first European university. The pioneering HEI, the University of Bologna, still exists and, since 1999, has been a symbol of the integration of the European area of higher education. The millennial tradition and the spread of this type of entity worldwide is a cultural phenomenon not found in other sectors. Today, more than 20,000 HEIs worldwide are dedicated to teaching students and conducting research (World List of Universities, 2006). The vision of expanding university formation in the 21st century has lost its explicitness. Researchers agree that HEIs are currently experiencing pressures of change, some of which are in crisis. Classical models of university functioning are being questioned. By analyzing the organization of universities and the pace of cultural and technological change, Peter Drucker predicted the twilight of universities by 2030 (Drucker, 1997). Although two decades have passed since this statement, we do not notice that universities are disappearing. Instead, the opposite is true—universities are growing but becoming more diverse. Therefore, we can say that there is an increase in differentiation between universities. We also deal with profound changes in universities' strategies, structures, and organizational cultures. I have devoted this book to the transformation of management processes of modern universities. Therefore, universities' diversity is nothing new in the higher education sector. However, the scale and depth of this diversification have increased since the end of the 20th century.

The monograph has cognitive and pragmatic objectives. First of all, it is intended to provide a new perspective on the changing academic organization and management, which will take into account the latest directions of transformation, also resulting from the formation of the digital university, catalyzed by the effects of the Covid-19 pandemic. The perspective here uses the counterpoint between the values rooted in academic tradition and the rapidly changing competitive challenges of the current market. The pragmatic objective is an overview of university management concepts that can be useful from the perspective of academic leaders and managers, as well as other stakeholders in the academic world.

The monograph consists of 5 parts and 14 chapters focusing on university management issues. The first part deals with the transition of contemporary universities toward digital HEIs. The integrated management model presented in the second part combines the university's governance, management, and leadership. The third part analyses the university's organizational system, seen universally as interdependent subsystems: strategy, structure, and organizational culture. The fourth part of the monograph describes the management of aspects of HEIs that are specific only to universities. This view concerns the management of the three streams of academic missions. The fifth management perspective focuses on the selected functional areas of the university organization, i.e., human capital, marketing, and finance management. The monograph closes with conclusions, each of which relates to the book's chapters (Sulkowski, 2022a; Lenart-Gansiniec and Sulkowski 2022b).

Part I

Past, Present, and Future of Academia

1 Ideals of universities

1.1 The essence of the university

Universities are understood as organizations that share many distinctive features. They are distinguished by their mission, structure, management mode, and academic culture. From the point of view of continuity and variability, they are stable and conservative organizations that have functioned for centuries. The medieval roots of universities have given these entities an identity that is transformed but continues to this day. Universities, being intentional social groups founded to explore knowledge and education, share some common characteristics:

- Are subordinated to the development of science and education, which are inextricably linked;
- Confer academic or professional degrees at a higher level;
- They use the Latin rooted name university, which means a whole, a community of teachers and students;
- Have a significant degree of autonomy, giving them a certain freedom of action.

Universities are long-lived organizations. If we analyze the list of the world's 100 leading universities 100 years ago and today, we can see changes in the list. Still, compared to the list of the top 100 companies, there are fewer changes in the ranking of the leading universities. On the other hand, however, the academic world was transformed after World War II. The massification of higher education, the rapid advancement of science and technology, globalization, and the wave of new private and public universities around the world are just a few factors that have influenced the development of universities in the second half of the 20th century. When reflecting on the management of universities, it is necessary to consider such dynamic change with a discontinuous form. Universities are changing in many directions, which makes it difficult to indicate the formation of a new, uniform type of organization. However, this was also the case in the past. Medieval universities were founded in different ways,

DOI: 10.4324/9781003366409-3

some by student guilds, such as the University of Bologna, others by monarchs, such as the Jagiellonian University, and still others by city guilds, such as the University of Cologne or others like Yale, Harvard, Princeton, Rutgers by different churches. They differed in their organization methods, type of governance, and management. It seems, however, that despite the significant differences, it is worth treating contemporary and historical formations of universities as ideal types to be analyzed from the point of view of organization and management. This "Procrustean bed" of organizational theory, constructed to understand the differences between various types of universities, despite the simplified way of describing them, will allow differentiating the methods of managing higher education institutions (HEIs).

An organizational discourse perspective, superimposed on university development, is needed from both a cognitive and a pragmatic point of view. The reflection on university management seems to be scattered. Depending on the type of HEI, different concepts need to be drawn upon. We take a different kind of consideration when studying public universities and another when studying private universities. We separate education management from science management, focusing on various missions. We distinguish multiple levels of reflection on the academic world, seeing the diversity of academic disciplines, national systems, types of universities, and relationships with the state, the market, and internal and external stakeholders. However, it seems worthwhile to create a general taxonomy of universities based on chronology to integrate concepts of organization and management. It will make it possible to distinguish universities of four waves (generations, formations, models), in which the organization, and thus the way of management, differ significantly (Wissema, 2009). The first historical wave of medieval universities, until the Enlightenment, is a very diverse set whose distinguishing feature—from the point of view of management—is, besides the community of mission, the lack of scientific reflection on the organization (Pedersen, 1997). The second wave, associated with the Humboldt-type university, is the 19th and 20th centuries. It is a model of the classical, traditional public university, in which the way of governance, management, and leadership was designed using philosophical reflection and historical experience (Anderson, 2020). The Humboldt formation university, like the other models, is an ideal type; within this group of HEI, the differences are significant. It is enough to mention the differences between countries and the Napoleonic university under state control or John Henry Newman's design of the American university in the middle of the 19th century (Newman, 2008). The second-wave university is firmly rooted in mentality, ethos, and academic culture. It has its distinctive features, related, for example, to collegiality and high autonomy, which also significantly influence, the idea of contemporary university management. In the 1980s, another form of the post-Humboldt university developed, called by Burton Clark the "entrepreneurial university" (Clark, 1998a). This university model results from changes in the environment and within the organization, into which management science's theoretical and practical discourse has been integrated. Just as first- and second-wave universities developed driven by academic values, ethos, and culture, third-wave universities are the fruit of reflections, experiences, and projects drawn from management. The question about the universities of the future remains open. We know they are very diverse because stratification and diversification of universities have been essential and ongoing trends for more than half a century. Among descriptions of new models, some refer to academic histories, such as civic university (Barnett, 2007; Goddard, Kempt, and Vallance, 2012), and some that transfer from the world of business: sustainable (Velazquez et al., 2006), responsible (Sørensen et al., 2019, p. 318), intelligent, smart (Berdnikova et al., 2020) and others referring to changes in the modern world: postmodern (Scott, 2006), virtual (Ryan et al., 2013), polymorphic, or fractal university (Bodunkova and Chernaya, 2012). Answering the question of what kind of university formation is emerging nowadays—I think it will be a digital university. I assume here the broadest understanding of this adjective, referring to the word *digitalization* and not the narrower *digitization*. We live in an era of digital transformation, which is the most important trend of change in the 21st century (Bloomberg, 2018). Digital, information and communication technologies (ICT), and networking have been evolving and radically changing social life, culture, and the economy for at least three decades. Digital universities are a model representation of fourth-wave universities.

University management is an area of organizational theory and practice that applies the more universal concepts of business management and public management to the field of academic institutions. It is also a specialized scientific discourse that seeks to develop specific theoretical concepts appropriate to academic organizations. Understanding the essence of university management requires deeper reflection and readiness to accept ambiguities and even organizational paradoxes (Alexander and Manolchev, 2020). The practice of university management, in turn, requires principals to combine managerial skills with the competencies of a scientist, teacher, and diplomat. When reflecting on university management, one should avoid the illusion of uniformity of models and continuity of transformation. Universities have always been diverse. Even in the Middle Ages, many founding patterns, complex relationships with church and monarchy, and modes of governance coexisted. The university understood as a *studium general,* differs from the college model of the medieval scholastic guilds (de Ridder-Symoens and Rüegg, 2003). National higher education systems have always varied considerably, especially regarding the level of autonomy of universities. Similarly, the issue of continuity of change is ambiguous. Universities have evolved in different directions throughout history, depending on their founding structure, mission, resources, and specialization. Therefore, the division into four waves of universities presented here has the character of a simplification, serving the analysis of the organization and management of the university.

1.2 First-wave universities from a management perspective

First-wave universities were established from the Middle Ages until the end of the Enlightenment. They were founded in various ways: by kings, popes, city guilds, and communities of teachers and students or churches. Reformed many times over the centuries, they persisted in their mission to educate the elite, with bachelors, within a collectively organized community (Cobban, 1989). An attempt to look at first- and second-wave universities from the perspective management discourse should consider the fact that scholarly reflection on the subject was lacking until the 20th century, which of course, does not mean that universities did not have their management and government. They had specific institutional characteristics, but universities were created, organized, and managed based on traditional, intuitively understood patterns. There were no management theories or experiences of business or public organizations to refer to. Conventional types of organization, rooted in culture: church schools, city guilds, scholastic guilds, became models for universities, which often received privileges from rulers: settlement, internal jurisdiction, cession and migration, tax exemption, autonomy, and the ability to issue degrees. The motivator for the establishment of universities, but also their activation, and the introduction of reforms to reorganize their work, were the development of markets and trade in university towns (Cantoni and Yuchtman, 2014), the relationship of many universities with the church, or with secular authority, the formation of scientific discourses and disciplines and curricula (Zhu, Jing, and Tang, 2010). The relationship of universities with the government evolved in the Middle Ages from dependence on the church towards autonomy and secularization in the Renaissance until the Enlightenment (Tian and Xiang, 2008). In France, reforms tended toward centralism and state control, and in Germany and Britain, towards the stable rule of an academic oligarchy. The power exercised in the university in the Middle Ages often resembled the model of the academic guild. It later transformed and diversified, taking different forms depending on the country and the university. The governance model varied greatly from university to university and country to country and evolved. The University of Bologna was under the control of the student guild from its inception, while the University of Paris was governed by academicians (Cardozier, 1968). The universities also differed in the dominant education profile regarding how they were managed and financed. For example, the University of Paris was dominated by theology, while the University of Bologna had much stronger practical faculties: law and medicine. The dominant disciplinary discourse in a first-wave university thus depended on the university; it could be theology, law, grammar, and rhetoric (trivium and quadrivium derived from roman and medieval education) (Proctor, 2021).

Medieval universities were characterized by a traditional, petrified organizational structure, with rigidly assigned academic roles. They were some of medieval Europe's most structured and specialized legal entities. They had at their disposal not only people capable of imparting and creating knowledge but also material, financial, and intellectual resources to fulfill their mission. The universities had lecture theaters, offices, libraries, dormitories, and archives, which management posed a challenge, forcing the universities to improve an organization culturally biased toward conservatism. The university organization was hierarchical and developed its academic patterns, it was characterized by a high degree of stability, and change took place through university reformation or gradual, spontaneous evolution. The strength mentioned above became part of the academic ethos over time, and the solutions developed were incorporated into the organizational identity of the universities. The basic organizational structure of the university, including faculties, schools, institutes, departments, and libraries, as well as functions, for example, rectors, and deans, dates back to the Middle Ages (Pan and Yang, 2009). People in the institution held positions that became part of the academic tradition and culture that gave these organizations a strong distinctiveness, reflected in high social prestige and professorial ethos. Governance was minimalist and was mainly regulated by tradition and culture, standard modes of organizational behavior. Supervision of universities in the Middle Ages was limited due to the privileges of autonomy they enjoyed. The Catholic Church and monarchs had some influence on their functioning through authority. In the Renaissance—until the Enlightenment—state governance of many universities somewhat increased with the development of the model of regional and then state and national universities.

First-wave universities differed in the funding of studies and the universities' activities. Historically, the first type of financing of studies was the model of paying and employing academic staff by students. This solution was the first to appear at the University of Bologna. The University of Paris was the first to adopt this financial model, with teachers being paid by the Catholic Church. In Great Britain, on the other hand, both universities, Oxford and Cambridge, were funded by the British Monarchy and the state (Gieysztor, 1992).

Universities enjoyed a relatively high degree of autonomy in various European countries, which was associated with the idea of academic freedom and self-government (Courtenay, 1989). They were also institutions with considerable academic freedom compared to all other medieval organizations. Some limits to intellectual autonomy were only provided by a hierarchical and petrified culture, limiting the non-conformism and creativity of researchers and students.

More pronounced changes in the organization of the medieval university took place during the Renaissance and Enlightenment periods. On the one hand, many universities ceased to be pan-European and internationalized, moving towards state concentration. On the other hand, they acquired a secularizing dimension in parts, often standing in opposition to the Catholic

Church (Guoqing, 2003). This was also linked to the diminishing importance of theology.

1.3 Second-wave universities—Humboltian type of organization

Second-wave universities are a formation that emerged as a result of the reform of academic institutions in Germany in the early 19th century. The model university became the University of Berlin, designed by Wilhelm von Humboldt, using the ideas of Friedrich Schleiermacher, German idealists, and Enlightenment thinkers. Second-wave universities are a broad and capacious category under which it places not only the Humboldtian university but also academic institutions designed by John Henry Newman in the United States, French universities after the Napoleonic reform, and many British universities (Schimank and Winnes, 2000; Shin, 2014). The University of Berlin, which opened in 1810 according to the design of Humboldt, Schleiermacher, and Fichte, can be considered the beginning of this academic formation (Anderson, 2020), while the transition to the final phase of the "post-Humboldtian university" would take place in the first half of the 20th century.

The university combined the thought of the German idealists with the values propagated in the Enlightenment. Humboldt's university was supposed to play a culture-forming role (Rothblatt and Wittrock, 1993) and shape national identity, which could be called inclusive and connected with the universal ideals of science. The university became a public institution whose mission was to unite the state around values rooted in history and tradition and to improve spirit and wisdom through philosophy and science (Anderson, 2020).

The Humboldtian university represents an ideal type through which we can trace the origins of the norms of current institutions with an educational function. The level of generalization and simplification does not allow for the diversification of university cultures caused of different founding values, cultural contexts, and the differentiation of institutions with the historical process. This model of the university, based on the concept of *Bildung* (perceived as culture and education), drew from the assumptions of the German idealists, Fichte, Schleiermacher, and Kant. *Bildung* is the refinement, the training of the spirit through philosophy and science to develop culture (Sorkin, 1983), which is the foundation of the Humboldt-type university and means "education through science." Its mission was brilliantly encapsulated in the maxim about the "unity of science" (Nordenbo, 2002). In the Anglo-Saxon cultural circle, on the other hand, the idea of the *cultural university*, developed by John Henry Newman, prevailed, reaching back to the liberal philosophy of the 18th century—the reflections of Hume, Lock, and Smith (Mlinar, 2013). Analyzing universities in different countries allows us to point out many differences. Guri-Rosenblit lists several types of national universities—French, German, English, or Scottish. Nineteenth-century North American universities were also different from the Humboldt type. Humboldt University emphasized research and the critical education of students, but it also belonged to a stable, hierarchical structure (Guri-Rosenblit, 2006). The hieratic nature of the system, linked to the differentiation between professorial and junior staff positions, is a feature of the Humboldtian model and its Napoleonic variant (Enders, 2006, p. 13).

This model is a cultural and ethos concept. The basic assumptions of the university include the values: the freedom of science, the autonomy of the university and the scientist, the community of students and professors, the culture-forming, and the national function of the university. Norms, cultural patterns, ideals of the university, and social institutions are derivatives of this axiology. The primacy of values is rooted in German idealism, focused on community spirit and its improvement through the historical process (Habermas and Blazek, 1987). The second-wave university is elitist and elite-forming. The academic culture and ethos are based on a community of masters and students improving themselves, educating themselves, and working together to develop science, culture, and society. This university elite exercises power over the autonomous academic community through a decentralized, collective decision-making system governed by the ethos and cultural norms. The academic identity of the university is very much linked to the ethos and identification of professors with the university, who constitute the academic oligarchy and hold power, reminiscent of the "republic of scholars" model, reminiscent of Plato's utopian *Republic* power structures (Gare, 2005). The dominant disciplinary discourse in the Humboldtian university related to the core idea of *Bildung*, where philosophy and the humanities, to the greatest extent, served to improve spirit and culture. The university's strategic goals were not explicitly formulated, but only the directions of improvement were outlined: Education linked to science and human and cultural development. Conceptually, the Humboldtian university had a complete character, meaning the representation of all major disciplines in one university. This is precisely due to the assumption of the unity of science and education. In the organizational structure, this translates into faculties representing areas of study or disciplines. The faculties are headed by deans who, like those managing the entire university, must have strong legitimacy to exercise the authority given by the academic community. This translates into the importance of collective bodies deciding, or at least co-determining, elections to leadership positions. Paradoxically, the organization of the university is loose and decentralized yet hierarchical and petrified. The traditional, very stable, and inflexible organizational structure reflects the regulation of management processes by the norms of academic culture. The structure is decentralized, as the burden of achieving the mission was entirely shifted to the level of faculties, institutes, and departments.

Research and education were conducted there, and most organizational decisions are made there. The university's identity tends towards a "federation of faculties," integrated by the imagined community of the university as a whole. Consequently, academic staff, whether engaged in core activities or holding positions, operate according to traditional divisions of roles and responsibilities. Nor was the exercise of functions generally the only, or often even the primary, occupation of staff elected as rectors or deans. The level of managerial specialization has proved to be low, as operational staff remain researchers and academics. This solution is far from the contemporary trend toward professionalization and administration specialization (Pechar, 2012). Governance has also become minimalist and limited by design, leaving much room for academic autonomy and freedom. First of all, the academic staff, but to some extent also the students, had the possibility of self-determination. The administration of the university was minimized and directed by academic functionaries. Central funds entirely financed the university's activities and the student's education. At the same time, the state had virtually no oversight over the university, funding its activities because of the development of science and its culture-forming and nation-forming role. The freedom of science and the university's autonomy was the guarantee of mission. The form of supervision was constituted by academic culture and ethos, creating conditions for the university community's control and the staff's self-control.

1.4 Post-Humboldt universities

In the mid-20th century, the previously dominant Humboldt-type university formation shifted toward other models that can be collectively described as post-Humboldtian (Chiang, 2012; Davis, 2018). There were several reasons for the erosion of the traditional university model. The most important ones include the massification and egalitarianism of higher education, the development of private HEIs, the growth of competition in higher education, the development of specialized universities, and the moving away from the model of the comprehensive university. For these reasons, we can add others that became visible in the following decades. First of all, the process of commercialization of educational activity progressed, and combined with the marketization of education, the importance of the third mission increased. Additionally, since the 1970s, the pressure to reduce unit costs of education grew, which was accompanied by successive reforms and changes in public policies in many countries (Nybom, 2012). Differentiating HEIs according to the following axes: Type of founder, mission, specialization, scale, and range of activities has become a permanent trend. Private universities, especially those recently created from the private, for-profit sector, have proven to be one of the fastest growing groups of HEIs. In contrast, public universities have come under pressure to restructure and cut costs (Davis, 2018). These transformations have been influenced by cultural, economic, and social changes in the modern world. The most important include demographic pressure and increasing competition in the education sector. The processes of acquiring knowledge, learning, improving, and conducting research are being modified. This implies the need to develop effective university management solutions.

The traditional form of the university is losing its importance and is being pushed out of the market (Pechar, 2012; Kobylarek, 2017). The state is increasingly abandoning funding for universities, which are becoming bureaucratized, learning is becoming more commercialized, and access to higher education is increasing, thanks to the rise of competitive institutions (Kiuppis and Waldow, 2008; Mehralizadeh, 2005). Public schools are increasingly facing funding problems rooted in the difficulty of reducing university operating costs, but there are also external causes. Since the 1980s, the welfare state model has no longer prevailed in many countries, and there has been a move to minimize the tax-funded cost of education (Hardy, 1988; de Pillis and de Pillis, 2001). Added to this is the increasing popularity of private universities, which also boast research success stories. We see this in the United States, with a group of "ivy league" universities, but also in many other places. In some developing countries, we can even speak of the dominance of non-public universities linked to the universality of higher education and the growing demand for educational services. Political and legislative decisions also contribute to the privatization of teaching. In many developing countries, education develops thanks to private sources of financing (Tilak, 2008a). The fastest growing privatization occurs in South America, the Middle East, Asia, Africa, and Central and Eastern Europe. New universities are also being established, which offer studies in specializations allowing for profitable education (Sagalyn, 2007; Altbach, 1999). Rankings of scientific achievements prove that these universities usually educate, but are less interested in conducting scientific research, so the classic university is being replaced by institutions responding to the needs of the labor market. This model does not seek to combine teaching and research work; it only focuses on education. Moreover, research activity is not currently limited to universities. Other entities can also offer commercial research, which is in demand in industry and economics. New private universities operating on a for-profit model have developed a third mission involving cooperation with business and teaching for the labor market. This trend, also present in public universities, has already existed for half a century (Nedeva, 2008). The universities themselves have also transformed—now, they are often bureaucratic institutions oriented toward educating specialists, and only some of them focus on research activities (Maassen and Stensaker, 2019). Universities' management, organizational culture, structure, and supervision are taking over many corporate solutions (Elliott, 2012; Czarniawska and Mazza, 2013; Zaitseva and Zapariy, 2016; Ramírez and Tejada, 2018).

The marketization of HEIs, budget problems, and privatization—are just some of the reasons for abandoning the academic oligarchy model. As the

Bologna Process develops, European Union universities focus on students, and motivation and control systems are being strengthened in areas of the quality of teaching, third mission, and accountability of research activity (Smagorinsky et al., 2004; Lim, 2018).

The area of university governance has not escaped change either. Universities are established not only by the state and private founders but also by third-sector entities, associations, and churches. The drive for ever-greater efficiency has reduced the freedom of staff and universities. Humboldtian academic autonomy, entailing research freedom and lack of government interference, is being eroded, and universities are subject to external accreditation and certification (Niemelä et al., 2014). "Professorial democracy" or "academic oligarchy," where a collegial body composed of faculty members, with a dominance of senior staff, elects academic leaders for a term of office, is being replaced by a "managerial-founder" model of university governance, characteristic of American universities. In this model, the founding body, supplemented by a collegial body (e.g., *board of trustees*), composed mainly of external stakeholders, elects the president. State universities still often use the collegiate model, while private universities more often resort to the managerial model (Meyer, 2007; Sahlin and Eriksson-Zetterquist, 2016), which may soon become the dominant type. The need to strengthen the competitiveness of universities also influences the transformation of their mission toward alignment with the labor market.

Thus, the progressive changes in contemporary university management can be described by three trends: shared management, corporate and entrepreneurial approach, and flexible and learning architecture (Sporn, 2007, p. 149). The concept of *Universitas* is sometimes displaced by market orientation, an attempt to meet the demand for educational services. Also, developing a knowledge-oriented economy has resulted in higher enrollment levels in societies. The elite teaching of intellectuals has given way to specialized education, subordinated to market mechanisms, with technical, economic, and non-public universities leading the way. The public in the 1980s began to be seen as bureaucratic and inefficient, leading to radical changes in academic governance in many countries. These reforms are sometimes stigmatized as creating a formation of the neoliberal university, which seems an overly capacious, imprecise, and ideologically charged term (Davies, Gottsche, and Bansel, 2006; Ball, 2015). Therefore, among the many names of the post-Humboldtian university, the most appropriate term for the formation that emerged in the second half of the 20th century seems to be "entrepreneurial university."

1.5 Third-wave universities organization—
Entrepreneurial challenge

"Entrepreneurial universities" are very diverse, depending on the type, specialization, mission, country of origin, and kind of founder, but they share several common characteristics, as described by Burton Clark. "Entrepreneurial HEI" is founded on the following assumptions: (1) Strengthening the steering center, (2) developing peripheral segments, (3) diversifying funding sources, (4) stimulating the academic core, and (5) creating an entrepreneurial culture (Clark, 1983, 1998b).

Among the distinguishing features of an entrepreneurial HEI, such as new governance, market strategy, and flexible structure, an entrepreneurial culture is markedly different from the traditional academic culture of the second-wave university. Shattock defines "academic entrepreneurship" as "the drive to identify and sustain a distinctive institutional agenda that is defined by the institution itself, rather than being a product of a state funding formula" (Shattock and Temple, 2006). Entrepreneurial universities are described based on the concepts of entrepreneurship, proactivity, adaptability, and competitiveness and are described as organizations: learning, intelligent, and knowledge-oriented (Sporn, 2001). This terminology refers to management science, which shows that organization and management have become the dominant disciplinary discourse for entrepreneurial universities. Management language, concepts, and methods have disseminated in thinking about the university's functioning, displacing the humanistic and philosophical discourse characteristic of the Humboldtian university (Arroyabe, Schumann, and Arranz, 2022). In the literature, there are also other, less popular terms for the "entrepreneurial HEI," for example, in the form of the "third-generation university" (Wissema, 2009).

Entrepreneurial universities should become technology hubs and focus on interacting with the technology environment, creating a commercial research base, enabling the transfer of research results to the business sector, and connecting the business and academic worlds based on the following:

- Stakeholder cooperation (Etzkowitz, 2003);
- Promoting an entrepreneurial culture (Kirby, Guerrero, and Urbano, 2011);
- Reward system for employees conducting commercial research (so-called knowledge commercialization) (Goldstein, 2010);
- Business-oriented university structure and adaptive strategies (Mainardes, Alves, and Raposo, 2011; Etzkowitz, 2003).

Strategic diversification and polarization in university management involve fundamental changes in universities, including increasing specialization. Research universities strive to develop science at an increasingly high, world-class level. Scientometric indicators and international rankings used to measure scientific output (such as the ARWU or THE rankings) encourage universities to hire researchers with the best productivity and promote the best disciplines (Luque-Martínez and Faraoni, 2020) and diversify their missions. Universities often turn to scholarly specialization as a kind of diversification strategy in response to the suggested public policy shift towards rewarding the university's scientific excellence. As a result, the brightest scientists apply to the most prominent research universities that compete in the global marketplace. Another type of university diversification is teaching and research specialization, seeking a balance between science and education. Some universities choose to focus on education or teaching combined with the development of a third mission. In turn, the polarization of the university is associated with a more profound stratification of internal stakeholder groups. The increasing tendency of a division into intermediated elite schools will be visible in differences in reputation, the value of degrees and jobs, and the so-called "economics of prestige" of scientific activity (Blackmore and Kandiko, 2011). The orientation of economies towards knowledge and entrepreneurship affects the higher education system and the role played by universities.

Third-wave universities focus on academic entrepreneurship, effective management, competitiveness, cooperation with the environment, inno-vation, and an integrated entrepreneurial culture (Zaharia and Gibert, 2005). Entrepreneurial universities are organizations: egalitarian, flexible, and dynamic, where power is exercised in a mixed model: managerial and collective. This involves taking advantage of external opportunities and managing change to adapt to the environment. In other words, HEIs are seen as dynamic and flexible organizations, in contrast to the static vision of first- and second-wave universities (Bratianu and Stanciu, 2010). The mission differentiates according to the specialization of the HEI. It may move towards emphasizing one aspect of the mission or even deeper spe-cialization and abandoning the development of a particular stream, for example, research in a teaching university. The exercise of power is based on a hybrid solution, combining a collective (participatory) and a mana-gerial model, with the latter still dominating in private universities (Bratianu and Stanciu, 2010). Universities usually develop formal strategies, at least in the form of mission and strategic objectives. Some organizations develop a basic strategic management process, while others remain open, evolu-tionary, entrepreneurial, and emergent strategies (Buckland, 2009). They emerge and are developed in the organizational processes of the university and take the non-formalized form of spontaneously emerging ideas, pro-jections, and visions for business improvement. An important concept for the third-wave HEIs is *accountability*, which assumes that the HEIs are accountable for their goals and that the effects of the HEIs' activities and their costs are measured and compared. This leads to control, development of the planning process, and project and process management (Sulkowski et al., 2020). Entrepreneurial culture is assumed to be pragmatic, strengthening cooperation with the business environment, and oriented towards change and innovation. The organizational structure often takes matrix forms, with a strong decision-making center but also strong peripheries. The managerially managed center is usually supervised or advised by efficient, not too numerous collective bodies. An example of this tendency can be seen in the reduction of the decision-making prerogatives of the senates, traditionally the most important collective structures of the university. Due to their size, collegial character, and dominance of the academic oligarchy, some of the powers are taken over by smaller groups, for example, university councils and boards of trustees. There is also an increasing role of specialized administration, which serves the development of accountability and operational management (e.g., quality of education) (Vogel and Kaghan, 2001). Structurally, third-wave universities represent an organizational paradox, attempting to combine centralization with decentralization. Strengthening and making the decision-making center more flexible serves efficient decision-making at the university-wide level. However, organizational units like faculties have delegated authority and responsibility for the management objectives. The matrix structure also stimulates the creation of project and process teams that go beyond the silos of the faculties. For example, the teams are created as network with economic environment, for implementation, and innovation, making education more practical, by including practitioners and academic staff from various units (Pinheiro and Stensaker, 2014; Pilbeam, 2008). Implementation, innovation, and cooperation with the environment can also be an example of combining centralization with decentralization. At the level of management of the whole system, the cooperation with the social environment is stimulated. Still, most of the implementation and project management is carried out at the level of departments (Pugh et al., 2018). The organization of a university combining concentration with dispersed control is often "strict" at the level of the head office and "loose" at the level of faculties (using K. Weick's distinction between loose and strict systems) (Weick, 1976). Academic staff in the university can play roles more flexibly, focusing on selected aspects of the mission at any given time while the administration is specialized. Management is gradually expanding to include planning, controlling, and directing various functional areas of the organization. It takes both planned and analytical forms and entrepreneurial and creative ones. The general tendency in management is to combine entrepreneurship with professionalization. The professionalization of management is served by the expansion and specialization of the university administration, which also includes professional managers who are not academic staff. This creates a potential threat to the bureaucratization of the university, devaluating the entrepreneurial culture, and employee participation in organizational processes (Vogel and Kaghan, 2001). Three trends are emerging in the area of funding. The first, apparent as early as the 1970s, is the restriction of budget funding, particularly from the state. This results in the search for new sources of funds needed to maintain and develop universities. Diversification of financial streams is made possible by (1) the development of a practical, third mission, consisting of cooperation with the economic environment, (2) the raising of funds from sponsors (fundraising), (3) the successful investment of endowment, financial surpluses, or profits in the case of for-profit universities, (4) the restructuring of universities, and (5) the introduction of payments or co-payments for studies. The third feature is the development of accountability of HEIs in the financial aspect, allowing for effective accounting and verification of the economic effectiveness of the implementation of objectives and activities of the whole university (Sotirakou, 2004). Supervision of third-wave universities depends on the system of education, the type of university (public, non-public), the statutes, and the adopted supervisory solutions (*governance*). In general, in non-public HEIs, there is usually less supervision by central authorities compared to public ones. Still, the control by the founder of a private HEI is often high (Donina and Paleari, 2019). The HEI's autonomy remains at a lower level compared to Humboldt-type universities, which, however, depends on the schooling system. One can point to a more general principle in the public policies of many countries of setting general rules, accountability, and quality standards for universities while leaving considerable autonomy regarding the methods of achieving the goals (Etzkowitz, 2016). Academic freedom is at a lower level compared to third-wave universities. Applying scientific policies and positive financial incentives as grants for scientific and implementation work on topics and projects that are strategic or profitable for the university is a limitation. It is more difficult to obtain funding for the development of non-priority research (Razvan and Dainora, 2009; Shattock, 2010a; Gaus and Raith, 2016).

A researcher in an entrepreneurial university acts as a member of research teams and a knowledge producer who may be involved in basic or applied research projects. These may include collaboration with external entities. Professionalization of management in science is a significant issue that concerns many aspects of the university organization, including teaching staff, administration, organizational structure and culture, organizational processes and projects, finance, and supervision (Lee, 2016).

1.6 Fourth wave—Digital universities

The fourth generation of HEI is born at the end of the 20th century and today is still in the process of formation. The logic of global changes towards networking and digitization of societies and people support this type of transformation. The development of the digital organization of universities was going from the last decades of the 20th century. Still, the catalyst for bigger and faster change, which will accelerate the crystallization of this formation, is Covid-19 (Altbach and De Wit, 2020; Antonopoulou et al., 2021b). The pandemic caused the transition of universities to remote activities. All streams of the academic mission have been conducted during lockdowns mainly remotely (Webb et al., 2021; Velásquez et al., 2021). The return to direct contact classes and research relations is taking place, but the competencies in using remote communication and cooperation methods will stay. This will push HEIs toward the development of hybrid models of teaching and research (de Vasconcelos Guedes and Séra, 2022).

The changes in organization, culture, and mentality will likely prove sustainable and contribute to the development of digital universities (Johnston, MacNeill, and Smyth, 2018; Davey and Galan-Muros, 2020; Sangster et al., 2020; Marin, 2021). This type of HEI arises due to the transformation of entrepreneurial universities, carried out often as a planned, long-term transition driven by digital transformation representing a civilizational change (Gehrke, 2014; Balakrishnan and Das, 2020). The fundamental values of fourth-wave universities are scientific and educational network, knowledge management, competitiveness, accountability, and open learning. Their foundations are ICT, knowledge management, and evidence-based decision-making. The values are based on digital transformation, leading to the development of intelligent digital organizations relying on network activities (Berman, 2012; Hazemi, Hailes, and Wilbur, 2012). The transformation of science and didactics leads to creating a scientific network, including virtual research teams, which will connect scientists but will also be open to practitioners. Many activities will grow to international scale. The basis for developing such teams will be research networks created through scientific and social media (e.g., ResearchGate, Academia.edu, Kudos). Similarly, in the area of didactics, forms of work and communication with students will develop through e-learning systems, internet communicators, and network software in the cloud. Informatics, together with management, will become the dominant disciplinary discourse (Khalid et al., 2018; Vial, 2019). Besides, the direction development of management sciences, focusing on knowledge management and competitiveness, will remain influential. The knowledge management methods lead to developing a networked intelligent organization that uses synergies with ICT (Jones, 2013). The activity of HEIs will increasingly shift to the Internet, where the following will be essential for the development and competitiveness of the organization in areas of science (Hassan, 2017), education, (Losh, 2014), third mission (Lundberg and Öberg, 2021), people management (Johnston, MacNeill, and Smyth, 2018, pp. 217–233; Bagdasarian et al., 2020), process and project management (Baltaru and Soysal, 2018), marketing and finance (Peters and Jandrić, 2018). The association of ICT and management in university workouts conducts to the idea of evidence-based management, which is the ground for accountability (Mihardjo et al., 2019a; Hoecht, 2021). The advancement of accountability is based on ICT concepts such as *big* data, *cloud computing*, the Internet *of things, crowdsourcing* (Mitchell, 2002), massive online courses (Akhmetshin et al., 2021), specialized educational and management software (LMS, SIS, ERP) (Mosteanu, 2020a). The digital transformation of HEIs is founded on disruptive innovations and communication technologies that relatively or even radically transform the practice of higher education (Arnold, Tanes, and King, 2010; Picciano, 2017; Maltese, 2018), research (Rakonjac et al., 2012), and also the university management (Gehrke, 2014; Hoecht, 2021) leading to the creation of ICT infrastructure of virtual campuses (Heckman, Crowston, and Misiolek, 2007; Mosteanu, 2020b).

Competitiveness and accountability foster organizational systems supported by knowledge and data management that will increasingly regulate the functioning of universities. Developing measurements of the effectiveness of HEIs performance will allow for the construction of assessment and motivation tools for employees to monitor the effectiveness of work (Canhoto et al., 2016; Bagdasarian et al., 2020). The spread of e-learning, remote work, and the globalization of science will probably lead to strengthening competition in higher education, where universities will compete for students, scientific achievements, and implementations in an international field.

The development of accountability connected with evidence-based management will also be necessary for scholarly activity. The professionalization of human capital management leads to quasi-corporate performance systems for academics, based on the analysis of big data on scientific output, compared on a global scale using scientometrics (Brewer and Brewer, 2010). The development of academic crowdsourcing, and cooperation in international networks, based not only on research but also on the co-creation of goods, will probably strengthen the open science approach, which is dominated by universal and free access to publications and research results on the Internet (Peters and Jandrić, 2018; Sitnicki, 2018). The significance of this practice is not just the democratization of science and widespread availability of knowledge as well as facilitation and reduction of costs of research and education but also more effective verification of scientific outcomes (Open Science Collaboration, 2015; Vicente-Saez and Martinez-Fuentes, 2018).

Open science is established on ubiquitous and unrestricted access to publications and information, data, research results, and application software for scientific purposes. The term "open science" was coined in 1998 and quickly spread, leading to the establishment and opening of access to many scientific journals and publications, the organization of open repositories and archives, legislative actions supporting the spread of access, the organization of conferences, issuing reports and declarations developing open science (Berlin Declaration of 2003, OECD report of 2007, and UNESCO conference of 2019) (González, 2006). Extrapolating from the growing scale and reach of open science, it is probable to be one of the fundaments of the digital university. With easy, free access to research outcomes, it will be quicker and more efficient to confirm, disseminate, plan and fund research (Fecher and Friesike, 2014). Scholar activities in a digital university will be included in organizational and management strategies founded on an information and communication system in HEIs delivering trustworthy data. Science using knowledge management ideas will stand on strategic, process, and project management, coupled with human resources management. Also, education and the third mission of the digital university will be organized and accounted for using an ICT system providing data for evidence-based decision-making. Teaching will use quality assurance systems and measures of educational performance and student satisfaction. The hybridization of education by combining remote learning and contact forms and using substantial informatic support is likely. The third stream will remain vital, particularly for applied sciences universities, and will likely also be included in the accountability system. Likewise, technology transfer, intellectual rights protection, and patents will become more and more refined and data analysis based (Raffaghelli et al., 2016). Power in the university will take managerial and team forms, a change from the third-generation HEIs, where there was a diminishing scope for collective governance. The executive and project teams, not numerous compared to the senates, will participate in the management and supervision of the university. It follows the example of business, mostly leaving the decisions on academic managers' shoulders. The strategy will consist of mission, objectives, plans, strategic analysis, and management relying on control. Controlling is an organizational process serving the accountability of achieving scientific, teaching, financial and other objectives. The ground for its implementation will be an integrated ICT system, processing data for managerial decisions at all levels (Hazemi and Hailes, 2001; Egoeze et al., 2018). Meanwhile, it is probable to preserve a strong center with departmental and administrative branches shifting towards advanced concentration. The organization will become more virtual with the full immersion of teams in the ICT system. Access depends on staff members' responsibilities in areas like managerial decisions, quality of education, academic performance, project management, etc. The digital university ideally will become a networked learning organization, concentrated, focused, and centralized, being, on the other hand, flexible and managerial. Depending on the university's mission, the HEI's staff will focus on the following roles: scientific, research and teaching, education, or cooperation with the non-academic environment. Again, the flexibility of HEIs in the forms of cooperation and employment of staff will be noteworthy (Sheail, 2018). It will be achievable to combine organizational roles with flexibility. Regardless, specialization is likely to be rewarded due to accounting for work results. Rarely an excellent researcher becomes an outstanding teacher and vice versa. The roles of executives and administrative staff will be durable and intensely focused (Mitchell, 2002). The degree of complexity in the management of a digital university is growing. The reason is that analyzing large amounts of data should reduce the uncertainty arising from operating in a turbulent and competitive environment (Günther et al., 2017; Maltese, 2018). Change management will be a permanent process using information analyzed to make managerial decisions (Karmoush and Theeb, 2013; Selwyn, Henderson, and Chao, 2018). Professionalization of management will be connected with a focus on administration, and the implementation of information systems servicing main processes in the HEI, with emphasis on functional areas of management (finance, human resources management, marketing, and information management). The university administration will grow both within the existing structures and by developing relatively new ones (e.g., the Information Department and the *Chief Information Officer*) (Shannon et al., 2008). Administrative staff not belonging to the research and teaching employees of the HEI will be able to perform managerial functions. The financing of the university will be diversified and founded on various streams: public and private funds, student tuition co-financing, grants for science and implementations, and revenues from cooperation with outside organizations. A more profound decrease in state funding is probable and associated with a trend of the proliferation to pay for performance in state accountability systems (Coy et al., 2001; Brown, 2018; Mosteanu, 2020a). Governance of HEIs will remain varied according to the type of university and the state system. However, there seems to be a convergence of global solutions in governance in this area. The general trend is to evolve toward universal regulations and establish objectives and performance models for the most effective institutions. Such a resolution leaves much autonomy to public HEIs in choosing ways to achieve goals. Non-public HEIs, which mainly have less funding from state budgets, will be subject to even looser regulations, especially accreditation and increasingly detailed central reporting (Nigsch and Schenker-Wicki, 2013; Aitchison et al., 2020). Academic autonomy, as in the entrepreneurial university, will be constrained by budgets, the HEI's strategy, public policies, and the direction of the third mission. Research for such type of university is not a priority, and unprofitable science will not be developed (McCluskey and Winter, 2014; Levine, 2018).

The model of the digital university leads toward effective, innovative organizations, focusing on knowledge creation, management, and distribution. Data-driven decision-making, constantly adjusted systems, processes, strategy, and structure, advanced ICT and accountability, and advanced management methods indicate a high level of professionalization in implementing the academic mission (Cantner, 2022; Ibragimovich et al., 2022; Yang et al., 2022). The pandemic facilitates the development of digital HEIs in 2020/21 (de Vasconcelos Guedes and Séra, 2022). Nevertheless, this evident organizational excellence has its borders. The tendency is growing, moving further away from second-wave universities and academic freedom toward fourth-wave HEIs in which control play a central role (Hassan, 2017; Rof, Bikfalvi, and Marques, 2022b, p. 269). It is the apparent danger that critics of the neoliberal university warn about (Rhoads, 2018; Laalo, Kinnari, and Silvennoinen, 2019). The digital HEI raises the essential threat of a "digital panopticon" of systemic control of knowledge workers. The dangers of alienation (Hopkins, 2015), the commercialization and corporatization of the academic world, and the erosion of university culture and ethos (Johnston, MacNeill, and Smyth, 2018, pp. 3 17). The trial to prevent the fall from the utopia of academic freedom of the Humboldt-type university into the dystopia of robust power control of the digital university, maybe the responsibility of academic stakeholders together with reflection, critical thinking, and discussion about the conditions of creating engaged HEI (Neilson, 2020; Sulkowski, 2022a; Lenart-Gansiniec and Sulkowski 2022b).

1.7 Four waves of HEIs from the organizational perspective

The idea proposed in this book on the long-term transformation of HEI from the standpoint of management discourse leads to several conclusions (Table 1.1).

The crucial mission of universities remains constant. However, strategic diversification leads to different types of universities focusing on selected aspects of the mission in their activities. Examples include research universities, applied sciences HEI, vocational colleges, and corporate universities. Universities have not lost their organizational identity and, despite profound transformations, remain intelligent organizations focused on science, education, and the third mission. A substantial change concerns precisely the design and implementation of differentiated missions of universities. The direction leads from consistently interpreting the university's role in the traditional university to diversification strategies in the third and fourth waves. For Humboldtian universities, the approved strategy, reflected in academic culture and assimilated by faculty and students, is education and science. For third- and fourth-wave universities, the mission is fulfilled by the composition of strategy, identity, and organizational culture, managed and developed for organizational effectiveness.

The role of academic culture and ethos, which for traditional universities was the organization's glue. However, it is changing. The integration of staff and students took place by entering a group of values and cultural norms. Despite the many transitions and various universities, tradition has regulated people's behavior, given them the identity, and determined how they govern and manage. The development of the third wave of universities in the 20th century caused the status quo-oriented traditional culture to change into an entrepreneurial culture that uses business patterns. There is a development of management concepts that radically transform the functioning of HEIs, previously based mainly on academic ethos. The professionalization of university management contributes to the growth of effectiveness of their operation. However, it creates resistance to bureaucratization, commercialization, managerialism, and corporatization of the academic world (Beckmann et al., 2009; Laalo et al., 2019; Peters et al., 2012). Critical management studies and other radical perspectives like gender studies, neo-Marxism, and postmodernism stigmatize and reject the neoliberal transformation of universities, growing out, as they claim, from the discourse of contemporary post-industrial "turbo-capitalism." The power of instrumental reason with primates for putting efficiency, competition, and the market on a pedestal pushes universities to shift away from focusing on their mission of reaching and proclaiming the truth and

Table 1.1 The four waves of universities—A comparative analysis

	First-wave university	*Second-wave university*	*Third-wave university*	*Fourth-wave university*
Name	Traditional	Humboldtian	Entrepreneurial	Digital
Creation and reforms	Spontaneous or established by rulers, public and rarely private founders	A plan for university establishment or reform based on the Humboldt project, mainly public founders	Strategic plan and change management project, public or private founders, and the influence of external stakeholders (state, public and private organizations)	Strategy, project management and controlling, public or private founders, the result of external stakeholders
Chronology	11th–18th centuries	19th to mid-20th century	1970 to present	21st century
Values	Training of students by masters, science	*Bildung*, cultural and nation-building ideas integrating nation, state	Competition, market, academic entrepreneurship	Research and education network, knowledge management, competitiveness, accountability, open science
Formation	Elite	Elite	Egalitarian	Egalitarian
Academic culture	Community of bachelors and students	The elite of professors (masters) and students	Competitive, flexible knowledge organization	Network organization of knowledge
Authority	Guild	Academic community	Managerial and academic, personal and less collective	Managerial, team leadership, and less academic collective
Missions	Education and research, Single	Education linked to science and culture, unified	Science, education, and the third mission, differentiated	Specialization: science, education, and third mission, differentiation
Strategy	Traditional objectives, spontaneous development	Ethos objectives, guidelines for development	Emergent strategy or strategic plan, mission, and objectives formulated	Strategy: plan, mission, evidence-based goals, controlling
Structure	Traditional, stable, ethos based	Traditional, hierarchical, established	Matrix, with an intense decision-making center, increasing level of specialization	Networked, with an intense decision-making center, flexible, specialized

Organization of the university	Hierarchical, stable, academic	Loose, bureaucratic, decentralized, stable, academic	Tight-central, loose-periphery, flexible, elements of centralization and decentralization, managerial-academic	Networked, flexible, centralized, managerial, ICT based
People in HEIs	Traditional roles and responsibilities	Traditional roles and responsibilities	Flexible, variable staff roles, specialized, and permanent administrations	Flexible, varying roles and fixed administrations, specialization
Management	Minimized, traditionally regulated	Limited, project-planned, ethos	Extensive, planned, and entrepreneurial professionalization	Extensive, analytical, planned, data-driven, and evidence-based professionalization
Administration	Very limited, guided by elected academic staff	Very limited, shown by elected academic staff	Extended and growing, specialized management functions	Extended and growing, specialized management functions
Funding	Miscellaneous, private, public, church	Public, governmental, both research and education	Various, often mixed, public universities—more often state	Different, often mixed, public universities—more often state
Governance, supervision	Limited, internal	Very limited, inner, academic	Various, public-state, private founders, external	Stronger, general, external, accountability
Autonomy of the university	Large, varied models	Extensive, various models	Large, varied models	Large, varied models
Academic freedom of faculty	Significant in relation to society, limited by a hierarchical culture	Very high freedom to choose research topics and methods, students and collaborators	Moderate, limited by finance and strategy of HEI	Moderate, limited by finance and strategy of HEI

Source: own elaboration.

transforming them into industrial knowledge producers (Berglund, Hytti and Verduijn, 2020; Hurd and Singh, 2020; Hosseini, 2021). Digital universities could raise their problems, compounded by the culture of control developing through the digital panopticon based on ITC controlling systems (Williams, 2013; Gourlay, 2020).

The organizational aspects of universities in the 21st century unite developing ICT with implementing management concepts and methods. HEIs advanced networking, digitization, and informatization are ongoing trends entangled with management through accountability, data-driven decision-making, and a culture of control. Despite resistance from parts of the academic community, progress in the development of digitization in universities is probable, as it will be pushed by increased efficiency in achieving goals and by technological and civilizational change.

HEIs refinement in applying management ideas is increasing. Founded on business concepts, new public management, and public value management, HEIs are professionalizing many aspects of their activities: human capital, finance and accounting, marketing, processes, projects, and knowledge management. The result is an expansion in managerial power and control but also a potential danger of bureaucratization of universities.

2 Transformations of higher education institutions

2.1 Dimensions of academic transformation

The management of organizations is dynamic even in the relatively stable higher education sector. Neither do universities remain in the *status quo* but undergo transformations due to the environment's influence and the organizational system's evolution. Although universities are long-lived organizations, by tradition tending toward a conservative academic culture and stable, ritualized management patterns, in the last few decades, they have been under the pressure of rapid changes in their closer and more distant environment (Meyer, 2002; Trowler, 2002; Howells et al., 2014; Olk, 2020). In this chapter, I take up the challenge to distinguish the most important change trends in the university world and analyze the consequences of these transformations for the management processes. The feedback loop of external and internal variables is shaping academic strategies, structures, and cultures, which are evolving from homogeneous, traditional Humboldt-type university patterns toward diverse models of entrepreneurial, virtual, research, teaching, corporate, and other forms of universities. Recent decades, particularly the time of the COVID-19 pandemic, have also seen an acceleration of the transformation toward the digital university (Mosteanu, 2020b; Sobral et al., 2021). Some trends are more universal and affect multiple sectors. This is the case with the proliferation of the neoliberal management model, the internationalization of activities, and the rise of the trend toward accountability in public institutions. Other trends are specific to the university sector. Diversifying and stratification in higher education are enduring trends that distinguish universities from different types of organizations.

The analysis of the directions of HEIs' transformation that has been carried out creates a broad background for the study of HEIs' governance processes. Presidents, rectors, members of university councils, academic managers and administrators, and all higher education system stakeholders should understand its transformation's key directions. This is needed not only for deeper reflection on the role and spirit of the contemporary academy but also for more effective university governance.

DOI: 10.4324/9781003366409-4

Among the directions of change, many different trends can be identified, seven of which I will discuss in this chapter.

1 From the humanist university in the Humboldt model to the neoliberal university (Sassower, 2022, p. 343);
2 From national universities to the internationalization of HEIs (Liu and Gao, 2022);
3 From the universal university organization to diversification and stratification (Shavit et al., 2022);
4 From elite education to the egalitarianism of higher education (Pickard, 2022);
5 From the ethos of academic science to commercial and industrial science (Lekka-Kowalik, 2021; Jaeger et al., 2022);
6 From academic trust to organizational control (Hoecht, 2021);
7 From academic to business orientation (Hil, Thompsett, and Lyons, 2022);
8 From collegiality to managerialism in management (Marquina, Centeno, and Reznik, 2022; Sims, 2022);
9 From bureaucracy to adhocracy in organizational structures (Mustafa et al., 2022);
10 From the "freelance," autonomous academic to the professional "knowledge worker";
11 From cultural conservatism to innovation (Fuad, Musa, and Hashim, 2022);
12 From quality culture to quality management in education (Liu, 2021);
13 From the expert evaluation of science to global scientometrics (Zerem and Kunosić, 2021);
14 From attitudes of researcher and student criticism to academic conformity (Hosseini, 2021);
15 From a university creating public goods to a university producing private goods (Smith, 2008; Sulkowski, 2016b; Choudaha and van Rest, 2018).

2.2 The neoliberal university—growth and a critique

The drive to marketize universities in the United States and Europe has led to criticism of neoliberal change (Rhodes, Wright, and Pullen, 2018). In many countries, the 1980s brought changes leading to academic capitalism (Jessop, 2018; Croucher and Lacy, 2020; Sigahi and Saltorato, 2020; Li and Liao, 2021). One thinks, for example, of Reaganomics in the United States and Thatcherism in the UK. In opposition, critical currents emerged—*Critical Management Education, Critical Management Study*, and *Critical Pedagogy*, institutionalized from the early 20th century in the social sciences. The narrative of these currents involved the development of a critique of neoliberalism in scientific, social, and political activity (Canaan and Shumar, 2008). For its critics, neoliberalism became a symbol of a change devoid of humanism, with instrumental reason, economization, and managerialism at its core. The Frankfurt School scholars initiated the criticism of instrumental reason, related to analyzing the effects of the economization of contemporary culture. Economization or marketization means that economic market criteria become the essential values in developing a particular area of social life. Managerialism consists in using the methods of management and the managerial approach in other aspects of the activity of social groups (Ridley, 2017; Mahony and Weiner, 2019; Busher and Fox, 2021).

Neoliberalism can be called market fundamentalism, based on the assumption that competitive and market-based solutions are effective and universal, regardless of the type of activity and sector (public or private). Dent and Barry connect neoliberalism with applying new public management and describe several trends. The restructuring of the public sector organization, carried out successively since the 1980s, was most often connected with decentralization and privatization of a part of public services (Broucker, De Wit, and Verhoeven, 2017; Tight, 2019a; Hodgins and Mannix-McNamara, 2021). In this sector, management methods and techniques borrowed from business emerged (Dent, Chandler, and Barry, 2004). Human resource management, strategic management, marketing methods, controlling, or benchmarking were used in management. Management's rhetoric, logic, and pragmatics gradually saturated the public sector. Its economization, expressed in the orientation toward efficiency toward savings, has been introduced through cost accounting and performance measurement, as well as through the use of productivity standards and norms (Lawrence and Sharma, 2002; Saravanamuthu and Filling, 2004; Lock and Lorenz, 2007; Giroux, Karmis, and Rouillard, 2015; Taberner, 2018).

Of course, there was no shortage of people citing the weaknesses of neoliberalism. For-profit, private universities, and tuition fees exacerbate social inequalities as financial barriers to higher education are created (Macdonald and Young, 2018; Richter et al., 2020; Morrish, 2020). There is talk of the precariat and the "lost generation" who face joblessness after graduation due to the crisis (Standing, 2011; Alvesson, 2013). Paid studies and quasi-corporate governance solutions destroy the autonomy of scientific and teaching activities and, as a result, the academic culture (Leys, 2000). Economization is not conducive to long-term scientific investment, as it is geared toward current revenues. The neo-liberal university contradicts the ethos of science and didactics. There is no place for the opposition, which conditions an autonomous and critical perception of the social world and lies at the basis of democratization, solidarity, and reflexivity of society. Universities have the task of carrying out research of a broad scope (more comprehensive than the current market needs) and an innovative nature and of training qualified workers equipped with the ability to perceive reality critically. The education of the citizens was provided in *Universitas*, which is being abandoned today by viewing higher education as a private, not a public good (Sani, 2021). The in-strumentalization of education and the pursuit of teaching specialists stems from the recognition of education as a market *commodity* (*commodification*) and the abandonment of its cultural or civic role—the foundations of democratic systems (Holmwood and Marcuello Servos, 2019). One should also look at the departure from universities' traditional culture and ethos in management. It was brought about by the managerial revolution that started in the mid-20th century—first in the United States and then in Europe, which was later intensified in the 1980s (Rourke and Brooks, 1966). There were efforts to implement instrumental business methods in university management—academics were to be managed by professional managers, and universities functioning in a corporate fashion should be subjected to the norms of economic efficiency (Shepherd, 2018). Market-oriented reforms were justified by the growing interest in higher education and the desire to report to the environment and maintain transparency, which resulted in greater complexity and size of universities (McKelvey and Holmén, 2009; Kwiek, 2010). Neoliberal reforms of the public sector (including universities) (Arnaboldi, Lapsley, and Steccolini, 2015) are based on the assumptions of managerialism, which has at its core new public management and involves social stakeholders from outside the organization in its evaluation using external quality criteria. Criticism of market tools in higher education is encouraged by the inability to prove that management will solve the problems of universities, involving mass education and emphasis on reporting and transparency (Becher and Kogan, 1992). Some researchers argue that corporately managed universities are unable to face the challenges of current civilization trends (Olsen and Maassen, 2007). In quasi-managerially organized universities, their cultural mission is less important. Thus research with social relevance is lacking, and students no longer develop the capacity for critical civic society participation and are not competent enough to do so. This is due to the preference for market solutions at the expense of the humanistic dimension of university culture (Davies, Gottsche, and Bansel, 2006). The implementation of "organizational cul-turalism" and "managerialism" in higher education institutions in Europe has, according to critics, been led by neoliberal reforms (Willmott, 1995). As Matts Alvesson believes, the reforms have at their core incorrect assumptions of the market and educational fundamentalism (Alvesson, 2013).

The objectives of higher education include creating conditions for developing a knowledge-based society and civilization but also meeting the challenges of the labor market. The *performance management* style, based on *performance indicators* and research *projectification* (Fowler, Lindahl, and Sköld, 2015), encourages employees to focus on their research rather than on creating an academic ethos or working on developing social ties or involvement in work and family life while maintaining a balance between the two spheres (Besley and Peters, 2006). As a result, not only the quality of education is lowered, and students obtain higher education without adequate competencies and knowledge but also the value of the scientific work of researchers is decreasing, focusing on the requirements of reporting, bureaucracy, and chasing in rankings. Academic work is increasingly about taking formal measures for the survival of specific organizations. We can agree with Pierre Bourdieu (Bourdieu, 1988), who mentioned the "ritualization of appearances" of university work, which is also emphasized by researchers of the critical current looking at European education. Let us recall the example of criticism of the use of ranking lists in assessing the quality of work of universities, which took place in the report of the *European University Association* (Van de Walle and van Delft, 2014).

The market orientation of the university has been replacing the perspective of general human values over the last few decades. Higher education is often paid for like other private goods, and an equal sign is put between universities and "customer-oriented corporate networks" (Rutherford, 2005). Critical researchers list several vital themes that suggest the wrong direction of change in the contemporary university:

- Universities expect students to pay tuition fees and, at the same time, look for other sources of financing, manifested, e.g., in the commercialization of research (patents, licenses, etc.) (Perkmann et al., 2013), which increases the commercialization of universities, commodification of education and causes a move away from the traditional academic ethos;
- Linking higher education to the needs of business and the labor market eliminates universal content in favor of specialized vocational training;
- Greater employment flexibility means little stability and contractual work, with teachers employed on temporary contracts (Shore and Davidson, 2014);
- Higher education as a private good becomes an investment in a career—one's own or one's family's (Marginson, 2011), the mission of civic education, the sense of cooperation and community are disappearing;
- Business management methods increase economic efficiency but also make universities quasi-corporations due to the application of the new public management concept (Guglietti, 2012);
- Neoliberalism leads to the privatization of the vast majority of public services, including education, and especially higher education (Angus, 2015);
- University activities are economically driven and subject to measures of efficiency, but creative work proves challenging to measure (Watermeyer, 2019; Bloemraad and Menjívar, 2022);
- The university and its employees are confronted with the need to compete with corporations or make research results available. The changing concept of knowledge adversely affects research and education in the humanities and social sciences, imposing on them the role of professional education (Zabrodska et al., 2011);

- Hierarchical and managerial forms of organization strengthen the power of managers, i.e., presidents or chancellors, at the expense of collegiate decision-making; they establish supervisory bodies that include representatives of business; they weaken academic freedom, autonomy, and the role of trade unions and collectives; they reduce employee participation in university governance (Deem et al., 2007);
- A culture of control and audit is developing, quantitative measures of effectiveness are increasingly being used, and measurement of scientific achievements (scientometrics), on which the promotion of university employees, and sometimes also their remuneration, depends. There is increasing pressure to publish among academics (Castree and Sparke, 2000);
- Universities seem to pursue the professional interests of groups. In disciplines (such as architecture, law, medicine, construction, psychology, and others), professional associations are formed to shape educational content, standards, certify professional credentials (Lynch, 2006);
- A new organizational hierarchy is taking shape in the university, a group of academic managers is coming to power, and the administration's contribution is increasing in quantity and importance (Webster and Mosoetsa, 2002).

Lynch reassesses the critique of the neoliberal university by referring to several scholars. The critical view of restricting access to education has a rich tradition in the social sciences. The Frankfurt School, and later Bourdieu and Passeron, point to the reproduction of elites through higher education as a social mechanism that limits mobility and deepens social stratification (Bourdieu and Passeron, 1990a). Similar themes appear in many studies of universities, pointing to a lack of inclusivity, the creation of class barriers to access to study, and the rise of fee-based payment, making study opportunities dependent on income (Shavit and Blossfeld, 1993; Clancy, 1988, 1995, 2001; Archer, Hutchings and Ross, 2002). Related to the problem of inclusivity and elitism is also profession-centrism, consisting of closing, hermitization, and implementation of social practices favoring the interests of elite professional groups (e.g., doctors, lawyers, university professors). This is often accompanied by restricting access to higher education in a given area (Clancy, 1988, 1995; O'Hanlon, 2002). The critique of the neoliberal university also highlights the problem of commercialization of the university mission (Dill, 2003; Steier, 2003; Dill and Soo, 2004). Paid education, the commodification of education and science, and the development of industrial research, commercialized by corporations and universities, the distance the latter from concern for the common good (Chubb and Moe, 1988). The characteristic of the neoliberal university is a kind of "servilism" toward power and corporations and unreflective application of business solutions in the public sphere, including universities (Giroux, 2002).

A critical and balanced view of the university's development may be more beneficial for the university than a radical approach. However, it is the most vocal, leads to questioning the obvious, and forces one to think. However, it does not encourage discussion and acceptance of compromise solutions. Constant criticism of the changes introduced by politicians may provoke opposition from part of the scientific community and, consequently, resistance and a tendency to reject the changes or distort them. It seems sensible to find a compromise on the issue of academic governance. The idealized Humboldtian university by academics critical of neo-liberalism will not return. Mass education has initiated changes that modify the world of universities. Still, it must be accepted that they need steering and a search for solutions by decision-makers and the scientific community. Criticism is raised not only by radical researchers but also by Philip Altbach (a leading representative of the mainstream) disagrees with treating higher education only as a marketable commodity or a private good and stresses the dangers of the lack of academic ethos and pauperization of the faculty (Altbach, 2015a, 2015b). However, the researcher does not stop at criticism and suggests solutions based on dialogue as a basis for democracy and on the realization that the model of the university has changed. The only thing that can be discussed is the degree of marketization of education and science. It is difficult to deny the value of the mechanism of coopetition of universities, primarily because of effective leadership, quality of education, and image.

2.3 Internationalization of higher education

One of the axes of change in modern universities and entire higher education systems, also observed in scientific research, is the deepening processes of internationalization (De Wit, 1999; Altbach and Knight, 2007; Knight and De Wit, 2018). With the development of globalization, the internationalization of science and higher education in its many forms is increasing. It can even be argued that in the last few decades, universities—from being nationally active and focused on the development mission of countries—have transformed themselves into internationalized and partly even global ones. This fundamental transformation is taking place according to different patterns around the world. Universities from Anglo-Saxon countries with the most developed educational systems (the United States, the UK, Australia) (De Wit, 2002) are expanding in developing countries and "importing" students. Australia has even created a model of internationalization of studies in which almost half of the students come from abroad, mainly from China and other Asian countries (Hong, 2020). The European Union focuses on intensifying internationalization within the EU (De Wit and Hunter, 2015; Tamtik, 2017). Universities from many regions of the world are developing international cooperation in all mission areas. Thus, universities from all over the world are looking for effective solutions for the internalization of higher education because, as many studies show, the above process can be managed in the university (Johanson and Vahlne, 1993; Taylor, 2010; Adel, Zeinhom, and Mahrous, 2018).

In 2020, the question of the future of higher education internationalization had been raised. In the context of the COVID-19 pandemic, the dramatic question was asked: "Is the coronavirus killing university internationalization?" (De Wit and Altbach, 2021; Li and Eryong, 2021). According to pioneering research, this is not the case, but forms of internationalization are undergoing significant modification (Ota, 2018; De Wit, 2019; Lin, 2019; De Wit and Deca, 2020; Finardi and Guimaraes, 2020). One could even say that a kind of e-internationalization is emerging, which precisely corresponds to the development of a new formation of the digital university (Altbach and De Wit, 2020; Finardi and Guimaraes, 2020; Mok and Montgomery, 2021; Mok et al., 2021). Pandemic thus becomes a catalyst for the digitalization and networking of all internationalization processes in universities (Abdulrahim and Mabrouk, 2020; Nurhas et al., 2021; García-Peñalvo et al., 2021).

The search for effective models for managing the internationalization processes of higher education should begin with the differentiation of forms and levels of internationalization according to the type of university and its mission. In the second half of the 20th century, trends toward the internationalization of universities and higher education on a global scale have developed. Internationalization is defined in many ways. Piercy (1985) describes it as the relocation of an organization's activities abroad, thus equating internationalization with establishing an organization outside the home country. Melin (1992) defines it as a process of evolutionary change leading to an increase in the level of international involvement of an organization, which is a function of an increase in knowledge of foreign markets. Welch and Luostarinen (1988) define internationalization as the process of increasing an organization's involvement in international activities, which includes both internal operations (passive, e.g., purchasing licenses, using franchises) and external operations (active, e.g., foreign direct investments, international strategic alliances, and acquisitions, various forms of capital and non-capital cooperation). At the level of higher education, Knight (2003) defines the process of internationalization as the integration of the international, intercultural and global dimensions into the functions, purpose, and specificity of universities and the harmonization of policies and programs implemented by universities and governments in response to globalization. The activities mainly concern the foreign exchange of students and lecturers, the establishment of campuses and satellite organizations, and engaging in various types of inter-institutional cooperation. Using these definitions, I propose to adopt the following understanding of the internationalization processes of universities. Internationalization is the integration of international, intercultural, and global perspectives into planning and organizing an HEI's activities and improving the quality of education, research, or third stream. Internationalization of higher education includes, among others, the following spheres: Strategic planning, international mobility of students and staff, foreign language teaching, joint curricula, global research, and intercultural educational content (De Wit and Hunter, 2015).

The following are the most important reasons for the development of internationalization in the higher education sector (Sulkowski, 2016a):

- Deepening globalization processes;
- The university's strategy to attract international students;
- Increasing the internationalization of research;
- Aiming to improve the quality of education through the internationalization of education.

Deepening globalization processes, manifested by: The development of the international economic market, increasing flows of goods, services, and labor, the evolution of knowledge-based economies and societies, as well as trade liberalization and the weakening role of nation-states (Stiglitz, 2002; Hirst, Thompson and Bromley, 2015), motivate the development of the internationalization of higher education (King, Marginson, and Naidoo, 2011). Globalization affects many aspects of HEIs, reinforcing the pressure for internationalization. First, due to the globalization of business and societies, many candidates choose universities outside their country. The number of students in international programs is also increasing. This is made possible by expanding English as the modern *lingua franca*. Secondly, global competition forces universities to promote their brands and develop educational programs aimed at foreign students. Thirdly, many universities in developed countries face the problem of demographic decline, which means that both labor markets and universities are looking for young people outside their own countries. Finally, the growth of multinational corporations and business activities in the global marketplace motivate the improvement of intercultural competencies that employees need. The global competition for talents, students, and academics occurs simultaneously in several segments. Some high prestige universities focus on attracting outstanding students and researchers worldwide. In the lower prestige university segment, marketing activities are developed to recruit as many potential students as possible. The bright side of the competition for outstanding scientists is the development of creative international teams, which can boast world-class scientific achievements. The downside, however, can be the brain drain effect that deprives less developed countries of talented researchers, exacerbating the inequality between rich countries and the rest of the world (Johnson and Regets, 1998). However, as noted by many authors, internationalization should not be understood as an end in itself but primarily as a way to improve the quality of education and research (Knight, 2001; Brandenburg and De Wit, 2011; Green, 2012). Many studies indicate that the development of various forms of internationalization promotes the development of the quality of education (Ota, 2018; Gorodilov and Chuchulina, 2018; Bowles and Murphy, 2020). In general, according to research by various authors, internationalization also correlates positively with the scientific productivity of academics employed at universities (Kwiek, 2015a; Ahn, Choi, and Oh, 2019). In most studies, the internationalization of higher education is presented as beneficial for the quality and development of higher education and science. Among the most critical assessments of the value of internationalization appear stimulation of intercultural relations, improvement of universities, global competition for talent among scientists and students, sources of economic development, and others. There is also a growing group of skeptical opinions about the internationalization of universities, which they criticize:

- International marketing, which focuses on attracting foreign students who pay for education (Lee, 2015);
- International rankings, which are becoming a fetish and an instrumental target for universities (Shafiepoor, Atashac, and Torabinahad, 2019);
- An intercultural ideology that deepens the domination of economically developed regions over the "periphery" (Luke, 2010);
- Dual and joint degrees, increasingly becoming mere "marketing products" and not requiring the implementation of additional learning outcomes and student effort (Tian, 2011);
- Treating educational programs as a pass to leave the country to obtain visas to more attractive countries.

The motives driving universities to increase internationalization vary quite considerably between different universities and regions of the world (Kim, 2009). For the United States and the UK, for example, internationalization has primarily a commercial aspect of attracting foreign students who pay for their education or how to attract global talents. Furthermore, English and American prestigious research universities are magnets for talented researchers worldwide (Schuster, 1994). In Western European countries, internationalization is seen as part of the Bologna agenda and is associated with strengthening integration processes and intercultural communication (Altbach, Reisberg, and Rumbley, 2009).

In the literature, we find many indicators, models, and measures of HEI internationalization (Bartell, 2003; Chan and Dimmock, 2008; Shafiepoor, Atashac, and Torabinahad, 2019). *The European Association for International Education* identifies eight main reasons for internationalization: (1) to improve the overall quality of education, (2) to prepare students for international work and for global study, (3) to attract more international students, (4) to improve the international reputation, (5) to improve the quality of research and development, (6) to increase competitiveness, (7) the demands of the labor market, and (8) financial benefits for institutions. The list of preferences is compiled based on a survey of universities in Europe. An interesting observation is that financial reasons last place (Engel et al., 2015).

According to Ph. Altbach, globalization has increased universities' international role and expanded campuses' internationalization (Altbach, 2014). It has become the strategic orientation of university schools in recent decades. The level of internationalization of universities depends on various factors such as country, type of school, and program. However, the general change trend toward an international HEI is constant (Jafari et al., 2018). The first substantial wave of internationalization was mainly based on business schools in the United States, UK, and Europe, followed by international accreditation processes. American business accreditations such as AACSB (*Association to Advance Collegiate Schools of Business Accreditation*), IACBE (*The International Assembly for Collegiate Business Education Accreditation*), British accreditations such as AMBA (*Association of MBAs Accreditation*), or European *accreditations* such as EQUIS (*European Quality Improvement System*) were developed and implemented internationally (Aggarwal, 1989). A strong factor for internationalization is the growing number of students studying outside their home country (Palmqvist, 2009). However, the trend of increasing numbers of students studying abroad was halted in 2020 by the COVID-19 pandemic, and the modified forms of e-internationalization of HEI could be observed (Lindsay, 2021; Yu, 2021; Takagi, 2022).

2.4 Diversification and stratification of university management

The change of academic governance results in an increasing diversification of universities, which is related to their strategic specificity. A group of stronger universities will be able to compete globally and will focus on their research mission (Harris, 2010; Huang, 2015). The main focus will be on the development of universities and the generation of innovation in a large number of disciplines and at a global level, as enforced by international rankings and indicators (Vidal and Ferreira, 2020). Research and teaching universities seek a balance between these aspects of the activity. This is a frequent cause of specialized HEIs. Economic universities can use their connections to business and offer mainly practical education, while technical universities can focus on innovations, education in applied sciences, and implementations. Other specialized universities also face similar decisions (e.g., military, art, music, or medical universities). Research and teaching universities are faced with the choice of disciplines in which they will strive to achieve high scientific positions at the expense of investing in others (Gómez et al., 2009). This is a big challenge for university leaders and their staff, as it means a change in mission and strategy and the identity of the research and teaching staff. Most non–public universities probably focus more and more on teaching (Adriansyah et al., 2022). The strategic diversification of universities entails specialization and stratification of the academic profession, which translates into a division between teaching and research staff. The polarization of universities entails a progressive stratification of internal stakeholders. The division into elite and average universities will deepen and lead to differences in prestige, the value of university diplomas, and future jobs for graduates (Mok, 2007; Davies and Zarifa, 2012).

Diversifying strategies translate into differentiated management depending on the organizational model of the university. When looking for some model management solutions, one can refer to K. Weick and the concept of *loosely coupled systems* (Orton and Weick, 1990). "Loosely coupled" management systems are characterized by flexibility, network linkage, and the possibility to reconfigure and replace elements without destroying the organizational system. The transformation toward a digital university seems to involve just such a networked design. Following I. McNay, S. Dopson, and L. Lomas, it is possible to describe four academic cultures that characterize differentiated management styles (Dopson and McNay, 1996; Lomas, 1999). The dimensions that differentiate the management of academic organizations are the definition of policies and strategies and the control over their implementation (loose versus tight).

- The college is characterized by a poor definition of policies and strategies and loose control over their implementation. Governance will take the form of "academic self-government," with significant participation of collegiate bodies. This model, similar to the traditional Humboldtian university, in the power triangle of B. Clark, distinguishes it by its orientation toward academic oligarchy.
- Bureaucracy is characterized by the loose formulation of policies and strategies accompanied by tight control over their implementation. The management of this type of university focuses on the operational and tactical level, capturing the organization's strategy in a traditional, general, planning, and often facade manner. The management model resembles administration, with an elaborate structure of specialists who perform detailed, procedural tasks, but there is no reflection on the strategy of the whole organization. When looking for a description of this management approach, the term "self-reproducing bureaucracy" can be used.
- An enterprise-like university is characterized by the strict formulation of strategies and policies and loose control over its implementation. It is oriented toward the market, the customer, and the organization's environment rather than its interior. The management model can be called "quasi-business" because measurable competitive results are essential. The power triangle of B. Clark's triangle is characterized by its market orientation.

- The corporation, understood as a complex market structure, combines the strict formulation of strategies and policies with solid control over their implementation. The management model is based on a strong central authority that designs and implements strategies and policies and delegates the implementation of measurable objectives according to the organizational hierarchy. When looking for a name for this mode of governance, the term "quasi-corporate" can be used (McCaffery, 2018, pp. 51–53).

Diversification of universities and their management has consequences in the form of increasing stratification. The differentiation of types of HEIs depending on: founders, specialization, prestige, mission, and range of activities. The variety of HEIs is increasing after the Second World War. In recent decades one can also point to the growing stratification of university management models. Corporately managed are "private-for-profit" universities, such as the University of Phoenix and Corinthian Colleges, but also training, often networked higher education institutions (Apollo, DeVry, Kaplan, Laureate Education), universities created by corporations (BAE, Disney, Ford, Microsoft, Motorola), as well as part of mega-universities (UK Open University, Academic University Turkey, University of South Africa, Indira Gandhi National University) (McCaffery, 2018, pp. 12–13). Following the American "Ivy League" example, research universities focus mainly on scientific prestige, acquiring central funds, and benefiting from scientific cooperation with business (Fernandez and Baker, 2017). Paradoxically the leading American university, because of rising prestige, competition, and research focus, is not increasing the numbers of students admitted in the last dozens of years (Mann, 2020). A reflection of this stratification process, measured by academic and scientific prestige, can be found in rankings of excellence such as *ARWU, QS Ranking, Times Higher Education,* and *US News and World Report.* For many countries, it is unattainable for their universities to achieve a position in the group of scientifically leading universities. Strategic diversification and stratification also take place in teaching universities. A group of leading teaching universities with different specializations and scope of activities is separating, and the "tail" is getting longer, i.e., the number of weak universities devaluing the degrees is growing (including the lowest category of the so-called *diploma mills*) (Ezell Jr, 2002).

Diversification and stratification of universities also relate to internal stakeholders. Academic staff, university administration, but also students of prestigious universities benefit from cultural and relational capital and the principle of "prestige inheritance." The results of this stratification are diverse, ranging from the reproduction of elites described by Bourdieu and Passeron, through the development of human capital driving socio-economic progress, to the creation of social networks allowing for the development of individual careers (Passeron and Bourdieu, 1970; Jenkins, 1982).

The processes of stratification according to the criterion of scientific prestige at the individual level are described by Marek Kwiek, who points first of all to the dimension of increased differentiation in terms of individual and collective scientific achievements (Kwiek, 2018). Conclusions from these studies are unambiguous; stratification according to the criterion of scientific prestige has been deepening in recent decades, which is reflected in the strategies of research universities that attract talent and outstanding researchers and create conditions for developing human capital in the university. Also, the measures and possibilities to compare the achievements of researchers are becoming more sophisticated, which is happening through scientometrics (Kretschmer, 1993).

To sum up, therefore, the processes of diversification and stratification have been deepening in higher education over the last few decades, leading from the Humboldtian model toward highly diversified types of organizations and modes of management. This diversified sector differentiates itself among many dividing axes. The critical variables are scientific and didactic prestige, business models, relations with the environment, mode of management, type of founder, university specialization, mission, structure, and academic culture.

2.5 Massification of higher education

The process of changing the elitist to the egalitarian model of higher education and its massification began after World War II. Its beginning and pace depend on the country, state policy, and other factors, including the level of national product per capita. Universal access to higher education was offered by the United States, where war veterans could take advantage of free college. The G.I. Bill of Rights Act of 1944 contributed to a considerable increase in the number of students and modified thinking about higher education (Olson, 1973). In addition to free college for veterans, the rise in the number of students in the United States was also linked to the emancipation of women and their growing participation in higher education (Pascall and Cox, 1993). Moreover, this trend occurred in most countries or even took the form of post-massification (Tight, 2019b; Mok and Marginson, 2021). Secondary mass education took hold in most developed economies, but the process took place over several decades, starting in the 1960s (Guri-Rosenblit, Šebková, and Teichler, 2007). In the 1990s, higher education became more widespread in Eastern European (former post-Soviet) countries (Scott, 2007). Then the rapid growth of number of students in Asia, Africa, and Latin America continues in the XXI century (Mohamedbhai, 2014; Varghese, 2015; Giannakis and Bullivant, 2016). The most significant increase has occurred over the last 30 years in India, China, the South East Asian region, and some African countries such as South Africa and Nigeria (Shin and Harman, 2009). More than 150 million people go to university every year. The rapid growth of higher education is one of the key phenomena of the second half of the 20th and the first half of the 21st century (Guri-Rosenblit, Šebková, and Teichler, 2007). The increase in the number of students is reported by analyses and statistics demonstrating this global trend, which has been gaining momentum in recent years (Schofer and Meyer, 2005). Differences in the timing of the start and the pace of expansion are still significant. The number of students continues to grow fastest in developing countries (China, India, and Indonesia) and slowest in countries with the highest education indicators. However, the number of students—per population—is consistently highest in developed countries.

T. Brennan cites three ideal types in higher education:

1 Elitism—educating the potential ruling class as the future social elite;
2 Massification—the transfer of professional skills and knowledge in universities to large sections of society;
3 Universalism—preparing the "whole population" for dynamic social and technological change.

Brennan and Trow argue that these stages coexist in one system or institution (Brennan, 2004; Trow, 2006). The saturation of the high number of students in the best-developed systems could lead to the post-massification stage. The number of students in the third decade XXI century begins to be stable. However, the student body is now very differentiated ethnically by gender, income, and type of education. It creates new challenges concerning financing and quality of higher education, proper inclusion, and stratification of students and HEIs (Gumport et al., 1997; Reiko, 2001; Wan, 2011).

2.6 Corporatization of the academic profession

Philip Altbach in his article "The deteriorating guru: The crisis of the professoriate" illustrates the negative impact of the changes of the last decades on the working conditions of academic teachers, so that not the best and the most talented express their interest in the profession. Of course, an academic staff member should not be perceived as a guru who has at his disposal revealed knowledge and whose dogmas are not to be questioned. But the ethos of such workers included features of a vocation and a sense of social mission. The traditional academic culture, which was losing its importance, attracted outstanding individuals because it could offer a lot, e.g., freedom of research, creativity, lack of routine or bureaucracy and autonomy, and high social status (Altbach, 2015a). The replacement of the traditional culture with a corporate-managerial one has resulted in the fact that the profession of an academic employee no longer seems so attractive to talented young people; it no longer means security and is not always associated with the perspective of development. A. Amaral and A. Magalhães mention the phenomenon of polarization of the academic profession, i.e., the erosion of its relative benefits linked to social status (Amaral and Magalhães, 2007, p. 8). In the UK and the United States, most academically qualified lecturers applied for tenure (the equivalent of a full professorship in European systems) after several decades of work. This position provided more prestige, security, and stability of employment. Universities are currently abandoning permanent employment in many places and opting for contract employment. In the UK, tenure is almost non-existent, and in the United States, only half of the workforce has chosen a route that will enable them to apply for tenure in the future. In the European Union, there are limited opportunities for promotion than there used to be (Altbach, 2015b). Younger staff face an even more difficult situation, as they are often employed only on temporary contracts due to budget reductions. University lecturers work casually, in various places, or earn extra money by doing other work (Welch, 2012). As a result, the focus on scientific and research activities is lacking or is carried out at a low level (which translates into less valuable publications). University salaries could never be compared with those offered in business, but they were compensated by a lower risk of dismissal and high professional status. International comparative studies show that academic salaries in relation to business have continued to decline in most of the countries studied (Altbach, 2012). Doctoral education has also lost its attractiveness because postgraduate students, just like other employees, have problems with unemployment in situations of crisis in the labor market. Those interested in the job of academic teachers have limited career prospects. The lack of job security and the lower prestige of the profession make academic work less attractive for the young and talented. However, it is also worth mentioning the possible positive effects of less job stability.

In 20 years, universities have undergone processes of formalization and standardization of work. Borrowed business solutions have transformed universities' organizational architecture, but they have brought little benefit to employees. The need for more and more work documentation takes time away from the creative work of lecturers. Excessive bureaucracy destroys the professional ethos, turning education and the work of scientists into a quasi-business activity. As a result, demoralization and the development of organizational cynicism progress, and the scientific community contests excessively formalized systems. According to Sloterdijk, organizational cynicism is developing in corporations based on instrumental reason and the manipulation of others in organizations (Sloterdijk, 1987, p. 389). The academic ethos has a value orientation that is the antithesis of business, clerical or corporate activity. Therefore, control systems do not have sound effects and are becoming increasingly costly. They must be continually re-regulated in the face of developing control avoidance practices. Attempts to use competition-oriented solutions that simulate the free market also have mixed results. Teamwork collapses if performance is assessed within a formalized system, encouraging circumventing the system. Increased control also means more stress for employees and higher levels of burnout (Kinman and Jones, 2003; Winefield et al., 2003; Tytherleigh et al., 2005). Universities experience lower job satisfaction, commitment, and identification with the institution. In addition, staff retention and absenteeism increase (Bozeman and Gaughan, 2011; Ryan, Healy, and Sullivan, 2012; Mello, 2013). Organizational cynicism only negatively affects work and academic identity and may lead to unethical behavior. It is caused, among other things, by the erosion of the traditional ethos of the academic staff member, who is under pressure to change to form a "professional knowledge worker" (Carvalho, 2017; van Winkel et al., 2018; Siekkinen, Pekkola, and Carvalho, 2020). It must be acknowledged that the traditional academic culture was also effective in the face of mass education in the 20th century. Professors combined teaching with the work of a scientist based on status, collaboration, and a commitment to work conceived as a vocation. Academics themselves created the curricula and worked on the quality of education while enjoying a high degree of autonomy and many privileges. In recent years, we have seen the replacement of the collegial academic culture with a quasi-corporate culture, in which the task of academics is to remain competitive and achieve appropriate scientific and didactic results (Parker and Jary, 1995). To this end, systems for controlling, evaluating, and motivating staff have been developed, and administration has been employed to implement them (Guenther and Schmidt, 2015). Particularly developed and diversified remuneration systems are introduced for university managers in the UK and the United States (Langbert and Fox, 2011). Incentive systems are no longer characteristic only of developed countries, subject to the revolution of new public management, but also of developing countries (Khan, Islam, and Husain, 2014). In addition, organizational strategies, quasi-corporate structures, and procedures had to be created. Formalized systems for the management of educational quality have been developed, which have become commoditized and result in increased bureaucracy, sometimes not conducive to the quality of teaching (Lichtenberger, 2013). Business solutions prevail among the fastest growing universities (i.e., non-public universities and especially private profit-oriented universities) (Lee, 2017; Pekkola et al., 2018; Shams, 2019; Cardoso, Carvalho, and Videira, 2019; Ajayan and Balasubramanian, 2020; Gaiaschi, 2021).

2.7 Industrial and academic science

The norms operating in universities and the social roles of academics make up a coherent social system derived from modern science and the idea of the university, through which we can know and change the world. The second half of the 20th century was the beginning of a time when the model of the traditional academic institution was considered anachronistic. Researchers cite symptoms of a crisis in science, steaming from rapid social change, which was brought about mainly by the development of science. J. Ziman argues that academic science has been replaced by "post-science" at this time. He believes that "post-academic science" (or "industrial science") is:

- Limited (*local*);
- Commercial;
- Authoritarian;
- Expert;
- Proprietary (Ziman, 2002).

Therefore, the creation of limited, practical, and proprietary knowledge to analyze detailed, often technical or administrative solutions to problems is happening. Scientists are now contractual and dependent experts who do not carry out basic or hardly pragmatic research. Such industrial science may degenerate into an unethical "post-science," which is the antithesis of the ethos of academic science based on the "CUDOS" standards of Robert Merton. "Post-science" negates academic norms, which induces scientific pathologies and casts doubt on the "moral integrity of science" (Ziman, 2002, pp. 28–50, 67–68, 330). The crisis of trust in science, progressing in recent decades, is due to the negation of the norms of academic science. Science, entangled in the network of economic or political interests, was forced to abandon the ideal of disinterestedness in order to pursue profits for business, power, politicians, owners, or managers. For these reasons, it is increasingly dehumanized and instrumental. What matters is research and education in practical disciplines, the educational profile is narrowed down to one specialization, and the canon of general education is omitted. The norms of communalism and the freedom of scientific expression are violated by financial dependence, and the decision-makers demand specific research. Principals expect research to give them a competitive advantage and do not intend to make the results available to competitors. One manifestation of the commercialization of science is the so-called "marketing of the intellectual property," whereby rights to intellectual ownership, often regarded as commercial brands, are sold and advertised using social engineering. The norm of universalism is undermined by: bureaucratic power structures in science, which are responsible for increasingly complex and formalized rules of scientific research funding, and the rise of the academic corporation, which creates authority based on a system of interests and dependencies. The bureaucratization of science changes the ethos of the scientific worker into that of a technocrat, focused on careers and scientific administration rather than on creative activities. This increases distrust of institutions and scientific authorities. The judgments of scientists are criticized as biased and subordinated to their interests, which is also linked to a more general crisis of trust in experts and the spread of false opinions online. The popularization of science is becoming less and less important, as people often give up exploring the world in favor of other aspects of social life. It must be acknowledged that the phenomena of escapism and scientific ignorance are a frequent danger associated with succumbing to the delusion of irrationalism (e.g., the phenomenon of post-truths, the fashion for alternative medicine or paranormal) (McIntyre, 2018; Lapsley and Chaloner, 2020; Lynch, 2020; Valladares, 2021). Academic science used to have an autotelic value. Still, now that the hybrid academic-industrial science model has undermined the traditional ethos of science, it has lost its strong identity and is characterized by a diversity of approaches. The next model of doing science may retain a pragmatic character—science will not be an autotelic value but may be a derivative of economic importance (Barnes and Dolby, 1970; Stehr, 1978; Kalleberg, 2007; Huff, 2007; König, Børsen, and Emmeche, 2017; Kim and Kim, 2018).

2.8 Privatization and specialization of education

The Humboldtian university did not aim to cooperate with the labor market. State financing of universities and focus on basic research did not bring universities closer to industry or applied research—unlike in the United States, where the Newman model related to the Humboldtian concept but also associated with religious education and focused on the student and the labor market, was dominant (Rothblatt, 1997). In the United States, there was a fundraising system from the beginning, and private funders also contributed to the establishment and development of universities. These universities maintained contact with their graduates after graduation. The European Union discovered the gap between the European and American systems in the Lisbon Strategy and sought to reduce its effects by implementing the Bologna process (Keeling, 2006; Dale, 2007). However, this may happen gradually due to the diversity of European higher education systems and the heterogeneity of the academic community's positions on forms of cooperation with employers. The multiplicity of ways of education results from the need to respond to labor market demands in different countries. Good universities apply standards of academic work, fight for the quality of teaching, and achieve an appropriate level for graduates, which often involves limiting practical training. Practice-oriented universities—to a large extent non-public ones—deal with education for business, reaching for flexible forms of teaching (e-learning, internships, practical profile of education, part-time studies, classes with practitioners). In general, however, an attempt is being made to adapt instruction to the labor market, and practical education is being promoted. This trend has many manifestations. The traditional university tended toward an academic, theoretical education focused on imparting essential knowledge. Graduates of key universities worked in administration in selected professions of usually high prestige (e.g., legal or medical). Employment was based on social and intellectual capital, social relations within the establishment, and in addition on competence. Knowledge transfer between universities and industry was indirect. Universities made available the results of their basic research, which enabled their use in business by industry or practically oriented universities (e.g., polytechnics), which were established later than universities. Graduates had no problem finding jobs and making careers, as they became the social elite. They were supported by associations or alums clubs, especially in the American system. Traditional universities used programs and education methods based on contact between the lecturer and the group, with practice only being a supplement. The group of lecturers was supplemented by full-time employees who combined teaching and research. In teaching, the full-time form prevailed, intended for education-oriented students. Extramural education was on the margin. Nowadays, universities educate both essential and vocational competencies and combine general education with adapted to the needs of the labor market. The university and education programs are assessed by the ability of the graduates to find a job. Many forms of cooperation between universities and the labor market have emerged, for example (Macioł et al., 2012):

- Job fairs;
- Associations and alums surveys;
- Academic career offices;
- University rankings from the employers' point of view.

In the area of transfer of research results to practice, institutional solutions linking universities directly with business (such as industrial parks, regulations supporting the commercialization of research, spin-offs, and spin-outs of universities, and business incubators) have also been successfully applied, although these solutions are subject to various barriers (Bigliardi, Galati, and Verbano, 2013; Link and Scott, 2017). In educational programs, the theoretical orientation harmonizes with the practical one, and an increase in the number of practical and specialized classes is observed. In our country, a large part of universities prepares programs in the practical profile and specialist fields. Lectures, and exercises are enriched with professional practice (which later helps students to find a job and start a career) or e-learning. The number of teaching staff with professional experience and those employed at the university on a contract basis is increasing. In the United States, reputable universities have long used practitioners (e.g., MIT, which leaves selected specialized classes to practitioners). Nowadays, part-time education is increasingly offered to students in various forms (e-learning, extramural mode, evening and weekend mode).

Universities will be increasingly oriented toward teaching professional competencies and providing the labor market with specialists. From the point of view of how well students are employed and how well they respond to the market's needs, both universities and teaching programs will be assessed. This will also make it possible to compare universities worldwide—an analytical system considering employment, salaries, and graduates' careers. Technology transfer will become crucial for research universities, which will collaborate with businesses in implementing innovations to maintain their position and attract funding from the industry. Alumni participation in university governance (on university boards of trustees, advisory or supervisory boards) will increase. Forms of education connected with professional work, i.e., part-time with e-learning or dual forms (combining practical learning and labor), are likely to develop. The structure of the teaching staff will change, as it is expected that training will be mainly the responsibility of practitioners temporarily employed by higher education institutions (adjuncts). The permanent staff will probably concentrate on either research or teaching activities.

There is a shift from considering higher education as a public good to a private interest. Among the developments that have influenced this are (Tilak, 2008b):

- Privatization of higher education;
- The university's move toward quasi-corporate management (up to the producer model of higher education services and research results);
- The globalization of higher education services, thanks to liberalization and the regulation of international competition through the World Trade Organization (WTO) or General Agreement on Trade and Services (GATS) agreements, which treat higher education as a private good or product of international trade (Altbach, 2015a, 2015b);
- Neoliberal education policies and new public management assume that students will pay for their education, and universities will rely on self-financing.

The social responsibility of universities is expressed in reliable research and the provision of high-quality teaching—this is the public mission of a university in crisis. Public universities are struggling with financial problems, constant restructuring, and market pressure, so in their concern for survival, they tend to treat the ideals of the public mission marginally. Non-public higher education institutions are usually development-oriented from the very beginning and want to benefit from financial surpluses from their activities (Balán, 2015). The assessment of neoliberal changes by part of humanists, i.e., philosophers, pedagogues, sociologists, and cultural anthropologists, turns out to be largely critical, in contrast to the assessment by economists. The criticism originates mainly within the universities and draws attention to the issue of HEIs neglecting their public mission due to the commercialization, commodification, and privatization of higher education (Calhoun, 2006; Dill, 2012). The critique of "academic capitalism" is based on concepts that go beyond neoclassical economics, and use neo-Keynesianism, to more radical concepts (critical theory, *Critical Management Studies*) (Slaughter and Rhoades, 2004). Bourdieu and Passeron have analyzed the education process, including the formal and informal aspects. Teaching is a vehicle for power, and its transfer occurs in institutions of learning, especially higher education. Hidden power structures are transferred in cultural patterns perpetuated in the educational process. We have the reproduction of the entire socio-cultural system, together with relations of subordination and domination (Bourdieu and Passeron, 1990a, pp. 58–125). Martin Carnoy and Henry Giroux treat education at the global level as a dialectic of imperialism and resistance (Carnoy, 1981; Giroux, 2001). According to Matts Alvesson, higher education gives students or graduates the illusion of guaranteed careers while burdening them with the high cost of education (Alvesson, 2013). S. Marginson stresses that the neo-liberal thought visible in higher education is connected with such an idea of the social world, in which there is no place for alternatives, in relation to the transformation of the university, moving away from the concept of the public good (Marginson, 2011). The formation of an "entrepreneurial culture" and, in addition, the restructuring in higher education have reinforced the pursuit of the interests of the educational institution rather than the public mission. This translates into the loss of social, democratic, and civic values that were previously intrinsic to the university. There is no focus on reducing social injustice, which was supposed to help disadvantaged groups find their way in the labor market and social life. Universities labeled "neoliberal" do not cultivate ideals of equality, striving for equal life chances, and helping the talented without paying attention to their origin or income. It is known that the offer of free university education does not work in itself to combat inequality and only contributes to social stratification to a certain extent. Still, it has become an essential part of the strategy to ensure social justice, to reduce the number of excluded people. Another aspect of moving away from the university's public good is the management of science. Steering investment in science can be a potential threat to the humanities. Funding only applied and quickly commercialized fields of research may lead to the erosion of humanistic thinking and, as a result, even the dehumanization of education and social life. A balance should be maintained in the development of different areas of science, as it is challenging to conclude their productivity in the future—therefore, it would be good to ensure conditions for the development of different areas. A policy of short-term, instrumental, and quantifiable scientific investment may prove to be a threat to its growth in the future. The experience of humanity demonstrates that a diversity of education is necessary—stable social development is ensured by people of different professions, whether entrepreneurs, scientists, engineers, or poets. It is in society's interest to impart skills and to offer courses that enable creativity to flourish in various fields. Furthermore, civil society's development can occur through critical social awareness provided by universities as communicative communities of researchers and students. Misappropriation of the ideal of the public good makes organizations quasi-corporations deprived of the option of criticality, abandoning the training of intellectuals in favor of specialists (Altbach, 2007). This threatens civil society, which should be built by critical, informed, engaged citizens who make political choices (Roksa, 2008; Jamshidi et al., 2012; Levine, 2018).

3 Digital transformation of universities

3.1 Digital transformation

Digitalization has been taking place for at least half a century. It is an ongoing tendency that has grown in importance and been transformed by the spread of the Internet and connected social and organizational practices, such as the Internet of Things, crowdsourcing, social networks and media, virtual communities, teleworking distance learning, and many others. The concept of digitization is vague and different meanings can be pursued (Vial, 2019). Some of them are narrow and concentrate on a detailed meaning of digitization, such as converting data from analog format to digital one (*digitization*). Others, broader, define digital transformation in terms of computers, networks, information technology, and communication transition (*digitalization*) (Bloomberg, 2018, Ebert and Duarte, 2018). For the first time, this term probably appeared in 1971, when the digitization of society was understood as the spread of digital and information technologies (Brennen and Kreiss, 2016). Choosing a more generalized meaning and looking for an understanding could lead to the definition that digitalization is using information and communication tools to effectively disseminate knowledge between social actors (Reis et al., 2018).

Digitalization is a technological, social, and cultural process that, via software, networks, and information and communication technologies (ICTs), allows fast sharing, dissemination, and collaborative work on all kinds of data, including texts, numbers, images, and sounds. The description of digital technologies in the literature varies. A simple definition is to enumerate a set of technologies, sometimes referred to by the acronym SMACIT (Sebastian et al., 2020).

1 *Social*: Group dimension of information and communication technologies (Oestreicher-Singer and Zalmanson, 2012).
2 *Mobile*: Using smartphones, mobile, portable and remote applications.
3 *Analytics*: Ability to gather and analyze big data, enabling evidence-based decision-making (Günther et al., 2017).
4 *Cloud*: Storing and processing data in the computing cloud.

DOI: 10.4324/9781003366409-5

5   *Internet of Things* (IoT): The ecosystem of interconnected and data-exchanging things (Tambotoh et al., 2016).

Most of these technologies are developing through the Internet, utilizing value co-creation methods. In addition, many digital transformation technologies include software, social networks, online platforms, and mobile applications (Jewitt, 2013; Heim et al., 2018).

It is worth raising the issue of the social, cultural, and organizational consequences of digitalization processes in the broad sense. The first effect will be the emergence of a *network society* based on new interactions by Internet technologies that get people together through virtual ties into virtual communities. The concept of the "network society" was coined by J. Van Dijk in 1991 and popularized by M. Castells end 20th and beginning of the 21st century (van Dijk, 1999; Castells, 2011). For Castells, networks driven by digital technologies are becoming the most critical nodes of social structures at all levels and gradually the basis for creating individual and collective identities. The concept of the network society is an extension of the ideas of the information society and the knowledge economy (Castells, 2004). One of the crucial aspects of the evolution of the network society is the construction of the *network economy* (de Man, 2004). The most vital resource of this economy is data development by strengthening the network market based on data processing via the Internet. At the individual level, transitions in the sphere of identity and the creation of interpersonal ties are a clear tendency (Burke, 1997). A similar process of shaping collective network identities exists at the level of organizations (Burke, 1997; Kohtamäki, Thorgren, and Wincent, 2016).

Virtualization is building virtual, rather than physical, models or things using computers and information technology (Kohtamäki, Thorgren, and Wincent, 2016). Virtualization can lead to the creation of music, films, books, photographs, and even works of art or money. It allows quicker, more widespread, and more affordable admission to many activities and services. Sectors of the economy founded on virtualization are emerging, such as computer and video games, scientific research, education, technical simulations, VR, e-books, films, and multimedia publishing (Heckman et al., 2007; Rodríguez-Haro et al., 2012).

The tendency to upgrade efficiency and reduce costs in the organization leads to systems of data-based decision-making. Digitalization improves intra-organizational efficiency in the coherence, quality, and precision of the realized processes. For managers, greater control is exercised over organizational functions at the operational and strategic levels. Such management practices happen by effectively accessing, collecting, and processing data (Mazurek, 2019, p. 23). Digitalization is closely related to evidence-based decision-making, revolutionizing management processes, culture, and social life.

The digital revolution has strong and weak sides. The optimism connected to developing a network society emanates from the pioneering ideas of the network revolution. It is reminiscent of the utopian socialist concepts of Charles Fourier, Henri de Saint-Simon, and Robert Owen (Jones, 2016). Network society emphasizes the potential for the growth of open online communication and digital democracy, permitting better participation in power and removing barriers to access to knowledge (van Dijk, 1999; Castells, 2011). Many hopes associated with empowerment and knowledge accession through the web have come true in the last decades. An example could be Wikipedia, a massive encyclopedia of humanity continuing the idea of a complete compendium of knowledge and universal access (Anthony, Smith, and Williamson, 2009). Popularizing access to scientific sources are the growing Google Scholar, Scopus, Web of Science platforms, and *open source* projects (Ávila, Teixeira, and Almeida, 2018). Examples of growing communication are networking social media like Facebook, LinkedIn, Instagram, Twitter, and communication platforms such as Messenger, Snapchat, and WhatsApp. They build foundations, for commercial reasons, for the creation of networking communities that provide universal, easy access to human contact (Jarvenpaa et al., 1999; Kenchakkanavar, 2015). ITC and mobiles are conquering business and social life. Computers and the Internet also bring several dangers. It could be the overproduction of vast amounts of redundant data, social transitions threatening alienation, and growing aspirations for conspicuous digital consumption (Reddy and Reinartz, 2017). Concerning this last characteristic, the case of "conspicuous consumption" defined by T. Veblen remains intriguing (Trigg, 2001; Bagwell and Bernheim, 1996). Does networking guide the democratization of consumption and shift away from " conspicuous consumption"? It seems that it does not. There are unique manifestations of it in the form of digital consumption "for the show," e.g., purchase of ownership of digital works of art. Internet conspicuous consumption creates elites, facilitates stratification, and outlines status differences (Ismail et al., 2018; Katsulis, 2010).

The digital transformation leads to various social, economic, and cultural changes (Barnatt, 2001). At the individual level, behavioral changes appear and significantly transform consumption patterns. People are becoming consumers of digital goods, which frequently take a dematerialized form during digital transformation. Information and educational services, e-commerce, films, computer games, texts, photos, and videos increasingly utilize dematerialized digital services, displacing older technological generations of products (Breeding, 2013). Dematerialization, virtualization, a departure from material products, and a shift toward services are other digital transformation features (Griffiths, 2013). Digital consumers are different from those of material products. New characteristics are flexibility, service co-creation (*crowdsourcing*), readiness for networking and virtualization, and sometimes even ephemerality in choices (Nicholas and Rowlands, 2008, pp. 1–13; Gilleard, 2017). The networked economy and the digital consumer are descriptions of aspects of the transformation of organizations towards digitality. The main characteristics of this transformation are virtualization, networking, agility, responsiveness, and co-creation of value (Berman, 2012; Lis, 2021).

Digital transformation sometimes supports the feeling of insecurity in organizations, as technology must be connected with the social and cultural sphere (Mazurek, 2019, p. 49).

- The complexity of digital transformation goes beyond the degree that describes the implementation of new information and communication technologies as it activates coupling processes.
- Organizational borders are blurring under the influence of networking.
- Physical and digital interdependence enrich innovation processes due to the coupling results of various technologies.
- Digital customer behavior is hard to predict.

Summarizing this review of the literature on the digital transformation of societies, one finds standard, universal features of this long-term transition. Essential characteristics of digital transition in social aspects can be capitalized in eight points.

1   The formation of new behavioral patterns of the digital consumer emphasizes the perception and utilization of digital goods (Zwick and Dholakia, 2004).
2   The network and information economy is growing, with the importance of dematerialized products and services (Moutinho and Heitor, 2007).
3   Digital services and innovation development proliferates in many economic sectors, and old generations of products are losing ground (Quattrociocchi et al., 2017).
4   The primacy of ICT in shaping the economy, society, and culture (Moreno, 2014; Barbet and Coutinet, 2001).
5   Forming new communities and social links based on digital competence (Feenberg and Barney, 2004).
6   The progressive change of organizations and networks towards digitalization supports the increasing uptake of ICT (Ballantyne and LaMendola, 2010).
7   The consolidation of information and communication technologies is critical in gaining a competitive advantage for organizations (Mu, Tang, and MacLachlan, 2010).
8   Advancing value co-creation by networking communities and co-creating value with the customer (Chan, Li, and Zhu, 2015).

3.2 Organizations of the digital age

Over the past 50 years, the digital transformation has gradually impacted all spheres of human relations. Its effect on the culture, economy, society (macro level), and human behavior (micro level) can be complemented by organizations (mezzo level). Organizations' assimilation of digital technologies is a multi-level process creating long-term revolutionary change and paradigm shift. Formerly critical for the competitive position was the proper combination and use of human, finance, knowledge, and natural resources. Today access to knowledge resources and competencies related to their processing and dissemination begins to play a dominant role. Digital technologies require effectively managing these unique resources at the strategic, tactical, and operational levels (Uzzi, 1996). Adapting digital technologies is an organizational means that impact many functional areas (Matt et al., 2014).

Organizations are under pressure from the fast development of ICT due to technological progress and the growth of competition in most sectors (Innes and Booher, 1999). The change has consequences: Developing a risk society, increased uncertainty, blurring organizational boundaries, and changes in economic and sociocultural systems. These changes are closely related to networking, digitization, automation, and robotization (Caruso, 2018). Many researchers point to several possible manifestations of new forms of digital organization related to the development of information and communication technologies, including *cloud computing*, the IoT (Samaniego and Deters, 2016; Tambotoh et al., 2016), *hyperconnectivity* (Collins and Kolb, 2013), *Software-as-a-Service* (SaaS) (Agarwal, 2011), *big data analytics* (Günther et al., 2017; Choi, Wallace, and Wang, 2018). The revolutionary changes taking place, which are rooted in ICT, are captured in differentiated cognitive frameworks. Examples of hybrids of management concepts with computer science ideas include agile, reengineering, NBIC, and many other perspectives (Yu and Mylopoulus, 1996).

Agile is an organizational and ICT approach for manufacturing high-quality software. The rules of the Agile Manifesto, a coupling of ICT with management concepts, can be summarized in eight points: (1) simplicity, (2) continuous adaptation to changing requirements, (3) working software delivered periodically as the primary measure of progress, (4) speed of software development to achieve customer satisfaction, (4) attention to technical aspects and sound design, (5) teams based on self-management, (6) team communication focused on direct contact, (7) daily close cooperation between developer and business, and (8) no disruptive effect of late changes in specification on the whole software development process (Gurusamy, 2016; Krehbiel, 2017).

Reengineering (also *Business Process Reengineering*) is a management method postulating radical reconstruction of organizational processes resulting from ICT implementation processes (Hammer and Champy, 2009). In ICT, reengineering could mean code *refactoring*, i.e., restructuring an existing program without changing its function and operation (Yu and Mylopoulus, 1996; Kumar and Gill, 2012).

NBIC from prefixes: *Nano-, bio-, info-,* and *cogno-* are technologies being the collection of practical solutions and the conceptualization and skills to apply them (*know-how*), as well as the methods, procedures, and technologies that use this knowledge (Dosi, 1982, p. 152; Volkova et al., 2017).

Several trends in the development of organizations in the digital age are a consequence of the absorption of ICT by people in sociocultural systems. Organization virtualization applies virtual methods and tools in management (Verdouw et al., 2015). In turn, agile is a management method for creating and implementing ITC projects (Javdani Gandomani and Ziaei Nafchi, 2016; Rigby, Sutherland, and Takeuchi, 2016). An example of the growth of digital management methods is the co-creation of values by network communities (*crowdsourcing, crowdfunding*) (Siala, 2013; Chan, 2015). From the point of view of management, the collection and processing of mass data (*big data analytics*) (McAfee et al., 2012) and data-based *decision-making* (*evidence based*) are also crucial (de Waal, 2015).

Organizations use digital transformation for different purposes. The first differentiation points to ICT as a digital product or process that supports its functioning. An organization's digital transformation may reduce costs, increase quality, efficiency, and effectiveness, expand communication with customers and the environment, or acquire new digital consumers (Nicholas and Rowlands, 2008; Berman, 2012). It can therefore follow different directions: strategy, technology, value, structure, and finance (Jewitt, 2013; Matt, Hess, and Benlian, 2014; Adner, Puranam, and Zhu, 2019).

Diverse management concepts accompany the implementation of new ICT. We point to reengineering among the ones gaining importance: Industry 4.0, Industry Revolution 4.0, SMART, Internet of Things (Shrouf, Ordieres, and Miragliotta, 2014). ICT, used as a foundation for management processes, includes the operations of digitization, computerization, virtualization, robotization, real-time processing and analysis of mass data, the ecosystem of the Internet of Things, and the Internet of Technology, inter-organizational relations, coopetition (Strategic Partnering, Knowledge Partnering, Artificial Intelligence, neural networks, fuzzy logic and soft computing, Machine Learning, Machine to Machine Communications and other (Adamik, 2016).

The market role of ICT directs to the building of relationships between customers and stakeholders, the management of strategic and operational actions of the organization in the areas of service delivery to the market, the delivery of new value to customers, the shaping of the business using digital methods, the co-creation of values with customers (Berman, 2012; Polo Peña, Frías Jamilena, and Rodríguez Molina, 2014; Breidbach and Maglio, 2016; Heim, Han, and Ghobadian, 2018; Mihardjo et al., 2019a).

The digital transformation in a company leads to strategic changes and a fundamental restructuring of strategic and operational processes (von Leipzig et al., 2017; Mazurek, 2019, p. 49). DT leads businesses to the creation and implementation of new business models. In organizations, DT usually changes the areas of technical infrastructure (*hardware*, equipment), application, user, and organizational software (*software*), system and communication infrastructure, integration of business processes with external contractors.

The strategic aspect could refer to an essential change in the core business, enriching it with entirely new activities. An organization's strategy is closely linked to digital transformation (Domazet, 2018; Trenkle, 2019; Tabrizi et al., 2019; Sebastian et al., 2020). It could be the development of an organization resulting from creating a new digital market. In the case of companies: Producing computer hardware and software and implementing solutions in the sphere of information and communication technologies, computer games, e-commerce, and social media (Kim, Yang, and Kim, 2008). The development of such a sector first takes the form of a blue ocean strategy, in which market leaders gradually appear and are followed by a group of imitators (Pillania and Chang, 2009).

The development of Industry and Society 4.0 in the 21st century also led to a change in business models. The direction of transition is from a product to a service orientation. Business models are founded on the integration and cooperation of companies, people, and machines in providing a service to customers. Collaboration between humans and digital machines leads to market value creation. It also enables flexibility and pushes the innovation process. Decentralized decisions built on constant communication and data examination advance flexibility in production and management. Networked and digital organizational methods play a critical role in this tendency (Lasi, 2014; Almada-Lobo, 2015; Morrar, Arman, and Mousa, 2017; Oberer and Erkollar, 2018).

The prospect for development is caught, among other advantages, in increased effectiveness. Industry 4.0 allows better allocation of resources and shorter downtimes, optimizes the organizational processes, and creates new products. Industry 4.0 shapes new sectors. In the economy, there is a growth of innovation. Technology is expanding abroad, which attracts investors. Latest jobs with high added value are being generated, centered around IT, automation, and new industries involving, for example, human–robot cooperation. Better quality products, as well as lower stocks, contribute to lower production costs. There is a focus on sustainability, efficient use of materials, and improved energy efficiency. Customer needs more customized products, which means manufacturing in small batches (*mass customization*). The digitization of large sectors of society is changing business practices and social services, education, health, social care, journalism, entertainment, and more (Larsson and Teigland, 2019, p. 378; Saxena, 2021).

Higher education is not immune to these changes. Digitalization processes are advanced, and the possibility of new market opportunities is significant. Many aspects of managing organizations in digital transformation are in the literature. Examples include several approaches and models: "cybernetic," "technological," "value creation," "structural change," and "finance" (Matt, Hess, and Benlian, 2015). The "Cybernetic" model of organizational management describes a process starting with data acquisition, then transformation (algorithmic or heuristic) towards information and the process closes with knowledge diffusion. Digital transformation means the choice of priorities related to technology, value creation, change, or finance. Technology use refers to a company's attitude towards new technologies and its ability to exploit them. The role of ITC is fundamental to a company's operations as it is the product core on which the company's strategy evolves. The strategy involves deciding what market position the entity is aiming for technological leader or follower. Being a technological market leader may lead to a competitive advantage. Still, it also involves uncertainty and risk because the technology to be the core of the business may not yet be developed, and its possibilities are unknown. From a business perspective, using new technologies often means changes in value creation. These relate to the impact of digital transformation strategies on the "value" of companies online, depending on how far the new digital activities diverge from the classic ones that are often still the core business. The changes create opportunities to expand and enrich the current portfolio of products and services and to transform the business model to fit better the changing market. Digitalization of products or services may require different forms of profit generation and even adjustments to the business scope of the strategy if products address other markets or new customer segments. Different technologies often go hand in hand with structural changes to provide a suitable basis for new operations. Structural transformations refer to changes in a company's organization and involve the need to locate a new digital operation within corporate structures. It is, therefore, crucial to assess the scale of the changes resulting from a company's digital transformation. If the range of change is quite limited, it could make more sense to adjust the new activities to existing corporate structures. In contrast, it would be better to create a separate subsidiary within the company for more substantial changes. The financial aspect relates to assessing which financing models will result from the company's digital transformation (Matt, Hess, and Benlian, 2015, Lenart-Gansiniec and Sulkowski 2022b).

3.3 Digital transformation in universities

A literature review indicates many meanings of digital transformation in HEIs (Benavides et al., 2020; Simonette, Magalhães, and Spina, 2021; Cantner, 2022). Categorizing these definitions and areas, we can identify a few dominant motives: change management, educational innovation, digital turnaround, customer alignment, and new business models.

Digital transformation is a change process in the university and involves dynamically understanding people, project strategies, and structures. DT is "a process that aims to change an organization holistically through a combination of information, computing, communication, and connectivity technologies" (Vial, 2019). The organization goes in the direction of controlling the DT that occurs through a planned change management process (Carcary et al., 2016; Tabrizi et al., 2019).

Digital disruption is transformation caused or influenced by digital technologies disrupting established ways of value creation, social interaction, business, and, universally, our thinking. The concept of digital disruption is strongly related to digital transformation and also to *disruptive innovations* (Lim, 2019). Implementing digital technologies in economic activities and social life rapidly changes how we do things. We are dealing with digital breakthroughs at the time of the pandemic when the actions of universities moved to the virtual world (Saxena, 2021; Telli and Aydin, 2021).

DT are also adaptations or investments in technologies and new business models to engage customers efficiently at every stage of the lifecycle (Balakrishnan and Das, 2020; Puriwat and Tripopsakul, 2021). Companies consider DT a "formal effort to renew business vision, models, and investments, moving towards a new digital economy" (Betchoo, 2016). A new strategy based on DT should include co-creating market value with customers (Malar, Arvidsson, and Holmstrom, 2019; Mihardjo et al., 2019a; Ruoslahti, 2020).

DT goes beyond the dematerialization of processes and includes the innovative application of new technologies to develop new services, redefine business models, and co-act with users. DT also creates and implements innovations that change organizations and markets and lead to new solutions (Hinings, Gegenhuber, and Greenwood, 2018; Nambisan, Wright, and Feldman, 2019).

DT of the HEIs should include the modernization of the governance, information management, and ITC infrastructure, which could contribute to innovation in education (Kaminskyi, Yereshko, and Kyrychenko, 2018). In recent years, a rapid increase in research on DT in higher education has occurred.

In the DT of the HEI, new solutions for modernization of the educational system with the help of ITC technologies and integration of digital technologies in teaching, learning, and organizational practices are essential topics (Fleaca, 2017). DT has been a significant subject in education during the last decades. The main issues are the didactics of e-learning, the analysis of interaction and digital communication in the learning process, and the application of information and communication solutions in education (Androutsos and Brinia, 2019; Simonette, Magalhães, and Spina, 2021).

DT is also the accelerated evolution of "selecting" management resolutions better adapted to the competitive environment and market. It is also a revolution because of its profound, critical structural implications for people and infrastructure, introducing new educational models (Gama, 2018). New organizational models and management methods usually demand rethinking and design of essential management items: strategy, target customers, and products (Sandhu, 2018; Tabrizi et al., 2019). From a management side, the influence of DT on business processes, public organizations, NGOs, and public policies is increasingly essential. Initially, the most considerable amount of research concerns business, but as DT advances, the share of public and non-profit sectors is growing (Kokkinakos et al., 2016; Mergel et al., 2018; Larsson and Teigland, 2019).

Summarizing analyzed ways of understanding the sense of digital transformation in higher education, it makes sense emphasize common subjects present in the publications. First, DT means breakthroughs leading to profound changes in strategies, structures, and cultures of HEIs. The variety of the changes caused by DT includes all three streams of academic mission. New teaching patterns, research, organization, management, communication, and implementation are born. In management, knowledge, human capital, marketing, finance, processes, and projects are perceived through the prism of DT. An inductive and analytical approach is dominant in contemporary research on digital transformation in HEIs. There is a place for a more synthetic and holistic view of DT in higher education (Holmwood and Marcuello Servos, 2019; Benavides et al., 2020, Sulkowski, 2022a, pp. 4–31).

Part II

Governance, management, and leadership of HEI

4 Universities management models

4.1 Relations between governance, management, and leadership

University governance is a complex organizational process, including exercising authority, making decisions, and allocating resources, which is carried out at three levels: academic governance, university management, and leadership (Muktiyanto, Hermawan, and Hadiwidjaja, 2020). The level of academic governance is related to the systemic solutions adopted in different countries and types of HEIs to supervise and manage universities (Rowlands, 2017b). Higher education is subject to relatively strong regulation, usually more detailed than most business sectors. Unsurprisingly, we are dealing with an activity crucial to society and in which public participation is significant. The science and higher education sector, like, for example, the health service, carries out a fundamental social mission for which the state takes responsibility. Universities enjoy social privileges associated with a sectoral monopoly or oligopoly, allowing them to award professional (e.g., bachelor, master, engineer, doctor) and scientific (e.g., doctor, professor) degrees. In non-profit activities, universities in many countries are exempt from taxation or benefit from significant concessions. Thus, they are a kind of "social investment" in developing human capital, civilization progress, cognition, and world improvement. The outlays for such an investment and its effects should be planned, controlled, and accounted for in some way. The process called accountability of HEIs serves this purpose. It is particularly important in the case of public HEIs, which are mainly maintained by the state budget. Academic governance includes legal and systemic solutions regulating the functioning of HEIs (Rowlands, 2017a). The term "external academic governance" could be used to describe the legal and systemic solutions governing HEIs in a national and sometimes broader framework (e.g., European Union) (Côme et al., 2018). "Internal academic governance" is the system of a university, regulated by its legal regulations, e.g., statutes. These internal regulations are shaped in a design of co-governance by the university's governing bodies (e.g., rector, president, senate) and supervisory bodies (e.g., founder, board of trustees,

DOI: 10.4324/9781003366409-7

supervisory boards, university councils). The academic governance system depends on the country, the type of university, and the legal and political solutions adopted. However, academic governance is evolving from public-administrative systems to business solutions modeled on agency theory and corporate governance (Schulze-Cleven and Olson, 2017; Kaplan, 2006).

The level of university governance is closely related to external and internal academic governance, as both personal and collegiate governing bodies are appointed in universities based on internal regulations, which must be by the law (Kozien, E. and Kozien, A., 2017). Several cognitive perspectives of understanding governance can be distinguished in university management (Renaudie, 2018). The systemic view combines the university's strategy and mission with the structure and organizational culture (Schmitz et al., 2018). Management levels start from strategic management through the tactical level to the operational one. The perspective of functional areas focuses on learning, teaching, and the third mission, realized using human capital, marketing activities, financial resources, information management, and many others (Rachman et al., 2017). It is also worth noting that many issues related to control are interdisciplinary. Academic leadership and the organizational identity of the university are good examples. The progressive marketization of the higher education sector on a global scale favors adopting management solutions adapted from business (Bileviciute et al., 2019, p. 5). However, it is necessary to critically reflect on their application and adjust them to the university with an awareness of the implications. Another critical area of research is the management of public universities with their specificity resulting from functioning within the stakeholder model. The *New Public Management* stream is based precisely on the assumption of transferring management concepts, methods, and tools from the business sector to the public sector (Broadbent and Laughlin, 2005), while *Public Value Management* is enriched with a critical reception of this process (Dent and Barry, 2017).

Leading people in the university short-circuits the process of exercising power at the micro-organizational level and includes human resources management processes. It refers to the managerial relationship and the employee perspective in the organization. It encompasses the classic elements of the HR process in organizations: employee recruitment, motivation, appraisal, and development (Ning and Lin, 2007). People management in universities can also be analyzed through the lens of different management paradigms, theories, concepts, and methods. The chronological overview leads from the philosophy of people administration, through personnel and human resource management, to human capital development (Bi, T., Han and Guan, 2014; Ahmady, Tatari, and Hosseini, 2016). Managing people also includes leadership processes, problems with leadership styles and patterns, and issues of organizational identity (Zhao, Chen, and Zhang, 2011). Other streams of people management that do not fit into the proposed classifications

Table 4.1 Methods of effective management in universities

Level	Scope	Method of implementation
Micro	Monitoring the quality of education, the value of research, and financial flows.	Applying management methods while maintaining the social mission. Not everything is controllable; a university's ethos, organizational culture, or identity are not measurable; they can only be encouraged to improve. Excessive pressure to change the culture and extreme control can arouse resistance and even lead to the development of countercultures in opposition to the solutions suggested by power structures.
Mezzo	Cooperation between universities and the environment.	Collaboration with business, third sector, and public organizations. Activities for the local labor market. Cooperation within clusters at the regional level. Technology transfer, development of career offices, business incubators. Collaboration with other regional universities.
Macro	Cooperation between the university and the state using management methods.	Co-creation of central strategies and public policies in education, health, security, economy, and science. Implementation of projects and innovations at the main level. Creation of national and international research and education networks.

Source: own elaboration.

are also important such as diversity and talent management or employer branding (Bradley, 2016).

What would be the role of governance in the case of the academic world? Universities should have methods for effective management at all levels. The sense of their use and limitations are shown in Table 4.1.

4.2 Concepts of management of HEIs

The management and organization of the university is a broad topic that requires a combination of synthetic and analytical insights. The synthetic view is a holistic perspective: the organizational system; the models of management; the links between governance, leadership, and supervision of the university; and the levels of management. The analytical viewpoint attempts to isolate more essential elements such as mission and strategic objectives, values, products, organizational participants, customers and stakeholders, decision-making process, and functional areas of management: human capital management, marketing, finance, accounting, and knowledge management.

A dynamic view of the university is also proposed, taking into account three formations, which are reference points for today's and future universities: the Humboldtian, the entrepreneurial, and the digital university. A comparison of the university's activities to a typical large or medium-sized enterprise was carried out to trace the changes in organization and management. Management theory and its application were primarily carried out in business activities, so the typical enterprise, managerially and corporately managed, can be taken as a reference. Public organizations and universities, as well as universities in general, are significantly different from businesses, so it is worth comparing management models and approaches. It will also answer the question about the directions and conditions of organizational changes in modern universities (Tsay et al., 2018).

The management levels of a university refer to the strategic and operational perspectives (Yudianto et al., 2021; Alavi et al., 2021). The strategic perspective concerns long-term development directions, planning, and implementation of strategic objectives, management of the entire organizational system, and relations between academic governance and leadership in the university (Parakhina et al., 2017). On the other hand, the operational horizon is shorter, related to decisions made on an ongoing basis in various functional areas or organizational units. In the case of both perspectives, important issues are the professionalization of management based on specialization, management by objectives, accountability, and decision-making based on reliable data analysis.

Analyzing modern universities' management transformation directions, it is worth pointing out a clear shift toward using the patterns developed for enterprises and business activities (Ashworth, 1984). This is related to several factors that make up the transformation, sometimes labeled ideologically as the "neoliberal university" (Taylor, A., 2017). The global trend toward privatization of a significant part of higher education is leading to business-like educational organizations. This is particularly evident in the case of private for-profit universities, which not only consider profitability as a key strategic goal and use a wide range of corporate management methods, but even in pursuit of their mission, abandon research activities, making a significant modification of the classical sense of the concept of the university. Another variable is the increase in competitiveness in providing educational services, combined with the reduction of state funding for universities and the development of substitute forms of education and science to the services offered by universities. The expansion of management as an instrumental but economically productive discourse in contemporary culture and society is also a key factor. Managers govern the world, and the insights of management science have become permanently embedded in social practice, not only in business but also in public organizations (new public management) and political and social activities (political and social marketing). Management concepts, methods, and tools permeate from business to university activities, creating a gradual professionalization of management.

The beginning of the 21st century is also marked by the acceleration of digital transformation, making a revolutionary civilizational change in social, economic, and cultural life and the condition of modern man. Universities are not exempt from the management changes by digital transformation involving the entire information and communication ecosystem. We are coming to the development of knowledge, information, and data management in organizations, leading to a profound change in companies and public organizations, and universities. Historically, one can see that the Humboldt-type university is the furthest from using management patterns taken from the business. In the 19th century, parallel to the development of Humboldt-type universities, the foundations of economic and corporate governance took shape, linked from the beginning of the 20th century to academic reflection on management. However, the Second-wave universities remained very far from the concept of governance in their spirit. On the contrary, drawing on the philosophies of German idealism and the Enlightenment, they represented a circle of non-instrumental ideas distant from economic and pro-efficiency thinking. The idea of progress in science and education referred to spirituality, culture, and human improvement. Such thinking remained constitutive of the model university until it entered the post-Humboldt phase, leading to the differentiation of the university and later to the formation of the entrepreneurial university. Third-wave universities became much closer to business; they absorbed management theory and practice. This can be seen in practically all spheres of activity of entrepreneurial universities (Cerver Romero, Ferreira, and Fernandes, 2021). The idea of entrepreneurship comes from the center of interest of management sciences, although it has an interdisciplinary character. Thanks to the fact that it combines discourses of various social disciplines, it is a load-bearing base for building on it a new organization of an entrepreneurial university, striving to make universities similar to enterprises in some respects (Audretsch and Belitski, 2022). They are characterized by an entrepreneurial culture, which differs significantly from the traditional academic culture. Values such as flexibility, innovation, management efficiency, and cost-effectiveness take precedence over the *Bildung* ethos characteristic of the second-wave university (Karhapää and Savolainen, 2017). While developing peripheral areas, the strong managerial core reflects the experience of efficient, managerial central management, combined with decentralization and delegation of operational authority to the level of departments and line units. The tendency to develop a third mission is an offshoot of entrepreneurship and the search for alternative funding streams other than the state. The opening of the third-wave university, which is supposed to be the opposite of the "ivory tower," consists of the intensive development of cooperation with the environment, with business, and the implementation of projects together with external entities (Rubens et al., 2017). In the classic model B. Clark's significant role is played by a shift toward the market and away from the power associated with the state's omnipotence or the academic oligarchy's collective decision-making (Clark, 1998a). Competitiveness, based on co-opetition rather than pure competition, is also important. The management mode of the third-wave university is thus motivated by entrepreneurship. It is accompanied by creating and implementing basic performance standards, professionalization and specialization of management, and a drive to account for the results. However, there are significant differences between universities and businesses in Clark's model. The nucleus of the university's activity remains the mission based on three pillars, which are a strategic priority and has precedence over the economic results of the activity. Decisions made in enterprises are mainly economically motivated. At the same time, third-wave universities may be justified by the development of science and teaching, the impact of public policies, and economic reasons. The management of the functional areas of an entrepreneurial university is also much closer to business solutions compared to a Humboldtian university. Entire spheres of activity are based on management concepts and methods, including human resource management, marketing, finance, accounting, and knowledge management. This is reflected in the professionalization and the corporatization of university management.

A theme of paramount importance in university governance is the differentiation of the shareholder model from the stakeholder model. The stakeholder model, which is characteristic of business and relates to corporate governance, assumes that those who own shares in a corporation, the shareholders, should oversee and manage the corporation to maximize the financial returns on their investment. This classical approach, defended by Milton Friedman, can be the basis for the business activities of private for-profit universities (Somers et al., 2018). Public universities' stakeholder model in which governance has a trade-off between the interests of different groups of influence seems adequate. Organizations should serve to maximize the broadly understood benefits for the stakeholders who make up the groups of influence, as well as work for the good of society, e.g., through social responsibility (Ramos-Monge, Llinàs-Audet, and Barrena-Martinez, 2017). In a public university, teaching staff, academic managers, administration, and students seek to gain benefits in the form of access to financial resources, material resources, power and influence, and symbolic goods using coalitions and social games in the organization. The development of the stakeholder model in universities, especially in public universities, is facilitated by collegialism in the way decisions are made. The advantage of the stakeholder model is the sense of participation, and internal democracy in the university, while the limitations include less flexibility and speed in decision-making. The entrepreneurial university significantly limits the scope of collegiality in decision-making, relying more on solutions adapted from business, managerial and corporate solutions.

The management of the digital university is likely to move toward business-modeled solutions, similar to the entrepreneurial university. However, these will be different organizations from the entrepreneurial university phase, as they will be at an advanced stage of digital transformation. As described in the previous chapter on the organization of the university, digital formation involves founding the whole management process on accountability, big data analytics, internet and intranet communication, and evidence-based decision-making. It leads to the reconstruction of the whole activity of the university, which nevertheless pursues its mission based on the three pillars (Table 4.2).

Integrated university management can be presented in the form of four triads. The first one describes the relationship at the level of the whole university, linking the HEI activities' governance processes with managing the organization and leading people. These elements are interdependent and are in a dynamic relationship with the university's organizational system, which consists of the subsystems: strategy, structure, and corporate culture, relatively separated from the environment and entangled in the process of material, financial, and symbolic exchange. The third triad is the three missions of the university: science, education, and relations with the non-academic environment. The last internal triad represents university management's dilemmas in the tension between the exercise of power and university autonomy and academic freedom. Such a synthetic view of the whole university organization and management, which resembles a star in the figure (Figure 4.1.), provides a basis for a deeper analysis of management processes, taking into account the perspective: of strategic *versus* operational, static *versus* dynamic (change management, process management, project management), and functional areas of the university organization (human resources management, marketing, finance).

4.3 HEIs governance

Governance is the supervisory, strategic decision-making process, or "making policies and rules to regulate institutions." It refers to the totality of management processes, which can be carried out by different actors, for example, the government, the market, or a network of organizations. Governance can be made effective through various means, including but not limited to law, cultural norms, or language (Bevir, 2013). The term *corporate governance* is used to refer to the regulation of enterprises, and the term *governance is* used more frequently to refer to public organizations.

In HEIs, *governance* means the fundamental principles according to which universities manage their affairs (Tierney, 2004; Shattock and Temple, 2006). The regulations for university governance are contained in external (e.g., laws and regulations) and internal (e.g., statutes) rules of law (Sporn, 2007). *Governance is* also intertwined with *university management*, as it concerns the participation of various stakeholder groups in control, the division of decision-making prerogatives, the appointment of powers of collegial and personal bodies, the principles of legitimacy and delegitimization of power in the university (Bianchi, Nasi and Rivenbark, 2021; Compton et al., 2022;

Table 4.2 Management of the three formations of the university *versus* management of the enterprise

	Company	Humboltian model university	Entrepreneurial university	Digital university
Management model	Shareholder model, business, commercial, private ownership	Stakeholder model, public universities, public good	Stakeholder model—public, stakeholder model—private	Stakeholder model—public, stakeholder model—private
Governance	Profit-driven and market-driven, performance standards, structured and advanced management, intensive and rational use of resources, economically accountable results	Driven by ethos, lack of performance standards, intuitive management based on tradition, unaccounted use of resources, and economic results	Entrepreneurial driven, basic performance standards, professional and intuitive management, fundamentally accountable use of resources, oriented on a mission and financial results	Guided by knowledge management, performance standards, structured and advanced management, intensive and rational use of resources, Accountable, mission and financial performance
Levels of governance and management	Strategic—shareholders, and objectives, operational—management principles	Strategic—vision, operational—tradition, and culture	Strategic—mission, objectives, operational—management of principles	Strategic—measurement, mission, plan, goals, operational—accountability, data, management
Organizational system	Integrated	Loose or mixed	Loose—large, public universities Miscellaneous—other universities	Loose—large, public universities Miscellaneous—other universities
Organizational objectives of the action	Economic profits, defined, accounted for	Non-economic values, generally inherent in the ethos, are unaccounted for	Miscellaneous—mission and operating costs, attempts at accounting	Multiple objectives, defined, quantifiable and manageable

Operating model	Business, profit generation, possible corporate social responsibility	Cultural and ethos driven	Missional, socially responsible, and competitive	Missional, socially responsible, and competitive
Values	Economic, various, shaped by owners and managers	The emanation of academic culture and ethos, traditional	Different, based on academic and entrepreneurial culture	Hybrid: university mission, ICT, innovation, management
Participants in the organization	Owners and shareholders, managers and executives, employees	Internal stakeholders: research and teaching staff, students, administration	Internal stakeholders: research and teaching staff, students, administration	Internal stakeholders: research and teaching staff, students, administration
Customers	Individuals, businesses, or public organizations	Lack of clients, perspective on serving science and culture	Students, external stakeholders, academia, society	Students, external actors, academia, organization, and network communities
External stakeholders	Customers (significant), influence groups, and society (usually negligible)	Central government and society (usually negligible)	Central and local government, business, influence groups (significant)	Networked influence groups, power, business (important)
Product or service	Differentiated, specific, measurable, profitable	No product, prospect of civilizational value	Knowledge, education, cooperation effects, difficult to measure	Knowledge, competence packages, project results, measurable
Decision-making	Economic rationale, economic decisions, little autonomy, decision-making systems	Cultural, political, ethos justifications, participation, significant autonomy, no systems	Political, academic, economic, participatory justifications, limited autonomy, rudiments of systems	Differentiated justifications, participation, limited autonomy, advanced systems based on: quantifiability and mass data analysis
The environment of the organization	Competitive, less vulnerable to environmental factors, results of transformational activities	Non-competitive, stable, most important scientific, other with low impact on university activities	Competitive, variable, most important scientific, others with growing impact	Competitive, volatile, significant, and mission-dependent, uncertainty and risk are minimized by data analysis.

(*Continued*)

Table 4.2 (Continued)

	Company	Humboltian model university	Entrepreneurial university	Digital university
Managing people and leadership	Managerial, corporate, HR, formal, and leadership	Authority of professors, master-student relationship, staff participation	Mixed: academic, collective, participatory and managerial-corporate	Mixed: managerial, network, digital and academic, participatory
Finance and accounting	Advanced financial management and management accounting based on controlling	Elementary accounts of university activities or unaccounted	Increasing scope for accountability, elemental financial analysis, and simple management accounting	Advanced financial management and management accounting based on controlling and mass data analysis
Marketing	Extensive, relational, network, product-specific, branding, targeting, strategy, and marketing research	Lack, creation of reputation, prestige, and renown of the university by the academic staff	Developed branding, marketing, promotion, and PR, targeting the public and potential university applicants	Extensive, networked branding, relational strategies, and research, reliance on data analysis and ICT
Knowledge management	Advancement increases as DT progresses, evidence-based	Virtually none, mainly tacit knowledge, individual and social	Elementary knowledge management using management information systems	Advancement grows with DT progress, evidence-based, mass data, quantifiability

Source: own with the use of Meyer Jr., V., An Analysis of Alternative Tuition Policies for Brazilian Public Higher Education, Houston: Univesity of Houston Press, 1982. Mainardes, E. W., Alves, H., & Raposo, M. (2011). The Process of Change in University Management: From the "Ivory Tower" to Entrepreneurialism. *Transylvanian Review of Administrative Sciences*, 7(33), 124–149.

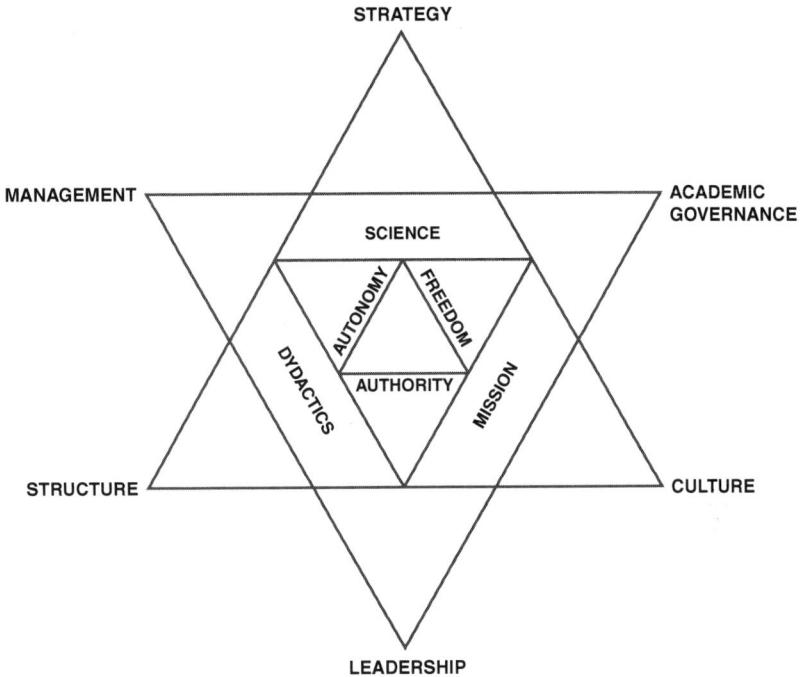

Figure 4.1 The four triads of university organization and management ("university management star").

Source: own elaboration.

Wang, Y., Liu and Chen, 2021). Among the stakeholder groups, one may indicate managers, scientific and teaching staff, administration, and students participating in the work of collegiate bodies. The involvement of these groups is implemented at the strategic and operational levels (Sporn, 2007, p. 143). It shapes a model of governance and management called *shared governance,* which, thanks to the participation of different stakeholders, makes it possible to achieve the mission effectively (Erickson, Hanna and Walker, 2021; Shattock and Temple, 2006). This is particularly important for the *stakeholder model,* which is characteristic of higher education institutions and dominant in the public sector (Mainardes, Alves and Raposo, 2012; Bacq and Aguilera, 2022; Yoshikawa, Nippa and Chua, 2021). As Peter D. Eckel believes, the involvement of all these groups is essential in moments of crisis (Eckel, 2000). It is worth distinguishing between *governance* and *government. Government* means, i.e., the collective entity exercising political power, while *governance* is the process of governing, supervision, oversight, dependence, and power sharing among all bodies involved in decision-making processes. The essence of such a regulatory system in a higher education institution is the ways of appointing and the powers of the collegiate and personal bodies, the regulations concerning the strategic and operational management of the organization, and the principles of supervision over the university. *Governance* can also be understood as *macro-level* and *policy decision-making* (Kezar and Eckel, 2004). A somewhat simplified understanding of governance refers to the internal power structure and the decision-making prerogatives of individual collegiate bodies and functions.

Governance of HEIs includes legal and institutional regulations, management prerogatives, and activities of various stakeholders to regulate power relations between *stakeholders* involved in the functioning of the higher education system. Among the key stakeholders of the higher education system who influence the governance processes are legislative bodies (parliament and senate), central executive power (government), local and regional government, university employees (in particular, scientific and teaching staff and administration), students, socio-economic environment, science institutions, and HEIs and other organizations and society. The degree of stakeholder participation in governance varies and takes on a direct or indirect character.

The most crucial systemic difference in the modes of academic supervision stems from the founding structure. Private and non-public universities are closer to the shareholder model, meaning their governance resembles *corporate governance* solutions. In contrast, public universities are closer to the stakeholder model, which translates into the model of supervision and management in which *stakeholders* participate. A.W. Rhodes distinguishes several sources of development of the concept of *governance* in organizations:

- reducing state interventionism (*minimal state*),
- corporate governance,
- new public management,
- good governance in the public sector,
- organization of the social and information system (*socio-cybernetic networks*),
- self-organizing inter-organizational networks.

Rhodes emphasizes the use of a way of understanding *governance* as self-organizing organizational networks, which fits the specificity of public universities. Several characteristics resulting from this interpretation of the concept of *governance* in universities can be pointed out. It refers to inter-organizational relationships in which the state is one among many stakeholders. Therefore, emerging governance is the result of diverse forces' influence, with relationships involving both the public, private, and third sectors. Continuous interactions between different actors result from processes of negotiation and transaction. The game's rules are also created in the negotiation processes between the various actors in the network. The degree of autonomy of the organizations forming the web in relation to the state is significant. They are self-organizing and autopoietic, although the state bodies, through regulatory action, can exert substantial influence on the activities of these actors. It seems that the other mentioned ways of understanding the essence of governance proposed by Rhodes are also adequate for interpreting the functioning of universities (Rhodes, R. A. W., 1996).

The governance of universities is key to achieving high-quality educational and scientific outcomes in the long term (Faraasyatul'Alam and Supriyanto, 2021; Castillo-Villar, 2021). The English term *university governance* describes precisely how the power structure in a university is regulated, which determines the organization and management processes. University governance is influenced by a number of factors, including but not limited to history and tradition, type of university, benchmarking, and internal and external legal arrangements (Xue and Zhu, 2022; Musselin, 2021).

4.4 Models of universities governance

The foundations of academic governance are the relationships between stakeholders, e.g., the state, staff, students, and the other stakeholders. These are reflected in *governance* models used in different countries and described by researchers: Burton Clark (Clark, 1983, p. 143), Frans van Vought, Robert Birnbaum (Birnbaum, 1988), Johan P. Olsen (Olsen, 2007, p. 30), Ivar Bleiklie, and Maurice Kogan (Bleiklie and Kogan, 2007, p. 488).

Burton Clark is the author of one of the fundamental approaches to academic governance models. He located this order in a triad consisting of an academic oligarchy, state power, and the market. The intersection of the three dimensions mentioned above gives us the following models: academic self-government, state control, and a model focused on the market (Clark, 1983). State control involves the state's key role in supervising universities and working out the regulations in force—this was the case, for example, in France. In the model of academic self-government, power is exercised collegially, and decisions are made this way. This system was adopted from the Humboldtian university, where collegiate bodies, composed mainly of professors, such as faculty councils and university senates, were responsible for decisions. University senates or other bodies elect rectors for the operational management of the university, develop strategy and watch over its implementation, and accept organizational or academic decisions taken. On the other hand, the market model aims at creating a regulated system, where market laws rule and university competition is allowed. This solution was inspired by the models found in the US and became a market-based modification of the Humboldt-type university. The triad proposed by Clark is the starting point for subsequent concepts of university governance.

Robert Birnbaum used functionalist and cybernetic approaches and described decision-making mechanisms that—through feedback—make it possible to maintain balance and the introduced order (Birnbaum, 1988). The rebalancing methods depend on the university and can be summarized in types of governance. Birnbaum distinguished four models of academic organization.

4.4.1 Collegiate

Power is held by collegiate bodies (university senates, faculty councils, boards, usually professorial dominance), which elect a principal or rector (*primus inter pares*) for a fixed term. The administration consists of academics who implement the decisions taken by the college. Unwritten, internalized norms regulate actions—hence the critical role of tradition and academic culture. Dominant leadership style is conciliatory, participatory, and group decision-making (which applies to operational and strategic levels).

4.4.2 Bureaucratic

Power is in the hands of the administration, appointed (by statute) by the founders or their representatives. It is a professional group that takes important decisions. Organizational culture operates based on measurement, formalization, and control; the level of academic entrepreneurship is sometimes limited (Birnbaum, 1988, pp. 87–101). The dominant leadership style is focused on the legal prerogatives of a single position in the structure, based on specialization and formal decision-making rights. Usually, the founder appoints a leader.

4.4.3 Political

Power is in the hands of key stakeholders (the most important are students, staff, administration, and founders). A dominant leadership style is based on negotiations; coalitions are formed to achieve goals.

4.4.4 Anarchic

It is based on weak, decentralized authority. The organization's structure is dispersed and resembles a Mintzbergian adhocracy (Mintzberg and McHugh, 1985). Dominant leadership style is leseferistic, evident in the weak culture of the organization.

Van Vought's 1989 breakdown (into two types of model strategies for supervision and university governance) is different (van Vought, 1989):

- the system of direct supervision that exists in most European countries,
- indirect supervision, as in the Anglo-Saxon countries (United States, United Kingdom, Australia, and New Zealand).

In turn, M. Kwiek applies J. P. Olsen's model: "stylized visions" of the university as a "community of scholars" with its own rules. We see this phenomenon in some research universities, dominated by the academic community of the predominant scientific schools. The university as a "vehicle for change" in the hands of political power is dominated by state supervision, which has its political, social, and economic objectives.

England, Scandinavia, the Netherlands, and other European Union countries emphasize the application of state control over universities and the implementation of social and education policies assumed by the state. Olsen's next vision is "representative democracy," similar to Birnbaum's collegiate model and Clark's academic oligarchy. The next vision is a "service enterprise" operating in competitive markets (Olsen, 2007, p. 30). The flagship example of the use of business solutions in universities is in the United States. Still, university competition mechanisms are found in many countries, helped by the massification of higher education and the privatization of parts of the sector.

I. Bleiklie and M. Kogan are the authors of a typology based on two dimensions to differentiate the ideal type of university and "knowledge regimes." Universities become "stakeholder organizations" or "republics of scholars." The dimension of "knowledge regimes" consists of "the regime of academic capitalism" (pursuing the interests of business, subordinated to the market and competition) and the "regime of public managerialism" (focused on the interests of government and administration, pursuing social policy) (Bleiklie and Kogan, 2007, p. 488).

The university's governance can be embedded in the stakeholder model, drawing attention to the diversity of participants making decisions—through representatives in collegiate bodies. Stakeholder groups include:

1   representatives of the authorities—central and local government,
2   academics and administrative staff,
3   students and graduates,
4   employers and other external stakeholders.

Their influence, of course, depends on the type of HEI, but it is the highest in public HEIs and the lowest in non-public profit-oriented universities. The degree of complexity of the mechanisms of governance, supervision, and management of HEIs is related to the long-lasting process of reaching a compromise between the authorities' aspirations for strict control and the autonomy of the HEIs and the pursuit of their own goals by different stakeholder groups.

4.5 Academic governance in different countries

Universities vary considerably in their modes of governance, depending on their country of operation, founding structure, and mission. Looking for sources in the most developed academic systems, it is worth looking at solutions in chosen leading educational systems: the UK, USA, and other European countries.

Many variables influence university governance, but first of all, legal and institutional solutions relate to the country's traditions and the type of university (public, private). Dating back to the Middle Ages, European universities and modern governance in the Humboldtian model have developed a tradition of autonomy, participatory authority, and collegiality (Stevens et al., 2014; Bruckmann and Carvalho, 2018, Marquina, Centeno, and Reznik, 2022).

Universities in the US also benefit from the assumption of participation in governance by representatives of key stakeholders, but it is still the president who has more lasting power—compared to European universities (Bleiklie and Kogan, 2007; Posselt et al., 2019). This can be seen, for example, in the prevailing solution of non-tenure and in the university senate's limited influence on the president's selection (Trakman, 2008; Parsons and Platt, 1973).

The way a university is managed depends primarily on its type. The differentiation comes from the legal specialization (Mora, 2001). The most straightforward division is public and private universities. *Private universities* can also be divided—following the American system—into *not-for-profit* and *for-profit*, which is connected with fundamental differences in management (Rhodes, R. A. W., 1997). The latter are examples of businesses. The former is controlled by supervisory or trustee boards made up of representatives of the economic or political community, the equivalent of social control. This is the case in numerous, often leading, private universities in the US (e.g., Harvard University), but also, for example, in the most successful Politecnico de Monterrey in Mexico and many more. Governance in this sense brings these universities closer to public universities.

Depending on the country, universities may have different founders and different supervisors. Public universities are usually established by either central or local government units. In the USA, public universities supervised at the state-regional level are predominant, while central state-founded and overseen public universities are the dominant case in most countries. The founders of a non-public higher education institution may include individuals and commercial law companies, churches, associations, and other third-sector organizations. The funding body greatly influences the institution's governance, especially in private universities. It is not possible to describe a single dependence model, but it is possible to notice a relationship between the type of founder and the applied governance solution. Commercial companies are often established by profit-oriented non-public universities—compared to universities created by third-sector entities or churches (Crow, Whitman and Anderson, 2020; Stamps, 1998; Sperling, 1998).

The legal solutions adopted in a given country regulate how universities are governed. Many countries have a pluralistic approach, assuming the existence of different forms of non-public universities alongside the public ones. In non-democratic countries and some democratic and market economy countries, public universities may dominate (this is the case in Central-Eastern Europe, Israel, France, Germany or Canada, and many more).

The degree of supervision over universities also depends on the country, ranging from a high degree of freedom to much stricter solutions.

In the UK, a number of historically contingent models of governance coexist, among which solutions emerging from the neoliberal reform of universities that took place in the 1980s and 1990s are gaining prominence:

- Oxbridge model (Oxford and Cambridge), which is dominated by "academic self-government" derived from the medieval concept of guilds of masters and craftsmen's guilds,
- the Scottish model involves a strict separation of powers between the council and the senate with dependent executive power in the hands of the principal, vice-chancellor, or president, elected with student participation (Universities of Aberdeen, Edinburgh, Glasgow, and St Andrews),
- the civic university model, the classic English bicameral system with the court as the oversight body, the council as the executive body, and the senate with weaker powers to oversee purely academic matters. The University of Manchester is an example of this arrangement,
- The HEC (*Higher Education Corporation*) model was established in the early 1990s after the Jarrat Report (Jarrat et al., 1985), followed by the *Education Reform Act* (1988) and the *Higher Education Corporation* (1992). As a result of the changes, polytechnics became universities and came out of local government control. The most significant change concerns establishing a unified, centralized structure of authority and oversight. This is the model of a *single-chamber board of directors* with a maximum of 24 members, of which the *vice-chancellor* is the *chief executive* (McCaffery, 2018, p. 38; CUC, 2020).

In the USA, in the first half of the 19th century, oversight and *governance of universities* began to be regulated, exemplifying the world's highest complexity and sophistication of university governance. A reference to the Enlightenment in the preparation of curricula was suggested by the Yale Report (1828), which denied the vision of religious education in universities. A statement by the *administrators of colleges and universities*, promulgated in 1920 by the *American Association of University Professors*, proposed solutions to educational policy, budget, or personnel matters. Its vision of *governance included creating management and supervisory structures and addressing* key educational issues. A statement related to staff governance, published by the National Education *Association* in 1987, covered the following matters (AAUP, 2014):

- staff participation in decision-making related to administration, remuneration, and budgeting,
- the responsibility of staff for scientific advancement,
- the preparation of educational programs—in cooperation with staff and administration,
- the development of degree-related educational requirements.

Currently, governance in the US is addressed in the Institutional Governance document published in 2010 by the *Association of Governing Boards of Universities*. It places the responsibility for oversight of the university on the *governing board*—the supervisory boards—but reminds them of the need to respect the decision-making culture of the university (AGB, 2014).

It is difficult to speak of single academic governance in the US. This is because we are dealing with great complexity of systems and solutions resulting from historical, political, social, and cultural conditions and the massive scale of the higher education sector. The diversity of regional solutions is related to the state political structure. Fundamental differences also arise from the different founding forms of universities and the type of legal constitution. The diversity of missions, styles, and specializations of universities also results in differences in governance. Extreme examples of differentiation might be California and, at the opposite extreme, Georgia. California, like Connecticut, Louisiana, and Nebraska, has three coexisting models of academic governance. One for research universities, one for teaching-oriented universities that provide graduate and undergraduate education, and one for *community colleges*. The state board coordinates all these arrangements. In contrast, states such as Georgia and Wisconsin have a single-state system of academic governance (McCaffery, 2018, pp. 39–40). Thus, the academic governance of US universities is dominated by solutions modeled on business, which take very different forms. The most common are hybrid systems in which public and private universities coexist, with various founders and diversified missions.

4.6 Governance and management

Governance is concentrated on the supervision of managers by the representatives of founders or owners (Cristofoli, Markovic, and Meneguzzo, 2014; Tihanyi, Graffin, and George, 2014; Provan and Kenis, 2008; Lynn Jr, Heinrich, and Hill, 2000). Management is focused on strategic and operational decision-making in organizations (Simon, 1960; Goodman, 1993). Looking at the practice of management in developed HE systems, we can find different state resolutions connecting governance and management in the United States. The US model proposed in the 2009 CUC *Governance Code of Practice* distinguishes between *governance* and *management*. The board, which oversees managers, is elected for a term and is usually composed mainly of external stakeholders. Its prerogatives include:

- The election and appointment of the person who governs the university,
- Setting management targets for the university (*key performance indicators*), monitoring, and holding the manager to account,
- Establish a system of oversight and accountability over the finances and operations of the university,

- Accepting the University's mission and strategy, annual budget, and long-term investment plans,
- Ensuring that the university operates appropriately, in line with the wishes of stakeholders, and creating mechanisms to resolve conflicts of interest (McCaffery, 2018, p. 41).

Depending on the system, the positions of general managers (CEO) are president (the USA, many English-Speaking Countries), vice-chancellor or principal (United Kingdom), provost (the USA, head of academic staff), rector (Central Eastern Europe, Latin America, Middle East). The responsibilities of the managing person usually include representing the HEI; managing strategically; managing the heads of functional departments, reporting on the implementation of the HEI's strategy to governing boards; appointing and leading persons to perform managerial functions and dismissing them; creating, transforming, and liquidating organizational units; the financial management of the HEI; the allocation of the organizational structure of the Academy and the division of tasks within this structure.

Governance, therefore, differs from management in many respects. It is about overseeing the organization and managers and creating conditions for accountability and development from a strategic perspective. Strategic and operational management of the university, which is the domain of managers, is about organizing work effectively, leading people in the university, achieving management objectives effectively, and allocating resources efficiently (Table 4.3).

Table 4.3 Differences between *governance and management*

Criterion	Governance	Management
Definition	Making key decisions on university oversight and strategic controlling	Making strategic and operational decisions in planning, organizing, leading, and controlling the activities of the university
The role of	Supervision of the organization and managers, selection of the principal, approval of the strategy, financial monitoring, and implementation of the strategy	Operational and strategic management of the university and cooperation with the supervisory body and external stakeholders
Structure	Supervisory board, board of trustees, collective, statutory body with external stakeholders	Rector, president, vice-chancellors, chancellors, deans, statutory management positions (top management)
Strategy	Approved and monitored	Prepared and implemented
Type of organization	Public and non-public universities	Public and non-public universities

Source: own elaboration.

4.7 Criticism of managerialism in university governance

Modifications of university governance have received a lot of research (Kezar and Eckel, 2004; Lapworth, 2004; Middlehurst, 2004). The last 20 years have borne fruit in the form of work on the application of new public management in higher education (Bleiklie, 1998), which is associated with the development of the idea of management of the university, which goes back to the concept of corporate governance (Ramírez and Tejada, 2018; Andrades, Martinez-Martinez and Jorg, 2020). S. Lapworth documents the growth of the concept of corporate governance, with a decline in the importance of consensus-based management and academic participation leading to managerialism (Lapworth, 2004; Poutanen et al., 2022; Law, 2019; Ajayan and Balasubramanian, 2020). Many other authors cite changes in university cultures. A. J. Kezar and P. D. Eckel point to a move away from collegial decision-making in most universities. Due to economization and the need for both rapid decision-making and detailed reporting, the corporate model of management is gaining importance (Kezar and Eckel, 2002). Researchers have also drawn attention to bureaucratic tendencies in the culture of modern universities. Some criticize the increased academic bureaucratization, linking it to the loss of university identity. Other researchers (J. Dearlove, S. Lapworth) are more optimistic, believing that given the massification of education, more bureaucracy and reporting are necessary and reconcilable with the mission of a modern university (Dearlove, 1997). The literature on the subject abounds with empirical illustrations of how university governance works.

Shattock looks at the clash between the corporate model and the English collegiate approach (Shattock 1994), beginning with a comparison of two publications describing university governance. G. C. Moodie and R. Eustace portrayed the British model, referring to collegiality and suggesting that university governance should be in the hands of academic staff (Moodie and Eustace, 1974). Meanwhile, Catherine Bargh, Peter Scott, and David Smith point to the corporate model as dominant in England, where power is exercised by the management and governing board of the university (Bargh, Scott, and Smith, 1996). The board consists of Vice-Chancellors, Bursar, and senior managers. Thus, the shift from an academic/collegiate to a corporate/managerial model has taken place over 30 years, with many economic, social, and cultural reasons behind it (in England, for example, the new public management and Thatcherism are worth mentioning). According to Shattock, the corporate-managerial model does not necessarily mean better-functioning universities. Oxbridge uses an academic-college model and achieves success. Conversely, sometimes reaching for corporate solutions has accelerated the loss of academic standing of some universities (Elton, 2000). It is worth recalling that this position can be measured by a scientific evaluation practice called *Research Assessment Exercise* in the UK. Universities in the best places are more likely to turn to collegial rather than corporate arrangements.

Shattock proposes a model of shared governance of the university—involving administration and academic staff. *Shared governance* has little in common with the neo-liberal model advocated by the new public management and instead moves toward public value management based on the economics of academic prestige (Shattock, 1994; Westerheijden, 2018; Curnalia and Mermer, 2018; Honu, 2018; Scott, R. A., 2020; Nabaho, 2019).

Peter Coaldrake, Lawrence Stedman, and Peter Little have conducted comparative studies of trends common in the US, Australia, and the UK. They draw our attention to the adverse effects of the growing importance of corporate governance in university management. The researchers suggest a rebalancing of university governance, advocating a move away from focusing solely on a managerial approach, and supporting a collegial approach (Coaldrake, Stedman, and Little, 2003). M. McMaster also suggests using a partnership between academic staff and administration in the management of public universities (McMaster, 2007). Roger L. Geiger, Frank Meier, and Georg Krücken point out that American research universities are just such hybrids, formed from the model of American Harvard, English college, and Humboldt University (Geiger, 1986; Meier and Krücken, 2006).

It can be said that the changing management and governance models of modern universities are a heterogeneous and multidirectional process. Globalization and phenomena related to the new public management led to the marketization of the university and its adoption of the corporate-manager model. However, the variety of state systems and types of universities force a differentiation of the models used. Therefore, it is possible to reach for hybrid models that combine universal and local tendencies (Bruckmann and Carvalho, 2018; Martini et al., 2020). This has already happened in higher education.

5   Academic leadership

5.1 Leadership in the university

Leadership is a vast, interdisciplinary area of research that interacts with many spheres of social practice (Sharma and Jain, 2013). Analyzing the definitions of leadership present in the literature, it is possible to extract some common features that reflect the essence of this phenomenon. Leadership is social as it involves influencing other people. It leads to cooperation and collaboration and is based on authority. It takes place through communication processes and is a form of exercising power. It aims to create a social bond that can last in organizations and other social groups. Thus, leadership can be defined as "the exercise of influence over other people, based on communication and authority, leading to the creation of bonds and cooperation in the pursuit of common goals." Depending on the type of bond and social group, many spheres of leadership can be distinguished, ranging from political or economical to academic.

In university management issues, leadership is one of the most important subjects on which rich literature has accumulated. It is the subject of thousands of studies and millions of publications, while academic leadership in universities is one of the most frequently discussed management topics in higher education. A quantitative analysis of the body of research on educational leadership in HEIs demonstrates that it has been an area developed longer than academic reflection in management, rooted in research since the early 20th century (Mumford, 1906; Blackmar, 1911; Terman, 1904). A qualitative literature analysis indicates that various leadership concepts are developed in universities, only partially converging with theories drawn from business and political organizations (Yielder and Codling, 2004; Devlin, 2013; Söderhjelm et al., 2018). The review of leadership theories and analysis of leadership roles attempt to characterize academic leadership. The logic of the argument will be based on the chronology of the emergence of the theory and its cognitive and practical potential in higher education. This pragmatic approach allows us to focus only on the more important leadership concepts such as trait theory, leadership styles, situational, behavioral, transformational, power-based, cultural, and charismatic approaches (Middlehurst, 2008).

DOI: 10.4324/9781003366409-8

Table 5.1 Academic leadership issues in the English language literature

Phrase/number of items	2000	2005	2010	2015	2021
Leadership	1 690 000	1 780 000	1 860 000	2 110 000	4 820 000
leadership + higher education	168 000	313 000	992 000	1 340 000	2 220 000
academic leadership	4 900	8 120	13 900	18 100	46 600
university leadership	4 860	7 300	11 100	15 200	28 800
digital leadership	32	95	179	583	4 560
digital leadership + University	20	62	119	413	3 490
digital leadership + higher education	9	21	41	143	1 060

Source: Retrieved from Google Scholar, https://scholar.google.com/, 08.08.2021.

The theory review closes with digital leadership, one of the most rapidly growing research areas of HEIs management in the 21st century (Table 5.1).

Definitions of academic leadership vary, but the differentiation between theoretical and practical interpretations is equally clear. Leadership in higher education can be interpreted as holding the following positions: presidents, provosts, principals, rectors, deans, chancellors, bursars, institute directors, and department heads, but also other managerial positions in the administration. Most researchers believe that leadership is not limited to a hierarchical position but is a dynamic social process of influencing and organizing people that develop through communication, collaboration, talent, energy, and commitment of group members (Thompson and Franz, 2017; Rowley and Sherman, 2003). Many researchers define a leader as a person who enables positive change and leadership as the progressive process (Thompson and Franz, 2017; Floros, 2015) or the values-based actions of supporting intended change (Astin, A. W., and Astin, H. S., 2000; Anthony, S. G., and Antony, 2017). Academic leadership is valued for creating positive social change, sustainability, social responsibility, and participation in the common good (Astin, A. W., and Astin, H. S., 2000; Bringle, Game,s and Malloy, 1999). Leaders are expected to influence the organization and people effectively, drive transformational change, and develop the university's vision (Green and McDade, 1994).

Academic leadership can therefore be defined as getting members of an organization to act together to achieve the university's goals. The concepts of academic leadership draw from a rich theoretical background in organization and management, psychology, and sociology. The fundamental research problem concerns effective leadership, which is analyzed from the perspective of different theoretical schools.

5.2 Concepts of academic leadership

Leadership research conducted over 100 years has resulted in many theories, some of which are used in higher education. A review of these concepts and an indication of their application in universities should also consider the evolution of the dominant formation of academic institutions (Marshall, Adams, and Cameron, 2000). The analysis will therefore focus on the traditional (second wave) university, which, although a historical formation, is embedded in the mindset, ethos, and identity of academia and many academic cultures. It will also cover the third-wave universities, which are the most numerous today and in which leadership concepts play a leading role. It will also offer some predictions about the direction of leadership development in fourth-wave universities, where academic leaders will be seen through digital leadership.

Charisma is a religious term derived from Hebrew and Greek, where it means "grace." It owes its popularity in leadership concepts to Max Weber, who defined it as: "a certain quality of the individual personality by virtue of which they are distinguished among ordinary people and treated as endowed with supernatural, superhuman, or at least particularly exceptional powers or qualities. These, as such, are not available to ordinary people but are regarded as of divine origin or as exemplary. Based on these, the person is treated as a leader" (Weber, 1947, pp. 328, 358). Charismatic leaders are seen as unique, distinguished, and chosen, and thus attract other people. The neo-charismatic leadership school goes back to the heritage of M. Weber. For example, R. House pointed to value orientation and trust building as the hallmarks of charismatic leadership (House, 1976). Charisma is often described as a characteristic of outstanding leaders who manage entire universities (Pounder, 2001).

In a Humboldtian university, charisma is reinforced by the authority and ethos of the professoriate, which is elitist and profession-centric. It paints a picture of an exceptional profession, which is about educating the elite and perfecting the spirit of a select few. However, the strength of this charisma and the scope of power is sometimes limited by collectivism, as this out-standing leader is only *primus inter pares* among his fellow professors (Bleiklie and Lange, 2010). Entrepreneurial universities need charismatic leaders who are first and foremost leaders of change, entrepreneurial and flexible, and ready to make a profound transformation of the management, strategy, and culture of the traditional university to seek competitive and market oppor-tunities for the managed university (Macfarlane, 2013; Doh, 2003). Network charisma and digital authority are terms used to describe the outstanding leadership competencies of digital university leaders. The development of authority, communication, and engagement, effectively leveraging the net-worked structure and essence of the networked organization is precisely network charisma, supported by digital authority meaning the respect, attachment, and work of the leader's followers for the benefit of the uni-versity and digital transformation (Antonopoulou et al., 2021a).

Trait theory looks for a configuration of personality traits, individual characteristics, and competencies that an effective university leader possesses (Stogdill, 1974). Today we know that this success-enhancing configuration of traits is not universal but depends on the type of organization, the formation of the university, the academic governance, and the cultural context. A private *for-profit university* will require managers who resemble the configuration of traits of leaders from other knowledge service businesses (e.g., consulting). In contrast, a public university will require a completely different set of traits (Yielder and Codling, 2004). The development of the historical concept of leadership traits has also moved toward the development of leadership competencies; a similar evolution can be observed in the study of academic leaders (Stogdill, 1950).

In the second-wave university, among the set of preferred qualities of leaders can be found: respect for authority and the ethos of teaching and research, integrity, stability, and cooperation. This set of universal characteristics reinforces traditional, conservative, and *status quo-oriented* management under collectivism. The third-wave university prefers an entirely different composition of features, focusing on entrepreneurship, innovation, and flexibility of change leaders (Bento, 2011). The fourth-wave university will first develop a social network and digital competencies connected with communication and managing other people's work (Montag and Elhai, 2019).

Situational theories reject attempts to find universal characteristics of leaders, treating leadership as a social relationship shaped by various variables (Afshari et al., 2017). Researchers seek answers to the question of effective leadership in a managerial relationship and the conditions for its implementation (Fiedler, 1967; Grudzinskiy, Zakharova, and Bureeva, 2016). The power triangle of B. Clark situates university governance between the influence of the state, the market, and the academic oligarchy, which can be seen as sources of power (Clark, 2001). Academic leaders also operate in the context of governance of HEIs and the influence of variables such as staff and team characteristics (e.g., maturity, openness to uncertainty, communication), university type, and environmental conditions. The common idealized aspects of academic leadership, stemming from the essence of the learning organization, are oriented toward the higher good, cognitive curiosity and willingness to share knowledge, the pursuit of efficiency gains, and participative management based on relationships (Parveen and Tariq, 2014; Birnbaum, 1989; Warrick, 1981). Situational leadership in a traditional university is a participative and directive orientation, emerging under status quo conditions and decision-making collectivism. An important variable is the maturity and experience of students and faculty, allowing them to select more participatory (less directive) leadership approaches (Muijs, 2011). Entrepreneurship can also be interpreted as a situational concept in which the leader seeks and reinforces conditions of flexibility and innovation. Therefore, achievement-oriented leaders are valued in the entrepreneurial university. Often also ready to select the way of leading to the situation for bringing out entrepreneurial opportunities (Pihie, Sadeghi, and Elias, 2011). Digital leadership in universities is, by definition, situational, as it focuses on effective action and improvement of the university by exploiting the opportunities inherent in digital transformation (Oberer and Erkollar, 2018). Depending on the conditions, leaders' attitudes are dominated by achievement and support orientation. Concepts of leadership styles have been developed since the 1940s. A leadership style is a manager's way of influencing subordinate group members, fixed in the manager's behavior and affecting the group and its performance. The pioneering theories were developed by R. Lippitt and R.K. White, and R. Likert (Likert, 1967a). The most popular concept of leadership styles is the two-dimensional leadership grid created by R. Blake and J. Mouton (Blake and Mouton, 1964). Universities are among the organizations that are more often managed using participative than autocratic leadership styles—compared to most business organizations (Ekvall and Ryhammar, 1998; Pounder, 2001; Randall and Coakley, 2007; Shahmandi, 2011). The traditional power of the principal of HEI is "first among equals" (*primus inter pares*) in academia, and the knowledge orientation requires significant stakeholder involvement and cooperation.

The traditional university is dominated by participatory leadership styles within the academic oligarchy, resembling patterns of "professorial democracy." Toward other stakeholder groups and outside the organization, autocratic and paternalistic styles are more often dominant, stemming from academic authority (Mohnot and Shaw, 2017). The entrepreneurial university is based on a flexible choice of leadership style for the situation, to the change management process, with a preference for an integrated style in Blake and Mouton's grid. Achieving high levels of task accomplishment by focusing on people is the ideal of the entrepreneurial leader. However, under conditions of radical change, it may be more effective to use an autocratic and participative style in situations requiring consensus. Undoubtedly, however, the leadership style in third- and fourth-wave universities must be oriented toward effective teamwork under conditions of change management in a turbulent environment (El-Kafafi, 2020, p. 33). The digital university will require leaders to select holistic and integrated leadership styles that combine people- and task orientation with ICT improvement under intensifying competition and digital transformation.

Behavioral concepts draw on the psychological stream of behaviorism and treat leadership as a learning process based on a single (conditioning) and double loop (anticipation, reflection) (Davis and Luthans, 1979; Fuqua and Newman, 2005). Leaders motivate followers through reinforcement, rewards, and learning processes, resulting in compelling performance and engagement. In higher education, behavioral leadership is seen through the lens of empowering and teaching: staff, students, and academic managers—effective actions for the university (Hyatt, 1969). Today, the behavioral approach draws on cognitive psychology concepts and behavioral economics, describing leadership's biological and evolutionary roots (Wrangham and Peterson, 1996; Van der Meij, Schaveling, and van Vugt, 2016).

In the second-wave university, leaders reinforce routine, tradition-based, and conservative behaviors that are part of ingrained values in the academic culture. In the third-wave university, reinforcements relate to entrepreneurial and innovative activities that shape followers' attitudes toward flexibility, tolerance of uncertainty, and readiness for change (Willmott, K. E., and Wall, 2014; Díaz, 2020). In the fourth wave of university, network cooperation, collaboration in virtual teams, and digital transformation are supported (Oberer and Erkollar, 2018; Heckman, Crowston, and Misiolek, 2007).

The behavioral approach is concerned with the functions of leadership and the specific behaviors of leaders to contribute to the organization's or individual's effectiveness. The functionalist view here involves integrating the organization through leadership actions. The leader has diverse functions, including monitoring the environment, organizing collective action, teaching, mentoring and coaching subordinates, motivating others, and actively intervening in the work of the group (Lord, 1977; Santos, Caetano, and Tavares, 2015; Hackman and Walton, 1985; Hackman, 1980).

Humboldt University can be seen functionally as a harmonious, integrated organization where the main functions of leaders are teaching others, mentoring, and teamwork. An entrepreneurial university changes and looks for opportunities in the environment, which means monitoring the environment, organizing, and motivating are key. The digital university, on the other hand, will focus on creating and testing a new organization, combined with work intervention and motivation (O'Mullane, 2011).

B.M. Bass and D.M. Burns proposed a distinction between transactional and transformational leadership, which has become a very influential concept in management (Bass, 1999). Transactional leadership is based on the proposal of exchange with subordinates—in return for completing the set tasks, they receive material or symbolic goods. In transformational leadership, a new quality of the social relationship is created through the joint commitment of the leader and his subordinates. Such a leader succeeds in changing the organization's values, realizing both his vision and the organization's goals, as employees become involved in their responsibilities. The transformational approach leads to employees' self-actualization and shapes their identity and organizational identity.

Transactional leadership is also a significant concept in university management because the expectations of academic stakeholders are often based precisely on the exchange of goods and services that satisfy the parties' interests (Brown, W. F., and Moshavi, 2002). Within the scope of transactional leadership are studies on students, academic staff, university administration, and academic managers (Harvey, Royal, and Stout, 2003).

Humboldt University saw academic leaders as inspiring, engaging, and showing role models not only professionally, both to students and to other researchers, but also people outside the academy. It can be said that a transformational and charismatic view of education, learning, and cultural activities was present in academic culture even before theoretical reflection on these forms of leadership (Ekman, Lindgren, and Packendorff, 2018). In the entrepreneurial university, on the other hand, transformational leadership is coupled with innovation, change management, strategy, and people management. Adaptation to the market, implementation of new projects, deconstruction and redefinition of the mission, a reorientation toward the third mission, and practical education—characteristic of the third-wave universities—are often implemented more effectively by transformational leaders (Williams, D., 2012; Rubins, 2007; Gibb, Haskins and Robertson, 2013). In the case of a digital university, transformational leaders will usually be effective in guiding the university and its stakeholders through a digital transformation process that touches all aspects of academic operations.

Cultural and symbolic leadership plays a unique role in the management of universities, as they are a type of organization with a distinct organizational and professional culture based on academic identity and ethos. The cultural strength of the academic world lies in its centuries-long continuity, its unique civilizing mission, and the importance of universities to the progress of humanity (Baker III, 1992). Cultural leadership has a rich literature on the subject, and the concept itself is ambiguous and intersects with other schools of leadership (Sergiovanni, 1987). At its core is recognizing culture as the most critical factor influencing leadership and searching for leadership concepts and methods that consider the cultural context (Festing and Maletzky, 2011). This can include society's values and their impact on leadership, as well as organizational culture and identity with its distinctive patterns. Culture can be understood in different ways, illustrated by the concept of cultural paradigms in management (functionalistic, interpretative-symbolic, and critical) (Sulkowski, 2009). Seen functionally, it is a variable that shapes leadership, but leadership also feedbacks on organizational culture. Comparative international studies of the impact of cultural context on leadership mainly adopt functionalist assumptions (e.g., the GLOBE project) (House, Wright, and Aditya, 1997), as do cross-cultural leadership projects (Guthey and Jackson, 2011; Chrobot-Mason et al., 2007) and organizational culture change management. Based on the interpretative-symbolic paradigm, cultural leadership will take the form of control of meaning, *sensemaking,* and *sensegiving* (Osland and Bird, 2000; Salicru, 2018). A leader can shape the perception and understanding of the reality of his followers and thus induce them to act. The critical paradigm reflects on the oppressiveness, coercive, and manipulative aspects of leadership being a projection and manifestation of power. In higher education, cultural concepts of leadership cover many management issues: people, relationships, processes, projects, strategy, quality, diversity, and other aspects of organizing (Amey, 2006; Roth and Ritter, 2015).

Second-wave university leaders shape a conservative culture based on values, authority, and academic participation, while third-wave leaders focus on cultures of innovation, change, and entrepreneurship (Stephan and Pathak, 2016). Digital leadership is oriented toward developing digitally based cultures and networked *sensemaking, sensegiving,* and *management of meanings* (Kirschner, Buckingham-Shum, and Carr, 2012).

Servant leadership combines the perspective of a leader who makes decisions in the organization with responsibility and support for people. A leader's actions, oriented toward positive management, are manifested by mentoring and developing people and expressing humility and authenticity in relations with people. Relationships, trust, and honesty are expected to be the essential mediating processes to encourage self-actualization, positive work attitude, productivity, and better organization focusing on sustainability and corporate social responsibility (van Dierendonck, 2011; Russell, 2001; Sendjaya and Sarros, 2002). In higher education, servant leadership is related to educating students and doctoral students, conducting research for the benefit of people, and social responsibility (Hannigan, 2007; Latif and Marimon, 2019; Aboramadan, Dahleez, and Hamad, 2020).

In a Humboldt-type university, the activities of a thought leader and champion, which is what each professor sought to be, were directed toward serving science, students, culture, and the nation. This idea of academic leadership taking the form of service was inextricably intertwined with the concept of *Bildung*. In the entrepreneurial university, on the other hand, the leader supports innovation, creativity, and work of both staff and students. The digital leader primarily innovates with the team, builds new competencies, and supports the development (Styron, 2015; Khatri and Dutta, 2020; Blayone et al., 2017).

Exchange theory in leadership refers to sociological exchange theory by G. Homans, P. Blau, and R. Emerson and symbolic interactionism by H. Blumer (Cook et al., 2013; Cropanzano et al. (2017). The interaction between leader and follower is viewed as transactive, as a fair exchange in which the leader provides benefits: support, compensation, help, rewards, and power, and the followers reciprocate by giving the leader respect, cooperation, commitment, and work outcomes. High-quality "transactions" should be developed within the group, while exchanges with the environment may be of lower quality (Erdogan and Bauer, 2015; van Breukelen, Schyns and Le Blanc, 2006; Lee, J., 2008). In higher education, exchange theory is used to interpret: relationships, communication, and power in organizational change management, learning, and collaboration with the environment (Peterson, T. O., and Aikens, 2017).

In the first-wave university, the leader primarily provides support, advice, and authority, and the followers reciprocate respect, cooperation, and commitment. In the entrepreneurial university, as in the digital university, the leader's essential exchange goods are salary, promotions, development opportunities, professional challenges, and support at work. The followers balance this with productive work, collaboration, and commitment.

The approaches of team leadership, leadership substitutes, and self-direction are based on the theory that the team performs a vital leadership function (Kerr and Jermier, 1978; Dionne et al., 2005; Howell et al., 1990).

Work teams are social groups operating in organizations. Their members— independent entities—strive together to achieve common goals. Following this definition, we will look at leadership in terms of the functions of motivating, coordinating, or administering. M.R. McGrath is the author of the theory of critical leadership functions. Their fulfillment is necessary for the work team to act effectively, and there is no need to institutionalize the leadership role (Hackman and Walton, 1986, p. 76). According to G.L. Drecksel, directing is about adapting the actions taken by the team to changes in the environment (Drecksel, 1991). Thus, leading here is not related to the social role. Other researchers, C. Larson and F. LaFasto developed 1989 the conditions for the emergence of self-directed as well as competent teams (Larson and LaFasto, 1989). Regarding team leadership, we can also include the theory of autonomous leadership of authors such as H.P. Sims, Jr. and Ch. C. Manz (Sims Jr. and Manz, 1996). In their opinion, modern companies take on a horizontal shape, which is connected to the processes of decentralization and "slimming down" of organizations; as a result, work teams are created, which exercise authority and are responsible for autonomous leadership of the group. The concept of leadership substitutes, which mentions situational factors replacing an effective leader, is also part of the concept of team leadership (Kerr and Jermier, 1978). In the same stream, we also find the ideas of bottom-up leadership (Helgesen, 1995). It should not be considered that the success of an organization is usually rooted in the manager's leadership abilities because the manager is not a leader by his position. It is not bosses but work teams that count, especially in the post-industrial era and the knowl- edge and service economy. The power distribution process is different as groups organize themselves, defining objectives and action methods, allowing them to respond to the challenges of rapid information processing. The concepts of team leadership and *self-leadership* are also evident in aca- demic leadership analyses of network activities carried out by research teams (Pearce, 2007; Ball, S., 2007).

In a Humboldtian university, the substitutes for leadership are academic autonomy and freedom, academic culture, collective decision-making, a tenure mechanism that weakens autocratic leadership, self-direction, and self-actualization. In an entrepreneurial university, self-direction can be based on rotational team coordination, where the functions of coordinators are performed interchangeably by different group members. Autonomy, the tenure mechanism, and the approach to self-actualization and self-direction remain similar to the second-wave university, at least for public universities. Self-directed and autonomous network teams will be created in the digital university and held accountable for results (Khamis and Kamarudin, 2014).

A developing cognitive perspective on leadership is the critical current, which includes issues of narcissistic leadership, and pathological leadership (*mobbing, bullying, harassment*) and can be seen as part of a management para- digm called *Critical Management Studies*. The CMS paradigm analyses leader- ship's oppressive, unethical, manipulative, and ideological aspects (Alvesson and Sveningsson, 2003a; Ford, 2005; Gedro, 2010). The leadership research of this paradigm started with a critical analysis of "The Nature of Managerial Work" by H. Mintzberg by two authors, M. Calás and L. Smircich. They draw attention to Mintzberg's masculinist interpretation of leadership (Calás and Smircich, 1991). This reflection continued, within the academic world, narcissistic leadership, the "glass ceiling," leadership pathologies, and, moreover, stigmatizing practices toward disadvantaged groups have been analyzed. Such research was conducted, among others, by the representatives of the critical movement (Willmott, H., 1995; Dominici, Fried, and Zeger, 2009; Alvesson and Sveningsson, 2003b; Khwaja, 2015; Labby, 2010).

Looking critically at the leadership at Humboldtian University, one can see that it is aimed at elites, i.e., students and professors. It can be an organization that is hermetic, non-transparent and treats pathologies as taboos, which can be described using the "ivory tower" metaphor. In the entrepreneurial university, the critique of leadership moves toward exposing and explaining the weaknesses of neoliberalism in higher education, with its limitations in the form of the threat of a culture of control, commercialization, commodification, and corporatization of the academic world (Collinson, 2017; Jameson, 2019; Goldman, 2020). An additional threat may be the Machiavellianism and even cynicism of leaders seeking to maintain influence at the expense of eroding academic values. A potential danger of leadership in the digital university will be the threat of surveillance or manipulation, bringing the organization closer to the metaphor of a digital panopticon (Johnston, MacNeill, and Smyth, 2018; MacNeill, Johnston and Smyth, 2020).

A synthetic summary of the interpretations of the concept of academic leadership in the three university models is found in Table 5.2. Three conclusions emerge from the comparison of perspectives. First, the diversity of leadership theories can be described using the metaphor of the jungle of theory and practice in which researchers and managers found themselves. Second, this multiplicity, even redundancy, could be cognitively and pragmatically useful. By fitting the academy into different frameworks of leadership theory, we can see its complexity. Third, academic leadership theories are derivative of leadership concepts in general. Yes—they need to be adapted to academic activities, which should take into account: value orientation, organizational culture, and ethos, mission specificity, human capital characteristics. Nevertheless, universities are organizations where rectors, chancellors, presidents, deans, and heads of department teams play managerial roles. Therefore, many leadership concepts created for other organizations are applicable in HEIs, of course, considering differences, e.g., public *versus* private, small *versus* large, local *versus* international, etc.

5.3 Leadership roles in universities

Peter Drucker almost 50 years ago, distinguished between leaders and managers, stating that the former know what to do ("do good things")

Table 5.2 Leadership theories applied to universities

The university wave / The concept of leadership	Humboldtian University	Entrepreneurial University	Digital University
Charisma	Strengthened by authority and ethos, limited by collectivism	Leaders of change, entrepreneurial, and flexible	Network charisma, digital authority
Leadership traits	Ethos, tradition, authority, stability, cooperation	Entrepreneurship, innovation, flexibility	Social networking and digital competence
Situational approach (e.g., F. Fiedler)	Participative and directive orientation dominates students' maturation process and reinforcement of the *status quo*.	Achievement orientation dominates, creating conditions for entrepreneurship	Achievement-oriented and supportive, use of ICT
Leadership styles	Participatory within the academic oligarchy, autocratic outside it	Integrated, flexible, change management	Holistic, integrated, network and digital
The behavioural concept	Reinforcement of routine behavior based on tradition	Strengthening entrepreneurial and innovative behavior	Strengthening network cooperation and digital transformation
Transformational leadership	In education, science, and cultural activities, *implicitly* accepted without scientific reflection about leadership	In change and people management, and strategy, adopted *explicitly*, subject to scientific reflection	In the digital transformation of all areas of the university, adopted *explicitly*, subject to scientific reflection
Functionalist leadership	Teaching and mentoring and teamwork dominate	Monitoring the environment, organizing, motivating	Dominated by the organization, work intervention, motivation
Cultural and symbolic approaches	Conservative, traditional culture develops leadership based on values, authority, and participation	Leadership based on the values of innovation, change, competition, entrepreneurship	Digital leadership, network sensemaking, and management of meaning
Servant leadership	A thought leader as a champion serves science, students, culture, and the nation	A leader supports and motivates creativity and work	Digital leadership builds competence and supports the development

Leader–follower exchange theory	Leader: support, advice, guidance Supporters: respect, cooperation, commitment	Leadership: remuneration, challenges, support, Supporters: efficient work, cooperation, commitment	Leadership: challenges, remuneration, support, guidance, network relations Supporters: efficient work, collaboration, involvement, network relationships
Substitutes for leadership and self-direction, team leadership	Academic culture, autonomy, collective decisions, tenure, self-direction as academic freedom	Rotational coordination, autonomy, cadences, mature self-direction	Networked, self-directed teams, autonomy
Talent management	The master searches and refines talents	Leadership focused on finding and developing talent	Finding and improving digital and online talent
Critical school, narcissistic leadership	Leadership for elites in a hermetic university, oppressiveness	Neoliberal leadership in a culture of control, Machiavellianism	Surveillance and manipulation leadership, the digital panopticon

Source: own elaboration.

while the latter knows how to do it (Drucker, 1974). This is also true in higher education institutions, where, however, one finds a great deal of complexity in organizational activities that are intertwined with the roles of researcher and academic.

Adopting the classic management perspective of manager and leader roles proposed by H. Mintzberg, it is worth looking at leadership in universities. Managerial activity can be described by ten roles, grouped into three main categories. These are presented in Table 5.3.

Academic leaders exercise power often based on charismatic legitimacy and strong informal authority (Liu, L. et al., 2020). Leaders operate at an organization-wide level but may also focus on selected mission areas, functional spheres, or even structural units (Risanty and Kesuma, 2019). Although

Table 5.3 Managerial roles, according to H. Mintzberg

Category	The role of	Role description
Interpersonal contact	Figurant	Represents and symbolizes the organization (e.g., ceremonial duties of the leader of HEI)
	Leader	Motivates and supports team members, helps them develop, and interacts with them (e.g., academic managers, HR development)
	Connector	Creates informal and formal networks to gain critical information so that the organization can succeed (e.g., leaders lobbying for HEI)
Information processing	Monitor	Collects internal and external information, compares and verifies it (e.g., Chief Information Officer)
	Disseminators	Provides information to employees (e.g., internal communication of leaders)
	Spokesperson	Provides information to the public, and people outside the organization (e.g., public, outside presentations)
Decision-making	Entrepreneur	Plans and implements organizational change (e.g., academic managers' innovations)
	Interference operator	Deals with organizational conflict and other disruptions (e.g., mediations of leaders with stakeholders)
	Resource allocator	Designs and controls the allocation of human, financial, and time resources (e.g., bursar, finance controlling)
	Negotiator	Represents the organization in external and internal negotiations (e.g., leader negotiate with outside stakeholders)

Source: adapted Mintzberg, H. 1979, The Structuring of Organizations: A Synthesis of the Research. Prentice-Hall, 54–99.

we often identify academic leaders who simultaneously hold the highest management position (rector, president, chancellor, principal), leadership may relate mainly to academic activities, teaching, or the implementation of the third mission (Yielder and Codling, 2004). It can also refer to finance, human resources, marketing, and ICT. A leader can also be a faculty dean, an institute director, or the head of a department, library, or another organizational unit (Willett, 2012; Hvorecký, 2017). The temporal perspective is long-term and strategic, although planning processes usually take on a heuristic and visionary character, which requires creativity, innovation, and originality of thinking. Tasks include leading change, team building, motivating and developing employees, and managing talent. A leader uses a rich arsenal of management methods, such as HR management, *sensemaking,* and management of meaning (Parrish, 2019; Degn, 2015). In corporate relations, leaders build a network of contacts and coalitions based on followers who act with commitment, recognizing the personal authority of the academic leader.

Managers of the whole organization may have leadership competencies and become leaders, but this is often not the case. Considerable power, legitimized legally and backed by formal authority, is often not conducive to enhancing charismatic legitimacy and informal authority. Managers have statutorily regulated prerogatives, which in some cases are also anchored in the external governance of the education system. The main tasks of top management include managing the organization, managers, and strategic projects and directing or supervising all functional areas. In the field of people management, for example, this means: developing personnel strategy and personnel planning and participating in: recruitment and selection, motivation and development of key staff. In general, they are synthetic managers who are expected to be creative and innovative. Managers use organizational methods taken from different management areas but focus on the organization as a whole rather than its parts. Alongside "hard" management methods, "soft" practices such as management of meaning can be helpful. The area of organizational relations is based on power, which is distributed through the managerial level, including vice-chancellors, deans, vice-deans, and other functional staff in the university.

Academic managers are the broadest category comprising leadership roles in the university (Bassnett, 2005). Leaders may or may not have managerial positions, and managers need not be leaders (Sidrat and Frikha, 2018). Taking into account the level of leadership, the differentiation indicates the following levels: managers (senior managers, top management), middle managers, and line managers (De Boer and Goedegebuure, 2009). Top managers in universities are rectors, presidents, chancellors, and vice-chancellors, and sometimes heads of key administrative divisions, e.g., bursars, chief information officers, and registrars. The highest level of responsibility for strategic decisions requires collecting and analyzing data, consulting with experts on decisions, and taking adequate time to study the consequences (Mehralizadeh and Shahi, 2004). Middle managers are heads of academic units and support divisions in universities. Examples are deans, vice-deans, directors of institutes, HR managers, and library directors. They are responsible for decisions at the tactical and operational levels, which are subordinated to the logic of strategic decisions. The responsibilities and authority they delegate are specialized and concern their functional division (de Schrevel and Jost, 2013; Sidrat and Frikha, 2018). Lower-level managers (line managers) are people who manage executive staff or even just projects, working directly with the university's stakeholders. This group of managers is often also identified with academic administration (Byarugaba, Bagiire, and Bagorogoza, 2012). Examples of positions located at this decision-making level could be deanery managers, project managers, heads of science departments, and heads of auxiliary units of faculties (Janković and Vuković, 2016).

The traditional separation in the university includes academic staff, who have general leadership and public policy making as potential prerogatives, and administration, who are responsible for implementing academic policies. Educational administrators are separate from leaders and faculty members and have many areas in common with academic managers (Moula, 2021). University administration is a term whose meaning is evolving. One can speak of a narrow and broad understanding of it. The narrow sense is the non-academic staff who operate support processes in the university. In the traditional university, these were groups of specialists led by an elected academic. For example, an elected or appointed dean of faculty oversaw the operation of the dean's office. In this narrow sense, the dean was not part of the university administration but was a link between the academic community and the professional administration. A similar situation often applied to the positions of rectors and vice-rectors, as well as to vice-deans, heads of institutes, and chairs. In many systems, the chancellor, and definitely the bursar, was already part of the administrative staff and was not involved in scientific or teaching activities. In a broader sense, the term administration and consequently the roles of administrators include professionals who are not academic staff and faculty members who have been appointed to perform functions in the university. Then the administrative responsibilities are also performed by: the rector and vice-rectors, deans and vice-deans, heads of institutes, and chairs. Nowadays, both ways of understanding administration interact, although a broader understanding of the term is more common (Wisdom, 2019).

The term university administration is associated with several concepts. Firstly, it is a link to the bureaucratic organization that primarily burdens public institutions (Lopdrup-Hjorth and Roelsgaard Obling, 2019). Bureaucracy here means a set of unelected officials exercising legitimized legal authority. In bureaucratic management, the principles of specialization, formalization, and delegation of decisions are implemented. Bureaucracy is the administrative system governing every large organization, public and private (Baekgaard, Mortensen, and Bech Seeberg, 2018; Wamsley et al., 2020).

The development of the concept of bureaucracy leads toward post-bureaucratic organizations, characterized by: evolutionary or emergent strategy, network structure, decentralized authority, distributed management functions, and flexible organizational culture (Maassen and Stensaker, 2019). The concept of the entrepreneurial university (referred to here as the third-wave university), usually understood as a non-bureaucratic organization, can be a point of reference here (Toshmali et al., 2020; Abidin, 2020). The second source of administrative concepts in universities are references to the executive and scientific management stream, within which the English term administration was understood as a synonym for management. Reminiscence of this way of understanding management is, for example, the most popular professional degree in management, namely the master of business administration (MBA). Thus, university administration meant the group of persons holding managerial positions in the university and their subordinates. Gradually the term university administration shifted toward the concept of bureaucratic organizations, also acquiring a somewhat derogatory meaning colloquially. The university administration was supposed to limit the autonomy of the academic staff with bureaucratic requirements for activity planning, reporting, and accountability (Kallio, T. J., Kallio, K. M. and Blomberg, 2020). A common diagnosis in university research has been the proliferation of administration as a trend of the last few decades (Baltaru and Soysal, 2018). However, interpretations of the causes and effects of these processes go in two opposing directions. The cause may be that universities are becoming more like commercial organizations and corporations. The commodification of higher education, market competition, and cutting public funds for universities contribute to the commercialization of their activities. The other trend is the professionalization of university management, which requires in-depth specialization, managerial competence, and many years of experience. According to many studies, a tenure-track research and teaching staff often cannot match professional academic managers in terms of work efficiency (Ikpesu and Ken-Ine, 2019). Thus, a tendency is developing toward expanding the administration and shifting power to its employees who are not academic staff (Carvalho and Videira, 2019). On the other hand, the administrative approach in universities is sometimes opposed to professionalization if it carries the dangers of bureaucracy (Scarlat et al., 2012). An entrepreneurial university would be based on a managerial approach, not a bureaucratic one, focusing on flexibility and change management (Secundo, Schiuma, and Jones, 2019; Wu, X., 2017).

Thus, when analyzing the organizational role of administrators, one has to note the orientation toward formal empowerment, combined with legal legitimacy and bureaucratically regulated prerogatives. In the narrow sense, administration employees (abbreviated as administrators) concentrate their activities on sections of the organization such as departments or smaller structural units. Administrators are less often recognized as leaders because they are, as it were, by definition entitled to coordinator rather than leader powers. Somewhat mythologized by tradition, academic leadership roles are assigned to academic staff with organizational functions. The main tasks of administrators include planning, controlling, and accounting for operational activities, coordinating, and accounting for people's work. The competencies needed for administration stereotypically do not require significant creativity or innovation and focus on data analysis and operational decisions. In management methods, algorithmic, repetitive, standardized processes are most important and are used in crucial relationships between administrators and academic staff and administrators and students (Egoeze et al., 2018; Lassabe, 2021).

In summary, there is a diversity of organizational roles in universities related to leadership. From management, we know the relationship between the roles of leaders and managers and leaders and managers. All relationships concerning administrators remain specific to the higher education sector. Table 5.4 illustrates the differentiated organizational positions in HEIs.

5.4 Digital leadership in universities

The concept of "digital leadership" is new and was born in the 21st century, gaining popularity as the digital transformation progresses. An offshoot of this, the term "university digital leadership" is new and still not deeply rooted in research, as it is only emerging with the early development of digital universities. Digital age organizations are also characterized by "digital leadership." In analyses of digital transformation, the concept of "digital leadership" emerges, which applies to different types of organizations, including universities (Promsri, 2019; Kane et al., 2019; Hensellek, 2020; Ahlquist, 2014). A closely related term in the literature is also "leadership 4.0"—the word derives from the fourth industrial revolution driven by data and information and communication technologies ("industry 4.0," "society 4.0") (Mihardjo et al., 2019b). Digital leadership ("leadership 4.0") is described as networked, flexible, team-oriented, with a strong focus on innovation. Concepts and methods combine management with information technologies and approaches such as *agile* and *scrum* (Gurusamy, Srinivasaraghavan, and Adikari, 2016). The leader's competence, mindset, and ability to apply new methods and instruments (like design thinking) are vital dimensions. Applied concepts, methods, but also intuitive approaches combine a high level of social orientation toward communication and cooperation with competencies in knowledge management and the use of information and communication technologies. *Design Thinking*, *Agile*, *Scrum*, and *Prince 2* are examples of approaches and methods managers use to solve complex organizational problems (Oberer and Erkollar, 2018). In management, digital leadership enables solutions to be found by managing people, knowledge, and projects.

Universities are facing the challenges of digital transformation, gaining momentum in the 21st century. Some universities, especially the part of

Table 5.4 Organizational roles of academic leaders, managers, and administrators

CRITERIA	Leaders	Managers	Coordinators	Administrators
Authority	Informal	Formal dominates	Formal dominates	Exclusively Formal
Legitimacy	Charismatic	Legal	Legal	Legal
Temporal perspective	Strategic, long-term	Strategic, long-term	Tactical and operational, medium and short term	Tactical and operational, medium and short term
Range of activities	The whole organization or a significant part of it	The entire organization	A structurally separated organizational unit	Organizational cell or service role for the whole organization
Prerogatives	Shaped by the leader	Regulated by statute	Organizationally regulated	Bureaucratically regulated
Main organizational role	Leading	Decision-making	Organizing	Coordinating, administering
Main tasks	Leading change, team building, motivating	Management of organizations, processes, and projects	Coordination of organizational units, people, and projects	Planning, controlling, and accounting for operational activities
Management of people	Motivation, development, talent management	HR strategy and planning, main tasks of HRM	Basic functions of HRM	Coordination, control, and accountability of people's work
Management practices	*Sensemaking, sensegiving,* management of meaning	Managerial and organizational techniques, management of meaning	Managerial and organizational techniques	Organizational techniques
Perception of universities	Synthetic	Synthetic	Analytical	Analytical
Organizational relationships	The leader and followers	Managers and subordinates	Managers and subordinate	University and administrators

Source: own elaboration.

public ones, culturally and mentally remain with their roots, with the Humboldtian, post-Humboldtian, or hybrid model, as they have not yet passed through the phase of the entrepreneurial university. Meanwhile, the competitive market, the rise of higher education substitutes, technological and social changes, and the transformation of management modes in business reinforce the pressure for digital transformation in higher education. Digital leadership has also taken on particular relevance under the uncertainty caused by the Covid-19 pandemic, where it has taken transformational forms using the opportunities of organizational digitalization (Bartsch et al., 2020). In higher education, change—associated with remote learning and online university operations—is a revolution and a catalyst for change on a global scale (Antonopoulou et al., 2021b). Developing digital leadership competencies in universities is a strategic challenge for today's academic world (Ehlers, 2020).

When looking for characteristics of digital leadership in HEIs, it is possible to synthesize the current literature that only partly relates to higher education and adapts this approach to the academic sector. This leads to the emergence of ten distinctive characteristics of positive digital leadership in universities.

1 A focus on people and relationships takes on the characteristics of an integrated leadership style that also assumes a situational approach, often with a preference for a participative and collaborative leadership style. University managers responsible for the selected functional area should develop social and leadership competencies to develop an integrated and participative style using network modalities and digital methods and tools.

2 Transformational, charismatic, trust-based leadership, especially in breakthrough processes and projects, uses network and digital modality in communication and cooperation (network charisma, digital authority) (Wilson III et al., 2004). Academic leaders, accustomed to slowly changing organizations, should learn to operate in turbulent change and breakthroughs that require transformational approaches.

3 Social and emotional intelligence, combined with network and digital intelligence, allows conscious and intuitive use of information technologies for social and organizational purposes (Saputra, N. and Saputra, A. M., 2020). A high level of intelligence combining social, managerial, and digital aspects is particularly desirable (Lee, J., 2020).

4 Using and combining knowledge management and ICT methods in leading and organizing. This emerging approach is gradually ceasing to be eclectic as ICTs become increasingly intertwined with management concepts and techniques. The academic leader, but also the digital manager, should have the ability to "tinker" (*bricolage*) (Baker and Nelson, 2005), combining and adapting methods drawn from different disciplines and discourses to situational needs.

5 Project and process approach in strategic and operational orientation. Digital leadership is a permanent attitude; in this sense, it is a strategic orientation consisting of supporting, motivating, and organizing people and activities to achieve the university's goals using ICT. However, the management is dominated by a process approach: dynamic, using change and knowledge management, sequential and project-based. Digital leadership in the university is also based on project and process management (Jarvenpaa and Leidner, 1999).

6 A networked and digital modality of operation characterized by proficiency in applying ICT to management. This includes many aspects of knowledge and information technologies at both the social (e.g., social media, *crowdsourcing*, Internet of Things) and management (e.g., *agile, scrum*) levels, the application of which enables effective change management in universities (Carcary, Doherty and Conway, 2016).

7 An internalized but also consciously applied "organizational philosophy" based on integrating information technology into management: *evidence-based management, accountability* methods, *big data* analytics, the use of artificial intelligence (AI), and others. So it is also a hybrid approach, combining management with IT to improve the university (Oberer and Erkollar, 2018).

8 Entrepreneurship and change management as well as flexibility and speed. An orientation toward entrepreneurship is mainly linked to digital transformation and even radical organizational change projects. In this sense, it is the continuity of the development of the digital university with the initial formation of the entrepreneurial university, popularized by B. Clark (Wessels, 2020).

9 Innovative, visionary thinking and readiness to implement disruptive innovations. The implementation of future technologies, the development of Industry 4.0 and Society 4.0, lead to accelerated implementation of new ICT technologies and related social and organizational changes. Universities developing: labs, incubators, research networks, and scientific cooperation with industry, and also participate in the creation and implementation of breakthrough innovations, which require visionary thinking and extensive collaboration in academic and non-academic networks (Wasono and Furinto, 2018; Abbu et al., 2020).

10 The ability to identify and improve digital talent and manage human capital, including online. This consists of competencies in attracting, selecting, motivating, supporting the development, and retaining people in the organization (Promsri, 2019; Maheshwari and Yadav, 2020).

The presented concept of digital leadership in the university is closely related to the development in the 21st century of a new formation of the digital university. The literature is dominated by a very positive image of digital leadership. It is seen as the result of optimal adaptation to digital transformation. It is mainly seen through the lens of the positive effects it brings to the organization, society, and employees. As is sometimes the case in the early stages of the development of a concept, positive opinion and often even enthusiasm dominate in the social sciences, with critical positions emerging over time. Pioneering essential texts refer to the role of digital leaders and the social, cultural, and organizational dangers of digital transformation (Sata, 1989; Cunningham, Hazel, and Hayes, 2020). However, it seems that the scope of the changes brought about by digital transformation (which affects organizations, societies, cultures, and people) is civilizational and universal. Thus, it is also worth taking a critical look at digital leadership and, in particular, digital leadership in universities. A fundamental threat arising from the universal progress of digital transformation is of developing a culture of control, which can be described using the metaphor of the "digital panopticon" (Portnoff and Soupizet, 2018; Calzada, 2020). The Internet, the vast amount of data on every individual and organization, makes it possible not only to control but also to manipulate people through information management. We experience this through contemporary online marketing: advertising efforts, targeting, product placement, and PR. People are less and less able to defend themselves against destructive social engineering and psycho-manipulation based on functioning on the Internet (Darmody and Zwick, 2020; Held and Germelmann, 2018). The virtualization of the world, moving work and life increasingly online, also makes people and organizations dependent on a small number of corporations, developing commercial and oligopolistic practices and controlling the entire online market. In seeing these dangers of digital transformation, it is also essential to recognize the role of the digital leaders who are its vanguard. Promoting a culture of control and a "digital panopticon" is a real danger that cannot be hidden under an ideological smokescreen of postulates: participation, team leadership, and trust management in networks. Digital leaders in universities may be threatened by the role of digital technocrats who gain more control over people and universities through the implementation of ICT. This may lead to increased productivity, but at the same time, it may limit academic freedom, creativity, and a sense of stakeholder participation in co-governing the university. The uncritical or unreflective transfer of management and IT concepts, methods, and tools from business to universities is also a threat. This may lead to erosion of academic culture in favor of a quasi-corporate approach, further commodification and commercialization of education and science, and projectification of university life (Maylor et al., 2006; Jensen, Thuesen and Geraldi, 2016). Avoiding these risks could be described by a rhetorical figure, a challenge for the digital leaders, a metaphorical journey between the Scylla of academic freedom and the Charybdis of power and management control. Awareness of the changes brought about by digital transformation should make us rethink how to preserve the civilizing mission of the university while adapting to the competitive changes.

Part III
The organizational system of the university

6 Academic strategy

6.1 Strategic management in the university

Managers of all types of universities strive to achieve long-term goals. The universal tasks of the organization grow out of the historical mission of the university, but they are also related to its improvement, i.e., effectiveness, quality, and efficiency of operation (Trapitsin, Granichina, and Granichin, 2017). Effectiveness means the ability to achieve goals, while efficiency results from the resources used compared to results. Apart from universal tasks reflected in the academic mission and effectiveness and quality of results, universities also have specific goals related to the specificity of their activities. Despite the diversification of university types, higher education is relatively homogeneous regarding missions and strategic objectives. Therefore, the tasks of the majority of universities are similar in their essential part and include the development of science and research, education and improvement of education quality, and forming valuable relations with a non-academic environment (Han and Zhong, 2015; Vallé et al., 2016).

Strategic changes in the functioning of universities are mainly catalyzed by external factors, i.e., the accelerating transformation of economies, societies, and cultures. The consequences are fundamental changes in the higher education and science sector globally. The diagnosis of the directions of strategic changes in higher education and science systems has been developed based on many conducted studies and is widely described in the literature (Rogers, 2001; Aldosari, 2020). Several significant trends can be identified through national and international research. Universities are characterized by differentiation. Organizations differ in size, activities, specialization, funding structure, and quality (Altbach, Reisberg, and De Wit, 2017). The educational sector strives for internationalization and, as a result, mobility of students, staff, programs, and, finally, the institution as a whole (Kwiek, 2001; Wang, 2008; Dakowska and Harmsen, 2015; Bondarenko, Kelemen, and Nesterenko, 2019; Zapp and Lerch, 2020). We can talk about the privatization and commercialization of education globally. Higher education is often treated as a "private goods" service, and learning is an intellectual product (Kornelakis and Petrakaki, 2020). This trend is sometimes followed

DOI: 10.4324/9781003366409-10

by the opposite direction of de-privatization in some countries—especially in public systems in a situation of demographic decline (Kwiek, 2016). An entrepreneurial university model is taking shape, often met with criticism and reluctance by the academic community. Entrepreneurial tendencies can be seen in the university culture in its orientation toward innovative and industry-driven scientific activity, in reaching for "quasi-business" and "quasi-corporate" organizational solutions, and in the orientation towards making profits from educational and scholarly activity (Marginson, 2014; Thornton, 2016). "Entrepreneurial universities" are guided by a market vision, work on competitive strategies, use accountability methods, and use a quasi-managerial model for decision making, whereby power is held by supervisors and a board of trustees, rather than a collegial model based on academic staff (Rowlands, 2015; Veiga, Magalhaes, and Amaral, 2015). The last 40 years have seen less state participation in financing universities. The *welfare state* model no longer applies, which means that public management has taken a new shape (Salminen, 2003). In many countries, multi-level systemic changes are taking place that will lead to more flexibility in the operation of public universities. The directions of change at the macro-transformation level of the higher education system are global, recognized, and guided by public policies in many countries, strengthening the competitiveness and entrepreneurship of universities. Local education systems (national level) differentiation occurs at the mezzo level. They are subject to change, but differentiation remains, which has its own if only historical, justification. For these reasons, university management has a national context and is mainly related to social, political, economic, and cultural issues (the context of university activities). However, most challenges come from the micro level of the university's functioning. Although the directions of changes are known, different types of higher education institutions (HEIs) may choose different strategies and be characterized by other structures. At the same time, this level is a field where management theory and practice expansion may occur. Reaching for very advanced management methods in universities is criticized, as is managerialism. The way out is to balance the social mission of HEI with a focus on university efficiency. Management makes it possible to adapt the concepts and organizational methods used in enterprises to the needs of universities. Restructuring, human capital management, strategic management, quality management, and financial and logistics management can increase the effectiveness of HEIs, provided the mission is fulfilled. It is no longer possible to negate drawing on management concepts in universities, but the point is to keep in mind the strategic objectives (improvement of science and higher education).

The factors that influence the shape of the university's strategy are its founder, type, specialization, resources at its disposal, the scope of its relations with the environment, and the country in which it operates. The difference between private and public universities is significant in strategic management. Private universities often operate under a solution similar to the shareholder model, where one of the most important goals is to generate financial surpluses from activities for the benefit of the founders (Zemsky, 2005). Public organizations move towards a stakeholder model and focus on a social mission: Learning, teaching, and a third mission, which may differentiate the two types of universities. However, there is a solution to this aspect in the form of a convergence of university missions. Both public universities and some non-public ones focus their activities precisely on the social mission. A particular exception may be the rapidly growing group of private for-profit universities, which operate according to the logic of the shareholder model (Chipman, 2000; Sanyal and Johnstone, 2011; Bleak, 2017). "New public management" treats university management as a complex process that can be compared to the business activities of companies (Dunleavy and Hood, 1994; Dunleavy and Margetts, 2006; Carvalho and Santiago, 2010; Broucker and De Wit, 2015; Yates et al., 2017; Van der Sluis, Reezigt, and Borghans, 2017). When we refer to the concept of public management, we can consider traditional "administration" as a thesis, "new public management" as an antithesis, and the "public value governance" will be a synthesis (Bryson, Crosby, and Bloomberg, 2014; Wiesel and Modell, 2014). Public value governance creatively makes adaptations of management concepts for public mission purposes.

The professionalization of strategic management began half a century ago, and it is a gradual process, now taking place also as part of the fourth wave of universities ("digital universities"). Long-term planning and controlling use an extensive IT and management ecosystem to collect and analyze data and subsequently make important decisions. Integration of systems: enterprise resource planning (ERP), *student information system* (SIS), learning management system (LMS), business intelligence (BI), and others ensure data flows between units; analyses are conducted to enable rapid decision making based on high-quality data. Strategic and operational decisions are given various priorities, and different access paths are developed, depending on the decision-making powers. Some activities take the form of decisions based on procedures and algorithms designed in the information and management system. Other actions take the form of heuristics, reflection, and consultation, but these actions also require the analysis of reliable data (Mutanov et al., 2020).

In academic governance, we can observe a trend that I already referred to in this book—a deepening diversification and strategic polarization of universities, caused by fundamental changes in higher education, increasingly centered around the HEI's high specialization strategies. Globally, it is noted that some regional universities are participating in international competition and orienting themselves to pursue a research mission. Already at the time of the emergence of Humboldt-formation universities, there were attempts to adapt the strategy to the culture or social conditions (e.g., at the Newman model university, which focused on development through learning and student participation in the academic community). Nowadays, the priority of universities has become the development of science and innovation at a high-world level. Universities, guided by indicators and international rankings, invest in the best researchers and disciplines with the most scientific achievements and diversify their mission and strategy of science development. This is possible if public policy rewards the achievements of universities.

It also seems that an essential thread of analysis should be the strategic changes catalyzed by the Covid-19 pandemic, which undoubtedly accelerated the development of the virtualization of education and work and also of management. In this sense, the pandemic may contribute to the faster growth and spread of a new formation of the "digital university." The understanding of strategic management can refer to the three missions of universities and the management of the whole organization and its different functional areas. In the sphere of didactics, a strategic change is a radical increase in the importance of e-learning and the virtualization of education. Shifting the burden of education to online forms involves vital challenges for managers and educators. In the long term, this means investing in and implementing at universities methods and tools for remote learning, providing synchronous and asynchronous e-learning opportunities and better control over the quality of online learning. The choice of form and way of learning, taking into account changes in the types of knowledge, is a strategic decision (Appolloni et al., 2021). The field of education is the development of networks of international and national collaboration, leading to high-value publications and implementations. Conditions for success are as follows: Rewarding and creating development conditions for productive researchers, talent management, and implementation of incentive systems (Webb, McQuaid, and Webster, 2021). The third mission may be a core element of the strategy in the case of universities specializing in applied sciences. In this strategic area, the pandemic did not lead to a revolution but only contributed to a radical increase in the importance of remote work and communication in research teams (Mosteanu, 2021).

Management of the whole organization should be based on the pillars: Professionalization, digitalization, and virtualization of universities. Professionalization of university management refers to the training and development of professional groups of managers in the spheres of strategic management (presidents, vice-presidents, chancellors, vice-chancellors), finance (bursars, CFOs), academic administration, and information managers (chief information officers, librarians) (Khademi Kolahlou, 2019; Liu and Preston, 2021). Digitization and virtualization of universities use systems: LMS, management information system (MIS), e-learning systems, SIS, data management systems (BI), as well as electronic examination systems, digital documents, and diplomas, mobile applications for universities, research information, and scientific evaluation systems, allowing to create of motivational techniques for academic staff (Maltese, 2018; Mosteanu, 2020a). Thus, the strategic management of a university consists of research, analysis, and strategic plans, as well as management methods and tools, which serve to implement the three streams of mission (Iliashenko et al., 2020; Mosteanu, 2020b).

Strategic management is playing an increasingly important role in universities. Digital universities of the 21st century will use formalized strategies and integrate them into the organization of HEIs with IT and analytical tools to measure activity and compare between universities. Systems consist of activities in the areas:

- Scientific;
- Financial;
- Competetitive (benchmarking);
- Educational;
- Organizational;
- Third mission.

Universities' management information systems are developing to provide market and strategic analyses using algorithms, massive data, and artificial intelligence (Konina, Tinkov, and Tinkova, 2020; Ge and Hu, 2020; Wang, 2021). Managers and university administration increasingly use new controlling, process, or project management tools to support decision making (Hladchenko, 2015). Strategic management is the planning and implementation of decisions in the allocation of an entity's resources that aim to:

- Fulfilling the mission;
- Achieving the entity's strategic objectives;
- Preparation and implementation of strategic plans;
- Long-term management of change;
- Increasing the degree of adaptation of the entity's activities to its environment.

The strategic management of a university (especially a public one) is to support the realization of the goals set by the type of organization or key stakeholders. In non-public institutions, the founding structure, to a large extent, determines the objectives. In contrast, it is the co-determination of managers, staff and student representatives, and policymakers in public institutions. The type of university, the statutes, and the power structure influence the degree of autonomy in strategic decision making. Strategic goals are, in other words, the most important undertakings for the organization, which are outlined in a long-term perspective. The mission is to reflect the meaning of the entity and justify its importance for the founders, society, employees, and other stakeholders. The university's strategic objectives depend on the type of organization that co-operates with the environment and realizes the scientific and educational mission. Strategic tasks and the mission of the public university focus primarily on the non-commercial area of activity, and the non-public usually more on the commercial one.

There is a widespread conception of schools in strategic management, which differ in concepts, methods, and tools for creating and implementing strategy. The planning school assumes that strategy should be reflected in a strategic plan, which consists of:

- SMART (*Specific, Measurable, Achievable or Ambitious, Relevant or Realistic, Time-bound*) strategic objectives (Morrish and Sauntson, 2016);
- Perspective on the implementation of actions;
- A sequence of steps to achieve objectives;
- Defining the resources needed to achieve them and how to use them.

In contrast, according to the evolutionary school, the strategic plan includes multiple options and is open ended and generic to enable the exploitation of strategic opportunities. Strategic planning should be based on the competitive advantage of the entity. The scope of the created strategy is determined by its levels. The organizational system relates to the university as a whole, and functional strategy relates to different aspects of the university's activities. The latter may be related to marketing, human resources, financial, and other functions. Complementary strategies and policies (scientific and educational) also play an essential role in the university.

6.2 Historical changes in academic mission and strategy

A vital element of the university's strategy is the mission statement. It reflects the vision and values, long-term plans, and organizational identity. The mission is, on the one hand, related to the type of organization specific to a particular HEI. Universities originating from a common root in the Middle Ages, followed by historical changes and subsequent reforms, the most important of which was the creation of the Humboldtian model, have had a similar, but not identical, mission for centuries.

Differentiating the missions and strategies of universities as types of organizations from a historical perspective, it is necessary to point out their several features. Firstly, mission and strategy are terms understood from the perspective of the discourse of management sciences developed in the 20th century, so they are secondarily applied to the analysis of the activities of medieval (first wave) and Humboldtian (second wave) type universities. In this sense, universities that operated before the 20th century used only implicit, tacit, and emergent strategies and missions. This was, on the one hand, a universal understanding of the role of the traditional university in society, which defined its most important goals and ways of achieving them. On the other hand, it was a peculiar, individual founding and developmental idea, often reflected in the university's name, the Latin phrase of its foundation, its erection act, and its coat of arms. Such a coupling of the universal with the particular is also characteristic of universities in the 20th and 21st centuries. However, mission and strategy are often formulated explicitly and do not need to be secondarily extracted and interpreted. Second, the strategies of most universities within the first and second waves were similar. In contrast, the third wave is characterized by considerable strategic diversification linked to the proliferation of universities and higher education. Third, the most critical common and universal elements of the university mission persist and include the following: Science, teaching, and the third mission, but there is an essential historical evolution of the mission. Science and didactics remain a very enduring and relatively unchanging element of the mission over almost a millennium, while the third mission is clearly evolving. The medieval university, derived in many cases from religious institutions, played a sacred role alongside learning and teaching (Magalhães, 2015). The third mission in the era of the "nationalization" of universities focused on state-forming aspects. On the other hand, the Humboldtian model was enriched by the cultural and civic role (Nybom, 2003; Östling, 2018, p. 312). In the case of an entrepreneurial HEI, the third mission gains importance, moving away from the vision of a hermetic, elitist university, metaphorically described as an "ivory tower" (Claes, 2005; Lam, 2010). Relations with the environment would be modeled on the implementation of scientific and technological solutions in the industry, the popularization of science, and participation in the development of civil society. The fourth distinctive feature of the university strategy is its connection with autonomy, i.e., the internal embedding of power, control, and supervision, which allows, in accordance with the ideals of scientific freedom, for the development of thought and education (Choi, 2019). The university's ability to fulfill its mission and values is based on freedom of research and teaching, which, historically, can be understood in many ways (Bayertz, 2006). The last feature mentioned here is the treatment of the university's strategy and mission since the 20th century as a search for ideas and ways to achieve success by the university understood as an organization (Allen, 2002; Shattock, 2010b). The perspective of the market, competition, co-operation (co-opetition), and the pursuit of established organizational goals have become a strategic premise for the university's existence in the last century.

The search for methods of historical classification of HEI development is fraught with the error of simplification, as we are dealing with an assortment of foundation ideas, development concepts, missions, and strategies. However, in an attempt to arrive at a particular synthesis, a historical description of the university's mission, values, and strategy can be proposed—included in Table 6.1. It provides a starting point for a detailed analysis of strategic management from the perspective of three university formations. The first one is the university of the past, i.e., the Humboldt type, whose ethos is also present in the academic environment and public awareness. The second, contemporary dominant and developing formation—is the entrepreneurial university and the formation of the "digital university," which is only just being formed.

Table 6.1 Historical transformations of the university mission and strategy

Historical stage	Mission	Values	Strategy
The first wave of universities	Common and universal: 1 and 2, specific foundation, 3 marginal	Community of Academics and Scholars	The traditional way of doing things, based on values and rituals
The second wave of universities	Reformed: 3, common and universal: 1 and 2	Master-student community, formation of elites	Incremental strategies, informal, based on the academic ethos
The third wave of HEIs	New: 3, transformed market adapted: 1 and 2	Competition, market, co-operation with the environment	Market success strategies, based on old and new objectives (scientific prestige, market share)
The fourth wave of HEIs	1, 2, 3 adapted to the network society	Digital transformation, networking	Restructuring, digital innovation, the radical redesign

Source: Own study, 1—first mission (science), 2—second mission (didactics), 3—third mission (relations with non-academic environment).

The missions and strategies of the first two waves of universities can be described as the primacy of academic culture over strategy and structure in the organizational system. The third and fourth waves represent an increase in the importance of HEI strategy, which in the case of entrepreneurial HEIs is based on management discourse, while digital HEIs are moving towards IT. The description of the emerging new digital formation points to distinctive features relating to the mission and strategy of HEIs, which will be analyzed in detail in the following subsection.

6.3 University formations and strategies

The Humboldtian-type university developed even before the scientific reflection on management. This means that at both the design and dissemination stages of this formation, the concepts, methods, and even language of strategic management, a sub-discipline of management science that emerged in the mid-20th century, were not used. However, this does not mean that "strategic thinking" was not present in the design and implementation of long-term university development plans. The term here represents the most elementary understanding of strategic planning for a long time. The mission of a second-wave university grows out of the academic tradition and ethos and, through the central idea of *Bildung,* combines science with learning and a cultural and state-forming role. It is difficult to say that "strategic thinking" was based on any school of strategy, but one can see that it was an orientation towards the status quo of a stable and static organization. If there was any long-term planning, it took the form of a single variant plan. A consequence of the absence of management discourse in the Humboldt-type university organization project was the absence of strategic management processes, analysis, planning, and strategic controlling (Thomas, Wilson, and Leeds, 2013). Functional strategies were absent, replaced by routine traditional patterns and modes of governance and decision making. For example, the university's finance had practices of accounting and payroll, but these did not translate to the level of financial analysis, ratios, and managerial accounting. In the system triad: Strategy, culture, and organizational structure, it was the culture that played a dominant role. The existing patterns and the university's ethos set the activity's objectives and the traditional academic structures and positions. A few staff members were nominated to the strategic level, holding elected tenure and sharing power with collegiate bodies such as senates. With a strategic horizon, long-term thinking was an area of interest for all academic staff, not just a limited group holding management positions. Similarly, intuitive and routine action characterized knowledge management strategies focused on libraries and archives, mainly collecting and sharing knowledge. They have been subject to strategic expansion projects to cope with the growing numbers of writers and readers. Second-wave universities use the discourse of classical humanities, German Idealism, and Enlightenment philosophy, which is far removed from management science. It is, therefore, difficult to speak of the professionalization of strategic management, which was entirely intuitive, rudimentary, and based on common patterns of action rooted in academic culture.

The formation of the entrepreneurial university developed in the final decades of the 20th century, when strategic management accumulated a considerable body of theory and practical applications. Using these concepts was possible not only for adapting solutions from the business sector, but the development of strategy in the stream of new public management opened the way for implementing organizational patterns in public universities (Groves, Pendlebury, and Stiles, 1997; Hatten, 1982; Shattock, 2000). Third-wave universities may approach strategy in two model ways, far from characteristic of second-wave universities (Lourens, 1990; Mainardes, Alves, and Raposo, 2011). First, by developing the idea of an entrepreneurial culture, they can move towards a strategy, emerging in action, evolutionary, and partly spontaneous, which is a creative response to opportunities in the environment. This way of interpreting strategy emphasizes openness, flexibility, innovation, and entrepreneurship, setting only more general directions of action resulting from the mission and strategic objectives (Fossatti et al., 2020). The second type of strategy, which can complement or replace the emergent strategy, is the planning perspective. The strategy is an elaborate, sequential, and sometimes multivariant plan of action to achieve the university's goals. The level of detail in long-range planning here is much higher than in tacit, emergent strategies. Strategic objectives are as follows: Formalized, formulated, disseminated, linked to the mission, and follow the postulates with the acronym SMART (Morrish and Sauntson, 2016). The adjective "smart" is also sometimes used to describe the strategy of the third mission of entrepreneurial universities, as the development of co-operation with the non-academic environment is a distinctive feature of the third-wave universities (Mali, 2000). Drawing on the classical concept of strategy schools by H. Mintzberg, we can see in the entrepreneurial university the use of not only the planning and evolutionary approach but also the positional and resource school (Clarke, 1997; Mintzberg and Lampel, 1999). The positional approach analyses the HEI's relative advantage and competitive position in the sector, considering the competitive strategy model created in the 1970s by M.E. Porter. The resource approach emphasizes the uniqueness of the university's resource composition, allowing it to strengthen its competitive position (Zhang, 2018). Both these ways of understanding strategy originate from business; in the case of an HEI, especially a public one, it seems appropriate to correct the pure model of competitive strategy and turn to the model of co-opetition between universities. Beyond the area of competition for students, researchers, financial resources, reputation, and prestige or scientific achievements, there is a wide field of co-operation: Scientific, didactic, implementations with industry, and even political, social, and cultural (position of the university and scholars in society) (Sulkowski, Seliga, and Wozniak, 2019). Strategic management in entrepreneurial universities is derived from understanding strategy (Parakhina et al., 2017). If it is interpreted evolutionarily, then strategic management is less formalized, and the process itself is flexible and does not take the form of an algorithm. In the case of the planning approach, strategic management has a cascading character, from the mission, through the objectives, a multi-variant strategic plan, with indicators of implementation that allow moving to the construction of operational plans and schedules implemented in the methodology of project management (Inga et al., 2021). Strategic analysis of universities has long used the most popular and oldest streangth, weanessess, opportunities, threats (SWOT) methodology based on basic market research and secondary data from university information systems. Other methods of strategic analysis, such as balanced scorecards or sector maps, appear much less frequently (Hladchenko, 2015; Morais, 2019; Hamzehpour et al., 2020; Abdolshad et al., 2020). Some of the universities implement more or less comprehensive strategic controlling systems, which most often monitor the processes: Financial, didactic (quality of education), conducting research and increase of scientific output, and human resources management (Sabau et al., 2009; Münch, 2015; Sulkowski, Fijałkowska, and Dziminska, 2019). Third-wave universities develop entrepreneurial culture as one of this formation's most important distinctive features. The way of understanding entrepreneurial culture varies, although it is generally derived from the discourse of management science. Organizational culture should be coupled with strategy, which means that entrepreneurship is reflected in the mission, objectives, and strategic plans. Quite ingrained is the belief that it is possible to shape and even manage an entrepreneurial culture to bring about market effects. Such instrumental, simplifying treatment of the hardly controllable phenomenon of culture often leads to confusion and unsuccessful attempts to implement culture and organizational identity management programs.

In the third-wave university, there is an increase in structural specialization in strategic management. In non-public universities and public ones, in various educational systems, there are more and more specialized academic managers who do not have term limits to hold the highest positions. There is also a larger group of decision makers at the strategic level through the specialization of divisions responsible, e.g., science, teaching, organization, finance, internationalization, and human resources (Tavernier, 1991). Functional strategies, which are components of the university-wide strategy, are also beginning to develop in the third-wave university. They are concerned with strategic investments in learning, teaching, and the third mission. Long-term planning also appears in the functional areas of finance, marketing, and human capital management. These are long-term investments, restructuring, projects, implementation, and other plans in the financial sphere. In terms of marketing, the planned development of the educational offer, expansion into new markets, investments in the university brand, relationship marketing, promotion, and public relations (PR) may take on a strategic dimension (Bratianu and Pop, 2007). In human capital management, multi-year plans may be created to develop employee competencies or to invest in attracting and developing academic or student talent. Combining different functional areas within a specialized university strategy is possible. An example may be the internationalization strategy related to the development of marketing (international students, mobility), teaching (double diploma programs, branch campuses), and science (international projects). Knowledge management strategy is quite rare in third-wave universities. Operational methods and knowledge management tools are mostly implemented based on distributed information systems (Choo and Bontis, 2002). When we also adopt the criteria of specialization, efficiency, and flexibility of management, the professionalization of strategic management increases in comparison with the Humboldt-type university. This is manifested not only by the application of concepts and methods of controlling, analysis, and strategic planning but also by placing the issue of strategy at the center of the university's interests and the growing specialization and competence of the management (Boldt, 1991; Sulkowski et al., 2020).

The digital university is founded on the information and communication revolution, which will be reflected in the interpretation of strategic management processes as the exercise of power over people and control over the organization to achieve long-term goals through data analysis and knowledge management (Sax, 2005; Peters and Jandrić, 2018). This means the strategy will be plan driven, multi-variant, highly detailed, and sequential.

The formalized strategy will be based on a data analysis approach leading to a synthesis in the form of objectives and plans to achieve them. It will be based on reliable data extracted from the university's information and communication system, using an interface to external knowledge bases. The premise will be strategic management based on accountability and evidence, which will integrate the insights of management science with the perspectives, concepts, and methods of computer science. Hence, the degree of absorption and application of management concepts and methods will remain as high as in the entrepreneurial university. Still, the coupling with information methods and tools will prove crucial. The theoretical basis here will be expanding knowledge management concepts and implementing these ideas into the academic world (Hazemi and Hailes, 2001; Mahjoub, 2004). The university's mission at the marketing level will probably remain quite general, but its detailing, goals, and strategic plans will exhaust SMART postulates. They will be subject to verification, both in implementation and through information analysis. The sophistication of strategic management, analysis, and strategic controlling processes will also increase. All these strategy elements will be characterized by: Accountability, analyticity, cascade, and reliance on mass data analyzed using algorithms, artificial intelligence, and other developing IT methods. The strategy will move away from heuristic and creative solutions, in the sense of human invention and entrepreneurship, towards algorithmic and quantifiable processes based increasingly on computers processing data into information. Computer-supported decision-making processes will become the basis of the university organization, which will contribute to the development of efficiency in every area of mission and management. Due to the development of information and communication technologies (ICT) and increased competitiveness in the sector, universities wishing to remain in the market will likely have to undergo a digital transformation phase (Safiullin and Akhmetshin, 2019). Regarding the use of the strategy school concept, all four can be used to describe strategic management in a digital university (Table 6.2). A planning approach based on the highest quality, reliable and detailed data and information will be the standard orientation, which must be complemented by constant monitoring of the environment (Bolisani and Bratianu, 2017). This trend tracking, benchmarking, and search for development opportunities is also based on the analysis of mass data compared with internal information. Scanning the environment for strategic opportunities is characteristic of the evolutionary school and the entrepreneurial orientation, which will be supported by permanent data analysis. The positional approach in strategy will result from increasing competition and diversification in the sector. Universities will increasingly compete within global or local strategic groups. Ivy league universities compete among themselves, universities of applied sciences form their co-opetition groups, and local and national universities compete and co-operate simultaneously (Ubi et al., 2012; Karwowska and Leja, 2018). The resource school will take on a new dimension in the information and network society.

Table 6.2 Evolution of strategic management in universities

Organizational criterion	Second-wave university	Third-wave HEI	Fourth-wave university HEI
Type of strategy	A traditional general mission, flowing from the academic culture and ethos, outlined development directions and intuitive "strategic thinking"	Emergent (evolutionary, spontaneous, tacit, opportunities in the environment) or planned (sequential, multi-variant) strategy	Planned, detailed, sequential, multi-variant, data-driven, quantifiable strategy
Degree of formalization of the strategy	No formalized university strategy, only "strategic thinking" about how to plan and how the university works	Different, formulated: Mission, objectives, and strategic plan	Extensive, analytical approach, evidence-based, and data-driven strategic management
Mission	Long-term action is based on academic values, *Bildung* as a core value of mission	Entrepreneurship, development of the third mission, possible specialization, preference for maintaining the science–education interface	Digital co-operation in developing the three streams of mission, possible specialization
Absorption of strategic management theory	Lack, universities development before academic reflection on management	Growing, concepts and methods of strategic management using	Large, advanced methods, coupling strategic management and ICT
Strategy schools	None, only intuitive "strategic thinking," going toward sustaining the status quo	Planning, evolutionary (entrepreneurial), positional (co-operation), resource based	Planning, positioning, resource based
Strategic management process	None, only intuitive "strategic thinking"	Different degrees and use, dual approach	High utilization rate, sequential, quantifiable
Strategic analysis	None, only intuitive "strategic thinking"	SWOT, basic market research, balanced scorecard	Extensive, based on external and internal mass data analyzed in the system
Strategic planning	None, only current plans and "strategic thinking"	Most HEIs create plans to achieve the objectives of the strategic management	An extensive, sequential, multi-variant plan

(*Continued*)

Table 6.2 (Continued)

Organizational criterion	Second-wave university	Third-wave HEI	Fourth-wave university HEI
Strategic controlling	None, only limited and intuitive operational control	Growing, varying degrees of development; finance, teaching and learning processes, human resources	Extensive, systematic, integrated, data driven
Strategic objectives	Default, academic mission	Formulated, disseminated, mission-related, SMART	Detailed, indicator based, SMART
Functional strategies	Lack, routine, traditional exercise of power based on cultural patterns	Created in the sphere of the three missions, less frequently finance, marketing	Designed for the university mission and functional areas
Strategy and organizational culture	Culture governs "strategic thinking," value orientation, and university ethos	Culture coupled with strategy attempts to "manage culture" through strategies	Culture coupled with strategy attempts to "manage culture" through strategies
Strategy and organizational structure	Functional, term, co-governance principals and staff with senates (reflection on the long-term plan of interest to all staff)	It is located in the structure at the level of managers, elected functions, tenure (more often public), or by appointment	Located at managerial levels and distributed, specialized administrative functions or by choice
Knowledge management strategy	None, only intuitive, routine operation	Rare, only operational methods and knowledge management tools	Advanced, integrated knowledge management system and strategic management, accountability
The professionalization of strategic management	None, actions ethos, intuitive, unplanned, tacit knowledge	Specialization, agility, and flexibility are increasing Project and strategic process management	Developed, specialized, measurable, quantifiable, and improving

Source: Own study.

Data is the most important resource leading to the smart university's strategic improvement. Thanks to it, all decision-making processes will be realized. This will happen both at the level of the strategy of the whole university and in formalized functional strategies. Science, teaching, third mission, internationalization, human capital management, finance, and marketing will have their functional strategies subordinated to the logic of knowledge management and holistic university strategy (Maxwell, Norton, and Wu, 2018). Setting management goals, creating strategic plans, and controlling their implementation process at the level of functional strategies will be a standard. It will probably be followed by further structural specialization, connected with creating specialized units and positions and developing non-cadre managerial functions subject to evaluation and motivation systems. A symptomatic example of the growth of managerial specialization and appreciation of the information sphere will be the common creation and location in the management structure of positions responsible for the information management division (Liu and Preston, 2021). In organizational culture, the tendency to develop network and digital orientation and coupling with strategy and structure will prevail. The question of cultural resistance to the threats of the "digital panopticon," privacy restrictions, and the "symbolic violence" of the information and communication system remains open (Manuel, 2017; Perakslis, 2017; Baranov, 2021). The knowledge management strategy will be advanced, elaborate, integrated with the other components of the organization, and based on the canonical assumptions: Accountability, mass data analysis, and evidence-based decision making. This will be the basis for further professionalization of strategic management, which should increase the efficiency of universities and the competitiveness of the whole sector and competition within it (Kazmina et al., 2020; Gorbunova, Timirgaleeva, and Khrulyova, 2021).

7 University culture

7.1 Evolution of academic cultures

According to the famous phrase of Peter Drucker, "culture eats strategy for breakfast," which means the primacy of organizational culture over planned and controlled subsystems of strategy and organizational structure. Cultures are spontaneously created by social groups, yet organizations are, by definition, social groups because people always make them. In universities and organizations built on values and ethos, this fundamental importance of culture is even more clearly reflected (Favaro, 2014).

The cultures of Humboldt-type universities were strongly oriented towards academic culture and values, which formed the organization's core. They were based on academic tradition, professorial ethos, and the idea of *Bildung*. These account for the coupling of individual identity and, therefore, the two vital social roles in the university: The professor (master) and the student (pupil), and the relationship between them. Organizational identity followed in the first instance, a sense of identification with the academy and the university, understood precisely as a community of professors and students. Disciplinary identity, related to the belonging of researchers to a particular field of science, also started to be important in the 19th century. Identification with the university was reflected in the image, i.e., its appearance presented to the outside world. The perception was based on a reputation usually derived from tradition and history, followed by scientific achievements and names of famous scholars. This was the case with the model University of Berlin. At the same time, it is a type of strong culture, thus homogeneous and conservative due to its permanence orientation, sometimes also with the beginnings of a bureaucratic orientation in the area of administration. The second-wave university did not have any management concept for organizational culture. It formed spontaneously and was not subject to control. As for the components of organizational culture, the academic ethos norms were derived from *Bildung*'s values. The two types of communication prevailed: Group communication, taking place in master-student relationships or small teams, and public communication, usually in the form of lectures. The discourse was academic and

DOI: 10.4324/9781003366409-11

profession centric, traditionally related to the area of research represented by the professor, with an overrepresentation of humanistic discourse. Stories and narratives were built around heroes, prominent academic figures, and their research achievements. Most academic life took on ritualized forms of customs rooted in the university's past, which regulated the teaching and research process, promotion of staff, and important events in the life of the university. Symbolism included Latin sentences forming the type of mission, the university's name, and graphic symbols (the university coat of arms). Conflicts over power, failures, and anything that could damage the image of the university and the academic oligarchy became taboo. Second-wave universities were strong, unified cultures in which countercultures were hard to discern. There may have been some subcultural aspects to the dominant culture of the professorial staff, the subcultures of academic disciplines and departments, and those of students. The "superiority" of the academic oligarchy and the elitism of professors and students over the rest of society were stereotypical. In the sphere of artifacts, mention may be made of the campuses, which were most often integrated into the cities in which they were built. Architecturally, they often referred to classicism and continuity of development, even from ancient Greece. The core metaphor of the Humboldtian model university can be seen as the ivory tower, the temple of knowledge, and the beacon of learning.

The cultures of entrepreneurial higher education institutions (HEIs) are market oriented, competitive and flexible, and innovative, as an ideal model because, in practice, some of them are nevertheless burdened with bureaucratic aspects. The identification sphere is dominated by the orientation toward scientific prestige, organizational effectiveness, and image related to outstanding achievements of scientists, implementers of innovations, teachers, and managers. Collective identity crystallizes at the level of the whole organization and, in the scientific staff case, at the discipline level. The entrepreneurial university is dominated by functionalist thinking about organizational culture by applying change management. Cultural norms, derived from the values of entrepreneurship and flexibility, constitute the principles of effective management and innovation in the university. They are cultural patterns that regulate the actions of organizational actors. The modes of communication are both group and individual, and the language is associated with management and the academic world of scientific disciplines. Stories, narratives, and myths are related to outstanding achievements in organizational, scientific, teaching, and implementation activities. Rituals do not play as important a regulatory role as in second-wave universities, functioning somewhat marginally as traditional ceremonial (promotions, inaugurations, senate meetings). Alongside them, new customs are formed, resulting from organizational practices related to management (e.g., recruitment and staff competitions, appraisal interviews, and organizational meetings). Symbols include the university's name, logo, visual identification, and founding sentences. Organizational heroes are not only outstanding academics but also managers who have contributed to the university's success. Taboo, as in the second-wave university, are organizational failures, particularly power pathologies, cronyism, corruption, and nepotism. In an entrepreneurial university, subcultures are formed around stakeholder groups (students, administration), researchers, academic staff, employees from different scientific disciplines, but also managers. The separated construction of campuses, derived from cities and often located outside the centers, can be regarded as artifacts. Another example of spatial artifacts can be the open architecture of business incubators, allowing flexible use of office space by partners co-operating with the university. Organizational stereotypes focus on the "superiority" of managers, their concepts, and management methods over other stakeholder groups. In other words, it is the construction of a mythology of the exercise of executive power in universities. Examples of core metaphors that a third-wave university may orient itself toward are knowledge factory, forge of human capital, and innovation producer.

In the digital university, the organizational culture will develop on the values of digital co-opetition and networked community, which are oriented towards communication processes, accountability, and effective management. Digital identity will be formed at multiple levels of the digital community, including different organizational roles: Researcher, teacher, organizer, implementer, and affiliation to various academic disciplines. This is combined with a network image based on relationships sustained by online communication and scientific and organizational achievements in implementing the third mission and social responsibility. Attempting to relate the numerous typologies of organizational culture to the fourth-wave university, it is possible to point to the complexity of the culture of the digital university, which will exhibit hybrid, sometimes paradoxical characteristics.

The culture of a fourth-wave university will be strong, innovative, and pragmatic. Strength will come from the drive to integrate organizations around virtual working, networked teams, and digital transformation. Innovation is an inherent feature of organizations relying on digital and networked technologies, which are changing rapidly, simultaneously resulting in profound adaptations of the organizations. Cultures of digital universities are likely to move towards pragmatism associated with effective management due to elaborate and, in the extreme, bureaucratic control systems. It is also possible that culture will move towards bureaucratization. Managing organizational culture will be seen as feasible by exerting influence through management methods and information and communication technologies. Around the values of digital co-opetition and networked management, cultural norms are formed to regulate the rules of effective networking. Modes of communication and language are characterized by: Networking (both group and individual), profession centricity, and links to management and information and communication technologies (ICT). Stories, narratives, and myths will often be about the "new" digital organization, online activities, outstanding scientific, teaching, third mission, and social responsibility. Rituals, customs, and more go in two directions. Traditional ceremonies and customs related to inaugurations, doctoral promotions, senate meetings, and others will become completely ossified rituals. In parallel, new network customs and mores will take shape, which regulate behavior in the area of digital transformation by creating routines and customs related to online activities. In the realm of symbolism, in addition to the name and logo, a growing number of network identities will emerge that are recognizable to users online. The functioning of symbolism can be measured by the awareness and brand image of the university online. Organizational heroes are both outstanding scholars and managers who achieve considerable success. Negative aspects of the university's activities will become taboo, as well as elements of a culture of control and surveillance. Subcultures will be able to form around stakeholder groups: Researchers, teachers, implementers, managers, students, and scientific discipline communities. Additionally, a distinct group with solid identification and a key role may become IT professionals responsible for central processes in the digital university. Stereotypes are likely to relate to the "superiority" of innovators, networks, and digital orientation, over previous university formations. The spatial artifact is expected to be the hybrid or networked organization of the campus. The core metaphors with which fourth-wave universities can be described are the positive reference emphasizing academic freedom and thus the "innovation network," and on the other hand, the threat of excessive managerial control—the "digital panopticon" (Table 7.1).

7.2 The disappearance of traditional university cultures

Significant changes in higher education systems, educational policy, and university governance also lead to far-reaching changes in the organizational cultures of contemporary universities. A deficit in cultural studies of universities and other HEIs can be discerned in the literature. Initially, between 1960 and 1990, organizational cultural studies focused on student cultures and then on the organizational cultures of universities (Corson, Foote, and Mayer, 1969; Clark, 1973; London, 1978; Nkomo, 1984; Whorton Jr, Gibson, and Dunn, 1986; Krimsky, 1987). B. Clark explored the diversity of HEIs' cultures, the role of beliefs and loyalties in universities, and organizational stories as tools for shaping institutional identity (Clark, 1998b). The last two decades have seen the development of international and comparative studies of academic cultures (Szelényi and Rhoads, 2013), studies of university leadership (Jones et al., 2012; Stensaker and Vabø, 2013), and changes in the educational system interpreted through the lens of culture and identity (Stensaker, Välimaa, and Sarrico, 2012).

D. Dill, in his pioneering research in the early 1980s, concluded that universities are ideological institutions immersed in strong organizational cultures. Academic culture cannot, in principle, be managed, but implicitly it influences identity, communication, and social ties. It mainly shows its

Table 7.1 Organizational cultures of universities

Organizational criterion	Second-wave university	Third-wave university	Fourth-wave university
The essence of culture and identity	Traditional academic culture, professorial ethos	Market, competitive, innovative	Networking, communication
Values	*Bildung*, learning with education, ideas integrating nation, state	Entrepreneurship, competitiveness, flexibility	Digital co-opetition, networked community
Organizational identity	A community of professors and students, academic staff identifying themselves with their environment and their university and research area	Prestigious, effective organization, managers and staff, image, disciplinary matrix	Digital identities, multi-level digital communities (disciplines, roles)
Organizational image	Traditional, based on reputation linked to the history and academic achievements or new projects of the university	Image, based on scientific prestige and achievements (three missions)	Network image, based on relationships, achievements, and digitalization
Type of culture	Strong, conservative, bureaucratic	Strong, innovative, pragmatic, or bureaucratic	Strong, innovative, networked, pragmatic, or bureaucratic
Organizational culture management	No concept, traditional culture, spontaneous, poorly controlled	Shaping organizational culture by management methods	Impact on organizational culture management and the internet
Standards	Professor's ethos	Principles of effective management and innovation	Principles of effective network management
Modes of communication and language	Group (master–student), public (lectures), academic, discipline specific, humanistic	Group and individual, scientific discipline language, management related	Network, group and individual, profession centric, management, and ICT related
Stories, narratives, and myths	Scholarly activity, outstanding achievements	Organizational, scholarly activity, and outstanding achievements	Networking, organizational, scholarly activities, outstanding achievements
Rituals, customs, and mores	The ritualized bulk of academic life	Rituals as traditional ceremonial, new organizational customs	Rituals as ossified ceremonial, new network customs

Symbols	Latin sentences, name of the university	University name, logo, mottoes	University name and logo, graphic identities on the web
Heroes	Eminent researchers	Eminent leaders and researchers	Outstanding innovators, leaders, managers, researchers, and teachers
Taboo	Conflicts over power, private life, organizational pathologies	Organizational failures, pathologies of power, cronyism, corruption, and nepotism	Negative aspects of university operations, the culture of control, and surveillance
Subcultures and countercultures	Professorial (dominant), student, scientific disciplines	Researchers, academic staff, scientific disciplines, students, managers	Researchers, educators, implementers, IT specialists, managers, students, scientific disciplines
Organizational stereotypes	"Superiority" of academic oligarchy, elitism of students	"Superiority" of managers, management concepts, and methods	"Superiority" of innovators, networks, and digital orientation
Artifacts	Classic campuses, integrated with cities	Separated campuses, separated from cities	Hybrid or networked campus
Core metaphors	Ivory tower, temple of knowledge, beacon of science	Factory of knowledge, forge of human resources, producer of innovations	Innovation network, digital panopticon

Source: Own elaboration.

importance in situations of crisis and resource scarcity. Commitment to a strong university culture can then protect against destructive conflicts and tensions, strengthening its integration and enabling its survival (Dill, 1982). In an environment of growing skepticism about the effectiveness of traditional planning management tools related to strategic management, finance, controlling, and marketing. There has been a concomitant growing interest in management by values. This orientation towards values and cultural variability is reflected in institutions operating in global and cross-cultural environments. As Dill notes, it is academic institutions in Western countries that most culturally resemble Japanese organizations. They are dominated by the employment of employees throughout their professional life, combined with fundamental mechanisms of team decision making and a sense of professional responsibility (honor, prestige). Characteristic, at least for public universities, is also the dominance of stable bureaucratic cultures, where organizational structures are permanent and relatively inflexible, and the system of evaluation and motivation of employees is not very formalized (Dill, 1982). To this diagnosis from the 1980s, we can add that the system in many universities is changing, becoming more like the corporate model, with formalized procedures for measuring quality, productivity, and motivating staff. There is also an increasing use of controlling, strategic planning, and management accounting methods in universities. Therefore, organizational cultures in universities are also evolving and diversifying.

B. Clark believed that a far-reaching complexity characterizes academic cultures compared to business organizations because they combine at least three spheres: The organizational identity as such, the professional culture of the academic community, and the culture of a given academic discipline (Clark, 1983). In describing the strength of academic culture, it is worth noting Western universities' rich tradition, continuity, and ethos. "Rites of passage," associated with student and academic life, refer to the centuries-old tradition of universities being *de facto* in a tiny group of institutions that have maintained continuity for so long (Dias and Sá, 2014). Universities build and reinforce a strong organizational culture by referring to this academic history and by socially legitimizing practice as an academic and teaching activity. The second area of organizational identity belongs to an academic community characterized by a strong and distinctive ethos rooted in university learning and teaching values. The academic degrees obtained, the academic ceremonies, the system of environmental evaluations, and many other practices build a sense of the value of the scholarly profession. Finally, most scientific disciplines create their scientific community, which has measures of prestige and recognition and develops norms of belonging and exclusion from a given area of research and didactics (Becher, 1981). At the turn of the 20th and 21st centuries, we witnessed the decline of traditional university cultures, which, despite the academic ethos, do not stand up to the changes brought about by the digital transformation (DT), massification of education, and the development of new public management practices.

Many of these critical publications accurately diagnose the problems of cultural transformation from the traditional ethos to the entrepreneurial university. But change is a fact, and the opinions of the academic community are not decisive in shaping the new order in higher education. The revolution in the form of higher education (HE) that has taken place worldwide has changed the conditions under which universities operate.

7.3 Culture of control in HEI

Academic culture during the heyday of the Humboldt-type university was hardly the subject of scholarly reflection because it existed as a prominent, assimilated pattern of the functioning of the HEI. First cultural research has begun to emerge with the symptoms of the profound change that the traditional university models have undergone in the last few decades. One axis of this change is the evolution from a trust-oriented culture to one based on verification, audit, and control. The traditional academic culture placed trust in academic staff based on the assumption that the professional ethos of a professor obliged them to do a decent job of research and teaching. Over the years, under the influence of many cultural, social, and economic factors, among which a significant role was played by the development of the new public management, the traditional university model was dismantled, and the patterns of the culture of trust disappeared. In its place, a new formation is developing, referred to as *evidence culture, audit culture, control culture*, or *assessment culture* (Farkas, 2013). The evidence culture is based on management control, process, and quality management at the university. At its core are assumptions taken from the new public management and applied to the university, namely:

- Building competitive mechanisms into the education system and the activities of universities;
- The economimization of the activities of the higher education sector, which will create a constant drive for savings in universities and result in a systematic reduction of the share of public finance in the activities of public universities;
- Privatization of a part of higher education through creating opportunities to open non-public HEIs and outsourcing part of the services in public universities;
- Transformation of university management systems from the traditional academic collegial-administrative system into a managerial-corporate management system modeled on business solutions;
- Implementation of a system of accountability, which will allow for the control of university management processes (financial, educational quality assurance);
- A change of orientation in education from academic to vocational by adapting programs to the needs of the labor market (Singh, 2001).

The strength of the culture of trust was embedding academic self-monitoring mechanisms in the university's operations. The effectiveness of the internalized tool of academic ethos was not 100%, but the costs of its functioning proved to be small. In the area of didactics, professors felt obliged to teach at an appropriate level, make demands on students, control and advise junior staff, and participate in developing educational programs. In the academic sphere, the need to conduct research and publish was linked to the pursuit of scientific advancement and flowed from intrinsic motivation. In practice, only part of the academic staff carried out research, while the rest concentrated on teaching. Faculty who did research enjoyed a higher professional status, commensurate with their academic standing (Altbach, 2015a). These were rewards rooted in a culture that was not reflected in material motivation. The academic work system was traditionally not very formalized and gave a lot of freedom in the choice of classes, working hours, and research topics. It was also characterized by collegiality and an orientation towards teamwork, which often slowed decision-making mechanisms. Still, it gave academics a sense of participation and involvement in the university's functioning.

The transformation towards a control culture involves a shift from trusting the employee to motivating and controlling mechanisms. The planned result should be a more effective and economical new system. The costs of introducing the solutions are primarily related to employing professional administration and training ICT systems, which should be compensated by higher productivity and quality of teaching and research work. In the sphere of values, productivity, efficiency, scientific and teaching work quality, and cost effectiveness are critical to the control culture. Thus, the principle of prestige based on the value of scientific output has survived. However, it has been transformed into the direction of the economy of prestige, i.e., valuing and ranking the achievements of academic staff and the whole university based on scientific productivity. The traditional collegial and team approach is being transformed into a quasi-corporate model. The academic staff is formally divided into research and teaching staff. Systems and mechanisms of evaluation, motivation, and controlling have been introduced in both the research and teaching streams. In the cultural sphere, the transparency of the system increases, as staff performance can be measured and compared, but at the same time, its oppressiveness increases. Academics are under pressure to produce output that is evaluated and used as a basis for employment renewal, promotion, and awards. The teaching staff is formally assessed by their superiors and students, which is a source of data for improvement but also a sometimes painful confrontation for the employee with the idea of the value of their own work (Kwiek and Antonowicz, 2015; Kwiek, 2015b). Drawing on the experiences of other countries, we can learn about the cultural implications of the changes in higher education.

Academic culture is changing under economic pressures. Marilyn Strathern calls this change—radical in relation to Humboldt-type academic cultures—a shift towards an "audit culture" (Strathern, 2000). It is associated with the development of an "audit society" in which all activities, if they are to be considered legitimate, must be audited and subject to potential public scrutiny (Power, 1997). In the case of academic culture, there is communitarianism and scholar skepticism in the Mertonian ethos of CUDOS, which is based on values similar to audit culture. Still, it applies only to science, not education and management (Merton, 1996). In the traditional academic ethos, education remained the individual responsibility of the professor. The formalization of educational quality management systems is eroding the culture of trust, and in its place, an audit culture is being introduced. The change in university ethos is connected with the assimilation of specific "rites of passage" from the culture of trust and academic ethics to the culture of control, supervision, and accountability (Power, 1997; Douglas, 1982). Thus, the heart of the system becomes the mechanism of bureaucratic control, which is enforced by the organization or the state, but at the same time can be a cause of inertia and demotivation of academics.

Related concepts of academic identities such as quality and evidence-based culture are also emerging. The UNESCO Dictionary of Quality defines quality culture as "a set of shared, accepted, and integrated quality patterns that form part of the organizational culture and management system of HEIs" (Vlăsceanu, Grünberg, and Pârlea, 2004, pp. 59–62). An alternative term is used to refer to quality culture, namely the *culture of evidence*, which can be contrasted with the traditional academic culture based on trust. An evidence-based culture would be a system of values, norms, and cultural patterns that characterizes a university and in which emphasis is placed on: Outside assessment and self-evaluation, learning outcomes, and involvement of staff and administration in collecting, analyzing, and interpreting data on the functioning of the university. According to some researchers, an evidence-based culture is the basis of a quality culture (Bensimon et al., 2004). Thus, as the Western Association of Schools and Colleges formulated, an evidence-based culture requires staff to provide data that verifies the achievement of strategic goals (Appleton and Wolff, 2004).

The expansion of the culture of control in modern universities is taking place rapidly in many countries. Still, at the same time, it is being met with criticism and even resistance from parts of the academic community. This is due to the fact that the culture of control, which is supposed to be derived from a change in the way universities are managed and held accountable, is imposed by the controlling bodies (state, ministries, accreditation agencies) and those holding power internally. The critique of the control culture focuses on several aspects such as:

• The economization of university activities;
• The decline of the ethos of the traditional university;
• The bureaucratization of education and research processes;

- An overly formalized system of education quality management;
- A facade and purely performance-based system for evaluating research results;
- A departure from the ethos of modern science (CUDOS);
- The reduction of the creative and prestigious aspects of the academic profession.

The culture of control is euphemistically called the culture of evidence, which means that the productivity and efficiency of the university and its employees must be proven and documented to the regulators. According to critics of the market model of the university, there is no research to prove that quasi-corporate solutions are more efficient compared to the academic tradition (Becher and Kogan, 1992; Mazza, Quattrone, and Riccaboni, 2008). Economic thinking thus becomes the dominant logic of the system, which forces the use of efficiency measures, controlling, and motivation systems. There is a shift away from the university's traditional values, mission, and ethos understood as an autonomous community of researchers and students serving the development of science and education (McLean, 2006). This is accompanied by a significant increase in educational processes and research formalization. Educational quality systems are expanding and autonomizing at a rapid pace by the employment of managers and administrators, the creation of documentation and reporting requirements, the enforcement of formal aspects of the quality system in accreditation processes, and the documentation requirements of HEI and regulatory bodies.

The pressure on universities to achieve scientific results in some countries takes on grotesque proportions and is sometimes criticized as "impact scoring." Instead of reflective and critical examination of scientific output, mass production of results is rewarded. The uncritical attachment to bibliometric indicators (citations) could create the danger of departure from the traditional ethos of science. This affects not only managers and administrators but also the entire scientific staff, consequently replacing critical dialog and reflection with mainly bureaucratic indicators (Weingart, 2004). The pressure solely to achieve scores is therefore dangerous for the values of academic culture, as top-down measures can stifle creativity and criticality. Cultural change also relates to the intellectual ethos, which loses authority and prestige by being subjected to a quasi-corporate supervision system.

7.4 The process of cultural change

Ernest Grady Bogue and Kimberly Bingham Hall describe the tension between two cultures in the contemporary US higher education system. On the one hand, there is the culture of stewardship, which sees higher education as a public good to be nurtured and its autonomy maintained. On the other hand, we are dealing with the idea of a culture of quality improvement, focused on: Educational efficiency, transparency of accounts, professional administration, and effective management (Bogue and Hall, 2003, pp. 224–225). The tension between these two cultures can be reflected in seven dilemmas:

- Improvement versus stewardship;
- Peer review versus regulation;
- Processes versus results;
- Enhancement versus compliance;
- Consultation versus evaluation;
- Trust versus evidence;
- General concepts (interpretation/holistic/synthetic) versus specific measurements (measurement/specifics/analytical) (Bogue and Hall, 2003, p. 229).

Attempts to reconcile the concept of servitude with an improvement orientation should combine an emphasis on entrepreneurship with a culture of academic ethos. A condition for sustaining the existence of universities in the future may be the creation of public–private partnerships to sustain the increasingly costly trend of scientific development and higher education. The attempt to reconcile these "two cultures" should take into account the following postulates:

- Continue to use peer assessments;
- The development and use of university performance indicators;
- Use of performance audits;
- Strengthening academic and market partnerships between universities;
- Holding the university accountable for achieving its goals and mission.

It is worth noting that culture changes relatively slowly compared to other subsystems. In an organizational system, changes in strategy, structure, and later procedures are usually done in a controlled way and relatively fast. Organizational culture operates *implicitly*, is assimilated, concerns the mentality of the cultural participants, and will therefore change much more slowly. Cultural change is also difficult to predict and has little control. Control culture arises secondarily, influenced by changes in structures, strategies, and procedures developed, but after a while, it autonomies and acts in coupling with other subsystems. This means that the interpretation of the university's functioning as an organization must also consider the influence of culture, which is not a passive medium subject to control, but an active subsystem. At the stage of transformation from a culture of trust to a culture of control, there is considerable resistance from a conservative academic culture. It is also difficult to predict whether cultural values, norms, and patterns, formed in the process of implementing change, will be conducive or rather a barrier to implementing change. Marvin Peterson and Melinda Spencer point to two aspects of the functioning of academic culture, which on the one hand takes the form of rational and planned activity, and on the other, is instead in the intuitive and unconscious sphere. The authors point to this tension in cultural discourse and describe a paradigm shift towards a qualitative and intuitive orientation (Peterson and Spencer, 1990).

Many problems with creating the new university model and its operation can therefore be interpreted at the level of organizational identity. The culture of control encountered considerable resistance from the academic community, which assimilated the values of a culture of trust. Autonomy and academic freedoms were reflected in a responsible but hardly formalized, restrictive approach to teaching and research. A tension emerges here between the formalism, accountability, and precision of the control culture and the openness, academic freedom, autonomy, and freedom of the trust culture. There are more such cultural confusions. The culture of trust is based on the authority of professorial staff, while the culture of control makes managers and centrally created regulations the source of authority. The level of power prerogatives, participation, and authority belonging to academics in the two cultural formations differs.

These cracks are permanent and lead to several possible options for implementing change, which can be described as repression, adaptation, hybridization, façade, or regression. Repression is the attempt to implement management change, mainly ignoring issues of resistance and cultural responses. This is rarely possible and even more rarely effective in knowledge-oriented organizations with dispersed power and loose structure (Weick, 1976). In implementing change in universities, the repressive model has happened, for example with M&A of HEIs. Still, it has led to escalating tensions in the form of, e.g., strikes or has contributed to the loss of strategic resources such as outstanding academics (Krause et al., 2008). In private universities, the repressive solution could be used due to centralized power. Compared to repression, adaptation is much more frequent in public universities, done through negotiation, which consists in making the change less painful and gradual and allowing the parties to the dispute to keep "face." For example, negotiations related to the slow transition from a collegial to a managerial model in the transformation of a university. They are a pretty common practice in many countries. The process of adaptation and negotiation is also accompanied by the evolution from a culture of trust to a culture of control. Hybridization means creating intermediate solutions that combine features of different models and cultures. In practice, hybridization also takes place through a negotiation process. It is a form of adaptation, but it is a more radical solution to finding one's way between the model and culture of academic trust and the principles of managerial control. The debate on university governance and the critical reception of some solutions from the realm of new public management applied to higher education has opened the way for such solutions in some developed countries. However, in many developing and emerging markets, moving away from public monopoly in university creation and legal changes have led to the transformation of HEIs that operate based on hybrid solutions. Façade change means an apparent change, i.e., only superficially carrying out small shifts that can be presented as significant changes if needed. Façade change means adding some wording that does not lead to a more profound transformation. A facade change of structures is the creation of positions that do not have power. In some HEIs, equality or diversity officers have been appointed in the last decade but have not been equipped with adequate prerogatives. Apparent change has little to do with organizational culture and only touches the realm of artifacts (e.g., rhetoric), leaving the core of values unchanged. Regression means a complete withdrawal from a planned or even implemented change. This solution is rarely practiced due to financial and legal costs and loss of prestige. The transformation from a culture of trust to a culture of control in many universities is part of a planned but also spontaneously occurring change in the higher education management model.

8 Organizational structures and power in universities

8.1 Organizational structures of the university

When analyzing power processes in universities, it is essential to pay attention to the types of organizational structures. Different concepts distinguish many kinds of structures in connection with power in higher education institution (HEI). In most organizations, we often deal with hybrid structures displaying various features. This is also the case in universities (Bacanu, 2011, p. 101). The linear structure is characterized by observing the management rules still proposed in a hierarchical, simple structure. The subordinates always have one superior. The team structure is characterized by the presence of advisory bodies that support the management process. In contrast, the functional structure is closer to the image of a bureaucratic and hierarchical division into specialized organizational divisions. In universities, we find features of all these structures. They seem to fit in particular with the second-wave formation in which, on the one hand, a simple hierarchy dominates. Still, on the other, the senate and collegiate bodies play a staff role, and the administration develops functional specialization. The answer to the limitations of the organization's classical, "Fayolian" types was to be a flexible matrix structure with an intersection of hierarchical departments and horizontal teams (Purwanto, 2016). Such two-dimensional subordination breaks with the principle of uniformity of management, as subordinates have two superiors, e.g., one within the hierarchical structure (functional, linear) and the other in the project team. Entrepreneurial universities should be matrix organized, where hierarchically arranged structures of faculties and functional administrative departments interact with the structure's project, scientific, implementation, and teaching teams (Cheng, 2009; Zhigang, 2012; Wang and Chang, 2019). The increased complexity of organizations, the pace of change and turbulence in the environment, and the digital revolution create pressure to form networked, virtual, and tensor structures. Types of hyper-flexible structures can be compared to "loose organizational systems" described by K. Weick within which there is no strong hierarchy or centralization (Weick, 1980). Network structures are organized based on loose heterarchy, with weak power ties, accompanied by flexibility and blurring of boundaries

DOI: 10.4324/9781003366409-12

between the inside of the organization and the network of cooperating entities. The term "networked" also has a more literal meaning, related to digitalization and virtualization. Virtual structures are networks of cooperation between entities, going beyond the system of a single institution, where different spheres of activity and functional areas are the subject of activity of cooperating organizations. On the other hand, the term tensor structure refers to a solution that develops and flexibilities the matrix approach and consists of creating structural cells in three dimensions. For example, it may mean the parallel existence of the functional, project, and territorial divisional teams (campuses) in organizational structure, whose participants operate simultaneously in three different groups and structural units. The group of hyper-flexible structures seems to be the most characteristic of the developing fourth-wave universities. Digital universities will develop networked and virtual organizational structures not only because of the volatility of the environment and the need for rapid change but also because of the activities based on information and communication infrastructure. The final structural solution worth mentioning is the divisional organizational structure. In the case of universities with a geographically dispersed organizational structure based on many campuses located in different cities, a divisional structure (Hill, 1985) functions frequently based on duplicating similar structural solutions in other locations (e.g., faculties and administration).

To sum up, the evolution of organizational structures towards increased flexibility and complexity is evident. However, several questions remain about other features of university structures relating to such dimensions as centralization, formalization, and departmentalization (Tao, 2010; Zhang and Wang, 2010). The last subsection includes a detailed analysis of these organizational structure aspects.

8.2 Changes in power structures in universities

The Humboldtian-type university is characterized by a traditional, petrified organizational structure that originates from the medieval university. The departmental systems and the positions of rectors, principals, and deans go back to the roots of the first universities. A functional and linear hierarchical structure with few (two or three) levels of leadership prevailed. The decision-making model can be described as strongly collectivist, and decision-making structures were not controlled and consciously shaped but were a continuation of academic tradition. The degree of formalization appeared to be relatively high, as the systems were stable and unchanging, with traditionally legitimized prerogatives of authority. However, formalization tended not to take bureaucratic forms as the role of administration, and the circulation of documentation became marginal. The degree of centralization was low, as the dominant authority was located at the faculty level. The decision-making model regarding teaching and learning was decentralized so that one could speak of dispersed power, with traditional prerogatives derived from the centuries-old history of the university. The weakness of oversight was due to the high autonomy of universities and the lack of structures controlling universities in which external stakeholders would participate. The legitimacy of authority takes traditional and legal forms, as the source of senates, principals, and deans derives from a long academic history and is accepted as complying with the rules of internal and external law. Administrative structures are limited, as all leadership and decision-making functions are staffed or collegially controlled by academics. Among the positions in the one-person authority structures, one can find, for example, rectors, presidents, deans, chancellors, and bursars, while among the multi-person collegial bodies, composed mainly of research and teaching staff, senates, faculty councils, and research councils played an important role. The systemic interdependence of structure, strategy, and organizational culture can be seen, for example, in the coupling of responsibility for long-term orientations, which rests with the management and the senates. The transmission of structural solutions concerning positions, their prerogatives, and divisions in the university took on a cultural character. These are customary power arrangements in universities, drawing on theoretical values. This flow of power occurs through academic leadership of a nature: Traditional, more spontaneous, also involving a transformation of the structure towards a second-wave formation. The degree of professionalization of power and organizational structures was low because facilities are tradition based, ethos based, intuitive, and unplanned.

Third-wave universities are characterized by growing professionalization of organizational structures, manifested by increasing specialization within the scope of science, didactics, and management and expansion of administrative structures supporting university processes. The types of organizational structures vary, but there is a preference for organizational flexibility, within which matrix solutions, better adapted to project and process management, are more frequent. The resolutions adopted range from single posts to multi-person bodies, cells, and departments. The structure is subject to planning and control by describing responsibilities and assigning authority prerogatives. The degree of structure formalization varies from HEI to another, but flexible and matrix solutions should protect against excessive bureaucratization. The degree of centralization of entrepreneurial universities is higher than the Humboldtian university, as the central authority is more substantial. There is an increase in the number of levels of the organizational structure where structural centers are located: Headquarters, faculties, and administration. Power in the university is dispersed and divided between different centers, but the aim is to maintain a solid and flexible central decision-making structure. Legitimate and charismatic legitimacy of power prevails, as are seen as authorities and leaders. The administration expands, specializes, and gains more power in the many activities that support the mission and fall within the functional areas of finance, human resources, knowledge management, and marketing. The collegiate bodies: Senates and councils have weaker decision-making powers than in the case of second-wave universities. Supervisory bodies are also emerging, in the form of a board of trustees, which increasingly includes external stakeholders. Individual power is concentrated in one-person university bodies, e.g., rector, president, chancellor, and other traditional positions, e.g., bursar and registrar—both staff representatives and increasingly also managers from the administration are staffed. Professional academic managers also have new functions not previously present in universities, such as Chief Information Officers. In the organizational structure, in the case of public HEIs, representatives of the research and teaching staff elected for management positions are most often responsible for strategy. In the case of non-public HEIs, more and more often, these are appointments of experienced academic managers who do not have to be scientists and teachers. A more flexible matrix team structure is also linked to an academic entrepreneurial culture and entrepreneurial leadership.

Digital universities will be characterized by a diverse, flexible, and networked organizational structure based on teams and projects that change according to needs. It will be crucial to control the rapid transitions of the structure, adapting it to changes in the turbulent environment and strategic objectives. There is likely to be an increase in the number of specialized jobs and an expansion of departments, cells, and teams, which will be able to form different configurations within the network, tensor, and matrix structures. Structural flexibility and the accompanying lower degree of formalization will bring fourth-wave universities closer to post-bureaucratic organizations in which heterarchy will replace traditionally entrenched hierarchy. Responsibilities and prerogatives of authority will change under the influence of extensive data analysis from the environment and within the organization. The degree of centralization of the organizational structure will be higher than in Humboldt-type universities by strengthening the decision-making powers of the head office and strengthening the single-person authority of a managerial and non-collegial nature. The degree of structural specialization realized in science, teaching, and management will be relatively high. There is also a tendency to create multi-level, variable network structures, which will not be hierarchical but cascaded to implement specific strategic tasks. Power in universities will tend to be concentrated in the head office and selected strategic centers (e.g., controlling and data analysis). The collegiate power structures in many HEIs are likely to retain senates or other collegiate bodies, but these will have minimal management powers. Increasing supervisory powers and external stakeholder participation in supervisory bodies are also expected. As far as single-person authority structures are concerned, their importance will increase with academic managers and administration representation. Professional academic managers will implement strategies at the managerial level more often. Network and tensor structures will be strengthened by digitalization cultures

Table 8.1 Evolution of power structures in HEIs

Organizational criterion	Second-wave university	Third-wave university	Fourth-wave University
Structure type	Traditional, petrified, functional and linear, collectivist, uncontrolled.	Differentiated, more flexible, matrix, collectivist and individualist, controlled.	Diverse, flexible, networked, individualistic and, team based, controlled.
Degree of formalization of the structure	Stable, relatively formalized, with traditional prerogatives of power, rather non-bureaucratic.	Variable and diverse, varying degrees of formalization, assigned prerogatives of authority. Depending on stabilization and formalization, it may move towards flexibility or bureaucratization.	Variable and differentiated, a lower degree of formalization, flexible prerogatives based on data analysis, post-bureaucratic.
Degree of centralization of the structure	Low power at the departmental level, dispersed among authorities.	Higher, more significant prerogatives of the central structure and administration.	Taller, more significant prerogatives of the main structure and administration.
Degree of structural specialization	Low, the staff carries out scientific, teaching, and organizational tasks.	Higher, increasing specialization within science, education, and management. Development of administration.	High specialization in science, teaching, and management. Field of roles in administration.
Levels of organizational structure	Flat structures, central, departmental authority.	Flexible structures, diverse, central, departmental, and administrative authority.	Networked, tensor, variable and differential structures at multiple levels.
Types of power in universities	Distributed, collective, loose governance, traditional prerogatives.	Centralized in headquarters and administration and dispersed departmentally, mixed, more substantial supervision, formal preferences.	Focused, managerial, intense supervision and governance, legal and variable prerogatives.
Legitimacy of power	Traditional and legal, based on authority, collegial.	Legal and charismatic, less collegial.	Legal and charismatic. Team based.

Administrative structure	Very limited, poor specialization.	It was expanded with increasing prerogatives and increasing specialization.	Extensive, specialized, post-bureaucratic, with great prerogatives.
Collegiate authority structures	Senate, academic councils, faculty councils, strong powers, and staff.	Senate and committees have weak powers, staff, and other stakeholders.	Senate and councils, weak powers, made up of staff and other stakeholders, including external stakeholders.
One-person authority structures	Rector, President, Provost, Principal, Dean, Chancellor, Bursar.	Firm, traditional, and academic managers and administration.	Academic managers and administration dominate.
Organizational structure and strategy	Functional, tenured, co-governance staff with senates.	Elective, tenure-track (often public universities), or appointed function level.	Executive level, specialized managerial roles, or by choice.
Structure versus organizational culture	The culture of the university is the transmission of structural patterns.	Academic entrepreneurial culture is related to structure.	A networked and digital culture translates into a networked structure.
Knowledge management structures	None, just intuitive, routine activities.	Rare, only operational methods and knowledge management tools.	A sophisticated, integrated knowledge management structure.
Academic leadership and structure	Traditional, spontaneous leadership transforms the structure towards a second-wave formation.	Entrepreneurial leadership strengthens structural flexibility.	Digital leadership constitutes network structures.
The professionalization of authority and organizational structure	Low, tradition-based structures, ethos based, intuitive, unplanned.	Specialization, agility, and flexibility are on the rise.	Developed specialization, measurement, quantifiability, and refinement of structures.

Source: Own elaboration.

based on communication values in virtual communities and advanced knowledge management. The professionalization of the organizational structure will be developed based on: The specialization of executive roles, advanced knowledge management, measurement, and work accountability, which lead to the adaptation of structures.

The evolution of organizational structures and power in the three waves of universities is shown in Table 8.1.

Part IV

University missions management

9 Science management

9.1 Importance of the scientific activities of the university

Scientific activity has been the essence of the university since its inception. Knowing and proclaiming the truth are the enduring foundations of academic values. The identity of the university, the social roles of researchers, strategies, and power structures have been primarily based on the development of the scientific activity. It is also the basis of academic prestige, which is the essential motive for the development of universities (Blackmore and Kandiko, 2011; Blackmore, 2015, pp. 171–184). The prestige consists of scientific and teaching excellence. However, the research component remains the most critical variable, reflected, for example, in the world rankings of university excellence (Liu, Cheng, and Liu, 2005; Benito and Romera, 2011). The research mission is evident in the activities of most universities, but its scale, quality, specialization, and relationship with teaching and practice vary significantly from university to university. Since the middle of the 20th century, this differentiation has progressed, and we are dealing on the one hand with "research super-universities" from the "ivy league" and the world's top, and on the opposite end with local universities not doing research at all or doing it on a small scale. Therefore, the description of science management processes is not easy with the progressive diversification of types of universities and their missions. Naturally, the described model of transformation, leading from one university formation to the next generation, is a considerable simplification. However, from a bird's eye view, it is possible to see fundamental changes in the essence of the operation of a university understood as an organization.

Historically, science development and the university's prestige were environmentally and socially recognized. They were connected with prestige. Reputation, image, and positive social opinions were given to universities associated with researchers with spectacular achievements. The university was seen as a center of science, teaching, and culture. There were no metrics to compare the scientific achievements of universities. The situation has changed radically in this respect in the last few decades. The development of the Internet, scientometrics, indexing of international journals, scientific

DOI: 10.4324/9781003366409-14

evaluation in universities, and rankings of excellence have created an ecosystem of accountability for the scientific activity of universities (Liu, 2006; van Raan, 1997; Bornmann, 2013; Mingers and Leydesdorff, 2015). It has paradoxically turned out that measuring the effectiveness of the most creative activity of a university, i.e., science, is much simpler than measuring the effectiveness of education, which aggregates many qualitatively diverse variables (quality of education, accreditation results, student survey results, employment and salary statistics of graduates, etc.) (Leontev, 2017; Vedder, 1994).

The issues of science management in a university are based on scientific evaluation (research exercise). Scientific evaluation is a set of concepts, methods, and techniques used to study, evaluate and measure the scientific activity's effectiveness, productivity, and quality. Evaluation can improve science management, research decision-making, implementing of programs of excellence, and comparing scientific disciplines, researchers, or even entire national science systems (Hai and Ye, 2003; Zhang and Yang, 2011; Chao, 2020). Evaluation can apply to many types of scientific units. Individual researchers (micro level), teams, departments, institutes, faculties, scientific disciplines (mezzo level), universities, national systems, European Union, and the world (macro level) (Cremonini, Horlings, and Hessels, 2018; Docampo and Cram, 2019). Scientific evaluation can mainly be based on expert evaluation, scientometrics measures, and a combination of previous elements. Evaluation of science is a criterion in the created systems of evaluation of universities, as well as employee evaluation, based on data on the increment of scientific output. Consequently, effective knowledge management depends on the reliability and effectiveness of data in the information system.

9.2 Management of the research activities of the HEI

Science management can be understood as a systematic process of organizing scientific work, leading to the improvement of the university in its research mission. In the traditional university, it wasn't easy to speak of science management because it was an area of researcher autonomy and creative freedom, where comparisons, peer reviews, and measurement of outcomes were impossible or, at best, very approximate. However, as universities grow, with the development of management practices and widespread trends toward economization and managerialism, HEIs are changing and introducing numerous management concepts, methods, and tools. This also becomes noticeable in the area of the first mission, i.e., science. Management of science is possible, and ICT and algorithmic solutions for the accountability of science can be added to heuristic solutions focused on academic creativity.

In the universities of the second wave, science was founded on the idea of arriving at the truth and formed the core of the organization, inextricably linked to education. *Bildung* meant "education through science" (Nordenbo, 2002). Learning is a creative and collective activity based on the academic ethos, which serves to improve humans, culture, and the nation.

Humboldtian-type universities had a kind of scientific mission, traditionally understood as the meaning of the organization and often reflected in Latin sentences and the university's symbols. Scientific activity was elitist and founded on the master-student relationship, leading to a focus on ethos and cultural solutions. There was no strategy for scholarly activity because, by definition, it was to be a creative activity, unplanned by the organization and the responsibility of the professorial staff. The whole mode of governance was centered on the model of the "republic of scholars," "professorial self-government" (Wolter, 2007). Comparing university models and looking for sources of legitimacy of power, the second wave universities gravitated most toward the "academic oligarchy" model, much less toward "state regulation," and were furthest away from "market competition" (Dobbins, 2009). The academic oligarchy of the "republic of scholars" presupposed the ethos regulation of academic work, which was the most important value of traditional academic culture (Višňovský, 2019). The university's mode of governance, based on strong professorial chairs, resulted in a relatively diffuse structure of central authority and the construction of the organization's identity and integrity precisely through ethos and culture (Welsh, 2010). The academic ethos and environmental pressures, rooted in the norms of academic culture, regulated the standards of academic work. There was no need for formal regulation in the form of systems of evaluation and management of science. The logic of traditional, cultural regulation of organizational practices is subordinated to all functional areas of the second wave university. There were as yet no conceptual or methodological approaches to people management. However, many areas of human resources management were working in the organization but took habitual, intuitive forms, often discontinuous and without a process for evaluating the outcome. The advantage of such a solution was that it was rooted in culture. People learned the academic ethos and acted habitually. It is an effective solution, deeply anchored in the university's tradition, which works well in a stable environment. In a situation of rapid change, increased intensity of competition, and pressure to reduce costs, and increase efficiency, the functional model of the Humboldtian university destabilizes, as we saw in the 20th century. This led to transformations and the emergence of post-Humboldtian forms of the university. The development of the "third mission" was also relatively weak because the Humboldtian university is innate. Power is held by an academic oligarchy holding positions according to a hierarchy of academic authority. This senior power structure goes hand in hand with the idea of university autonomy, i.e., self-determination, without the possibility of significant interference from outside persons or institutions. At the same time, state funding of scientific activities is a condition of university existence. The second wave HEI is also founded on reputation and image, which stems from a tradition dating back to the Middle Ages and continues to this day as the "economy of prestige." To the greatest extent, this reputation is derived from the position in science, which in the traditional university was perceived primarily through the prism of outstanding scientific achievements of the academic staff (Blackmore, 2015, pp. 171–184). These took the form of discoveries, publications, the creation of scientific schools, and, to a lesser extent, building up authority in culture and society; professors who spoke in public were a source of enlightened opinions and popularized science. Such an organizational solution was far removed from contemporary marketing management but well adapted to the existing social and cultural norms, communication modes, and state organization principles. The lack of mass communication media, corporations, and managers resulted in different solutions to information dissemination and power stratification than modern ones. In the Humboldtian solution, universities were autonomous and public, which meant state funding of scientific activity. In research, knowledge creation took place in master-student relationships and small, informal scientific teams, working under the guidance of informal authority. The organization's scientific activity was based on customary activities, which translated into the importance of tacit knowledge. Discoveries and publications were usually made individually, but their creative process was rooted in discussions held in chairs, seminars, and science schools. The researcher played the role of authority and mentor, and thought leader. In summary, the organization of research activity in a Humboldtian-type university was founded on traditional academic culture and ethos. Culture, with its central and inseparable value—science and didactics—regulates organizational processes in all spheres, which makes the second wave university an organization based on academic freedom.

The third wave university in the areas of ideas focuses on agile and flexible management, competition and efficiency, innovation, and an integrated entrepreneurial culture (Clark, 1983, 1998b). Scientific activity remains a vital mission of the entrepreneurial university, but to a much greater extent, compared to first- and second wave universities, it includes implementation, applied science, and innovation (Etzkowitz and Zhou, 2008; Shattock, 2010a; Thorp and Goldstein, 2013; Pinheiro and Stensaker, 2014). Research becomes embedded in the HEI management system, leading to efficiency, flexibility, and competitiveness (Mascarenhas et al., 2017). However, this is at the expense of academic freedom as universities introduce strategic management in the area; of planning, funding, and accounting for priority spheres of scientific development. The strategic management processes develop and contain the formation of a mission, strategic goals, allocating of resources, plans, and schedules, and controlling (Kristensen, 1999; Svensson, Klofsten, and Etzkowitz, 2012). This strengthens efficiency and competitiveness through planning and accounting in scientific activity. The entrepreneurial culture, central to the organization, stimulates change management, the development of implementations, cooperation projects with the environment, and innovations inseparable from research (Taylor, 2012). In the organizational structure, there is a clear trend toward more streamlined and flexible management, which involves the possibility of networking scientific teams. The development of the periphery means in science: the creation of network teams, strengthening flexibility and entrepreneurship, the establishment of entities and the formation of third mission activities in the form of joint projects and spin-offs and spin-outs, and the structural expansion of entrepreneurial activities in the university (e.g., business incubators, business parks; Pilbeam, 2008; Pinheiro, and Stensaker, 2014). Organizational practices include introducing many solutions that draw their sources from business and later from the stream of new public management. Among the fast-growing management aspects are the research process, project management, and specialized science management systems (Gjerding et al., 2006). In science, concepts, approaches, and practices adapted from business and new public management are developing in science's sphere of human capital management. They include basic methods: recruitment, motivation, and development of scientific staff. Marketing in science closely links the university brand with its scientific achievements. This solution, based on the university's reputation, coming from scientific achievements, was already characteristic of the second wave universities. The case of the third wave has been further strengthened by the globalization of the university sector and the internationalization of scientific activities. Other aspects of marketing are the development of Public Relations, Employer Branding, and University Social Responsibility based on scientific prestige. Entrepreneurial universities have significantly more science funding streams than second wave universities, which also concern research. It also develops universities' accountability, allowing for more effective accounting of scientific activity (Sulkowski, 2016b). Knowledge management of academic achievements and implementations linking research to the third mission is one of the developing aspects of knowledge and data management in the entrepreneurial university (Centobelli et al., 2019). Crucial for science accountability is an introduction and use on the strategic and operational levels of the ICT for research management like Research Information Systems.

A researcher in an entrepreneurial university plays the role of a member of research teams and a producer of knowledge who can operate within basic or applied research projects, where cooperation with external entities can be undertaken. The professionalization of management in science is a significant issue, which, according to the conducted review, concerns many aspects of the university organization (teaching staff, administration, organizational processes, and projects).

In summary, the digital university, in the implementation of its research mission, will be a learning and knowledge management organization based on integrated, advanced information and communication systems, coupling it with its environment. In scientific activity, the foundation remains accountable, based on reliable and massive data, which is the pillar of all decision-making processes. A fourth wave university is a professional, flexible, networked organization focused on efficiency and improvement of management (Table 9.1).

Table 9.1 Management of science and research activities

Organizational criterion	Second wave university	Third wave university	Fourth wave University
Strategy and science	Science is a creative activity based on academic ethos, a scientific mission, without a strategy, unmeasurable	Planning practical lines of the research mission crucial in the economy of prestige	Science strategy embedded in university strategies, evidence-based, controllable and accountable
The organizational structure of accountability for research	All academic staff responsible for scientific achievements	Centre, periphery, and specialized staff and administration	Managers, academic managers, staff, and science administration
Culture and identity linked to science	The value of truth and science in the spirit of ideas integrating nation, state	The value of applied research, academic entrepreneurship, and accountability	The value of the scientific network, scientometrics, open science, knowledge management, and accountability
Relationship between science and the third mission	Moderate researchers may occasionally collaborate with the environment	Significant, stronger in science-focused universities, weaker in teaching-focused universities	Strong, growing emphasis on applied research
Human capital in science	Staff improving relations with other researchers, reputation based, lack of formal HRM practices.	Formal practices of HRM: recruitment, development—education, and training of researchers, reward systems	High-performance systems based on controlling and accountability, talent management
Marketing in science	Reputation created by the academic staff and ethos of science	The economy of prestige, PR, marketing for researchers, global	The economy of importance is extensive, specialized, networked
Finance in science	No accountability, basic budgeting, financed by the state	Diversification of sources, growing accountability of science, budgeting, co-financing	Real-time accountability and budgeting, multiple sources of science funding

Knowledge management in science	Limited, only library, tacit knowledge, individual and social, informally co-produced knowledge dominates	Knowledge management of scientific achievements (publications and implementations), library	Advanced science knowledge management, ICT system and accountability, digital library
Professionalization of management in terms of science	None, academic ethos, intuitive, unplanned	Significant specialized staff, administration, processes	Advanced specialization, measurement, and improvement, controlling, ICT
The role of the researcher	Leading thought leader, champion, authority, mentor, and master	Knowledge producer, *publish-or-perish*, member of research teams	Co-creator of knowledge, a participant in research networks
Research relations	Master-student	Members of the research team	Participants in the research network

Source: Own study. ICT: information and communication technologies; HRM: human resources management.

9.3 International rankings of scientific excellence

International rankings are now used to get an idea of a university's reputation and academic prestige on a global scale. The rankings compare not only universities but also countries or scientific disciplines and observe long-term trends related to changing a given position. However, the selection of the criteria of the methodology can be called arbitrary, as it forces a positive evaluation for selected types of improvement and does not provide an opportunity to value others (e.g., appreciation of Nobel prize-winning achievements, measurement of citation and publications), which follows the development of scientometrics. More complicated is the evaluation of educational activities, which can be described by variables that are difficult to measure, such as the added value of education, the quality of education, student satisfaction and staff opinion, or employability and salaries and careers progress of graduates. Universities seem to drive knowledge-based economies. Therefore their value also influences the competitive position of a country. Scientific excellence rankings such as Times Higher Education World Universities Ranking (THE WUR) and Academic Ranking of World Universities (ARWU). It is worth mentioning that the ARWU was created to measure the distance between Chinese universities and the world's top universities; only later was it realized that it could be used to measure academic achievements worldwide. The rankings are not free of limitations, so it needs to be complemented by other methods of evaluating universities. The methodology makes it possible to appreciate the accumulation of scientific output or exceptional achievements, favoring the orientation toward creating large universities (Salmi, 2016). For higher education institutions and national public policy managers, promotion in the ranking is an essential measure of success (Münch and Schäfer, 2014). Researchers who criticize rankings point out that they are sometimes more important than the strategic, incremental, actual organic development of universities (Badat, 2010; Lynch, 2015) and can lead, for example, to destructive restructurings, radical changes in strategy or mergers that can weaken rather than strengthen the potential of the university (Ordorika and Lloyd, 2015). Rankings provide policymakers with a yardstick to prove to the public the advancement of a country and universities to world-class. Publications provide a simplistic measure of the achievement of complex university missions (Rauhvargers, 2014). This simplicity of steps proves illusory, as it can provoke public policymakers into radical actions that can destroy a university's ethos (Douglass, 2016).

International rankings began in the United States—A "ranking culture" emerged in various areas of social and economic life. The European University Association, while preparing a report on university rankings, identified different types of ranking (Rauhvargers, 2013). They are presented in Table 9.2.

According to researchers critical of rankings, they have been the primary measure of university effectiveness for public policymakers worldwide in the last decade. According to representatives of the radical current, under

Table 9.2 Rank types by EUA

Type of ranking and criteria	Examples of rankings
League tables according to research excellence measures (Buela-Casal et al., 2007)	Academic Ranking of World Universities (ARWU)—Shanghai Ranking Consultancy (Shanghai Ranking Consultancy, 2003) THE World University Ranking—Times Higher Education (NJ MED, 2016) World's Best Universities Ranking—US News & World (US News, 2017) U-Multirank (pairwise comparison) (U-Multirank, 2017)
Research quality, scope, and intensity according to research excellence measures	European Multidimensional University Ranking System (U-Multirank) U-Map—CHEPS Assessment of University-Based Research— European Commission (European Commission, 2010) Leiden Ranking—Leiden University (Leiden University, 2017) Performance Rankings of Scientific Papers for World Universities—Taiwan Higher Education Accreditation and Evaluation Council (NTU Ranking, 2017) CHE University Ranking—Centre for Higher Education Development/die Zeit (Zeit Campus, 2017)
Citability in Google Scholar, with Scopus or Web of Science indexing	Webometrics ranking (Cybermetrics Lab, 2017)

Source: Own elaboration based on the sources in the table.

the guise of neutral and non-valuing classification systems, the dominance of the elite model of the Anglo-American university is reinforced, which leads to stratification in the education system and American cultural imperialism (Ordorika and Lloyd, 2015). In the education sector, this drives commercialization and a culture of control at the expense of the traditional culture of the university (Kehm, 2014). We may be threatened by a return to "educational reproduction" in elite universities (Passeron and Bourdieu, 1970). The prevalence of rankings is a discursive phenomenon, along the lines of Foucault's knowledge-power phenomenon and power over discourse (Foucault, 1980; Revel, 2002). International university rankings are often a fact for us, a marketing frame of reference, or merely, as critical scholars have argued, interpretations and social constructs are deemed objective. In public perception, a school's ranking position is increasingly associated with a high academic level and, mistakenly, with a teaching level.

The importance of rankings in higher education is growing—some call this phenomenon ranking madness or obsession (Hazelkorn, 2015; Tilak,

2016; Stack, 2016). The emphasis on academic excellence in this issue supports a competitive group of elite universities—the "world-class university." They operate on the model of the American research university, primarily from the "ivy league" (Cole, 2012, p. 44).

9.4 A critical look at science governance

The last two decades have brought with them processes of standardizing scientific and teaching work and formalization. Business-derived solutions have changed the organization of universities but have not got many benefits to staff. Efforts to obtain credits and citations, which are the basis for evaluation but do not affect the remuneration of the team, are often a struggle against bureaucracy, as employees waste time documenting their work at the expense of its creative execution. Excessive formalization is not conducive to the professional ethos and brings scientific work closer to clerical and business work (Mcculloch, 2017).

Scientific governance is, by definition, a restriction on academic freedom and researcher autonomy. When academics are regularly evaluated for publications, grants, and inclusion in teams, the focus is on the cumulative development of scientific output rather than on outstanding individual achievements (Hallonsten, 2021; Lizotte, 2021). Spectacular achievements often reveal their value after years, being "life's work" and not the effects of repeated "scientific production" and are subject to community and expert evaluation rather than algorithmic summing of points awarded for publications (Metze, 2012; Khomyakov, 2021). The value of international indexing, citation statistics, and rankings of scientific excellence is also problematic. These are based on criteria of research reputation, which are environmental and conventional. Journal lists are dominated by English scientific periodicals, where scientific achievements published in local languages are ignored. The appreciation of citation statistics may encourage solutions based on the reciprocity of citations rather than the scientific merit of works. Rankings of scientific excellence operate according to the Mertonian mechanism of the self-fulfilling prophecy. Universities rated higher for scientific achievements thanks to orders strengthen their position in the rankings themselves, fitting better into the criteria, which do not have to be objective measures of scientific quality.

The vision of the digital panopticon, which in the scientific activity of the university means a system of scientific control, providing complete knowledge of achievements and possibly comparing and analyzing them, is also disturbing. It is the control and self-control of scientific production for which staff is evaluated and rewarded. This leads to transforming the academic ethos into a culture of control, where academic freedom is replaced by the executive power, where researchers become "employees of a knowledge-producing corporation."

10 Management of learning

10.1 Importance of higher education management

Teaching is the heart of a university's mission. Good quality of education is an essential service of most universities. In terms of prevalence, the education stream plays a more important role for far higher education institutions than the scientific achievements and the third stream. In the Humboldtian university, the value of quality of teaching is embedded in the university culture and academic ethos. By design, elite universities were interested in the quality of teaching by selecting students on entry and during studies. The massification of higher education has changed the approach to the quality of education (Li and Yang, 2013; Seng et al., 2018). The importance of managing the teaching process in the higher education institution (HEI) has become vital. The teaching is shaped through quality assurance systems (internal and external), educational rankings, accreditations, staff improvement, surveys of students, teachers, employers, salary surveys, and graduate employability data analysis (Federkeil, 2008; Avralev and Efimova, 2015). However, methods of measuring the effectiveness of universities' scientific activities have developed rapidly in the last two decades through scientometrics. Accountability of effectiveness of a university's teaching activities is going on much slower, facing many difficulties. Managing the quality of education is a costly, complex process that requires several approaches. It demands aggregating many incommensurable indicators (Titov and Tuulik, 2013). Quality assurance methods and tools could prove the importance of university education management (Tarí, 2011).

10.2 Quality management in education

There are many definitions of quality and educational quality. The most general descriptions of the quality of teaching are mentioned below:

- Quality of education is the degree of excellence in achieving learning outcomes.
- The quality of education results from the educational process achieving its objectives.

DOI: 10.4324/9781003366409-15

- Educational quality means acting according to established norms and standards.
- Educational quality is the level of satisfaction with teaching and learning as perceived by key stakeholders (Kumar, Raju, and Kumar, 2016).
- The quality of education results from the effective management of the teaching process.
- The quality of education is the relevance of graduates' competencies to the labor market and measures of their employability and remuneration.
- Educational quality is the adequacy of the delivery of the educational service and the commitment to its objectives within accepted standards of accountability, soundness, and integrity (Bogue and Hall, 2003, p. 14).

Several diverse methods of quality management of teaching exist, reflecting the complexity of this activity and the complexity of improving, assessing, and measuring quality:

- Quality strategy and policy—embedding quality in the mission of the university (O'Mahony and Garavan, 2012);
- Quality system—the internal quality of the education management system (Kalimullin, Khodyreva, and Koinova-Zoellner, 2016);
- External quality management systems for higher education;
- Accreditations—external audits examining the achievement of learning outcomes (Jani, 2012; Nigsch and Schenker-Wicki, 2013);
- Rankings—assessing the reputation of HEI according to pillars: scientific, teaching, or integrated (Shin, 2011; Blanco-Ramírez and Berger, 2014);
- Learning outcomes—verification of learning outcomes and the effectiveness of the teaching methods used (Duque, 2014);
- Certification and licensing—the test of achieving professional standards by external assessment (Habánik and Jambor, 2014);
- Program evaluations—the result of expert environmental research to evaluate and improve (*peer review*) (Paliulis and Labanauskis, 2015);
- Benchmarking—comparisons to other high-quality programs or HEI;
- Customer/stakeholder research—student opinion and staff satisfaction survey (Voss, Gruber, and Szmigin, 2007; Chalaris et al., 2013);
- TQM, total quality improvement—implementation of continuous improvement methods in the HEI (Bogue and Hall, 2003, p. 16).

Strategies and quality policies seek to embed and legitimize educational quality improvement as a strategic goal of the HEI. This can be reflected in the mission statement and strategic objectives and should be communicated appropriately in interaction with the university's stakeholders (Harvey and Green, 1993; Pramono et al., 2018). The consequence of establishing a quality and its assurance, as well as managing the didactic process as a strategic value, is the organization of internal systems of educational quality management in universities (Habánik and Jambor, 2014; Ulewicz, 2017). The assumption is to construct these systems based on reliable data collected on an ongoing basis by the information system. Thus, educational decision-making would be based on data and evidence. One of the most important manifestations of the evolution of university systems toward quality management is the rapid development and dissemination of accreditation. Higher education accreditations can be divided according to several criteria: program and institutional evaluations, national and international, sectoral, mandatory, and voluntary accreditations. National accreditation commissions are an example of an agency conducting the following assessments: curricular, institutional, and compulsory. Examples of industry, institutional, and voluntary accreditation are EFMD, AACSB, AMBA, and many others (AACSB, 2021; Association of MBAs, 2021; EFMD Global, 2021). Accreditations are peer assessments based on quality standards and expert evaluations. Their value is not only recognition, increasing the university's reputation, but also the process of learning and exchange of experience, which is the result of accreditation. W. Selden lists challenges of contemporary education, putting them in seven points, mainly related to accreditation mechanisms. These are as follows:

1   Need for emphasis on innovation and improvement, less so on meeting minimum educational standards;
2   Accreditation is intended as an essential tool for motivating higher education institutions in the pursuit of proquality solutions;
3   Focus on the universality of the accreditation system—educational institutions will be able to choose the agency where they join the accreditation;
4   The number of accreditation agencies does not need to be increased; what matters is their openness to different specialized and professional programs;
5   The need to simplify the accreditation process while maintaining efficiency;
6   The effect of accreditation is to provide information on significant educational programs and institutions;
7   Promoting interest in accreditation by administrations and authorities without compromising the autonomy of accreditation agencies (Bogue and Hall, 2003, p. 39).

Selden's analysis should be enriched with other challenges not related to accreditation but connected, for example, with the need for greater involvement of external and internal stakeholders in quality improvement. Equally important is university management focused on the process of education and development of students (*student-centered learning*). The essence of studying is changing, but the necessity of involving students in deciding on the university's functioning remains. Their role in university management in many HEIs is still not appreciated.

The problem of excessive bureaucracy and formalization of the process of educational quality management needs to be solved. The EU has implemented the principles of educational quality management and focused on its effects, which involves the obligation to document these processes (the so-called *European Standards and Guidelines*). This proves to be time-consuming and limits the innovation and flexibility of universities in decision-making. There is also the problem of state interference and narrowing accreditation bodies' autonomy. An additional issue is the quasi-monopoly of many national accreditation agencies in Europe—they are by law the only institutions responsible for the accreditation that is compulsory for higher education institutions in a given country. The accreditation role can also get mixed up with legal supervision.

G. Bogue and K.B. Hall draw attention to the myths about the quality of education at universities, commonly held by academics and accepted by the American public. One believes that only universities charging high tuition fees offer good quality education. According to another myth, high quality is provided only by more prominent universities. According to another concept, quality education is associated with high selectivity. Then there is the assumption that only nationally and U.S.-wide accredited universities provide quality. There is also the belief that educational quality is related to ample material resources. What do these statements have in common? Indeed, the idea of a limited supply of quality, according to which educational quality is a unique good and limited to a specific, elite number of institutions and programs (Bogue and Hall, 2003, p. 5).

The mentioned researchers point to eight dilemmas conditioning the improvement of the quality of education in universities (Bogue and Hall, 2003, p. 10):

1   Can quality education be considered a scarce, limited good, so only a few institutions can offer excellent education? Are selectivity and the size of the university associated with greater prestige? Can one expect an improvement in the quality of education given the multiplicity and diversity of universities?
2   How to verify the quality of education, who decides on educational quality standards, and what should they look like?
3   Can quality be captured in a single performance indicator, such as a rating or ranking? Or are diversity and complexity of data and indicators required to measure the individual and institutional effectiveness of teaching quality?
4   What information related to the quality of education can the university keep secret from the public, and to what extent?

5   What is the critical decision-making motive for nurturing educational quality—servitude, mission fulfillment, or perhaps the drive for improvement? To whom do universities need to account, and where do they report data?

6   What should be a good relationship between the university and external stakeholders? How do we combine accountability and reporting with the autonomy of higher education institutions?

7   What challenges does the market pose to teaching quality? Is conceiving students as customers and diplomas and degrees as market products a threat to quality?

8   Do higher education quality guarantees remain external or internal? What role do evaluation and accreditation play in quality assurance? Is there a place for commitment and academic ethos (academic culture)?

A culture based on results (therefore also on control) leaves questions about the issue of the quality system. Some researchers consider quality culture part of this system, while others link the quality system to formalized subsystems consisting of structures, standards, strategies, or procedures (Shore, 2008).

The scientific community generally does not question the second mission of the university, i.e., the quality of education, only that its understanding is different. Assessing the value of quality management also gives rise to disputable opinions. Some researchers advocate the perspective of management and the implementation of quality management methods from business. However, some authors do not share the desire to implement management concepts in the academic world (Watson, 2001; Monaghan and Cervero, 2006). Researchers of the critical stream consider the borrowing of methods for improving the quality of education from business as a manifestation of "quasibusiness of education," "university capitalism," or even "McUniversity." Two decades ago, M. Parker and D. Jary warned that targeting the administration and quality of teaching in the university's development entails the necessity to transform bureaucratic control regimes into motivational systems and management by objectives (Parker and Jary, 1995, p. 328).

10.3 Changes to quality systems in HEIs

Concepts of educational quality changed with the development of systems for control and management of teaching quality. Traditional universities of the 20th century, which approached the Humboldtian type, were concerned with the quality of education through an academic culture consisting of university values and norms. The quality of teaching flowed from both the academic ethos and the professor's authority—it had not been formalized before. Cultural norms, action patterns, and values were considered non-negotiable. Quality management was therefore based on unplanned, customary, and intuitive action, yet the quality of education was usually satisfactory, or at least the effects of higher education were rarely questioned. The quality system was local, involving the culture of the university and opinions about the value of the university and the staff or students, as well as the graduates. In some countries (e.g., the U.S.A. at the turn of the 20th century), external quality control of education (accreditation commissions) was gradually introduced. Still, this process was often voluntary, and most universities were not subject to it.

A different approach to educational quality began in the 1980s in developed countries. The dominance of culture was replaced by a formalized administration of educational quality with a network of formal procedures and processes supporting educational development (Bonvillian and Dennis, 1995, pp. 37–50). The quality of education is understood as the educational results achieved through managing teaching methods previously assumed by specific standards. A quality system's components include standards, procedures, strategies and quality policies, and internal regulations that shape interdependencies and supervise documentation flows. Such systems usually operate locally, within a single university, and there are limited possibilities for quality comparisons within universities (for example, employability surveys and employer feedback). A quality system is used to examine educational outcomes and, therefore, also to assess quality. The external control model over the mentioned system includes institutional program accredited universities granted by the state and international accreditation agencies.

The current concept of educational quality management lays the foundations for a new formation, according to which educational quality is a subject of management based on controlling, benchmarking, and knowledge management. Quality management will be a controlling system, providing the knowledge needed to manage quality and the entire university. The system will be fed reliable data from the whole university, external databases, and the Internet. Quality management will be possible through process and project management in education. What counts here is measurement and comparison, but also corrective action, which can be taken using performance measures and indicators of effectiveness in combination with defined standards or procedures and other quality system components. The global application of the measures will ensure benchmarking and comparison with other universities. It will be possible to compare educational results through internal and external indicators, such as students' and graduates' achievements. Moreover, external accreditation may be replaced by an internal system of educational quality management and self-accreditation, giving universities the opportunity for transparency. This will result in abandoning the previously applied system of academic values perpetuated by custom. Instead, we will get a formalized quality measurement and management system that will apply to teaching and research. The difficulty may be maintaining a balance between a value-based culture of quality and a bureaucratic system of procedure-based management.

Starting from strategy, policy and structures, personnel, educational content, learning outcomes, and programs, and arriving at resources, we can also try to analyze the university's activities in successive waves.

In the first- and second-wave universities, the role of didactic management was marginal, as the organization itself can be said to the university rather than to manage it. Structures or strategies designed to handle the quality of education were essentially nonexistent. Although teaching was important, it was organically intertwined with the research mission. Instead, staff was selected to conduct research. However, universities frequently give teaching and research teams a choice between a greater focus on teaching and research. Teachers proposed educational content, and therefore it was individualized in nature. For example, many monographic lectures were offered to upper-year students. The course offerings prepared by the staff depended closely on their research interests. Curricula and descriptions of their effects were not extensive. The most common teaching methods used were lectures, exercises, conversation classes, and seminars, and students were encouraged to self-educate through reading.

Nowadays, universities use formalized strategies and formulate their missions. The complexity of quality systems encourages using an organizational unit to manage the quality of education. Of course, the involvement of the staff is essential. The level of their specialization is increasing. They may be primarily oriented toward scientific activity or education, although both are important in contemporary universities. The educational content does not result only from the scientific interests of the staff. The current program determines it, so it is consistent with the assumed educational outcomes. Practical specialist classes increasingly replace monographic lectures related to the staff's research fields. The offer may be individualized only to a certain extent due to the needs of the labor market and competition. The curriculum and the educational content that goes with it result from a compromise between the program administration and the academic staff. Universities emphasize diversifying educational methods, and e-learning and multimedia education are being added to traditional forms. As a result, the infrastructure is also changing; e-libraries and IT infrastructure are being created.

The fourth-wave university will use formalized strategies and be equipped with analytical tools for measurement and comparison between institutions. Educational, financial, and market activities are part of the strategy. The structure of the quality system can be called the equivalent of management information systems in companies. It will consist of analysis and controlling departments, corresponding with the goals of the university management. The method of selection of employees will also be modified—it must be adapted to the needs of education. Therefore, probably, there will be an increase in the degree of specialization for teaching or research employees. It will be the program administration that will choose the educational content according to the criterion of market attractiveness. This will involve less individualization, standardization, and employment of the best lecturers. Therefore, the offer of traditional studies will be considered unified, corresponding to market needs and bench-marking. Due to the development of e-learning and multimedia education, we will deal with greater flexibility in the offer, educational content, and more excellent choices for students. Social, cultural, and institutional changes in HE sectors caused by the reaction to the Covid-19 crisis are going toward digitalization and hybridization of teaching. In the teaching infrastructure, systems enabling e-learning, blended learning, remote and hybrid learning will gain in importance.

10.4 Methods and tools for quality management in education

The description of the quality management methods of education at the university depends on the management methodology, so the analysis can focus on quality management or refer to the characteristics of university management. The first way assumes the use of methods for the creation, implementation, and improvement of the quality system, upgrade of the service system (Roger, 2014, p. 26), controlling processes, and determining the management responsibility.

However, to properly select quality management tools in the education sector, it is better to refer to the university level. Publications on this topic allow us to identify such methods as:

- Benchmarking of best practices;
- Management evaluations, audits;
- Student evaluations (Stinger and Finlay, 1993);
- *Total Quality Management* (TQM; Storey, 1993);
- National, external, and international accreditations;
- Implementation or development of internal or external educational quality standards (such as ISO 9001);
- Validation of education (Gibson, 1993);
- Awards and quality certifications;
- Strategic and operational controlling;
- Evaluations and consultations with external stakeholders (such as employers).

M. Brooks and N. Becket analyzed the use of management methods to care for the quality of education at universities (Becket and Brookes, 2006). The analysis shows that the most common groups of strategies adopted from business are under the umbrella of TQM (Motwani and Kumar, 1997; Cruickshank, 2003). Also, due to the links with industry, re-engineering, EFQM, ISO, balanced scorecard, SERVQUAL, or Malcolm Baldrige Award are used. The EFQM Excellence Model is a business-derived method that uses nine criteria to evaluate organizational improvement processes (Wongrassamee, Simmons, and Gardiner, 2003; Hides et al., 2004). The ISO standards (ISO 9000) are internationally recognized norms that make it possible to simultaneously apply comparable measurement methods and quality principles in various sectors, including higher education. The quality system aims at continuous improvement and customer satisfaction. *The Balanced Scorecard* was developed and popularized by consulting as a strategic and quality management method. It uses a management system and evaluates performance in four areas: financial, learning and growth, customer, and internal processes. SERVQUAL is used in higher education and service management to measure customer satisfaction, perception, and expectations. The method is used in five dimensions: service adequacy, responsiveness, value, guarantee, and empathy (Becket and Brookes, 2006).

The Malcolm Baldrige Award is used to assess performance improvement using the following seven criteria:

1   Customer and market focus;
2   Knowledge management;
3   Process management;
4   Results;
5   Leadership;
6   Strategic planning;
7   Improving human resources (Wilson and Collier, 2000).

Jonathan D. Fife analyses quality management methods in universities using two models already in the U.S.A. These are presented in Table 10.1.

The objectives for the implementation of AQIP are as follows:

1   Internal supporting processes in the university for quality assurance;
2   Identification and acceptance of the needs of the quality system by stakeholders—staff, administration, managers, students, but also external stakeholders-;
3   Shaping partnership and cooperation relations between key and other stakeholders;
4   Leadership and communication between internal and external stakeholders;
5   Planning a continuous improvement process through proquality changes;
6   Supporting students to learn, to reach for new competencies, skills, attitudes;
7   Evaluating, valuing, and motivating employees;
8   Enable the implementation of changes;
9   Operational management of the quality system;
10   The pursuit of various other objectives.

Table 10.1 Quality improvement models

Model name	Abbreviation	Origins	Brief description
Academic Quality Improvement Project of The Higher Learning Commission of the North Central Association	AQIP	Academic improvement project used by U.S. accreditation commissions.	A set of criteria must be applied together for the quality system and culture to work well.
Malcolm Baldrige National Quality Award	Baldrige	A criterion of educational quality is used in the U.S.A. to reward the best educational programs.	Implementing a quality culture is possible with the 11 quality principles of the university.
Total Quality Management	TQM	Integrated education quality management was taken from the business.	Introduction of strategies, policies, and procedures in the improvement cycle.

Source: modified from Fife J.D., Qualitative and quantitative measures: one driver of a quality culture, New Directions for Institutional Research 2001, vol. 112, pp. 103–105.

This model could be described by the principles that support the functioning of a quality system in HEIs. The system is based on the university's mission, which stakeholders should also recognize. Continuous improvement of the commitment and competence of human resources is essential— the readiness to work in many different groups, decision-making, conflict resolution, and using quality-centered methods. According to the following rule, leadership should harmonize the top-down perspective (strategic and systemic solutions) with the bottom-up view (executing quality culture through organizational practices). The subsequent direction is constant learning, on group level (units or the whole university) and individual level (faculty, administration, and students). Knowledge becomes the most crucial organizational process for development. Improvement of human capital could be established by reaching for the system of assessment and motivation of employees, consisting of comparing and systematic use of rewards for staff professional development. Cooperation between the people but also the organization's units should be supported. The constructed quality assurance system cannot resist changes and stakeholders' creativity. The stress is on organizational flexibility, agility, and readiness to introduce changes. To organize systemic proquality changes, it is required to anticipate the demands of changes in the environment. Planning should consist of obeying the trends of HEIs and their stakeholders in terms of performance. A quality assurance system in an HEI can work by systematically evaluating its effectiveness. Measurement is intended to provide current and valuable information of a qualitative and quantitative nature.

Trustful *information* will contribute to decision-making and quality improvement. The last principle is the social responsibility of the HEI, related to the awareness that higher education is valuable for society and needs continuous support (North Central Association of Colleges and Schools, 2000). The described principles will ensure the development of a formal quality assurance system and a quality culture within the HEI.

The AQIP join the Quality System in Management Practice and University Quality Accreditation, the Baldrige Award (Baldrige Performance Excellence Program, 2001). There are 11 principles of this resolution.

1 *Learning-centered education* concentrates on learning processes, students' potential development, and satisfaction from the learning;
2 *Organizational and personal learning*—at all levels, organizational units (i.e., teams, departments, faculties, or institutes), individuals (students, faculty, administration), and the whole HEI;
3 *Focus on results and creating value*—focus on effects appropriate to main stakeholders and creating value for them and the organization;
4 *Agility*—sensitivity and flexibility—readiness to satisfy stakeholders' needs and make necessary changes in the organization;
5 *Focus on the future*—monitoring change to recognize and analyze the factors that impact the organization and its position;
6 *Visionary leadership*—a visionary *leadership* founded on engagement, motivation, communication, and value orientation;
7 *Managing for innovation*—an orientation toward innovation and change, i.e., improving programs, social services, or processes to create new value for stakeholders and society;
8 *Management by fact*—decisions rely on evaluating the efficacy of actions. This is achieved by comparing outcomes with those considered in the organizational strategy. Key administrative processes should be investigated, and trustworthy information must be provided;
9 *Valuing faculty, staff, and partners*—involving the development of stakeholders and professional satisfaction;
10 *Public responsibility and citizenship*—binding significance to ethical action, social responsibility, safety, environmental protection, and the public good;
11 *Systems perspective,* i.e., managing the entire organization by its elements to achieve the objectives. The goals are attainable by coordinating the mission, vision, processes, and organizational values (Baldrige Performance Excellence Program, 2001).

J.D. Fife made a comparison between the two standards characterized above. He highlighted the function of evaluation and considered the evolution of a quality culture in educational quality management. Fife recognized four primary sorts of information to assess quality. The data must be trustworthy, proper for the management method, and needed for decision-making.

- *Baseline* and input data enable the appraisal of the organization's current position at a given phase of its evolution. This information is applied to evaluate the influence of proquality steps, which are carried out based on the acquired baseline data.
- *Process measurement determines* the examination and size of processes, i.e., the analysis of what takes place and how it works to enhance the quality of HEI actions. Data on processes is frequently delivered qualitatively and ready to reply to open inquiries.
- *Contextual outcomes or result trend data consist of* data obtained over many years by analyzing output information and process measurement.
- *Comparison data means information about* other HEIs through which we make a positional comparison. The mentioned author lists three elemental types of comparative data. They predominantly reference to actions of HEI competing in the same market. The first class is *peer group data,* i.e., data about other—similar—institutions, related only to the achieved results.
- The next sort is *aspirational data,* comparable market data, combined with information on equivalent groups of academic entities, i.e., those which attract research and teaching funds and students. The last kind of information is *benchmark measurement,* benchmarking measures, i.e., comparison to best practices in the group and best HEIs. The comparison involves only a distinct kind of organizational mission.
- Examining the selected quality of education management methods shows the growth of more robust trends: accountability, data analytics, and a culture of control. This change in direction is in line with the expansion of the fourth wave of HEIs (Sulkowski, 2022a, pp. 104–110, Lenart-Gansiniec and Sulkowski 2022b).

10.5 Critical perspective on educational quality management

Critical Management Studies, Critical Management Education, or *Critical Pedagogy* unite groups of researchers who radically criticize the use of business methods in higher education, considering them as contributing to the decline of academic culture and the ethos of science (Canaan, 2013). These researchers draw attention to teaching in the spirit of opportunism, devoid of reflexivity or criticality, without impact on civic education (Beckmann, Cooper, and Hill, 2009). They also raise the problem of excessive formalization and bureaucratic educational and research processes in universities, which limits effective leadership and creativity. Added to this is the flourishing facade of marketing in the education sector, which copies business solutions (Duignan, 1988). Employees and students are viewed instrumentally, resulting in shallow education programs (Perriton and Reynolds, 2004). Economic pressure causes an interest in financial results at the expense of general education and humanities. Corporations implement supervision and human resources management schemes. These mechanisms increase control over the costs of the organization but also over the organization itself and the content of education (Giroux and Myrsiades, 2001).

Some authors consider traditional humanistic teaching, referring to the mission of the Humboldtian university, as an anachronism (Donoghue, 2008). However, we must admit that voices of criticism concerning the adoption of business methods at universities should be considered in discussions on public management. It is worth betting on the dialogue between various academic circles and reaching for reflection based on many perspectives (Fenwick, 2005). Given the massification of education and dynamic growth of the HEI sector, an adaptation of management methods to education seems justified. The experience of countries with different types of public services, such as social care, health care, or general security, testifies to this. This does not mean that discussions with the scientific community on effective solutions can be abandoned (Parker, 2002).

It is impossible to manage the quality of education only in an administrative and deterministic way. Education and research are areas of creative processes and, therefore, also elements of organizational culture and identity, which management methods can reinforce. However, the imbalance between a bureaucratic, proquality management system and a value-based quality culture has given rise to the difficulties many universities face today.

11 Third mission management

11.1 The essence of the third mission

Historically, the third mission derives from the concept of the university's involvement in social, political, and economic life. It also flows from the close connection between the application of scientific research and the educational process, i.e., the first two missions (Laredo, 2007). From the beginning, universities have educated and engaged elites who have demonstrated participation in non-academic activities. However, a socially engaged university requires openness from all stakeholders. The formation of the medieval and later Humboldtian universities developed concepts of autonomy, self-government, and independence from political power. This leads to a tension between the idea of an open and engaged university versus a hermetic, "ivory tower." Thus, the third mission, or as it is often called in literature—the third stream—is a natural task of the university. However, it was not intensively systemically developed until the 1980s. The third mission was sometimes underestimated in the past because prestigious universities mostly regarded it as an applied activity for polytechnics and universities of applied sciences (Roessler, Duong, and Hachmeister, 2015). The last quarter of a century has seen the rise of the third mission, widely recognized as a key aspect of the functioning of any university (Kesten, 2019). However, how the third mission is understood has changed significantly (Lebeau and Cochrane, 2015). Since the 1990s, it has been assessed and valued in the UK by universities' funds and ranking mechanisms (Lockett, Wright, and Wild, 2013). If we add to this the funds from patents and licenses and cooperation with industry, the outside activities of universities become of strategic importance (Molas-Gallart et al., 2002). Similar activities are implemented by the public policies of many countries, including Australia, Sweden, Germany, Italy, Japan, and Chile (Nedeva, 2008). The orientation toward the development of the third mission is a global trend. It can be found both in the form of systemic actions on the scale of national public policies and as a priority in university strategies in non-democratic systems such as China and Russia (Egorov, Leshukov, and Froumin, 2020). China, due to the vital importance of universities for the development of the economy, knowledge, and human

DOI: 10.4324/9781003366409-16

capital, but at the same time, the robust state control over them focuses on selected aspects of the third mission. The dominant approach is industrial development and applied research (Wu and Zhou, 2012). Universities also play a role in public policies and political communication with society. However, it isn't easy to point to a positive role in the development of civil society. In the following section, the terms "third mission" and "third stream" will be used interchangeably.

The broadest way of defining the third mission of an HEI is based on its understanding of interaction or relations with the non-academic environment (Görason, Maharajh, and Schmoch, 2009; Vidal, Ferreira and Vieira, 2017; de la Torre, Casani, and Esparrells, 2021). The cooperation of an HEI with the environment covers many aspects of its activities beyond its scientific and teaching missions. The spheres of cooperation refer to economic, social and cultural activities. Collaboration with the environment is also differentiated depending on strategy and specialization. Research universities focus on the first mission, while the second and third implementation is often very closely related to scientific activity. The scope of the university's cooperation with the environment may be diversified. Leading universities are brands recognized worldwide, and their impact on the environment may be global. Large universities often cooperate with outside stakeholders and shape their relations locally.

The second relatively broad definition of the university's third mission is "the creation, application and use of knowledge and other capabilities of the university for non-academic activities" (Molas-Gallart et al., 2002, p. 2). The emphasis here is on the creation and implementation of knowledge, so the third mission is to be derived from the first and second missions, i.e., the development of science and didactics. In practice, the third mission often goes beyond the creation and use of knowledge, the development of cultural and social activity, and the popularization of science.

An example of a narrower way of understanding the third stream of university activity is the definition, linking it directly to academic entrepreneurship. The third mission is "the social, entrepreneurial, innovative activities that universities carry out alongside teaching and research, where additional benefits are created for society" (Montesinos et al., 2008). Another is "the formulation of new tasks relating to research and education that transform traditional universities towards greater social engagement" (Nedeva, 2008).

The development of the third stream concept can be seen in the context of the fundamental dilemma described in this book. The utopia of academic freedom is the third stream, understood as the idea of university involvement in positive social, economic, and cultural changes. In this sense, universities should move toward developing and popularizing the ideas of scientific progress, justice, civil society, emancipation, sustainability, diversity, and tolerance. It may be a utopian aspiration, but it is deeply rooted in the timeless values of a university founded on the ideas of truth and the emancipation of humanity. However, we are dealing with a dystopia of power and control over universities, which limits autonomy, imposes patterns of development of a university engaged in economic activity, and limits freedom of research by pushing practical issues. Many authors point to the rise of the third mission, associated with the development of the formation of entrepreneurial universities (Vefago, Trierweiller, and Barcellos de Paula, 2020). Researchers suggest that the development of academic entrepreneurship led to the rise in the importance of the third mission in the late 20th century. However, there is growing criticism of managerialism, new public management, and neoliberal ideology in implementing the third mission and, more broadly, in the academic world (Shore and McLauchlan, 2012; Steenkamp, 2017; Jones et al., 2021). Nedeva and Boden point out that the rise of neoliberal rhetoric pressuring economics and utilitarianism in universities and science, in general, would lead to short-sightedness related to obtaining immediate results and excessive control limiting the freedom of science (Nedeva and Boden, 2006). The pressure toward commercialization of research, collaboration with industry, and reducing the costs of teaching and scientific activity makes the development of the third mission a method of promoting a neoliberal vision of the academy (Thorn and Soo, 2006). This central tension of the third mission is also reflected in the dual interpretations of such trendy terms as *Community-Based Research, Social Entrepreneurship, Technology Transfer, Widening Participation,* and *Knowledge Triangle* (Unger and Polt, 2017; Maier, 2018). Thus, the development of the concept of the third mission and the increase of its importance in modern universities is a global trend related to the development of the neoliberal university. However, the development of the concept of an engaged, socially responsible, civic university (Breznitz and Feldman, 2012; Leja, 2010; Karlsen and Larrea, 2019; Barnett, 2007) accentuates the opening of the university to the environment but does not question the core of values in the form of academic freedom. Identifying this tension between instrumental and subjective approaches to the third mission makes managing this sphere a key challenge for the organizational identity of the university.

11.2 Objectives of the third mission of the university

The third mission includes cooperation with the environment and participation in social, political, and economic life, spin-offs and spin-outs, academic entrepreneurship, commercialization of research, patenting and licensing, and involvement in regional development (Benneworth, 2018), popularization of science. Making some synthesis of different studies on the third mission, ten objectives, and areas of their implementation can be proposed (Schoen et al., 2006).

- Transfer of human capital and competencies to industry and the public sector.

The main interest in this area is the transfer of competencies and people from the university to industry or the public sector. This concerns the education of doctoral students and postgraduates, students of courses who work outside academia. It is related to the development of knowledge-based economies and organizations, which require competencies from employees who are *lifelong learners*. Indicators of this objective may be the number of graduates, the quality of their competencies, and their relevance to the needs of the labor market. One can cite the example of graduates of studies, and doctoral schools, educated in practical disciplines, who, moving into the labor market, bring their research experience and competencies related to scientific work (van Laar, 2014).

- Creating intellectual capital and intellectual property.

It focuses on creating and managing codified knowledge produced by the university (patents, copyrights, licenses) (Meyer and Tang, 2007; Neumann, 2021). Innovation is also important—as part of creating and licensing intellectual capital (El-Kafafi and Gular, 2016; Kortov et al., 2019). Measures of the effectiveness of implementing this criterion can be the number of patents, licenses, and the value of royalties paid by other entities for using the university's intellectual property. This area can be illustrated by the examples of many universities which create technoparks and obtain significant revenues from this type of activity (Baycan and Olcay, 2021).

- Initiating and developing spin-offs and spin-outs.

Universities also transfer knowledge to practice through academic entrepreneurship, creating or co-creating economic activities (Miranda, Chamorro, and Rubio, 2018). Spin-offs are economic activities designed thanks to competencies or resources originating, at least partly, from HEIs. Universities can play the role of founders or shareholders of such companies. The intellectual capital of the emerging entity is often based on innovations developed at the university. This means that the employees come from the HEI. The key challenge here is to balance the benefits, risks, and resources of the university and other stakeholders (Cadavid, Díez-Echavarría, and Valencia, 2017). When examining the effectiveness of the mission in this area, it is worthwhile to calculate not only the revenue and costs from the business but also to look at: The impact of the spin-off on the region and the sector, the number of HEI employees involved, the innovations created, the market share and the growth rate of the business entity (Fuster et al., 2019). Descriptors are also needed to characterize the involvement and support of the university: Dedicated teams, incubator, and funding provided (in any form, including shares). Universities can also be involved in creating new business ventures that are incubated using academic resources but become independent entities (spin-outs).

An example is the significant number of spin-offs successfully created by US universities. In the United States, the effectiveness of this type of academic entrepreneurship is one of the critical measures of the performance of the university as a whole (Link and Scott, 2017). The rising tide of university spin-offs is typical in many countries and business sectors (Jung and Kim, 2018).

- Execution of contracts with industry and relations with economic organizations.

This area is focused on the co-production and transfer of knowledge from academic activities to industry. This is the primary determinant of the attractiveness of universities for existing economic entities. Co-production in business most often concerns applied research resulting in the implementation of innovations and creation of a new product or service (Malmberg and Serger, 2021). Indicators of the effectiveness of the fulfillment of this criterion may be the value and number of contracts, the type, and scale of projects, the value of partners (global, large companies, SMEs), the level of concentration (branch and on several partners), the types of contracts (research, consulting, services) and their duration. This is often complemented by a "soft" dimension in which the university is a member of professional associations and industry networks, produces industry publications, and implements training, consultancy, internship, and student placement activities. A successful example of the development of such systemic implementations in modern technologies are universities in Taiwan and development programs carried out with the industry (Wong, Wan, and Chen, 2018).

- Contracts and relationships with the public and third sectors.

Another critical area for realizing the third stream of the university's activities is the relationship between the public and third sectors (Zomer and Benneworth, 2011; Kola and Leja, 2017). An HEI may carry out activities for or in cooperation with these sectors in the form of, for example, a "public service." This may be a one-off activity or repeated or even permanent activity. The indicators of mission fulfillment are based on similar measures as in the case of cooperation with industry, i.e., scale, number, and value of implementations. An additional important criterion here is the social impact, social innovations, or, generally, the change created thanks to these relations (Klofsten et al., 2019). The university must complement the implementation activities with industry with public contracts, mainly when university laboratories focus on social and cultural issues. Examples of such activities could be cooperation with public and third sector organizations in health prevention, tourism, social care, and civil society (Appe and Barragán, 2017). Other activities could be projects of third-age and children's universities, created and managed by universities (Petrova, Popova, and Dejniak, 2020).

- Participation in the development and implementation of public policies.

An objective related to the previous one, but emphasizing the leading role of universities in public policies, is the participation in creating and implementing public procedures. Universities are often the leading partner, source of expertise, human resources, and competencies, allowing them to develop and enforce public policies (Vorley and Nelles, 2008; Nelles and Vorley, 2010). The advantage of universities is competence and relative impartiality resulting from a lack of political involvement. Universities often actively prepare reforms and public policies in the following areas: Health and social care, education, and security (Montesinos et al., 2008). Formalizing participation in the creation of public policies can be problematic. Because apart from preparation, cooperation in creating expert opinions and reports are activities such as scientific conferences and seminars, expert and academic communication, and consultancy in the sphere of public policies. In the preparation and implementation of public policies at the national and international level, an important role is played by leading universities. In contrast, in the practice of public policies at the regional level, more important local universities play a more significant role (Dan, 2012).

- Involvement in social and cultural life.

Universities are most often involved in social and cultural life at the regional and city levels. This is done through campus infrastructure and social and cultural activities. Academic centers have facilities such as sports buildings, libraries, exhibition halls, lecture theatres and halls of residence, specialized workshops and laboratories, and even museums, which can be used for more than just university activities. Social and cultural activities may include concerts and events organized by academic teams (e.g., sports, arts). Community involvement may also include expert activities the university pro bono carried out as part of the university's social responsibility or charitable activities (Montesinos et al., 2008). Accounting for this type of activity is tricky, and there is little experience in measuring the effects of such actions. The tested solutions estimate the added value from social and cultural activities, confronted with their relative share in all costs.

- Popularization and understanding of science in society.

The third mission function of popularizing science is based on the interactions of universities, researchers, lecturers, and students with the public. The deep specialization and complexity of modern science mean that the level of its understanding in society is low. Consequently, the complex opinions of experts and researchers are beginning to be dominated by "post-truth," propagated through social media. The danger of manipulating the opinions of people who do not understand science for commercial or political purposes increases. There is also a crisis of trust in experts (Michael, 1996). Traditionally, the university has focused on science and education, to which only the elite had access. The science and university didactics language remained hermetic because it was supposed to be addressed to a narrow group of experts or at least well-educated people. With the massification of education and the development of science, the demand for the dissemination of science increased, which, however, from the point of view of the identity of researchers and the strategic objectives of universities, still played a marginal role. Nowadays, there are more and more methods and examples of the dissemination of science by universities. The most important types of interaction with the public aimed at popularizing science include public debates, open seminars, webinars, open days, science festivals, fairs, popular publications, magazines, websites, podcasts, video podcasts, networks, and communities of "friends of science" and the dissemination of research through social media (Bauer, 2009). Universities do not have adequate measures of science dissemination and rarely make this aspect of their activities strategic. However, there are spectacular examples of universities organizing dissemination activities and cooperating with other organizations (such as BBC television, science dissemination associations, and business sponsoring events). One example of the institutionalization of this aspect of the mission was the creation of a chair in public understanding of science at Oxford University in 1995, headed by Richard Dawkins (Wikipedia Contributors, 2017).

- Commitment to regional development.

The third mission of most universities includes diverse activities at the regional level. HEIs are often large organizations with significant cultural, social, and economic influence at the regional level. The main focus of most HEIs is on the local level, which is usually reflected in solid links with the local community and governments and the organizational identity of the HEIs themselves (Fongwa and Marais, 2016). Examples include projects implemented at the regional level, with local governments and enterprises, aiming at regional development (Karlsen, 2007). They concern practically all aspects of the third mission, described in the following analyzed areas, but their concentration is on the regional level only (Profiroiu and Brişcariu, 2021). Regional implementations, partnerships with business and public organizations, regional spin-offs, and economic, social, and cultural activities at this level are only selected examples (Fuster et al., 2019). It is difficult to speak about the accountability of this type of activity, as they are scattered in different departments and organizational units.

• To accomplish a civilizing mission.

Universities are an emanation of the ideas of wisdom and justice. They carry a civilizational mission of reaching and proclaiming the truth, which translates into a responsibility related not only to the development of science, it's teaching, and popularization but also to taking the side of justice, goodness, and emancipation of humanity. In this sense, universities should be the vanguard of ideas and projects crucial for civilization. Nowadays, such ideas are, for example, sustainable development and ecology (Neary and Osborne, 2018), human rights and civic activity (Motala, 2015), fighting against the problems of humanity (e.g., diseases, hunger, wars), tolerance and diversity (Meyer and Sporn, 2019). Therefore, the challenge of the third mission is also the public engagement of universities to improve and enhance the world (Watermeyer and Lewis, 2018; Frazzica and La Spina, 2019). Different methods can be used for this purpose: popularization of science, cultural, social, and economic involvement, projects, and implementation. The effects of such activities may be more challenging to measure. Still, it seems that due to the importance of the university in society and the ethos of the academic profession, the mission to change the world for the better lies at the core of the idea of the university (Entradas, 2015; Huxster et al., 2018).

11.3 Management of the third mission

The processes of managing the third mission are connected with the implementation of concepts, methods, and organizational techniques, allowing for the shaping of non-academic activities of the university. They are located in different areas of the university's action, starting from the creation and implementation of strategies, through the design and implementation of measures of impact on society and the economy, to activities related to the improvement of human and intellectual capital and marketing.

Apart from measurable aspects of implementing the third mission, which is reflected in rankings, statistics, and evaluations of universities (Marhl and Pausits, 2011; Kotosz et al., 2015), many activities remain challenging to measure. In addition to commercializing research, patents, and licenses, implementing public policies, stimulating the development of a knowledge society, and popularizing science, the university influences society through its civic and culture-forming role. The university's activity is based on academic ethos and values: Criticality, the pursuit of truth, democracy, and civic spirit. It isn't easy to measure this type of activity, although it can be managed and shaped. For universities in autocratic systems, the aspect of the third mission—related to the development of civil society—is absent.

Implementing the third mission is also of interest to HEI management and is used to evaluate its activities. A set of accountability indicators can be used to monitor the effectiveness of the implementation of the third stream

(Molas-Gallart and Castro-Martínez, 2007). Specialized rankings of higher education institutions are also developing based on criteria related to the third mission, e.g., *Times Higher Education Impact Ranking* (Times Higher Education, 2021; Urdari, Farcas, and Tiron-Tudor, 2017).

When attempting to analyze the processes of third stream management, it is worth looking from the point of view of the change from the second wave university through the third wave to the crystallizing formation of the fourth wave. Third, mission management can be analyzed from the perspectives of strategic and operational, organizational system (strategy, structure, and organizational culture), corporate practices and processes, and selected functional areas (human capital, marketing, finance, and knowledge management) (Table 11.1).

Second wave universities exhibited limited third stream activity as they focused on research and teaching. Nevertheless, the Humboldtian university was supposed to perform a state-forming and culture-shaping function, using the authority of science and the academic ethos. The university's central role is reflected in the Humboldtian metaphor that the university is "the apex where everything that happens directly in the interest of the moral culture of the nation converges" (Wittrock, 1993, p. 317). Second wave universities did not have a strategy but were based on values and an academic ethos that set the direction and goals for action. *Implicitly* adopted, the most crucial third stream objectives were the readiness to interact spontaneously with the environment for the nation's and society's good. Thus, the organizational culture, derived from the academic culture and ethos, focused the third stream activities of the university on cultural, national, and state-forming values. In the traditional power structures of the university, there was individual responsibility, but some decisions were also made collectively by senates and councils. Therefore, the responsibility for culture- and state-forming activities rested with the entire academic staff. Managers were not assigned strategic organizational roles related to cooperation with the environment, except perhaps for representing the university externally and fundraising in the case of American universities. In the third stream sphere, unplanned and intuitive activities, guided by values and academic identity, predominate.

The third wave university is oriented toward academic entrepreneurship, management, competition, and cooperation with business become precious. This configuration of values favors the third mission's development, especially in academic entrepreneurship and cooperation with industry. Hence, among the organizational practices of third wave universities appear implementations and joint projects with business, as well as the first specialized managerial roles among administration and academic staff. Also, managers started to see cooperation with the environment as part of their responsibility. In the field of human capital management, the importance of the project, implementation, and business cooperation competencies and the importance of marketing is increasing. In the area of the third mission,

Table 11.1 Management of the third mission (3M)

Organizational criterion	Second wave university	Third wave university	Fourth wave university
The role of the third stream	Marginal	Growing, important	Relevant
Values of the third stream	State- and culture-forming role, academic ethos	Academic entrepreneurship, management, and cooperation with business	The role of digital cooperation networks
Strategy and third stream	Collective and individual will to act with the environment, spontaneous	Commitment to business relationships, planned	Data-driven, specialized, planned and controlled
Culture and identity associated with the third stream	A strong ethos. The value of creating ideas that integrate the nation, the state	Values: market, competitiveness, entrepreneurship, innovation	Values: universal communication and accountability
Responsibility structure for third mission	All academic staff	Managers, specialized staff, and administration	Managers, academic managers
Organizational practices related to the third stream	Marginal, public statements, expert opinions, lobbying	Developing, cooperating with business, projects, and implementations	Extended and accountable
Human capital and third stream	Lack of competence, lack of specialization in the third stream	Design, implementation, and business competences	Management, organizational, and IT competencies of staff and administration
Marketing—third stream	None, reputation created by academic staff ethos	Growing PR and promotion through third-stream activities	Extensive, specialized, networked
Finance—third stream	Lack of accountability and basic budgeting	Limited responsibility, advanced budgeting	Accounting and budgeting in real time
Knowledge management—third stream	None, tacit knowledge dominates, individual and social	Elementary knowledge management about relations with the environment	Advanced knowledge management about concerns with the environment
Professionalization, third stream management	None, actions ethos, intuitive, unplanned	Partial project management, strategic planning	Complete specialization, planning, measurement, and improvement

Source: Own elaboration.

marketing starts to be a tool for public relations and the promotion of the university. In finance and accounting, budgeting and accountability of implementations are at an elementary level. In entrepreneurial universities, other aspects of the third mission are also developed. However, the most important is still implementation, cooperation with business, and knowledge transfer between the academic sector and the economy. Thus, when analyzing the level of professionalization of management in terms of the implementation of the third mission, one can see that it is partial. The following have appeared: The foundations of strategy and structural specialization (responsibilities and organizational roles) and the first corporate practices based on management methodology and theory, such as project and quality management. The third stream gradually, with the development of the formation of the entrepreneurial university from the 1970s to the beginning of the 21st century, gains in importance, becoming one of the forms of transformation of the academic world toward neoliberalism.

The fourth wave universities are a continuation of the third wave in terms of neoliberalism's ideological basis and management's increasing role. Still, they are driven by digitalization and the development of networks and IT in a broad sense. Thus, the critical value will become the university's digital cooperative network with the environment, and this will be both academic and non-academic. This places the third mission at the center of the HEI's activities, as the effectiveness of the university's actions depends on the quality of its relations with the environment. Advanced processing of large amounts of data will be required to sustain intensive interaction with the environment. The organizational culture will go in the direction of strengthening the importance of communication processes and networking. There will be further development of accountability based on evidence, leading to third-stream measurement and evaluation. Consequently, the third mission will also be embedded in the developing audit and control culture. In organizational structures, it will not only be the responsibility of managers but also of specialized units and positions in both administration and academic staff. Organizational practices, controlled in a system of accountability based on real-time data collection, will construct a system of digital educational bureaucracy, which will, however, be heavily involved in cooperative networks with the non-academic environment. In the functional area of human capital, the third mission will be relevant, fostering the professionalization of management: Specialization, controlling, and the quality improvement process. A manifestation of this professionalization of the implementation of the third stream will also be the development, data-based, and integration into an information system of all essential aspects of the organization related to the cooperation of the university with the environment.

Part V

Management of functional areas of universities

12 Human capital and talent management in universities

12.1 Humans in the university

Human capital management is a sub-discipline of management science with the trite motto that "people are the most important resource of an organization." Indeed, the very existence and all the achievements of universities are made possible by people. Centuries of academic continuity and tradition are generations of scientists, teachers, students, and administrators in universities. This logic of continuity and accumulation was based on the academic ethos, serving the mission of scientific development and educating social and political elites. Today, management has entered the world of academic culture, with its patterns taken from the business. Man treated as an organizational resource is a tool for achieving the organization's goals. This instrumental approach, criticized by representatives of the radical management trend, has also become established in the academic world (Bolton et al., 2011).

This chapter attempts to answer the question about the possibility of seeking a balance between the traditional ethos approach to university employees and contemporary methods and tools of human capital management. It carries out a synthetic account of the area of human capital management in the university world, followed by an analytical reflection on the evolution of the HR function in HEIs.

12.2 Transformations of human capital management in universities

The fulfillment of the university's three missions requires the development of human capital. However, applying a simple scheme of transferring business solutions in personnel management to the academy does not bring good results (Gao and Haworth, 2019). Research, reflection, adaptation processes of management concepts and methods to the university world, and learning and change management in the academic environment are necessary. In the traditional university culture, it is difficult to talk about applying people management methods because social relations are based on established values, rituals, and academic behavior patterns. This means that

DOI: 10.4324/9781003366409-18

human capital management processes are carried out *implicitly* based on norms established in the organizational culture. They then usually take less formalized forms, although this depends on the aspect of the HR function. HR administration is necessary for a formalized aspect, irrespective of the type of HEI, because employment contracting, welfare and health and safety, as well as personnel records with data protection and payroll accounting are legal requirements. The data administered in the traditional system function in digitized or paper form, and their collection is a bureaucratic burden for employees. In a traditional university, we will find human resource functions in recruitment and talent management, motivation and appraisal, and staff development. Still, they are not process-managed and take an informal shape. Recruitment of staff for research and teaching activities is a process that rests on the shoulders of chairs heads, with the support of collective bodies that decide to hire a staff member communal and conciliatory. Attracting talent is possible through social practices: Master-student relationships and the image of authority figures. Outstanding students, inspired to academic work by their academic masters, undertake tasks in the form of working on a dissertation in cooperation with a supervisor. The image of authorities and scientific schools attracts researchers from other academic centers and increases the prestige of those universities with the most outstanding achievements. Knowledge of authorities and research schools is not global and spreads only environmentally, limiting the opportunities to draw from the international talent pool. In academic activities, recruitment is also a system of enrolling and selecting students for entry. In traditional universities, students are recruited through an examination system and are forced to persevere through a selection regime of study. Undoubtedly, the cost of this solution is the high selectivity in the study process, which is necessary to maintain its quality. Employee motivation and appraisal in the traditional university culture lie in academic ethos and personal leadership. A research and teaching employee of a university should be subjected to the evaluation of the scientific community, which serves the purpose of obtaining further academic degrees. Such assessment concerns academic achievements and outputs and, to a small extent, covers teaching and organizational activities. The academic ethos as a system of values imposes on the university professor cultural norms of academic and didactic "good work," which is not subject to formal evaluation (Fassin, 1991). Sometimes, in special cases, the intervention of superiors is necessary. There is also a system of academic prizes awarded by academic bodies, but their main aspect is symbolic and prestigious rather than realistically differentiating salaries. Generally, the traditional university system is characterized by hierarchically arranged and flattened salary levels, which are not very differentiated between salary groups or even less within the same employee group. In such a system, for example, every full professor at a university earns similarly, regardless of their academic achievements. The university trusts its employees provided they comply with the standards of "good work." In the situation of the organization's expansion and increase in the scale of its operations and the gradual dismantling of the cultural patterns of the academic ethos, trust is not enough, and there is a shift toward an audit culture rooted in business activities (Kok et al., 2010). The failure to differentiate salaries according to performance assumes that academic prestige will be the most important motivator in scholar activity. The belief in autotelic motivation in the form of scientific curiosity does not consider that salaries are one of the measures of social prestige (Blackmore and Kandiko, 2011). The academic activity offers prospects for development in many respects, which is a value of this profession. The opportunity to pursue the truth, realize one's passions, satisfy one's curiosity about the world by conducting research, and work with students and scientists are privileges belonging to academic work (Sulkowski and Dziedzic, 2020). Additionally, the development of employees means chances to benefit from international contacts, perspectives for employee promotion based on scientific achievements, and recognition. However, universities nowadays have limited resources in the growing competition. The need for rational allocation of resources and investment in staff development leads to two powerful model solutions. The first characteristic of traditional universities is allocating development resources according to the position in the hierarchy and striving for the collective and common use of development funds. The second solution, closer to the entrepreneurial university, is allocating resources based on scientific achievements, which is crucial in the case of the university's focus on its research mission (Mcculloch, 2017; Xu, 2020). The development of scientometrics and worldwide indexing and ranking systems for scientific journals allow for a quick, regular, comparable, and not too costly assessment of scientific achievements (Giri and Chaudhuri, 2021).

The functioning of human capital management in a traditional university is a system adapted to the specifics of an organization created in the spirit of the Humboldtian model and educating social elites. It is a dysfunctional solution in the conditions of the growing competition and the digital age. The massification of education, the digital transition, the commercialization of the university mission, market competition, and the proliferation of human capital management methods have posed new challenges to universities regarding the staff function.

The philosophy of human capital management in third-wave HEI is based on the assumptions of the culture of an entrepreneurial learning organization, with its market approach to people treated as an organizational resource serving the fulfillment of the mission. Competitiveness is connected with acquiring and developing competencies and implementing effective systems of evaluating and motivating employees, which allow achieving the organization's objectives. HR strategy takes the form of a formalized plan for human capital development, which considers the impact of supply and demand on the labor market. It is based on objectives that concern human capital but are closely linked to the strategic objectives of the whole university. HR administration is an increasingly complex information process involving legal, accounting, social policy, data protection, insurance, and employee health care.

In advanced DT shaping fourth wave universities, these changes influence the implementation of information systems that allow the processing of employee data, integrated into the entire management and information ecosystem of the university (Rodríguez, Osorio, and Berriel, 1994). Employee recruitment is a formalized process of searching for and selecting employees with competencies to meet strategic objectives. Such searches for staff and talent are conducted on a large scale and the select team from a global pool (Bradley, 2016; Al Rahahelah and Al Mubarak, 2017). The processes of student recruitment or, even more broadly—student process management—are carried out as part of the university's teaching mission and function and are supported by complex IT systems such as SIS and LMS. Here, the advantages from an IT perspective are speed, scope, and complexity of data processing and analysis (Ning and Lin, 2007). In recruiting students, the university's marketing also plays a key role, serving the purpose of image building and attracting an appropriate number of students at a satisfactory level. Marketing carried out primarily on the Internet allows reaching large groups of potential candidates for studies, from among which students are recruited. Research and teaching staff evaluation is formalized and implemented as part of internal motivational systems, reflected in the IT solutions implemented. Evaluation is permanent, regular, and carried out frequently (e.g., annually, every few years as part of a complete staff evaluation). The evaluation criteria are coupled with the mission and strategic goals. In the case of emphasis on research activities, evaluation using scientometrics dominates. In teaching, it is aggregated data from student surveys, employability and salary statistics of graduates, accreditation results, and employee evaluations created as part of internal education quality management systems (Hava and Erturgut, 2010). The employee motivation system is based on measurable and regular assessments of employees, focusing on their specialization. It combines motivators related to staff development, potential promotions, fixed and variable remuneration, and rewards of a tangible and intangible nature. Remuneration is based on performance. Base salaries vary much more than in a traditional university and depend on specialization and performance. Specializations of staff related to university missions and organizational activities are possible. Salaries of research, teaching, implementation, and administrative staff are differentiated, but it is also possible to combine areas of specialization. Variable salaries are extensive bonus systems based on a measurable assessment of achievements taking into account annual and several years of measurements and comparisons (Gläser et al., 2010; Collan, Stoklasa, and Talasova, 2014). Employee development is geared toward specialization and increased performance in the long term. It considers opportunities for promotion, the creation of differentiated career paths, and supporting the development of employees within their specialization. Employee development serves the logic of allocating resources to support employee development based on achievement, selection, and differentiated approach (Rahyasih and Kurniady, 2017). Talent management attracts, develops, and motivates outstanding individuals to stimulate achievements within their specialization. This often applies to scientific activities, but there are numerous examples of attracting great academic leaders and teaching staff. The concept of talent management in universities is based on systems of assessment, motivation, development, and attracting human capital (Bradley, 2016; Hojjati et al., 2018). A summary of the transformation process of the human capital management process in the university can be found in Table 12.1.

12.3 Human capital management professionalization

The ongoing professionalization of human capital management was a gradual process that emerged in the formation of the entrepreneurial university half a century ago and is now developing as part of the fourth wave of universities conventionally called—"digital universities" (Hassan, 2017; Khalid et al., 2018). HR management functions are an extensive information and management ecosystem for collecting and analyzing data that are the basis for HR decisions. Integration of such class systems: HRM, ERP, SIS, LMS, BI, and others rely on the ability to flow data between systems to produce analyses that allow decisions to be made based on high-quality data in a short time (Scholtz and Kapeso, 2014; Kasim and Khalid, 2016). It is also possible to give different priorities to strategic and operational decisions and create differentiated access paths depending on decision-making powers. Some activities make decisions based on procedures and algorithms developed in the information and management system. Others are heuristic, requiring reflection and consultation, but should still be made based on reliable employee data. Digital learning will have an extensive networked information system, of which the human capital management subsystem will be a part (Bagdasarian et al., 2020; Sitnicki, 2018; Gama, 2018). It will be a university using sophisticated solutions in terms of personnel strategy, HR administration, recruitment, and development of employees and students. A kind of "digital post-bureaucratization" will become a threat, synonymous with overburdening people and organizations with data processing that can operate according to a "dustbin" approach. It also potentially threatens the freedom and creativity of academics with excessive standardization and instrumentalism (Anderson, 2006; O'Reilly and Reed, 2011; Brunsson, Rasche, and Seidl, 2012).

Therefore, the question may be asked whether it is worth moving toward the professionalization of human capital management and digitizing university personnel functions. We see threats in the form of departing from

Table 12.1 Transformation of human capital management of HEIs

Areas of human capital management	Traditional university	Entrepreneurial university	Digital HEI
Philosophy of human capital	The Humboldtian model is a traditional culture based on the university's ethos	Entrepreneurial, competitive, market-driven, flexible culture	Network culture, learning organization, market culture, relaxed culture
Personnel strategy	Informal, the pursuit of intuitively understood, traditional, organizational rules	Formalized, generic, and flexible human capital development plans	Formalized and flexible human capital development plans based on IT metrics and HR systems
Personnel administration	Processes for collecting and reporting basic data on paper	Mixed paper and electronic documentation model. Varying degrees of bureaucratization and formalization	IT processes for analyzing mass data are integrated into a management and information system
Recruitment of staff	Informal processes of attracting researchers and PhD students by authority and prestige	Formalized recruitment and selection process. In public universities, competitive procedures	A formalized process for finding talent internationally, online with an assessment based on scientometrics data
Recruitment of students	University image-based bureaucratic processes of paper-based data collection and analysis	University image-based student attraction and selection processes	Mass data analytics-based network selection processes and online marketing Attracting by the reputation of the university
Employee evaluation	Informal, self-evaluation, collective and individual, sporadic, conditioning of academic promotion	Regular, formalized, according to established criteria for employee evaluation	Using scientometrics and network methods are permanent, regular, frequent, and based on the university's mission criteria
Motivating employees	An ethos system based on recognition and prestige	Differentiated, more or less advanced reward system	An appraisal-based system motivates employees for their performance within their area of expertise

Remuneration of employees	Poorly differentiated pay, hierarchical pay structure, token rewards	Gradual increase in pay differentiation according to merit and specialization	Varied, strongly stratified, merit-based salaries, extensive bonus systems based on the measurable evaluation
Employee development	A hierarchical, universal, collective system for sharing resources to support workforce development	Hierarchical, progressively differentiated development system. Can accommodate staff specialization and allow for differentiation (accommodate individual development)	Staff development considers opportunities for promotion, creating diverse career paths, and supporting staff development within their area of expertise, emphasizing networking
Talent management	Based on master–student relationships, scientific authority, and personal leadership	Based on finding and attracting talent to prestigious scientific centers and entrepreneurial academic activity	Based on systems to evaluate, motivate, develop, and attract human capital from a global talent pool by the network

Source: Own elaboration.

academic ethos, the instrumentalization of people in universities, degradation of traditional academic culture, and the development of "post-bureaucratic digitalization." It seems that, at least from a critical perspective, the balance toward traditional ethos solutions prevails (Gill, 2014; Kane, Sandretto, and Heath, 2002). However, reality cannot be criticized. Universities are not ivory towers. For long decades they have undergone transformation processes that have permanently distanced them from the utopia of traditional academic culture. In a changing market environment, operating in conditions of competition and limited resources, universities have been increasingly forced to implement organizational methods aimed at optimizing decisions and the use of resources. The last half century has seen accelerating digitalization processes that have revolutionized not only the entire organizational world but also culture and society. Universities are adapting to these changes, moving ever deeper into the new model of the digital university. In the sphere of human capital management, this means balancing the effects of digital instrumentalism with constructive solutions from the realm of organizational culture and identity.

12.4 Human capital management in universities and enterprises

Analyses of organizational management usually start with processes considered more deterministic and subject to solid managerial control—to move on to indeterministic methods with much weaker administrative control (Marks and Mirvis, 2011). Strategy and organizational structure are subject to more substantial managerial control. Although they are not entirely deterministic, they can be sequentially described by algorithms. People management concepts in universities draw from human capital theory and knowledge-oriented organizations (Dayan, Heisig, and Matos, 2017). Global competition and cooperation influence universities, modifying their intellectual and human capital management processes.

In the area of human capital management in universities, assessing the role of employees seems controversial. Research allows two positions to emerge: Critical and functionalist (Aspara, 2014). In the functionalist perspective, a person in an organization is a subject, enabling the realization of collective goals. Human resource management is nothing else than the coordination of organizational functions focused on results. Pursuing a good place in the university race leads one to agree to many principles or conventions that can hardly be considered unquestionable. The value of a university and its employee measured by scientometric parameters, the commercialization of culture, the transformation of the academic and scientific ethos, the advantage of the scale of an institution's scientific activity, and its size over other areas of its functioning—these are just some of the more controversial themes of human resource management.

The critical perspective abandons the instrumentalism of functionalist people management, drawing attention to the negative consequences of the transformation of the university, which we can include:

- The bureaucratization of teaching and the pursuit of research in such a way that it contributes significantly to the restriction of creative activity (Duignan, 1988);
- Unreflective and opportunistic student education (Beckmann, Cooper, and Hill, 2009);
- Attaching importance mainly to current economic performance, at the expense of general education and humanities content;
- Instrumental treatment of students and staff, use of human resource management and control systems taken from business, which results in control over the organization and content of teaching, not only over finances (Giroux and Myrsiades, 2001);
- Delivering vocational training programs without simultaneously teaching critical thinking skills (Perriton and Reynolds, 2004).

Human capital management in higher education institutions differs from people management in other organizations, if only by the activity's objectives. Businesses are guided by economics: Competition, profit, and market share, so employees are the entities tasked with producing economic goods. However, universities strive to create social goods—that is, science and education; the logic of higher values is balanced here with economic thinking. Employees are part of the systems that create higher education, science, and cooperation with the environment. Universities fit into the stakeholder rather than the shareholder model that characterizes companies. The choice of model impacts human capital management; external and internal stakeholders contribute to decision-making, including personnel decisions. Staff, students, administration, and often external stakeholders—all these links can influence critical decisions such as selecting managers for a term of office and implementing developments and projects. The enterprise is about being competitive, which is a sector requirement. Universities belong to a network ecosystem, as the creation of science is based on the continuous development of cooperative networks. Universities compete for good students and researchers, funding, recognition, and prestige, reflected in the structure, organizational culture, and strategies of a cooperative nature, which allow employees to network. In human capital management, it is also worth highlighting another difference between companies and public universities, which is the focus on internationalization and institutional autonomy (Kristensen, 2016; van der Wende, 2014).

The threads of economics, organization and management, psychology, and sociology meet in human resources management. The scope of the discipline is formed by the personnel function in an organization, i.e., the activities undertaken by employees and managers in the pursuit of personnel development. Therefore, the area of the personnel function in universities can also be approached from a more general social science perspective or a detailed, systematic, and instrumental insight into human capital management. Cognitive psychology, behavioral economics, and sociology provide theories to explain people's organizational behavior. The motivations, perceptions, interpretations, and therefore actions of university employees will differ only slightly from the behavior of people in other organizations. However, besides pursuing achievements, respect, and valuable social relations, scientific prestige, cognitive curiosity, and willingness to transfer knowledge will be significant motivators in universities. From the perspective of the instrumental discourse of human resources management, it is possible to indicate the possibility of adapting and using at least some of the methods initially developed for business organizations.

13 Marketing in higher education

13.1 Ambivalence of academic marketing

The approach to marketing in higher education is ambivalent and multi-dimensional (Hemsley-Brown and Oplatka, 2006; Hawkins and Frohoff, 2010). First, marketing activity derives from business logic, where commercial, market-driven organizations promote products and services in a competitive environment. This way of thinking is far from the academic tradition, which understands scientific and teaching activity as a mission, and whose rationality is based on social responsibility. Therefore, marketing activity is sometimes treated in the academic world as inconsistent with the university and professor ethos and sometimes even morally "suspicious" (Gibbs and Murphy, 2009). The development of social marketing, referring to non-commercial activities, has opened up opportunities for a more comprehensive story of communication and marketing activities in universities, making them part of the theoretical and practical discourse of management in higher education (Krachenberg, 1972). The rapid growth of non-public HEIs has reinforced this trend, mainly private, for-profit HEIs. They use increasingly sophisticated concepts, methods, and tools for promotion, image building, and branding. Marketing activities have become crucial for attracting students and gaining a competitive advantage in the market (Litten, 1980). Thus, it is possible to speak of a tension between a traditional approach, which focuses on developing the reputation of the university solely based on academic prestige, culture, and ethos, and an entrepreneurial approach focused on market competition and involved many marketing activities using branding, promotion, and PR.

Marketing of HEIs is multidimensional as it involves: Different spheres of activity and diverse stakeholder groups and uses many areas, concepts, methods, and marketing tools (Canterbury, 2000; Nicolescu, 2009; Filip, 2012). The multitude of aspects of marketing in higher education stems from the complexity of activities carried out by universities (Brooker and Noble, 1985; Hayes, 2007). The competition for prestige in the scientific and didactic sphere favors the implementation of concepts, methods, and tools for building the university's image. The need to attract students and

DOI: 10.4324/9781003366409-19

talents strengthens the value of practical promotional and communication activities (Nadiri, 2006). In this context, there is a radical increase in the importance of social media and online communication in general (Constantinides and Zinck Stagno, 2011). The drive to collaborate with the community, attract sponsors, and implement partnerships with businesses leads to the development of Public Relations. Increasing competitive pressure focuses on employee loyalty through applying the employer brand concept. The trend toward a digital university shows universities using IT-based marketing tools such as customer relationship management (CRM) systems, deanery, enrollment systems (part of *student information system* [SIS]), and project management software. Also, the growing internation-alization of the higher education sector favors an orientation toward recruitment development and international promotion (Clark, Fine, and Scheuer, 2017). These are just a few trends that illustrate and justify the reasons for the growing importance of marketing in universities in recent decades. It is worth looking at what theories, concepts, methods, and marketing management tools are finding broader application in the higher education sector. This growth is exemplified by the increase in university marketing applications and the development of theories, academics, and practitioners specializing in these activities. Examples include the prolifer-ation of marketing departments, the emergence of consultancies and IT solutions focused on university promotion, the creation of a community of professional university marketers, and the development of research and journals such as the *Journal of Marketing for Higher Education*.

13.2 Concepts of university marketing activities

Pointing out the most important objectives of the marketing activity of an HEI, one should notice its relationship with the mission. Subordinating the marketing strategy to the educational institution's mission specificity translates into focusing on various areas of marketing. The most developed marketing activities are undertaken by private universities operating for profit. They often treat teaching activities as a market product, which requires promotion and is positioned in terms of price and sold on the market to customers. Of course, it is a service that requires appropriate quality, connected with the market segment in which the university operates. Shaping the university's offer is product management, where the following must be considered: Quality, competition, costs, competence, reputation, and image of the university. Product portfolio management is therefore not a purely market-driven process. In many countries, the development of curricula, especially in selected fields of study (e.g., med-icine, technology, architecture), also requires the approval of central authorities, professional associations, or accreditation bodies. Promoting educational services involves advertising and various forms of marketing communication to reach the target group (student candidates) and the influence group (parents of potential students). Nowadays, the Internet and social media are the most important in promotion, and this tendency will increase with the development of the "digital university" formation. Pricing policy in higher education is determined by the type of university, the area of activity, and the education system. It is worth noting that universities operate according to the *matching markets* model (Demange and Gale, 1985), which means that the condition for using an educational service is not, even in the case of paid studies, only to pay for it. First, the entry selection system implies that a university candidate not only has to want to enter education but also that they have to meet the qualifying criteria (exams, grades, points etc.). The process of "acquiring" an educational service is stretched over time, takes several years, and is conditioned by the requirements of students. So, in education, the supply-demand curve does not work. "Ivy League" universities are limiting access and raising enrollment criteria for an elite group of candidates, even if demand for their services is growing. From the classic 4Ps in marketing-mix, the distribution (*placement*) also changes and takes specific forms. In the case of domestic students, it is usually their direct contact with the higher education institution, while applicants from abroad may also be recruited through intermediaries (agents). In the case of public HEIs, marketing activities usually take forms less oriented toward direct sales and more toward marketing communication. It serves the purpose of building the university's image, reputation, and prestige, which are reflected in: The profile of candidates for studies and rankings. Effective improvement of the quality of education, combined with efficient marketing communication, should upgrade the image based on reputation and increase brand awareness (recognition of the university name). It is worth noting that marketing is a practical perspective created in commercial and market sectors. The direction of higher education development for almost a century has been the gradual marketization of higher education. Therefore, marketing in higher education and other non-commercial areas (social marketing, political marketing) can serve practical, pragmatic concepts. However, the logic of *matching markets* and the non-commercial product means that transactional references to business cannot be applied indiscriminately. In other words, higher education marketing has its specificity, related not only to the type of educational service but also to the characteristics of the university and the higher education system. Thus, among the areas of marketing activities of higher education institutions, we can indicate the following:

- Building image, reputation, and prestige;
- Marketing communication with internal (Cook and Zallocco, 1983) and external stakeholders;
- Creating the university's marketing mix (shaping and promoting products, setting prices and sales channels);

- National and international student recruitment (Tang, 2011; Kalimullin and Dobrotvorskaya, 2016; Wu and Naidoo, 2016);
- Conducting marketing research and market analysis;
- University social responsibility.

The development of contemporary marketing in higher education is connected with concepts and methods that initially appeared in business activities. They are applied to selected aspects of university management. The marketing methods used in the higher education sector include the following:

- Public Relations;
- University brand management;
- Relationship marketing (Helgesen, 2008);
- Employer branding.

13.3 University brand

A university's reputation is often built through marketing, communication, and those connected with shaping an internal brand (*employer branding*). Terms such as image or brand are close to reputation and associated with shaping identity and organizational culture (Aula and Tienari, 2011). The functioning of organizations in these scopes is undergoing profound modifications to build a new formation of the digital university. The area of the brand, which is essential for various aspects of the organization, is usually analyzed on the grounds of marketing.

Managing the university brand proves to be strategic in various respects. A university's national and international recognition among students and other external stakeholders depends on its brand. The university's name shapes its image, giving a message that reflects the university's identity. The cultural character of the university brand is connected with providing uniqueness to the organization and employees and shaping the university's image externally. The brand is a kind of denotation of a higher education institution's culture. For example, the Jagiellonian University supports its organizational identity on its cultural role and tradition, which is evident in its name derived from its founders' royal dynasty. The name Université Grenoble Alpes, on the other hand, was created to ensure international recognition and openness. The university was formed by merging three universities: University Joseph Fourier, Université Stendhal, and University Pierre Mendès-France. The new brand is based on the globally recognized symbol of the Grenoble region, the Alps. The name Aalto University originates in the name of the famous Finnish architect Alvaro Aalto, a Helsinki University of Technology graduate who designed the university's campus.

A brand, as defined by the American Marketing Association (AMA), is a mark, name, symbol, term, design, or a combination thereof that enables the seller's goods or services (or a group of them) to be identified and distinguished from those of competitors (AMA, 2017). In the literature on the subject, one can find another approach to the brand, which identifies it with the concept of a trademark (Crass, Czarnitzki, and Toole, 2019). The idea of a brand is sometimes associated with a product (Yi and Oh, 2021). According to this notion, the brand buyer analyses three different planes of the product: Basic, functional, and enriched. The core need is the basic benefit that the service buyer receives. For example, the product in a university is the higher education, the diploma documenting it, and the competencies. On the functional plane, the functions of the product are analyzed in terms of how it satisfies the requirements of use. The available product is the market value of education, which is associated with helpful knowledge and competencies. The enriched plane presents those features that stand out from other services. Enriched products are features that distinguish universities, their programs, diplomas, and scientific achievements from other universities fulfilling the needs of building social networks of graduates (Schofer, Ramirez, and Meyer, 2021).

Students choosing a university are increasingly suggesting brand value and the benefits of a university degree. To verify the brand value, the Aaker model may be helpful. According to this approach, brand value is determined by five basic elements: Brand associations, brand awareness, perceived value, loyalty, and other assets associated with the brand. Regarding brand associations, we mean associations related to the brand compared to other brands (Aaker, 1997). The university's relationships with students, staff, alums, and external stakeholders all contribute to strengthening the university's brand. In terms of brand awareness, brand recognition is analyzed. The greater the number of positive associations associated with a brand, the stronger its position (brand image). This includes characteristics such as favorable study conditions, recognition of the diploma in the labor market, qualified staff, and high quality of education (but it could also be a well-known sports team). In the case of perceived brand value, the perception of the university as an institution offering products and services of adequate quality is analyzed. In most cases, the recognition, brand image, and perceived quality of education determine the choice of university. Loyalty is made visible in the attachment to the university by brands aimed at the public, staff, and students, which build a bond with the university. HEIs benefit from loyalty programs for students and alums. Other brand assets are, in other words, the brand-added features (accreditations, certificates, signed cooperation agreements). They reinforce the name, logo, and brand.

Brand positioning depends on how consumers perceive the brand's quality, value, price, advantages, and disadvantages (Dibb and Simkin, 1993; Ries and Trout, 1993). Manufacturers of high-quality products—also in the higher education sector—increasingly have elements that distinguish their product from international brands, the number of which continues to grow (Agrawal, 2011). Universities strive to obtain international accreditation abroad or in the sector and to have international partners to offer *double, dual,* or *joint degrees* to differentiate themselves from other universities in the market (Hogan and Lucke, 2006). The universities verify the satisfaction of students/ graduates with the quality or conditions of education through quantitative (e.g., questionnaires) and qualitative (e.g., in-depth interviews) methods. The results of the surveys are used not only to assess the university management methods but also the effectiveness of marketing activities undertaken by dedicated units.

The brand of a university has a direct bearing on the market value of the diplomas obtained there. The literature on the subject uses various brand terms that can be applied to the HEI. The literature on the subject also suggests that a brand is just a sign: Commercial, utilitarian, of a socio-cultural nature, which is a reflection of the symbolic and imagined value of the product (Jian, Zhou, and Zhou, 2019).

Four key brand strategies can be identified in management:

- Individual brand strategies—typical for products that have separate brands (rare in HE);
- Brand family strategies—all the products of the organization exist in the market under one brand (typical for HE);
- Common brands—similar product groups are present on the market under a single brand (rare in HE);
- Mixed strategies, dual branding involve combining a brand and an organization name (use in HE, university name plus name of the program).

Four types of brand development strategies can also be distinguished: Brand expansion strategy, market position exploitation and withdrawal strategy, and a selective brand development strategy. Expansion and exploitation are common for HEIs.

Five key objectives related to brand strategy are given as follows (Iyer et al., 2019):

1   Creating the conditions for implementing a specific pricing policy (e.g., high tuition fees);
2   Using the brand as a means of communication (e.g., name of HEIs as prestige vehicle);
3   Stimulating demand and sales (e.g., high demand for a university degree);
4   Using the brand to differentiate the impact on the market through the product (e.g., new programs);
5   Creating trust in the brand (e.g., high reputation of university).

The analysis of the higher education sector leads to the conclusion that the competitiveness of HEIs is reflected and connected with the strength and, therefore, the image and awareness of the brand (Sulkowski, Seliga, and Wozniak, 2019). The university brand is frequently visible in the mission and development strategy. Universities increasingly offer flagship products, shaping the image of individuals or the university itself. Brand expansion is also often used to develop communication, trust, and differentiation.

13.4 Marketing communication in universities

The marketing activities of universities are not only brand management but also public relations, marketing communications, and employer branding, which consist of many marketing concepts and areas. Universities increasingly use marketing concepts and tools to build their brand image and attract customers. Marketing activities aim not only at promoting the educational offer but also at relational activities that shape the university's idea in its operation areas. Special units and positions are established in universities dealing with marketing activities, which often do not have marketing in their name. These are, for example, departments of communication, promotion of studies, and positions of press spokespeople. Not infrequently, universities use the concept of relationship marketing, adapted from other sectors, which emerged as a result of analyses of the issue of contact and communication with the customer, combined with a partnership approach and strategic orientation. The literature shows that the criticism of classical marketing-mix and transaction marketing has contributed to the development of relationship marketing. Nowadays, different approaches to the relational current in marketing can be discerned. The concept undergoes modifications as it has to respond to trends in marketing communication. Table 13.1 illustrates the essential definitions of the relationship marketing concept and links them to the higher education sector.

The implementation of relationship marketing concepts in higher education is not without its difficulties. In the area of theory, one notices a focus on the operational and tool side of the idea, while few generalizing theoretical models can be applied in higher education. Among the problems of the practical sphere, organizational barriers to the implementation of changes in the field of marketing at the university can be pointed out, as well as the fact that academic managers and university employees are unfamiliar with relationship marketing methods and techniques. It turns out to be necessary to overcome stereotypes persisting in communication between students and university employees and bureaucratic restrictions. Deficiencies in the customer service system are also a problem, which is associated with the use of traditional approaches to the system.

Table 13.1 Relationship marketing in universities

Researcher(s)	Definition	Applied to higher education
Ph. Kotler	Forming profitable and long-lasting relationships with necessary parties (customers, suppliers, distributors) to maintain the company and generate income.	The key stakeholders involved in relations are staff, students, administration, employers, local government, and central government.
L. Berry	Building, maintaining And enriching customer relationships. Convincing a new customer is only the first step in the marketing process.	Sustaining the relationship and participation of the university's key stakeholders. E.g., the student is not recruited; they are the subject of complex communication, enrollment, and educational processes.
M. Armstrong	The concept adds quality to the traditional marketing mix.	A fundamental variable in the functioning of a university is the quality of education and research.
Ch. Grönroos	Building, maintaining, and enriching the relationship with the client and its partners aim to achieve both parties' goals through exchange and the fulfillment of promises.	The formation of stakeholder relations is based on the assumption of trade-offs aimed at achieving the goals of the university and the stakeholder groups.
R.M. Morgan, S.D. Hunt	Any marketing activity designed to establish, maintain and deepen a mutually beneficial exchange.	The university provides a platform for beneficial exchange between stakeholders.
P. Zeller	Relationship marketing has three features: It no longer sees marketing as an effort to acquire a buyer but directs attention to the existing customer and seeks to improve its service. It captures the market game as a relationship—within a network of interrelationships.	The marketing approach to university activities consider the links between universities, the improvement of scientific and educational activities, and the abandonment of purely pro-transactional activities.
T. Cram	The consistent application of updated customer knowledge to the design of a product or service is then communicated interactively. It is about creating and continuing a mutually beneficial relationship.	The dynamic change of educational services, which will include individualization and virtualization, involves redesigning the product and teaching and communication methods to best achieve the intended educational outcomes.

Source: Own work based on Leonard, 1983; Grönroos, 1990; Copulsky and Wolf, 1990; Armstrong, 1993; Cram, 1994; Morgan and Hunt, 1994; Kotler, 2005; Zeller, 2006.

13.5 Internal marketing and social responsibility of the university

The development of the concept of relationship marketing in universities is connected with the recognition of the role of research and teaching and administrative staff in the process of educational service delivery. This is how the idea of internal marketing is implemented. The literature emphasizes the role of employees in the activities of companies, paying attention to their knowledge of the activities of the company and the sector in which it operates (Sekerin et al., 2018).

Park and Tran think internal marketing flows from believing that service companies should hire the best employees to sell services to buyers and operate effectively (Park and Tran, 2018). The origins of internal marketing were in the 1980s (Berry, 1981) when the concept of relationship marketing also developed. It can also be seen that internal marketing is a tool that consists of all the company's activities, directed to the employees who contact customers and support them to ensure the highest possible level of customer service (Sadchenko et al., 2020).

Marketing activities of HEIs often emphasize the relationship between society and business in the context of social responsibility, modeled on business sectors and *corporate social responsibility* (CSR). CSR is a response to society's expectations in the area of organizations' commitment, the reasons for which lie in (Arena, Azzone, and Mapelli, 2018): Environmental degradation and climate change, the spread and massification of education, the development of the network society, the processes of globalization of the economy, threats to democracy and civil society, the growing awareness of consumers and the formation of consumer organizations, as well as the implementation by a business of sophisticated marketing activities toward customers.

There is also a shift in the understanding of the role of CSR among university managers. Universities are learning that competitive advantage can be built through a positive image. The literature on the subject emphasizes that running a company based on the CSR concept ensures its credibility and thus fosters cooperation with stakeholders. Similarly, emphasizing the social responsibility of universities in communication processes contributes to image enhancement.

Employer branding is also visible in the marketing activities of universities. The literature indicates two groups of activities within this concept - external and internal- supported by new technologies. In shaping their image, universities use recruitment advertisements, internet search engines, and social media (Sulkowski, 2017, pp. 236–245). Employer branding activities in HEIs result in a better reputation and consequently favor the attraction of quality staff and students.

14 The accountability of universities

14.1 The concept of accountability

Accountability in public institutions is about sustained responsibility, clarity, transparency, and efficiency. The prerequisite is implementing an accountability concept, methodology, and tools and using a defined, practical accounting and reporting system. The word itself is the combination of "accounting" with "ability" or even "responsibility." The term has become very popular in the social sciences, especially in the public sector, especially concerning higher education, but also in the health sector. Melvin Dubnick's discursive analysis argues that the meaning of "accountability" is ambiguous and entangled in valuation. Dubnick brought together different types of narratives, definitions, the work of other scholars, and the contexts they emphasize. On this basis, he argued that accountability represents a commitment to increased efficiency, more effective control, and more significant equity or democratization of organizations (Dubnick, 2012). It is a general concept exploited in many areas of public management by many researchers (their names are in this subchapter in brackets). The discourse here focuses on motivating, evaluating, and rewarding. It is used for this purpose:

- Standards (David Kassel);
- Performance management (Melvin Dubnick);
- TQM (handled by Mark Zbaracki);
- Performance measurement (Harry Hatry).

Accountability understood as solutions, standards, or measures influencing organizational behavior, is supposed to contribute to higher efficiency and effectiveness in university activities. Accountability as methods and concepts serves to predict and guide actions and operations in an institution, and allows for an increased degree of control. The discourse focuses on standardization, repeatability, and measurement. The following solutions are reached here:

- Reporting (Ciaran Connolly, Noel Hyndman, Stuart Cooper, and David Owen);

DOI: 10.4324/9781003366409-20

- Auditing (Robert Schwarz, Raanan Sulitzeanu-Kenan, Michael Power, Robert Ashton);
- Administrative control (Herbert Kaufman);
- Rule-making (Louis Kaplow);
- Formalization of operations and bureaucratization (James Baron, Ralph Hummel, John Markoff, Shmuel N. Eisenstadt, Diane Burton, Michael Hannan).

To increase the sense of fairness and to use better internal regulation, accountability is used, understood as formal procedures and rules (e.g., in the form of bylaws, codes, guides) to prevent the effects of unwanted organizational behavior. The discourse of accountability is about governance but also internal lawmaking. Principles can help create such internal regulations:

- Rule-making and accountability (Cornelius Kerwin);
- Formalization of internal regulations (Arthur Stinchcombe);
- Reinforcing and motivating correct actions (David Malone);
- Truth and settling conflict situations (Alfred Allan, Marietjie Allan, Jeremy Sarkin);
- Criminalization of infringing activities (Marcel Dekker).

Increased democratization, or at least wider participation in decision-making, is possible if we take transparent solutions and actions that limit the omnipotence of power through social accountability, whistleblower activity, fostering sensitivity, and the willingness of those in power to give public explanations. The discourse focuses on institutionalization with:

- Self-determined state (Larry Diamond and Marc Plattner, Andreas Schedler);
- Horizontal responsibility (Guillermo O'Donnell);
- Accountability forum (Mark Bovens);
- Constitution-making (Jürgen Habermas).

In many countries, public universities spend state funds, and other HEIs combine public and private funding streams. This raises the need for transparency in university accounts (this is one of the goals of *accountability*). The public should have access to knowledge about funding in universities; therefore, institutions and mechanisms are being created to enable such insight and accountability. Numerous state and institutional regulations are also being prepared, specifying the assessment of the quality of education, scientific activity, and teaching staff. An increasing number of states require universities to be accredited and to report on the results and assess whether the university funds were spent effectively and appropriately. This may be interpreted as actions serving the efficiency and transparency of universities, but on the other hand, they may limit universities' autonomy (Bogue and Hall, 2003, pp. 224–228).

14.2 University accounting

There is a gradual increase in the accounting complexity of higher education systems, which results from the multiplicity of funding sources, the numerous and diverse activities of universities, and the marketization of the higher education sector (Sulkowski, 2016b). Research shows that the complexity of accounting and reporting systems is increasing in public and non-public universities worldwide. This is due to growing economic pressures and, in the case of the public sector, the advent of the *new public management* trend. Financial strategies are becoming similar to business strategies, using income from fee-based education, teaching international students, state and international funding for research, and funds from cooperation with business and implementation (Parker, 2012). Arthur M. Hauptman sees that market strategies, performance-related financing, regulatory performance measures, and, additionally, auditing and monitoring (Hauptman, 2006) are manifestations of the growing orientation toward accountability.

The Gallup Institute in the United States surveyed bursars of American universities (*Chief Financial Officers*) in 2015. Their findings demonstrate the increasing complexity of financial analytics and accounting in management. The controlling systems of US HEIs enable the control of costs, revenues, and debt, which is essential in the face of the financial crisis that periodically occurs in the sector. Although as many as 81% that they believe the schools they work for are not threatened with liquidation. At the same time, 56% of the respondents confirm the media information on the financial crisis that the higher education sector is experiencing, and 19% see the possibility of liquidation. The transparency indicators of the surveyed sample are high, as 57% of the respondents admit that the HEIs publish financial data concerning their condition (35% non-public and 74% public). Over 7% of HEIs use economic indicators to assess the institution's condition, the state of debt, cost, and control. Of the respondents, 45% admitted to having made profound budget changes in the last four years (while 16% plan to do so). Due to economic pressures, the respondents aim to increase revenues by increasing recruitment (82%), taking advantage of new profitable programs (70%), reducing the cost of tenure (14%), obliging professors to teach more, or increasing the teaching load of the staff (19%). It is worth mentioning that according to 61% of the bursars surveyed, restructuring the university's costs is crucial. Yet, the financial challenges involved are understood by senior administration and board members (79%) and to a much lesser extent by research and teaching staff (32%) (Jaschik and Lederman, 2015). University financial management in the United States is similar to other business sectors. It is a professional activity managed by specialized financial administration staff using an extensive controlling system based on analytical indicators. The financial aspect of university governance mostly remains outside the college system; consequently, academic staff is unlikely to influence financial decision-making. University governance systems worldwide are evolving toward complex and professionalized accounting using business models (Tomkins and Green, 1988).

Peter Ling, the author of a comparative study of the higher education system in Australia and the UK, highlighted the disjuncture between the aspirations for university autonomy and the issue of accountability. Using an empirical illustration, Ling identified several systemic actions—based on the logic of new public management—that support university accountability. It becomes possible to establish national institutions that support, evaluate and disseminate good practices or innovations in process improvement but also control and accredit higher education.

Financial mechanisms are also used to promote effective practice—a system of grants awarded for quality and improvement. Another proposal is a system of training, certification, development, evaluation, and rewarding of university teachers for the quality of education (Ling, 2005). Ling finds it paradoxical that the greater importance of accountability clashes with less funding for universities from public funds. This trend seems to repeat itself in other sectors that have public financing. Problems of accountability include the development of adequate performance measures, the influence of politicians on the learning process, the rise of financial responsibility pressures in public opinion, and the power of stakeholder groups on the management mechanisms and costs of implemented changes.

Maintaining a balance between efficiency and transparency of higher education funding and its autonomy is a fundamental problem for the management and development of accountability systems. It is experienced not only by developed countries (mentioned the United States, UK, and Australia) but also by developing countries. It usually concerns the dominance of the state in the system and a large share of non-public universities. In China, for example, extensive state control, little university autonomy, and increasing complexity of external reporting systems. In India, universities are subject to central and regional management and reporting systems—different universities have varying degrees of autonomy and reporting requirements (Gandhi, 2013). The focus on using controlling methods to increase efficiency also applies to the quality of education, research, and fulfillment of social mission (Sandu et al., 2014).

Accountability systems provide oversight of HEIs, with the help of institutions that co-finance HEIs (state, local government, third sector organizations). They are also used for controlling, i.e., strategic and operational management of the institution. Opinions differ, however, on the effectiveness of these systems and the funding policies underpinning performance measurement. Researchers seem to demonstrate the effectiveness of the university's accountability systems while emphasizing the need for their continuous improvement (King, 2000; Zumeta, 2011). However, there is no shortage of researchers questioning the lack and benefits of accountability in higher education. Its opposing sides include bureaucratization and destruction of the culture of trust (Coy, Fischer, and Gordon, 2001; Craig and Amernic, 2002). Thomas Rabovski, using data from the *Postsecondary Education Data System,* concludes that accountability has little impact on the restructuring of higher education finances and equally little use in management (Rabovsky, 2012). Onora O'Neill has asked questions about the downsides of accountability, highlighting the declining public trust in universities and academics (O'Neill, 2005). According to O'Neill, accountability systems should not determine how a university organizes its teaching and research activities (O'Neill, 2013). This activity has many unquantifiable aspects, and only apparent or marginal effects can be assessed. For example, it isn't easy in the accountability system to appreciate scientific successes that require many years of teamwork. The costs of accountability systems in terms of staff time commitment and bureaucratization of university activities may prove too high and disproportionate to the benefits (Strathern, 2000).

In summary, university performance accounting systems for supervision and effective management are used to collect and process information for strategic purposes. The accountability of universities formalizes and bureaucratizes their activities through the use of performance measures (Carter, 1989).

However, these systems are not without limitations. Their implementation in higher education is costly and labor-intensive (Sinclair, 1995). In academic activities, they imply replacing a culture of trust with a culture of control, from which staff morale, commitment, and identification with the university often suffer (Currie and Newson, 1998). Strong accountability is another way of saying standardized and instrumental oversight, which can counter the concept of creative academic work and stifle innovation (Murphy, 2009). Accountability systems can provide apparent performance measures and hide the more valuable aspects of the university and its staff (Savoie, 1994).

14.3 Accountability and professionalization of management of public universities

The concepts of accountability emerge from the New Public Management (NPM) stream and concern: Control of public expenditure, transparency, effectiveness, and efficiency of public universities. Accountability as an idea and a methodology stems from the NPM because it is based on making public organizations accountable in the same way as business sectors. Accountability involved the creation of objective and measurable criteria for implementing public policies, allowing for the evaluation of university activities and, in effect, leading to the basing of funding on quantitative and qualitative management objectives (key performance indicators). The NPM was inspired by economic theories of public choice, transaction costs, and agency theory, which created concepts of state administration reforms based on competitiveness, transparency, and motivating employees through an incentive system. The idea of NPM also drew from managerialism based on business management techniques, the logic of managerial action taking precedence over bureaucratic-administrative solutions. However, in the case of public university operations, the accountability system does not reflect purely administrative solutions, as it operates within a stakeholder rather than a shareholder model. Thus, accountability in public universities is accompanied by a decision-making model using networks of influence groups that interfere in decision-making, often disrupting the logic of management by objectives (economic, scientific, teaching). As a result, to a much greater extent than in business organizations, accountability is also a political process based on the game of influence in public universities.

The accountability of HEIs can be seen as part of the professionalization of management growing out of the logic of applying managerial concepts and methods to the public HE sector. The professionalization of university management is taking place in many countries due to the DT and transition of the sector. Its manifestations include the development of management concepts in public and private universities, the implementation of theories and methods of strategic and operational management in universities, and the strengthening of managerial professions and functions in higher education. The concepts of NPM popularized business management methods in the public sector, and the educational sector indicated good practices in managing universities. However, management's professionalization can be considered contradictory to traditional academic thinking. As evidenced by their recent market expansion, private, profit-oriented universities often cling to inspiration from the business sector. We experience changes in university management by observing the administrative structures of universities, legal regulations of their functioning, missions, and strategies, and values of universities, as well as changes in academic ethos. These modifications shed new light on the previous view of university governance and its autonomy. The changes in this area are a consequence of the transformation in the university environment, especially in the society where there have been changes in the hierarchy of values, standards, customs, or even life priorities.

14.4 Measuring the performance of universities

Recent years have brought with them the popularity of accountability systems based on performance indicators in university funding, scientific activity, education quality, and research commercialization (Darling-Hammond and Snyder, 2015). Attaching importance to reporting and controlling are international trends in education. Adapted business models are used to account for finances and manage the quality of teaching and research achievements and other processes in higher education (Welsh and

Dey, 2002). The basis for effective university management seems to be proper accountability systems, which require appropriate performance indicators. According to Serge Cuenin, performance indicators are a mathematical formula providing a numerical value underlying the assessment or measurement of the system's effectiveness (Cuenin, 1987). The changing value of an indicator is information about a system operating more or less efficiently. Filip Dochy and Mien Segers are the authors of three postulates of an adequately formulated performance indicator:

- It must be related to the function of the organization concerned;
- It is used to assess only a selected area of the institution's functioning; therefore, the whole group of indicators must be interpreted;
- It provides an appropriate operationalization to measure and analyze the performance of a particular aspect of the organization (Dochy and Segers, 1990).

The Dictionary of Educational Quality and Accreditation provides a different definition and typology of performance indicators. Indicators are operational variables that refer to specific, empirically measurable characteristics of a higher education institution or its programs. These provide information to establish that a set standard has been met. Performance indicators are a set of statistical parameters that measure the extent to which a HEI (or its program) is completing a set standard (Vlăsceanu, Grünberg, and Pârlea, 2004, pp. 59–62). A simple indicator takes the form of a number and provides a "simplified, relatively objective measure" (Vlăsceanu, Grünberg, and Pârlea, 2004, pp. 59–62). This would be, for example, the number of applicants for a place at the university. Performance indicators are used to track trends and compare HEIs, making it easier to identify areas for improvement. Indicators help develop quality standards and procedures for managing the quality of education (operationalization). It is necessary to differentiate between an indicator and a measure. The latter is only a numerical value reflecting a particular aspect of efficiency, which must be revalidated depending on the scale or tool used. The standard assumes an acceptable level of efficiency, given in the figures. In addition to budget-related economic indicators, we distinguish efficiency indicators, which verify the degree to which the objectives set have been achieved, and performance indicators, which help to calculate the productivity of inputs (per unit).

Another distinction makes it possible to distinguish the indicators that make up the CIPO model:

- *Context*—which refers to the environment of the university or program related to social, economic, political, etc. aspects,
- *Input*—equal to the resources held by universities,
- *Process*—meaning how the university's resources are used to achieve its goals,

- *Output*—related to the effects and scientific achievements of the higher education institution.

The indicators used are, for example, points awarded for publishing articles or scientific monographs, the ratio of the number of university lecturers to the number of students, finances spent per student, employee or organizational unit, and scientific grants (Cave, Kogan, and Hanney, 1990).

Such a set of performance indicators will make it possible not only to look at the distribution of changes over time but also to make comparisons between organizations. It can therefore be an effective method of control. However, the development of indicators is a challenge, influenced by the diversity of educational institutions and not easy access to information. It is also accessible to misuse indicators (Ball and Wilkinson, 1994). A considerable role is played here by the developing information and communication systems and the possibility of using networks and external databases containing mass data (so-called *big data*). In perspective, the digital university will have a very sophisticated data processing system for accountability purposes in all aspects of university management.

The neoliberal changes moving toward university accountability in England in the 1980s were provoked by the central government (DES, 1985; Linke et al., 1991). A group called the Jarratt Commission was then set up to produce a report to drive change. In the information, there was a recommendation for universities to use performance indicators (Jarrat et al., 1985). The United States uses a number of them, the most common being the assessment of the quality of education, return on investment in education, degree of response to the labor market demand, a measure of the value added by schooling (i.e., student output relative to the input) (Reindl and Reyna, 2011, p. 7). The list of performance indicators for universities in the UK includes as many as 39 items, including the cost of teaching students, hiring staff, equipping staff, spending on administration, library, repairs, buildings, the percentage of students on a particular degree program relative to all, the ratio of students to staff, employment of graduates six months after leaving education, etc. (Elton, 1987; Johnes and Taylor, 1989; Ball and Wilkinson, 1994).

One of the most critical challenges of university accountability is the measurement of intellectual capital. Universities, being knowledge-oriented organizations, create, transform, and disseminate knowledge. This happens as part of their scholarly activities, as well as their teaching and implementation of their third mission. Accountability-based management should therefore seek to find methods to measure the university's intellectual capital on which the system of management by objectives, motivation, and funding will be based (Ramírez, Tejada, and Manzaneque, 2016).

In summary, the development of the accountability of universities is an ongoing trend and applies to all aspects of their activities. The biggest challenge is accounting for universities' intellectual capital, the concepts used in universities for two decades. The development of digital university formation in the 21st century leads toward extensive, analytical, and comprehensive university accountability systems that will serve as a basis for decision-making. Such systems founded on data management will form university information and communication ecosystems that draw and process information from within the organization and compare it with external data.

Conclusions

The monograph presents an integrated and multilevel view of university management, which is seen as a universal process of managing an organizational system that is a coupling of strategy, structure, and corporate culture. It consists of governance, university management, and leadership, which are realized in different aspects of organizing. The diversity of forms of academic management includes various levels of activity, i.e., strategic and operational management and functional areas including, among others: marketing, logistics, finance and accounting, human capital, knowledge, and information management. On the other hand, the sectoral vision of university management refers to the particularistic aspects of organizing, which constitute the specificity of the activities of higher education institutions (HEIs). In the book, I focused on managing the three pillars of the university's mission, i.e., organizing scientific activities, organizing teaching activities, and cooperation with the nonacademic environment. The analyses conducted in this book can be synthesized as brief conclusions, each summarizing a chapter of the book.

1 Analyzing chronologically waves of university development, it is possible to identify—after the historical first wave—consecutive ones related to the development of a Humboldtian university (wave II) and an entrepreneurial university (wave III), as well as a new formation of a digital university emerging in the 21st century (wave IV). The future university is probably the digital university, characterized by several distinctive features. It is based on a network organization, combining data analytics with advanced controlling and accountability methods, allowing evidence-based and data-driven decision-making. This involves the development of strategies, structures, and organizational cultures that enable the formation of flexible, innovative organizations that quickly adapt to changes in a turbulent environment.

2 The higher education sector is characterized by longevity. The core values and missions of universities have lasted for centuries. However, it isn't easy to say, especially in the last few decades, that the activities of universities are not changing. On the contrary, there is a profound,

multidirectional transformation on a global and national scale that several enduring megatrends can describe. The message of this book is the change in the formation of universities in the digital direction, which seems to be one of the most important megatrends. Undoubtedly, there is also a shift toward a neoliberal university, oriented toward a logic of competitive and market-oriented action, of course taking into account the diversification of strategic objectives. Strategic diversification, stratification, and specialization of the roles of HEIs and academics is another universal trend. Internationalization processes are continuously deepening in all aspects of the university's mission. Competition, the spread of higher education, and the development of digital transformation and management methods are transforming the university's social and cultural role from a "temple of knowledge and culture" to a "factory and network of intangible goods." The consequence is the managerialism and corporatization of academic life, with all its positive and negative effects, if only in the form of increased productivity and, at the same time, the atrophy of the culture of the free academic profession. This is accompanied by the development of industrial science and the privatization, commercialization, and professionalization of education and management.

3 Digital transformation, the most critical social, economic, and cultural trend in recent decades, also leads to a permanent organizational change in the higher education sector. Digital universities will develop the professionalization of management through the application of increasingly sophisticated organizational methods using network and digital orientation. This will be done through implementing communication and creating network communities, developing digital management methods based on the Internet of Things, crowdsourcing, big data processing, and AI. A threat may be the dehumanization of science and academic activity in general, which—based on instrumental management and data processing that is more and more perfect and less comprehensible to humans—may lose the values of striving to improve humanity and reach the truth.

4 The management of a university should be considered from multiple perspectives, joining: governance and management with leadership. A pragmatic view of the management process makes it essential to combine different viewpoints, leading to a process of decision-making and organizing. This can be served by an integrated view of the university management process, in which the level of supervision is combined with the management of the organizational system and the group of leadership and directing people. The synthesis of these three perspectives also translates into managing the triads: organizational subsystems (strategy, structure, and culture) and mission streams (learning, teaching, and cooperation with the environment). The challenge of managers at the whole organization level is precisely the harmonization of the various aspects of the university organization.

5 The leadership of the 21st-century university is moving in a networked direction, which is closely related to the universal digital transformation trend. It is increasingly based on combining social competence and transformational leadership with data- and network-based communication and organization. Digital leaders transform organizational strategies, structures, and values by engaging, improving, and organizing people's work in a rapidly changing technological, social, and cultural context.

6 The strategies of a university are closely linked to its mission and academic values. In a Humboldt-type university, the academic culture was the organization's core, encapsulating its mission and objectives. With the development of management science discourse and practice, strategic management concepts and methods took root in HEIs, reinforcing the entrepreneurial orientation (third-wave universities). The centrality of strategy in university management reflects a more general trend of moving from organizations based on values, culture, and academic ethos toward organizations of power exercising power through the increasingly professional use of concepts and methods of controlling and data analysis.

7 Academic cultures have constituted the continuity of universities for centuries. People who perceive themselves as part of the academic community identify values, norms, and patterns in learning, education, and cooperation with the environment. Academic cultures grow out of the utopia of freedom of learning and teaching, where autotelic values of truth and improving the world are supposed to create communities, engage and motivate people. However, universities, like any other organizations, are created by people. So they are not free from conflicts, power struggles, bureaucratic tendencies, and organizational pathologies. They are therefore increasingly subject to a process of supervision, control, and management that is the antithesis of academic freedom and autonomy. The danger of overextending controlling systems is to move toward cultures of control, leading to a dystopia of power and hindering freedom of thought and creativity. The instrumentalization of university activity also threatens the decline of critical values, leading to servility toward political or economic power.

8 An exemplification of the danger of the university's drift toward the dystopia of power may also be the development of organizational structures, which may favor surveillance and control of academic activity. The new formation of the digital university no longer uses only corporate methods of management but couples them with increasingly perfected data collection and analysis processes, which may threaten to move toward a Goffmanian total institution, which I metaphorically describe as a "digital panopticon." This danger can probably be avoided by leaving areas of creative freedom and academic autonomy in the realm of structure and power. This would be a search

for the "golden mean" between the development of control systems and the freedom of creators, teachers, students, and universities themselves.

9   The management of science would seem to be a challenging area. It concerns a complex, not very tangible, and creative activity, the effects of which we see years later. How to manage something so ephemeral and yet so meaningful as creativity? And yet developments, such as information networks, the digital transformation, the publishing and journal market, and academia, have made science management a competitive advantage. International indexing, impact measures, and scientometrics allow for a quick and cheap measurement of the value of the output created, or instead, only the measurement of the value of the publication of scientific output accepted by the scientific community in given disciplines. We are thus missing out on undervalued and unrecognized results that are not published in the relevant journal or publishing house. Yet, unconventional research results can be the most innovative. Founding science management systems on scientometrics and excellence rankings has several limitations, but this does not change the fact that it is a very fast-growing area of university management. It provides a quick and relatively straightforward measurement of scientific achievements, allowing multilevel comparisons of universities, countries, disciplines, or staff. This favors the development of controlling systems in science, leading not only to the measurement of results but also to basing on them the systems of evaluation and motivation of science employees and steering the science policy. Therefore, it is also worth drawing attention here to the danger of excessive scientific accountability, which may limit the creativity and independence of researchers.

10   The management of education has developed over several decades, focusing on the organization of the teaching process and the quality assurance of education. Measurement methods enabling the application of the controlling concept cover various aspects of didactic activity, such as analysis of data on education (grades, retention, sifting of students, didactic added value, and others), information from surveys of students and academic staff, data on employability and salaries of graduates, results of accreditations, and expert evaluations. In the development of didactics in the digital university, the foundation for improving education will be based on data, controlling, and using online didactics with digital educational resources and methods.

11   Third, mission management is developing dynamically in forming entrepreneurial HEIs. In the case of digital HEIs, it should grow on a large scale, but in forms and types of specialization depending on the strategy and type of the university. Progressive internationalization and the formation of cooperation networks between HEIs and the environment will probably increase the scope and field of this type of activity. If the growing trends in modern universities continue,

managing diversity and sustainability may become an increasingly important aspect of the activities of the fourth-wave universities.

12 Human capital management in a university is figuratively also a journey between the Scylla of creativity and the Charybdis of control. Academic staff is characterized by a relatively high degree of motivation based on autotelic values, i.e., the desire to learn the truth and change the world for the better. People management concepts and methods should reinforce these motivations, possibly adding others, but must not weaken the sense of mission and value from the activity performed. Therefore, material or career-related motivations can often play an additional rather than a critical role. Therefore, employee evaluation and motivation systems are needed in academic activities. Still, they should not be a simple translation of corporate strategies in which motivations play a fundamental role: financial, career-related, and professional development. Talent management is also beginning to play a vital role in university management. However, it should mainly be connected with attracting outstanding scientists, building authority and reputation of the academic center, and focusing less on short-term benefits and motivators.

13 Marketing has been underestimated for many decades by universities, particularly those operating in the public sector. With the development of entrepreneurial universities, their importance is growing due to the increased intensity of market competition. The digital university's communication and brand management forms are changing rapidly. The universities will learn the value of brand management and image building in the marketing sphere in the network. Digital universities will bet on network communication and image development, which will translate into a hierarchy of prestige and market value in the higher education sector, both on regional and global scales.

14 The finance and accounting in universities are moving toward an increase in accountability, typical to the management of the higher education sector in general. It is worth asking a question about the evaluation of this management model. Undoubtedly, the strength is the foundation of decisions on data and their analysis, which serves measurable objectives and economic rationality. The weakness of this approach is the move toward a culture of control, which can limit academic freedom and the cost of expanding the organization's control apparatus. A good solution for fourth-wave universities will probably be to balance accountability with the autonomy of universities and academics.

Bibliography

AACSB (2021). *AACSB international*. Available from: www.aacsb.edu [1 August 2021].

Aaker, J. L. (1997). Dimensions of brand personality. *Journal of Marketing Research*, 34(3), pp. 347–356.

AAUP: American Association of University Professors (2014). *AAUP Policies & Reports*. Available from: www.aaup.org/reports-publications/aaup-policies-reports [30 August 2014].

Abbu, H. et al. (2020). DIGITAL LEADERSHIP – character and competency differentiates digitally mature organizations. In: *2020 IEEE International Conference on Engineering, Technology and Innovation (ICE/ITMC)*. Piscataway: IEEE, pp. 1–9.

Abdolshad, M. et al. (2020). Codification and selection university management strategies using Blue Ocean approach (Case study: University of applied science and technology). *The Journal of Modern Thoughts in Education*, 14(1), pp. 45–61.

Abdulrahim, H., Mabrouk, F. (2020). COVID-19 and the digital transformation of Saudi higher education. *Asian Journal of Distance Education*, 15(1), pp. 291–306.

Abidin, M. (2020). Reinventing higher education bureaucracy through entrepreneurial values. *Universal Journal of Educational Research*, 8(12), pp. 6482–6490.

Aboramadan, M., Dahleez, K., Hamad, M. H. (2020). Servant leadership and academics outcomes in higher education: the role of job satisfaction. *International Journal of Organizational Analysis*, 29(3), pp. 562–584.

Adamik, A. (2016). The mechanism of building competitiveness through strategic partnering. *Management*, 20(1), pp. 292–310.

Adel, H. M., Zeinhom, G. A., Mahrous, A. A. (2018). Effective management of an internationalization strategy: a case study on Egyptian-British universities' partnerships. *International Journal of Technology Management & Sustainable Development*, 17(2), pp. 183–202.

Adner, R., Puranam, P., Zhu, F. (2019). What is different about digital strategy? From quantitative to qualitative change. *Strategy Science*, 4(4), pp. 253–261.

Adriansyah, G. et al. (2022). Strategic regulation and planning analysis of stratification in private colleges. *Corporate Governance*, (2), pp. 113–122.

Afshari, J., Moein, Z., Afshari, F., Sharifi-Rad, J., Balouchi, A., Afshari, A. (2017). A comparison of leadership styles with respect to biographical characteristics. *SA Journal of Human Resource Management*, 15(1), pp. 1–7.

Agarwal, P. (2011). Continuous SCRUM: agile management of SAAS products. In: *Proceedings of the 4th India Software Engineering Conference*. New York: Association for Computing Machinery, pp. 51–60.

AGB (2014). *Association of governing boards of universities and colleges*. Available from: agb. org [30 August 2014].

Aggarwal, R. (1989). Globalization of financial markets. *Foreign Trade Review*, 24(1), pp. 120–126.

Agrawal, J. et al. (2011). A cross-country study of signals of brand quality. *Journal of Product & Brand Management*, 20, pp. 333–342. DOI: 10.1108/10610421111157865

Ahlquist, J. (2014). Trending now – digital leadership education using social media and the social change model. *Journal of Leadership Studies*, 8(2), pp. 57–60.

Ahmady, S., Tatari, F., Hosseini, S. A. (2016). Human resource management models for recruitment of faculty members: a critical review. *Biosciences Biotechnology Research Asia*, 13(1), pp. 417–428.

Ahn, J., Choi, H., Oh, D. H. (2019). Leveraging bridging universities to access international knowledge: Korean universities' R&D internationalization. *Scientometrics*, 120(2), pp. 519–537.

Aitchison, C. et al. (2020). Tensions for educational developers in the digital university: developing the person, developing the product. *Higher Education Research & Development*, 39(2), pp. 171–184.

Ajayan, S., Balasubramanian, S. (2020). "New managerialism" in higher education: the case of United Arab Emirates. *International Journal of Comparative Education and Development*, 22(2), pp. 147–168. DOI: 10.1108/IJCED-11-2019-0054

Akhmetshin, E. et al. (2021). Massive open online courses as the initial stage of development of a digital university. *Journal of Social Studies Education Research*, 12(2), pp. 126–151.

Al Rahahelah, A. R. S., Al Mubarak, A. Y. (2017). The impact of talent management application on the strategy of human resources management at northern border university. *International Knowledge Sharing Platform*, 9(32), pp. 81–114.

Alavi, M., Leidner, D. E. (2001). Knowledge management and knowledge management systems: conceptual foundations and research issues. *MIS Quarterly*, 1(10), pp. 107–136.

Alavi, S. M. et al. (2021). Designing a third-generation university governance model using total interpretive structural modeling. *Journal of Management and Planning In Educational System*, 14(1), pp. 213–254. DOI: 10.52547/MPES.14.1.213

Aldosari, S. A. M. (2020). The future of higher education in the light of artificial intelligence transformations. *International Journal of Higher Education*, 9(3), pp. 145–151.

Alexander, A., Manolchev, C. (2020). The future of university or universities of the future: a paradox for uncertain times. *International Journal of Educational Management*, 34(7), pp. 1143–1153. DOI: 10.1108/IJEM-01-2020-0018

Allen, M. (2002). *The Corporate University Handbook: Designing, Managing, and Growing a Successful Program*. New York: AMACOM.

Almada-Lobo, F. (2015). The Industry 4.0 revolution and the future of manufacturing execution systems (MES). *Journal of Innovation Management*, 3(4), pp. 16–21.

Altbach, P. G. (2007). *Tradition and Transition: The International Imperative in Higher Education*. Chestnut Hill: CIHE Boston College.

Altbach, P. G. (2012). Higher education in the age of massification. *Brown Journal of World Affairs*, 19, pp. 183–193.

Altbach, P. G. (2014). Research and training in higher education. *Studies in Higher Education*, 39(8), pp. 1306–1320. DOI: 10.1080/03075079.2014.949541

Altbach, P. G. (2015a). The deteriorating guru: the crisis of the professoriate. *International Higher Education*, 36. DOI: 10.6017/ihe.2004.36.7426

Altbach, P. G. (2015b). The intricacies of academic remuneration. *International Higher Education*, 54. DOI: 10.6017/ihe.2009.54.8411

Altbach, P. G. (ed.) (1999). *Private Prometheus: Private Higher Education and Development in the 21st Century*. Westport: Greenwood Publishing Group.

Altbach, P. G., De Wit, H. (2020). COVID-19: the internationalisation revolution that isn't. *University World News*. Available from: https://www.universityworldnews.com/post.php?story=20200312143728370 [14 March 2020].

Altbach, P. G., Knight, J. (2007). The internationalization of higher education: motivations and realities. *Journal of Studies in International Education*, 11(3–4), pp. 290–305.

Altbach, P. G., Reisberg, L., De Wit, H. (eds.). (2017). *Responding to Massification: Differentiation in Postsecondary Education Worldwide*. Rotterdam: SensePublishers. DOI: 10.1007/978-94-6351-083-7

Altbach, P. G., Reisberg, L., Rumbley, L. E. (2009). *Trends in Global Higher Education: Tracking an Academic Revolution. A Report Prepared for the UNESCO 2009 World Conference on Higher Education*. Paris: United Nations Educational, Scientific and Cultural Organization.

Altınay, F. et al. (2019). A study of knowledge management systems processes and technology in open and distance education institutions in higher education. *The International Journal of Information and Learning Technology*, 36(4), pp. 314–321.

Alvesson, M. (2013). *The Triumph of Emptiness: Consumption, Higher Education, and Work Organization*. Oxford: Oxford University Press. DOI: 10.1093/oso/9780199660940.001.0001

Alvesson, M., Sveningsson, S. (2003a). The great disappearing act: Difficulties in doing "leadership". *The Leadership Quarterly*, 14(3), pp. 359–381.

Alvesson, M., Sveningsson, S. (2003b). Good visions, bad micro-management and ugly ambiguity: Contradictions of (non-)leadership in a knowledge-intensive organization. *Organization Studies*, 24(6), pp. 961–988.

AMA (2000). Available from: www.ama.org [21 July 2017].

Amaral, A., Magalhães, M. (2007). Market Competition, Public Good, and State Interference. In: Enders, J., Jongbloed, B. (eds.). (2007). *Public-Private Dynamics in Higher Education. Expectations, Developments and Outcomes*. Bielefield: Transcript Verlag.

Amey, M. J. (2006). Leadership in higher education. *Change: The Magazine of Higher Learning*, 38(6), pp. 55–58.

Anderson, G. (2006). Carving out time and space in the managerial university. *Journal of Organizational Change Management*, 19(5), pp. 578–592.

Anderson, R. D. (2020). German (Humboldtian) university tradition. In: Teixeira, P.N., Shin, J.C. (eds.). *The International Encyclopedia of Higher Education Systems and Institutions*. Dordrecht: Springer, pp. 546–551. DOI: 10.1007/978-94-017-8905-9_4

Andrades, J., Martinez-Martinez, D., Jorge, M. L. (2020). Corporate governance disclosures by Spanish universities: How different variables can affect the level of such disclosures?. *Meditari Accountancy Research*, 29(1), pp. 86–109.

Androutsos, A., Brinia, V. (2019). Developing and piloting a pedagogy for teaching innovation, collaboration, and co-creation in secondary education based on design thinking, digital transformation, and entrepreneurship. *Education Sciences*, 9(2), p. 113. DOI: 10.3390/educsci9020113

Angus, L. (2015). School choice: Neoliberal education policy and imagined futures. *British Journal of Sociology of Education*, 36(3), pp. 395–413.

Anthony, D., Smith, S. W., Williamson, T. (2009). Reputation and reliability in collective goods: The case of the online encyclopedia Wikipedia. *Rationality and society*, 21(3), pp. 283–306.

Anthony, S. G., Antony, J. (2017). Academic leadership - special or simple. *International Journal of Productivity and Performance Management*, 66(5), pp. 630–637. DOI: 10.1108/IJPPM-08-2016-0162

Antonopoulou, H. et al. (2021a). Transformational leadership and digital skills in higher education institutes: During the COVID-19 pandemic. *Emerging Science Journal*, 5(1), pp. 1–15. DOI: 10.28991/esj-2021-01252

Antonopoulou, H. et al. (2021b). Associations between traditional and digital leadership in academic environment: During the COVID-19 Pandemic. *Emerging Science Journal*, 5(4), pp. 405–428. DOI: 10.28991/esj-2021-01286

Appe, S., Barragán, D. (2017). Universities, NGOs, and civil society sustainability: Preliminary lessons from Ecuador. *Development in Practice*, 27(4), pp. 472–486. DOI: 10.1080/09614524.2017.1303035

Appleton, J. R., Wolff, R. A. (2004). Standards and Indicators in the Process of Accreditation: The WASC Experience - A United States Higher Education Accreditation Perspective. In: Vlasceanu, L., Barrows, L. C. (eds.). *Indicators for Institutional and Programme Accreditation in Higher/Tertiary Education*. Bucharest: UNESCO-CEPES, pp. 77–101.

Appolloni, A. et al. (2021). Distance learning as a resilience strategy during Covid-19: An analysis of the Italian context. *Sustainability*, 13(3), p. 1388. DOI: 10.3390/su13031388

Archer, L., Hutchings, M., Ross, A. (2002). *Higher Education and Social Class*. London: Routledge. DOI: 10.4324/9780203986943

Arena, M., Azzone, G., Mapelli, F. (2018). What drives the evolution of corporate social responsibility strategies? An institutional logics perspective. *Journal of Cleaner Production*, 171, pp. 345–355. DOI: 10.1016/j.jclepro.2017.09.245

Arnaboldi, M., Lapsley, I., Steccolini, I. (2015). Performance management in the public sector: The ultimate challenge. *Financial Accountability & Management*, 31(1), pp. 1–22. DOI: 10.1111/faam.12049

Arnold, K. E., Tanes, Z., King, A. S. (2010). Administrative perceptions of data-mining software Signals: Promoting student success and retention. *The Journal of Academic Administration in Higher Education*, 6(2), pp. 29–39.

Arroyabe, M. F., Schumann, M., Arranz, C. F. (2022). Mapping the entrepreneurial university literature: A text mining approach. *Studies in Higher Education*, 47(5), pp. 955–963.

Ashworth, J. M. (1984). The university as a business. *IEE Proceedings A (Physical Science, Measurement and Instrumentation, Management and Education, Reviews)*, 131(8), pp. 635–641. DOI: 10.1049/ip-a-1.1984.0084

Aspara, J. (2014). Struggles in organizational attempts to adopt new branding logics: The case of a marketizing university. *Consumption Markets & Culture*, 17(6), pp. 522–552.

Association of MBAs (2021). *What is accreditation?*. Available from: www.associationofmbas.com/business-schools/accreditation/ [1 August 2021].

Astin, A. W., Astin, H. S. (2000). *Leadership Reconsidered: Engaging Higher Education in Social Change*. Battle Creek: W.K. Kellogg Foundation. After: Thompson, N., Franz, N. K. (2017). Decision Points in Academic Leadership Development as an Engaged Scholar: To Lead or Not to Lead. *Journal of Higher Education Outreach and Engagement*, 9(2), pp. 78–80.

Audretsch, D. B., Belitski, M. (2022). A strategic alignment framework for the entrepreneurial university. *Industry and Innovation*, 29(2), pp. 285–309. DOI: 10.1080/13662716.2021.1941799

Aula, H. M., Tienari, J. (2011). Becoming "world-class"? Reputation-building in a university merger, *Critical Perspectives on International Business*, 7(1), pp. 7–29. DOI: 10.1108/17422041111103813

Ávila, L., Teixeira, L., Almeida, P. (2018). A methodological approach to dematerialization of business processes using open-source technology. *International Journal of Industrial Engineering and Management*, 9(3), pp. 121–128. DOI: 10.24867/IJIEM-2018-3-121

Avralev, N., Efimova, I. (2015). University rankings as a tool for assessing the quality of education in the context of globalization. *Asian Social Science*, 11(10), pp. 292–298. DOI: 10.5539/ass.v11n10p292

Bacanu, B. (2011). Organizational structure and performance: A predictive study on the transformation of the romanian public universities. *Bulletin of the Transilvania University of Brasov. Economic Sciences. Series V*, 4(2), pp. 101–106.

Bacq, S., Aguilera, R. V. (2022). Stakeholder governance for responsible innovation: A theory of value creation, appropriation, and distribution. *Journal of Management Studies*, 59(1), pp. 29–60.

Badat, S. (2010). Global rankings of universities: A perverse and present burden. In: Unterhalter, E., Carpentier, V. (eds.). *Global Inequalities and Higher Education: Whose Interests Are We Serving?*. New York: Palgrave Macmillan, pp. 117–141. DOI: 10.1007/978-0-230-36507-0_5

Baekgaard, M., Mortensen, P. B., Bech Seeberg, H. (2018). The bureaucracy and the policy agenda. *Journal of Public Administration Research and Theory*, 28(2), pp. 239–253.

Bagdasarian, I. S. et al. (2020). The university digital transformation as a tool for human capital development. *Journal of Physics: Conference Series*, 1691(1), 012184.

Bagwell, L. S., Bernheim, B. D. (1996). Veblen effects in a theory of conspicuous consumption. *The American Economic Review*, 86(3), pp. 349–373.

Baker III, G. A. (1992). *Cultural Leadership: Inside America's Community Colleges*. Salisbury: American Association of Community and Junior Colleges.

Baker, T., Nelson, R. E. (2005). Creating something from nothing: Resource construction through entrepreneurial bricolage. *Administrative Science Quarterly*, 50(3), pp. 329–366. DOI: 10.2189/asqu.2005.50.3.329

Balakrishnan, R., Das, S. (2020). How do firms reorganize to implement digital transformation?. *Strategic Change*, 29(5), pp. 531–541.

Balán, J. (2015). The crisis of the public mission in higher education. *International Higher Education*, 80, pp. 4–5. DOI: 10.6017/ihe.2015.80.6130

Baldrige Performance Excellence Program (2001). *Education Criteria for Performance Excellence*. Gaithersburg: National Institute of Standards and Technology.

Ball, R., Wilkinson, R. (1994). The use and abuse of performance indicators in UK higher education. *Higher Education*, 27, pp. 417–427.

Ball, S. (2007). Leadership of academics in research. *Educational Management Administration & Leadership*, 35(4), pp. 449–477.

Ball, S. J. (2015). Living the neo-liberal university. *European Journal of Education*, 50(3), pp. 258–261.

Ballantyne, N., LaMendola, W. (2010). Human services in the network society: Introduction to the special issue. *Journal of Technology in Human Services*, 28(1-2), pp. 1–6.

Baltaru, R. D., & Soysal, Y. N. (2018). Administrators in higher education: Organizational expansion in a transforming institution. *Higher Education*, 76(2), 213–229.

Baranov, N. (2021). "Digital Panopticon" as an Objective Reality of the Global World: The Dilemma Between Social Control and Civic Engagement. In: *Proceedings of Topical Issues in International Political Geography*. Cham: Springer, pp. 22–30.

Barbet, P., Coutinet, N. (2001). Measuring the digital economy: State-of-the-art developments and future prospects. *Communications and Strategies*, 42(2), pp. 153–184.

Barbosa, L. S., Santos, L. P. (2017). Networks of universities as a tool for GCIO education. In: *International Conference on Electronic Government*. Cham: Springer, pp. 117–127.

Bargh C., Scott P., Smith D. (1996). *Governing Universities. Changing the Culture?*. London: Society for Research into Higher Education and Taylor & Francis.

Barnatt, C. (2001). The second digital revolution. *Journal of General Management*, 27(2), pp. 1–16.

Barnes, S. B., Dolby, R. G. (1970). The scientific ethos: A deviant viewpoint. *European Journal of Sociology/Archives Européennes de Sociologie*, 11(1), pp. 3–25.

Barnett, R. (2007). Recovering the civic university. In: McIlrath, L., Labhrainn, I. M. (eds.). *Higher Education and Civic Engagement: International Perspectives*. Burlington: Ashgate, pp. 25–36.

Bartell, M. (2003). Internationalization of universities: A university culture-based framework. *Higher Education*, 45(1), pp. 43–70.

Bartsch, S. et al. (2020). Leadership matters in crisis-induced digital transformation: How to lead service employees effectively during the COVID-19 pandemic. *Journal of Service Management*, 32(1), pp. 71–85.

Bass, B. M. (1999). Two decades of research and development in transformational leadership. *European Journal of Work and Organizational Psychology*, 8(1), pp. 9–32.

Bassnett, S. (2005). The importance of professional university administration: A perspective from a senior university manager. *Perspectives*, 9(4), pp. 98–102.

Bauer, M. W. (2009). The evolution of public understanding of science-discourse and comparative evidence. *Science, Technology and Society*, 14(2), pp. 221–240.

Baycan, T., Olcay, G. A. (2021). Linking the performance of entrepreneurial universities to technoparks and university characteristics in Turkey. *Region*, 8(1), pp. 97–117.

Bayertz, K. (2006). Three arguments for scientific freedom. *Ethical Theory and Moral Practice*, 9(4), pp. 377–398.

Becher T. (1981). Towards a definition of disciplinary cultures. *Studies in Higher Education*, 6(2), pp. 109–122.

Becher T., Kogan M. (1992). *Process and Structure in Higher Education*. London: Routledge.

Becket N., Brookes M. (2006). Evaluating quality management in university departments. *Quality Assurance in Education*, 14(2), pp. 123–142.

Beckmann, A., Cooper, Ch., Hill, D. (2009). Neoliberalization and managerialization of "education" in England and Wales: A case for reconstructing education. *Journal for Critical Education Policy Studies*, 7(2), pp. 311–345.

Benavides, L. M. C. et al. (2020). Digital transformation in higher education institutions: A systematic literature review. *Sensors*, 20(11), 3291. DOI: 10.3390/s20113291

Benito, M., Romera, R. (2011). Improving quality assessment of composite indicators in university rankings: A case study of French and German universities of excellence. *Scientometrics*, 89(1), pp. 153–176.

Benneworth, P. (2018). Definitions, approaches and challenges to community engagement. In: Benneworth, P. et al. *Mapping and Critical Synthesis of Current State-of-the-Art on Community Engagement in Higher Education.* Zagreb: Institute for the Development of Education, pp. 16–46.

Bensimon, E. M. et al. (2004). Designing and Implementing a Diversity Scorecard to Improve Institutional Effectiveness for Underserved Minority. In: Vlăsceanu, L., Grünberg, L., Pârlea, D. *Quality assurance and accreditation: A glossary of basic terms and definitions.* Bucharest: UNESCO-CEPES.

Bento, F. (2011). A discussion about power relations and the concept of distributed leadership in higher education institutions. *The Open Education Journal,* 4(1), pp. 17–23. DOI: 10.2174/1874920801104010017

Berdnikova, L. F. et al. (2020). Strategic management of smart university development. In: Uskov, V. L., Howlett, R. J., Jain, L. C. (eds.). *Smart Education and e-Learning 2020.* Singapore: Springer, pp. 293–303. DOI: 10.1007/978-981-15-5584-8_25

Berglund, K., Hytti, U., Verduijn, K. (2020). Navigating the terrain of entrepreneurship education in neoliberal societies. *Entrepreneurship Education and Pedagogy,* 3(3), pp. 208–213.

Berman, S. J. (2012). Digital transformation: Opportunities to create new business models. *Strategy & Leadership,* 40(2), pp. 16–24.

Berry, L. L. (1981). The employee as customer. *Journal of Retail Banking,* 3(1), pp. 33–40.

Besley, T., Peters, M. (2006). *Building Knowledge Cultures: Education and Development in the Age of Knowledge Capitalism.* Maryland: Rowman & Littlefield.

Betchoo, N. K. (2016). Digital transformation and its impact on human resource management: A case analysis of two unrelated businesses in the Mauritian public service. In: *Proceedings of the 2016 IEEE (EmergiTech).* Piscataway: IEEE, pp. 147–152. DOI: 10.1109/EmergiTech.2016.7737328

Bevir, M. (2013). *Governance: A Very Short Introduction.* Oxford: Oxford University Press, 2013.

Bi, P., Jiang, W. (2012). Research on application of knowledge management in public sectors. In: Zhu, R., Ma, Y. (eds.). *Information Engineering and Applications.* London: Springer, pp. 506–513. DOI: 10.1007/978-1-4471-2386-6_65

Bi, T., Han, J., Guan, H. (2014). Research countermeasures of human resources management in university. In: *International Conference on Education and Management Science (ICEMS2014).* Lancaster: DEStech Publications, pp. 253–257.

Bianchi, C., Nasi, G., Rivenbark, W. C. (2021). Implementing collaborative governance: Models, experiences, and challenges. *Public Management Review,* 23(11), pp. 1581–1589.

Bigliardi, B., Galati, F., Verbano, C. (2013). Evaluating performance of university spin-off companies: Lessons from Italy. *Journal of Technology Management & Innovation,* 8(2), pp. 178–188.

Bileviciute, E. et al. (2019). Competitiveness in higher education: The case of university management. *Journal of Competitiveness,* 11(4), pp. 5–21.

Birnbaum, R. (1988). Administrative commitments and minority enrollments: College presidents' goals for quality and access. *Review of Higher Education,* 11(4), pp. 83–174.

Birnbaum, R. (1989). The implicit leadership theories of college and university presidents. *The Review of Higher Education,* 12(2), pp. 125–136.

Blackmar, F. W. (1911). Leadership in reform. *American Journal of Sociology,* 16(5), pp. 626–644.

Blackmore, J. (2010). Research assessment: A calculative technology governing quality, accountability and equity. In: Blackmore, J., Brennan, M., Zipin, L. (eds.). *Re-Positioning University Governance and Academic Work*. Rotterdam: Brill Sense, pp. 67–83. DOI: 10.1163/9789460911743_002

Blackmore, P. (2015). *Prestige in Academic Life: Excellence and Exclusion*. London: Routledge.

Blackmore, P., Kandiko, C. B. (2011). Motivation in academic life: A prestige economy. *Research in Post-compulsory Education*, 16(4), pp. 399–411.

Blake, R. R., Mouton, J. S. (1964). *The Managerial Grid*. Houston: Gulf.

Blanco-Ramírez, G., Berger, J. B. (2014). Rankings, accreditation, and the international quest for quality: Organizing an approach to value in higher education. *Quality Assurance in Education*, 22(1), pp. 88–104.

Blayone, T. J. et al. (2017). Democratizing digital learning: Theorizing the fully online learning community model. *International Journal of Educational Technology in Higher Education*, 14(1), pp. 1–16.

Bleak, J. (2017). *When For-Profit Meets Nonprofit: Educating Through the Market*. London: Routledge.

Bleiklie, I. (1998). Justifying the evaluative state: New public management ideals in higher education. *Journal of Public Affairs Education*, 4(2), pp. 87–100.

Bleiklie, I., Kogan, M. (2007). Organization and governance of universities. *Higher Education Policy*, 20(4), pp. 477–493.

Bleiklie, I., Lange, S. (2010). Competition and leadership as drivers in German and Norwegian university reforms. *Higher Education Policy*, 23(2), pp. 173–193.

Bloemraad, I., Menjívar, C. (2022). Precarious times, professional tensions: The ethics of migration research and the drive for scientific accountability. *International Migration Review*, 56(1), pp. 4–32.

Bloomberg, J. (2018). *Digitization, Digitalization, and Digital Transformation: Confuse Them at Your Peril*. Available from: www.forbes.com [August, 28, 2019].

Bodunkova, A. G., Chernaya, I. P. (2012). Fractal organization as innovative model for entrepreneurial university development. *World Applied Sciences Journal*, 18(12), pp. 74–82.

Bogue, E. G., Hall, K. B. (2003). *Quality and Accountability in Higher Education*. Westport: Praeger.

Bojinov, B. V. (2017a). Evolutionary entry of information technology in universities: Key findings and research. *SSRN Electronic Journal*. Available from: https://ssrn.com/abstract=3192899. DOI: 10.2139/ssrn.3192899

Bojinov, B. V. (2017b). The role of IT managers in higher education-preliminary results from CEE universities survey. *SSRN Electronic Journal*. Available from: https://ssrn.com/abstract=3192907. DOI: 10.2139/ssrn.3192907

Boldt, D. B. (1991). University strategic management: A businessman's view. *International Journal of Educational Management*, 5(5), pp. 10–12.

Bolisani, E., Bratianu, C. (2017). Knowledge strategy planning: An integrated approach to manage uncertainty, turbulence, and dynamics. *Journal of Knowledge Management*, 21(2), pp. 233–253.

Bolton, S. C. et al. (2011). Critical human resource management. In: Tadajewski, M. et al. (eds.). *Key Concepts in Critical Management Studies*. London: Sage Publication, pp. 74–78.

Bond, M. et al. (2018). Digital transformation in German higher education: Student and teacher perceptions and usage of digital media. *International Journal of Educational Technology in Higher Education*, 15(1), pp. 1–20.

Bondarenko, T., Kelemen, G., Nesterenko, R. (2019). Project current trends and prospects of the development of the internationalization of higher education. *R&E-SOURCE Online Journal for Research and Education*, 17, pp. 60–64.

Bonvillian, G., Dennis, T. L. (1995). *Total Quality Management in Higher Education. Is It Working? Why or Why Not?*. Westport: Praeger.

Bookstein, F. et al. (2010). Too much noise in the times higher education rankings. *Scientometrics*, 85(1), pp. 295–299.

Bornmann, L. (2013). *Is There Currently a Scientific Revolution in Scientometrics?*. arXiv preprint. arXiv:1307.6307. DOI: 10.48550/arXiv.1307.6307

Bourdieu, P. (1988). *Homo Academicus*. Stanford: Stanford University Press.

Bourdieu, P., Passeron, J. C. (1990a). *Reproduction in Education and Society*. London: Sage.

Bowles, H., Murphy, A. C. (2020). EMI and the internationalization of universities: An overview. In: Bowles, H., Murphy, A. C. (eds.). *English-Medium Instruction and the Internationalization of Universities*. Cham: Palgrave Macmillan, pp. 1–26.

Bozeman, B., Gaughan, M. (2011). Job satisfaction among university faculty: Individual, work, and institutional determinants. *The Journal of Higher Education*, 82(2), pp. 154–186.

Bradley, A. P. (2016). Talent management for universities. *Australian Universities' Review*, 58(1), pp. 13–19.

Brandenburg, U., De Wit, H. (2011). The end of internationalization. *International Higher Education*, (62), pp. 15–17. DOI: 10.6017/ihe.2011.62.8533

Bratianu, C. (2020). Designing knowledge strategies for universities in crazy times. *Management Dynamics in the Knowledge Economy*, 8(3), pp. 209–223.

Bratianu, C., Pop, N. A. (2007). Strategic university management and marketing. *The Amfiteatru Economic Journal*, 9(22), pp. 9–17.

Bratianu, C., Stanciu, S. (2010). An overview of present research related to entrepreneurial university. *Management & Marketing*, 5(2), pp. 117–134.

Breeding, M. (2013). Cloud computing: A new generation of technology enables deeper collaboration. In: Gathegi, J. N. et al. (eds.). *International Symposium on Information Management in a Changing World*. Berlin: Springer, pp. 25–35. DOI: 10.1007/978-3-662-44412-2_3

Breidbach, C. F., Maglio, P. P. (2016). Technology-enabled value co-creation: An empirical analysis of actors, resources, and practices. *Industrial Marketing Management*, 56, pp. 73–85.

Brennan, T. (2004). *The Transmission of Affect*. New York: Cornell University Press.

Brennen, J. S., Kreiss, D. (2016). Digitalization. In: *The International Encyclopedia of Communication Theory and Philosophy*. New York: John Wiley & Sons, pp. 1–11. DOI: 10.1002/9781118766804

Brewer, P. D., Brewer, K. L. (2010). Knowledge management, human resource management, and higher education: A theoretical model. *Journal of Education for Business*, 85(6), pp. 330–335.

Breznitz, S. M., Feldman, M. P. (2012). The engaged university. *The Journal of Technology Transfer*, 37(2), pp. 139–157.

Bringle, R., Games, R., Malloy, E. (1999). *Colleges and Universities as Citizens*. Boston: Allyn and Bacon.

Broadbent, J., Laughlin, R. (2005). Public service professionals and the new public management: Control of the professions in the public services. In: *New Public Management*. London: Routledge, pp. 107–120.

Brooker, G., Noble, M. (1985). The marketing of higher education. *College and University*, 60(3), pp. 191–200.

Broucker, B., De Wit, K. (2015). New public management in higher education. In: Huisman, J. et al. (eds.). *The Palgrave International Handbook of Higher Education Policy and Governance*. London: Palgrave Macmillan, pp. 57–75.

Broucker, B., De Wit, K., Verhoeven, J. C. (2017). Higher education research: Looking beyond new public management. In: Huisman, J., Tight, M. (eds.). *Theory and Method in Higher Education Research*. Bingley: Emerald Publishing Limited, pp. 21–38. DOI: 1 0.1108/S2056-375220170000003002

Brown, G. (2018). Online education policy and practice: The past, present, and the future of the digital university. *American Journal of Distance Education*, 32(2), pp. 156–158. DOI: 10.1080/08923647.2018.1440475

Brown, W. F., Moshavi, D. (2002). Herding academic cats: Faculty reactions to transformational and contingent reward leadership by department chairs. *Journal of Leadership Studies*, 8(3), pp. 79–93.

Bruckmann, S., Carvalho, T. (2018). Understanding change in higher education: An archetypal approach. *Higher Education*, 76(4), pp. 629–647.

Brunsson, N., Rasche, A., Seidl, D. (2012). The dynamics of standardization: Three perspectives on standards in organization studies. *Organization Studies*, 33(5-6), pp. 613–632.

Bryson, J. M., Crosby, B. C., Bloomberg, L. (2014). Public value governance: Moving beyond traditional public administration and the new public management. *Public Administration Review*, 74(4), pp. 445–456.

Buchbinder, H. (1993). The market oriented university and the changing role of knowledge. *Higher Education*, 26(3), pp. 331–347.

Buckland, R. (2009). Private and public sector models for strategies in universities. *British Journal of Management*, 20(4), pp. 524–536.

Buela-Casal, G. et al. (2007). Comparative study of international academic rankings of universities. *Scientometrics*, 71(3), pp. 349–365.

Bührig, J., Schoormann, T., Knackstedt, R. (2018). Business process management in German institutions of higher education: The case of jade university of applied science. In: vom Brocke, J., Mendling, J. (eds.). *Business Process Management Cases*. Cham: Springer, pp. 577–592. DOI: 10.1007/978-3-319-58307-5_31

Bulaitis, Z. (2017). Measuring impact in the humanities: Learning from accountability and economics in a contemporary history of cultural value. *Palgrave Communications*, 3(1), pp. 1–11.

Burke, P. J. (1997). An identity model for network exchange. *American Sociological Review*, 62(1), pp. 134–150. DOI: 10.2307/2657456

Busher, H., Fox, A. (2021). The amoral academy? A critical discussion of research ethics in the neo-liberal university. *Educational Philosophy and Theory*, 53(5), pp. 469–478.

Butnariu, M., Milosan, I. (2012). Preliminary assessment of knowledge management in universities. *Procedia - Social and Behavioral Sciences*, 62, pp. 791–795.

Byarugaba, J. K., Bagiire, V. A., Bagorogoza, J. K. (2012). Line manager involvement in human resource management issues in public universities in Uganda. *African Business and Development in a Changing Global Political Economy: Issues, Challenges and Opportunities*, vol. 13, pp. 343-352.

Cadavid, L., Díez-Echavarría, L., Valencia, A. (2017). Spin-off activities at higher educational institutions: performance implications from a modeling perspective. *Journal of Developmental Entrepreneurship*, 22(02), pp. 1–21. DOI: 10.1142/S108494 6717500133

Calás, M., Smircich, L. (1991). Voicing seduction to silence leadership. *Organization Studies*, 12(4), pp. 567-502.

Calhoun, C. (2006). The university and a public good. *Thesis Eleven*, 84, pp. 7–43.

Calzada, I. (2020). Pandemic citizenship amidst stateless algorithmic nations: Digital rights and technological sovereignty at stake. *Post-Covid Europe, series 4*. Brussels: Coppieters Foundation. DOI: 10.13140/RG.2.2.36196.19849/3

Canaan, J. E., Shumar, W. eds. (2008). *Structure and Agency in the Neoliberal University*. London: Routledge.

Canaan, J. E. (2013). Resisting the english neoliberalising university. What critical pedagogy can offer. *Journal for Critical Education Policy Studies*, 11(2), pp. 16–56.

Canhoto, A. I. et al. (2016). The co-production of value in digital, university-industry R&D collaborative projects. *Industrial Marketing Management*, 56, pp. 86–96.

Canterbury, R. M. (2000). Higher education marketing: A challenge. *Journal of Marketing for Higher Education*, 9(3), pp. 15–24.

Cantner, U. (2022). Challenges on the digitalisation of the universities in the European higher education area: The case of Germany. In: *Transformation Fast and Slow*. Leiden: Brill, pp. 78–102.

Cantoni, D., Yuchtman, N. (2014). Medieval universities, legal institutions, and the commercial revolution. *The Quarterly Journal of Economics*, 129(2), pp. 823–887.

Cantu-Ortiz, F. J. ed. (2017). *Research Analytics: Boosting University Productivity and Competitiveness Through Scientometrics*. New York: Auerbach Publications.

Carcary, M., Doherty, E., Conway, G. (2016). A dynamic capability approach to digital transformation: A focus on key foundational themes. In: *The European Conference on Information Systems Management*. Reading: Academic Conferences International Limited, pp. 20–28.

Cardoso, S., Carvalho, T., Videira, P. (2019). Is it still worth working in academia? The views from Portuguese academics. *Higher Education Policy*, 32(4), pp. 663–679.

Cardozier, V. R. (1968). Student power in medieval universities. *The Personnel and Guidance Journal*, 46(10), pp. 944–948.

Carnoy, M. (1981). Education, industrial democracy and the state. *Economic and Industrial Democracy*, 2(2), pp. 243–260.

Carter, N. (1989). Performance indicators: 'Backseat driving' or 'hands off control?. *Policy & Politics*, 17(2), pp. 131–138.

Caruso, L. (2018). Digital innovation and the fourth industrial revolution: Epochal social changes?. *AI & Society*, 33(3), pp. 379–392.

Carvalho, T. (2017). The study of the academic profession-contributions from and to the sociology of professions. In: Huisman, J., Tight, M. (eds.). *Theory and Method in Higher Education Research*. Bingley: Emerald Publishing Limited, pp. 59–76. DOI: 10.1108/S2056-375220170000003004

Carvalho, T., Santiago, R. (2010). New public management and 'middle management': How do deans influence institutional policies? In: Meek, V. et al. (eds.). *The Changing Dynamics of Higher Education Middle Management*. Dordrecht: Springer, pp. 165–196. DOI: 10.1007/978-90-481-9163-5_9

Carvalho, T., Videira, P. (2019). Losing autonomy? Restructuring higher education institutions governance and relations between teaching and non-teaching staff. *Studies in Higher Education*, 44(4), pp. 762–773.

Castells, M. (2000). Toward a sociology of the network society. *Contemporary Sociology*, 29(5), pp. 693–699.

Castells, M. (2004). *The Network Society: A Cross-Cultural Perspective*. Cheltenham: Edward Elgar.

Castells, M. (2011). *The Rise of the Network Society*. New York: John Wiley & Sons.

Castillo-Villar, R. G. (2021). Contemporary challenges to university governance models. In: *Governance Models for Latin American Universities in the 21st Century*. Cham: Palgrave Macmillan, pp. 59–71.

Castree, N., Sparke, M. (2000). Introduction: Professional geography and the corporatization of the university: Experiences, evaluations, and engagements. *Antipode*, 32, pp. 222–229.

Cave, M., Kogan, M., Hanney, S. (1990). The scope and effects of performance measurement in british higher education. In: Dochy, F. J. R. C., Segers, M. S. R., Wijnen, W. H. F. W. (eds.). *Management Information and Performance Indicators in Higher Education: An International Issue*. Assen/Maastricht: Van Gorcum and Comp, pp. 48–49.

Centobelli, P. et al. (2019). The mediating role of knowledge exploration and exploitation for the development of an entrepreneurial university. *Management Decision*, 57, pp. 3301–3320.

Cerver Romero, E., Ferreira, J. J., Fernandes, C. I. (2021). The multiple faces of the entrepreneurial university: A review of the prevailing theoretical approaches. *The Journal of Technology Transfer*, 46(4), pp. 1173–1195.

Chalaris, M. et al. (2013). Extraction of rules based on students' questionnaires. *Procedia - Social and Behavioral Sciences*, 73, pp. 510–517.

Chan, K. W., Li, S. Y., Zhu, J. J. (2015). Fostering customer ideation in crowdsourcing community: The role of peer-to-peer and peer-to-firm interactions. *Journal of Interactive Marketing*, 31, pp. 42–62.

Chan, W. W., Dimmock, C. (2008). The internationalization of universities: Globalist, internationalist and translocalist models. *Journal of Research in International Education*, 7(2), pp. 184–204.

Chao, X. (2020). Measurement and evaluation of science and technology innovation efficiency. In: *2020 16th Dahe Fortune China Forum and Chinese High-educational Management Annual Academic Conference (DFHMC)*. Piscataway: IEEE, pp. 30–34.

Chen, S. H., Yang, C. C., Shiau, J. Y. (2006). The application of balanced scorecard in the performance evaluation of higher education. *The TQM Magazine*, 18, pp. 190–205.

Cheng, M. (2009). University organizational structure innovative design. *Journal of Chengdu University of Technology (Social Sciences)*, 3, pp. 95–99.

Chiang, K. H. (2012). Research and teaching revisited: A pre-Humboldtian or post-Humboldtian phenomenon? The cases of France and the UK. *European Journal of Education*, 47(1), pp. 139–152.

Chipman, L. (2000). Academic freedom and the well-managed university. *Policy*, 16(1), pp. 22–30.

Choi, B., Lee, H. (2002). Knowledge management strategy and its link to knowledge creation process. *Expert Systems with Applications*, 23(3), pp. 173–187.

Choi, S. (2019). Identifying indicators of university autonomy according to stakeholders' interests. *Tertiary Education and Management*, 25(1), pp. 17–29.

Choi, T. M., Wallace, S. W., Wang, Y. (2018). Big data analytics in operations management. *Production and Operations Management*, 27(10), pp. 1868–1883.

Choo, C. W., Bontis, N. eds. (2002). *The Strategic Management of Intellectual Capital and Organizational Knowledge*. Oxford: Oxford University Press.

Choudaha, R., van Rest, E. (2018). *Envisioning Pathways to 2030: Megatrends Shaping the Future of Global Higher Education and International Student Mobility*. Studyportals. Available from: www.studyportals.com.

Chrobot-Mason, D. et al. (2007). Illuminating a cross-cultural leadership challenge: When identity groups collide. *The International Journal of Human Resource Management*, 18(11), pp. 2011–2036.

Chubb, J. E., Moe, T. M. (1988). Politics, markets, and the organization of schools. *American Political Science Association*, 82(4), pp. 1065–1087.

Claes, T. (2005). Defining 'the university': From 'ivory tower' to 'convenience store'. In: Claes, T. (ed.). *Probing the Boundaries of Higher Education*. Oxford: Inter-Disciplinary Press, pp. 35–49.

Clancy, P. (1988). *Who Goes to College?: A Second National Survey of Participation in Higher Education*. Dublin: Higher Education Authority.

Clancy, P. (1995). *Access to College: Patterns of Continuity and Change*. Dublin: Higher Education Authority.

Clancy, P. (2001). *College Entry in Focus: A Fourth National Survey of Access to Higher Education*. Dublin: Higher Education Authority.

Clark, B. (2001). The entrepreneurial university: New foundations for collegiality, autonomy, and achievement. *Higher Education Management*, 13(2), pp. 9–24.

Clark, B. R. (1973). Development of the sociology of higher education. *Sociology of Education*, 46, pp. 2–14.

Clark, B. R. (1983). *The Higher Education System: Academic Organization in Cross-National Perspective*. Berkeley: University of California Press.

Clark, B. R. (1998a). The entrepreneurial university: Demand and response. *Tertiary Education and Management*, 4(1), pp. 5–16.

Clark, B. R. (1998b). *Creating Entrepreneurial Universities: Organizational Pathways of Transformation*. Oxford, New York: Published for the IAU Press by Pergamon Press.

Clark, M., Fine, M. B., Scheuer, C. L. (2017). Relationship quality in higher education marketing: the role of social media engagement. *Journal of Marketing for Higher Education*, 27(1), pp. 40–58.

Clarke, G. (1997). Reassessing resource allocation strategies in higher education: Methods for analysis. *International Journal of Educational Management*, 11(6), pp. 286–292. DOI: 10.1108/09513549710186920

Coaldrake, P., Stedman, L., Little, P. (2003). *Issues in Australian University Governance*. Brisbane: QUT.

Cobban, A. B. (1989). The role of colleges in the Medieval universities of Northern Europe, with special reference to England and France. *Bulletin of the John Rylands Library*, 71(1), pp. 49–70.

Cole, J. R. (2012). *The Great American University: Its Rise to Preeminence, Its Indispensable National Role, Why It Must Be Protected*. Oxford: PublicAffairs.

Collan, M., Stoklasa, J., Talasova, J. (2014). On academic faculty evaluation systems-more than just simple benchmarking. *International Journal of Process Management and Benchmarking*, 4(4), pp. 437–455.

Collins, P. D., Kolb, D. G. (2013). Hyper-connectivity: How choice, response norms and technology do (and don't) matter. *Academy of Management Proceedings*, 2013(1), 15245. DOI: 10.5465/AMBPP.2013.15245abstract

Collinson, D. (2017). Critical leadership studies: A response to Learmonth and Morrell. *Leadership*, 13(3), pp. 272–284.

Côme, T. et al. (2018). University governance in Europe: Managerial convergences or political harmonization?. *Journal of Intercultural Management*, 10(3), pp. 61–81.

Committee of University Chairs (2020). *The Higher Education Code of Governance*. London: Committee of University Chairs.

Compton, M. et al. (2022). New development: Walk on the bright side - what might we learn about public governance by studying its achievements?. *Public Money & Management*, 42(1), pp. 49–51.

Constantinides, E., Zinck Stagno, M. C. (2011). Potential of the social media as instruments of higher education marketing: A segmentation study. *Journal of Marketing for Higher Education*, 21(1), pp. 7–24.

Cook, K. S. et al. (2013). Social exchange theory. In: Delamater, J. (ed.). *Handbook of Social Psychology*. New York: Kluwer Academic/Plenum Publishers, pp. 61–88.

Cook, R. W., Zallocco, R. L. (1983). Predicting university preference and attendance: Applied marketing in higher education administration. *Research in Higher Education*, 19(2), pp. 197–211.

Corson J. J., Foote C., Mayer H. (1969). Culture of university-governance and education. *Journal of Higher Education*, 6, pp. 493–494.

Cuenin, S. (1987). The use of performance indicators in universities: An international survey. *International Journal of Institutional Management in Higher Education*, 11(2), p. 117–139.

Courtenay, W. J. (1989). Inquiry and inquisition: Academic freedom in medieval universities. *Church History*, 58(2), pp. 168–181.

Coy, D., Fischer, M., Gordon, T. (2001). Public accountability: A new paradigm for college and university annual reports. *Critical Perspectives on Accounting*, 12(1), pp. 1–31.

Craig, R., Amernic, J. (2002). Accountability of accounting educators and the rhythm of the university: Resistance strategies for postmodern blues. *Accounting Education*, 11(2), pp. 121–171.

Crass, D., Czarnitzki, D., Toole, A. A. (2019). The dynamic relationship between investments in brand equity and firm profitability: Evidence using trademark registrations. *International Journal of the Economics of Business*, 26(1), pp. 157–176.

Cremonini, L., Horlings, E., Hessels, L. K. (2018). Different recipes for the same dish: Comparing policies for scientific excellence across different countries. *Science and Public Policy*, 45(2), pp. 232–245.

Cristofoli, D., Markovic, J., Meneguzzo, M. (2014). Governance, management and performance in public networks: How to be successful in shared-governance networks. *Journal of Management & Governance*, 18(1), pp. 77–93.

Cropanzano, R. et al. (2017). Social exchange theory: A critical review with theoretical remedies. *Academy of Management Annals*, 11(1), pp. 479–516.

Croucher, G., Lacy, W. B. (2020). The emergence of academic capitalism and university neoliberalism: Perspectives of Australian higher education leadership. *Higher Education*, 1-17, pp. 279–295. DOI: 10.1007/s10734-020-00655-7

Crow, M. M., Whitman, K., Anderson, D. M. (2020). Rethinking academic entrepreneurship: University governance and the emergence of the academic enterprise. *Public Administration Review*, 80(3), pp. 511–515.

Cruickshank, M. (2003). Total quality management in the higher education sector: A literature review from an international and Australian perspective. *TQM & Business Excellence*, 14(10), pp. 1159–1167.

Cunningham, C. M., Hazel, M., Hayes, T. J. (2020). Communication and leadership 2020: Intersectional, mindful, and digital. *Communication Research Trends*, 39(1), pp. 4–31.

Curnalia, R. M., Mermer, D. (2018). Renewing our commitment to tenure, academic freedom, and shared governance to navigate challenges in higher education. *Review of Communication*, 18(2), pp. 129–139.

Currie, J. K., Newson, J. eds. (1998). *Universities and Globalization: Critical Perspectives.* Thousand Oaks: Sage Publications.

Curtis, S. (2019). Digital transformation-the silver bullet to public service improvement?. *Public Money & Management*, 39(5), pp. 322–324.

Cybermetrics Lab, Consejo Superior de Investigaciones Científicas(2017). *Webometrics Ranking of World Universities*. Available from: https://www.webometrics.info/en [3 July 2017].

Czarniawska, B., Mazza, C. (2013). Consulting university: A reflection from inside. *Financial Accountability and Management*, 29(2), pp. 124–129.

Dakowska, D., Harmsen, R. (2015). Laboratories of reform? The Europeanization and internationalization of higher education in Central and Eastern Europe. *International Journal of Higher Education*, 5(1), pp. 4–17.

Dale, R. (2007). Changing meanings of "the Europe of knowledge" and "modernizing the university, from "Bologna" to the "New Lisbon". *European Education*, 39(4), pp. 27–42.

Dan, M. C. (2012). The third mission of universities in the development strategy of Vienna City. *Informatica Economică*, 16(4), pp. 49–56.

Darling-Hammond, L., Snyder, J. (2015). Accountability for resources and outcomes: An introduction. *Education Policy Analysis Archives*, 23(20), pp. 1–4. DOI: 10.14507/epaa.v23.2024

Darmody, A., Zwick, D. (2020). Manipulate to empower: Hyper-relevance and the contradictions of marketing in the age of surveillance capitalism. *Big Data & Society*, 7(1), pp. 1–12. DOI: 10.1177/2053951720904112

Davey, T., Galan-Muros, V. (2020). Understanding entrepreneurial academics-how they perceive their environment differently. *Journal of Management Development*, 39(5), pp. 599–617.

Davies, B., Gottsche, M., Bansel, B. (2006). The rise and fall of the neo-liberal university. *European Journal of Education*, 41(2), pp. 305–319.

Davies, S., Zarifa, D. (2012). The stratification of universities: Structural inequality in Canada and the United States. *Research in Social Stratification and Mobility*, 30(2), pp. 143–158.

Davis, R. A. (2018). Ethics, epistemology and the post-Humboldtian university. In: Smeyers, P., Depaepe, M. (eds.). *Educational Research: Ethics, Social Justice, and Funding Dynamics*. Cham: Springer, pp. 11–24. DOI: 10.1007/978-3-319-73921-2_2

Davis, T. R., Luthans, F. (1979). Leadership reexamined: A behavioral approach. *Academy of Management Review*, 4(2), pp. 237–248.

Dayan, R., Heisig, P., Matos, F. (2017). Knowledge management as a factor for the formulation and implementation of organization strategy. *Journal of Knowledge Management*, 21(2), pp. 308–329.

De Boer, H., Goedegebuure, L. (2009). The changing nature of the academic deanship. *Leadership*, 5(3), pp. 347–364.

de la Torre, E. M., Casani, F., Esparrells, C. P. (2021). Measuring universities' engagement: A revision of the European research projects and the actual use of the so-called 'third mission' indicators. *Revista de Estudios Regionales*, 1, pp. 97–128.

de Man, A. P. (2004). *The Network Economy: Strategy, Structure and Management.* Cheltenham: Edward Elgar.

de Pillis, E. G., De Pillis, L. G. (2001). The long-term impact of university budget cuts: a mathematical model. *Mathematical and Computer Modelling*, 33(8-9), pp. 851–876.

de Ridder-Symoens, H., Rüegg, W. eds. (2003). *A History of the University in Europe. Volume 1: Universities in the Middle Ages.* Cambridge: Cambridge University Press.

de Schrevel, M., Jost, T. (2013). The role of university managers for a successful university development. *The Open Management Journal*, 5(1), pp. 1–8.

de Vasconcelos Guedes, T. S., Séra, J. (2022). Digital university: Investigating the impact of the pandemic on the acceptance of E-learning. *Athens Journal of Technology & Engineering*, 9, pp. 1–23.

de Waal, A., Kerklaan, L. (2015). Developing an evidence-based management approach for creating high-performance higher educational institutions. *Academy of Educational Leadership Journal*, 19(3), pp. 85–103.

De Wit, H. (1999). Changing rationales for the internationalization of higher education. *International Higher Education*, (15), pp. 2–3. DOI: 10.6017/ihe.1999.15.6477

De Wit, H. (2002). *Internationalization of Higher Education in the United States of America and Europe: A Historical, Comparative, and Conceptual Analysis.* Westport: Greenwood Publishing Group.

De Wit, H. (2019). Evolving concepts, trends, and challenges in the internationalization of higher education in the world. *Educational Studies Moscow*, 2, pp. 8–34. DOI: 10.17323/1814-9545-2019-2-8-34

De Wit, H., Altbach, P. G. (2021). Internationalization in higher education: Global trends and recommendations for its future. *Policy Reviews in Higher Education*, 5(1), pp. 28–46.

De Wit, H., Deca, L. (2020). Internationalization of higher education, challenges and opportunities for the next decade. In: Curaj, A., Deca, L., Pricopie, R. (eds.). *European Higher Education Area: Challenges for a New Decade.* Cham: Springer, pp. 3–11.

De Wit, H., Hunter, F. (2015). The future of internationalization of higher education in Europe. *International Higher Education*, (83), pp. 2–3. DOI: 10.6017/ihe.2015.83.9073

Dearlove, J. (1997). The academic labour process: from collegiality and professionalism to managerialism and proletarianisation?. *Higher Education Review*, 30(1), pp. 56–75.

Deem, R. et al. (2007). *Knowledge, Higher Education, and The New Managerialism: The Changing Management of UK Universities.* Oxford: Oxford University Press.

Degn, L. (2015). Sensemaking, sensegiving and strategic management in Danish higher education. *Higher Education*, 69(6), pp. 901–913.

Demange, G., Gale, D. (1985). The strategy structure of two-sided matching markets. *Econometrica: Journal of the Econometric Society*, 53, pp. 873–888.

Dent, M., Barry, J. (2017). New public management and the professions in the UK: Reconfiguring control? In: Dent, M., Chandler, J. (eds.). *Questioning the New Public Management.* London: Routledge, pp. 7–20.

Dent, M., Chandler, J., Barry, J. eds. (2004). *Questioning the New Public Management.* Aldershot: Ashgate Publishing.

DES (1985). *The Development of Higher Education until the 1990s.* Cmnd 9524, HMSO.

Devlin, M. (2013). Effective university leadership and management of learning and teaching in a widening participation context: Findings from two national Australian studies. *Tertiary Education and Management*, 19(3), pp. 233–245.

Dias, D., Sá, M. J. (2014). Initiation rituals in university as lever for group cohesion. *Journal of Further and Higher Education*, 38(4), pp. 447–464.

Díaz, E. R. (2020). Entrepreneurial leadership in Indian and Mexican graduate students. *Latin American Business Review*, 21(3), pp. 307–326.

Dibb, S., Simkin, L. (1993). The strength of branding and positioning in services. *International Journal of Service Industry Management*, 4, pp. 25–35.

Dill, D. (2012). *Assuring the Public Good in Higher Education: Essential Framework Conditions and Academic Values.* Available from: www.unc.edu [12.01.2016].

Dill, D. D. (1982). The management of academic culture: Notes on the management of meaning and social integration. *Higher Education*, 11, pp. 303–320. DOI: 10.1007/BF00155621

Dill, D. D. (2003). An institutional perspective on higher education policy: The case of academic quality assurance. In: Smart, J. C. (ed.). *Higher Education: Handbook of Theory and Research.* Dordrecht: Springer, pp. 669–699. DOI: 10.1007/978-94-010-0137-3_12

Dill, D. D., Soo, M. (2004). Transparency and quality in higher education markets. In: Teixeira, P. et al. (eds.). *Markets in Higher Education.* Dordrecht: Springer, pp. 61–85. DOI: 10.1007/1-4020-2835-0_4

Dionne, S. D. et al. (2005). Substitutes for leadership, or not. *The Leadership Quarterly*, 16(1), pp. 169–193.

Dobbins, M. (2009). Comparing higher education policies in Central and Eastern Europe. In: Jakobi, A. P., Martens, K., Wolf, K. D. (eds.). *Education in Political Science.* London: Routledge, pp. 58–75.

Docampo, D., Cram, L. (2019). Highly cited researchers: a moving target. *Scientometrics*, 118(3), pp. 1011–1025.

Dochy, F., Segers, M. (1990). *Selecting Indicators on the Basis of Essential Criteria and Appropriate Assessment Methods or a Quality Assurance System.* Paper prepared for the CHEPS Conference, "Quality Assessment in Higher Education" at Utrecht, March 16th, 1990.

Doh, J. P. (2003). Can leadership be taught? Perspectives from management educators. *Academy of Management Learning & Education*, 2(1), pp. 54–67.

Domazet, I. (2018). Digital transformation of business portfolio through DCRM. In: *Digital Transformation: New Challenges and Business Opportunities.* London: Silver and Smith Publishers, pp. 214–235.

Dominici, F., Fried, L. P., Zeger, S. L. (2009). So few women leaders. *Academe*, 95(4), p. 25–27.

Donina, D., Paleari, S. (2019). New public management: Global reform script or conceptual stretching? Analysis of university governance structures in the Napoleonic administrative tradition. *Higher Education*, 78(2), pp. 193–219.

Donoghue, F. (2008). *The Last Professors: The Corporate University and the Fate of the Humanities.* New York: Fordham University Press.

Dopson, S., McNay, I. (1996). Organizational culture. In: Warner, D., Palfreyman, D. (eds.). *Higher Education Management.* Buckingham: Open University Press, pp. 16–32.

Dosi, G. (1982). Technological paradigms and technological trajectories: A suggested interpretation of the determinants and directions of technical change. *Research Policy*, 11, p. 147–162.

Douglas, M. (1982). *In the Active Voice.* London: Routledge.

Douglass, J. A. (2016). How rankings came to determine world class. In: Douglass, J. A. (ed.). *The New Flagship University.* New York: Palgrave Macmillan, pp. 9–29. DOI: 10.1057/9781137500496_1

Drecksel, G. L. (1991). Leadership research: Some issues. In: Anderson, J. A. (ed.). *Communication Yearbook 14.* Newbury Park: Sage, pp. 535–546.

Drucker, P. F. (1974). *Management: Tasks, Responsibilities, Practices*. New York: Harper & Row.

Drucker, P. F. (1997). *'Seeing Things as They Really Are'*. Interviewed by Lenzner, R., Johnson, S. *Forbes*, 159, pp. 122–128.

Dubnick, M. (2012). *Accountability as Cultural Keyword, University of New Hampshire*. Paper presented at a seminar of the Research Colloquium on Good Governance, Netherlands Institute of Government, VU University, Amsterdam, 9 May 2012.

Duignan, P. A. (1988). Reflective management: The key to quality leadership. *International Journal of Educational Management*, 2(2), pp. 3–12.

Dunleavy, P., Hood, C. (1994). From old public administration to new public management. *Public Money & Management*, 14(3), pp. 9–16.

Dunleavy, P., Margetts, H. (2006). New public management is dead: Long live digital era governance. *Journal of Public Administration Research and Theory*, 16(3), pp. 467–494. DOI: 10.1093/jopart/mui057

Duque, L. C. (2014). A framework for analysing higher education performance: Students' satisfaction, perceived learning outcomes, and dropout intentions. *Total Quality Management & Business Excellence*, 25(1-2), pp. 1–21.

Ebert, C., Duarte, C. H. C. (2018). Digital transformation. *IEEE Software*, 35(4), pp. 16–21. DOI: 10.1109/MS.2018.2801537

Eckel, P. D. (2000). The role of shared governance in institutional hard decisions: Enabler or antagonist?. *The Review of Higher Education*, 24(1), pp. 15–39.

EFMD Global (2021). *Accreditations*. Available from: www.efmdglobal.org/accreditations [1 August 2021].

Egoeze, F. et al. (2018). Impact of ICT on university administrative services and management of students' records: ICT in university administration. *International Journal of Human Capital and Information Technology Professionals*, 9(2), pp. 1–15.

Egorov, A., Leshukov, O., Froumin, I. (2020). 'Regional flagship' university model in Russia: searching for the third mission incentives. *Tertiary Education and Management*, 26(1), pp. 77–90.

Ehlers, U. D. (2020). Digital leadership in higher education. *Journal of Higher Education Policy And Leadership Studies*, 1(3), pp. 6–14.

Ekman, M., Lindgren, M., Packendorff, J. (2018). Universities need leadership, academics need management: Discursive tensions and voids in the deregulation of Swedish higher education legislation. *Higher Education*, 75(2), pp. 299–321.

Ekvall, G., Ryhammar, L. (1998). Leadership style, social climate and organizational outcomes: A study of a Swedish University College. *Creativity and Innovation Management*, 7(3), pp. 126–130.

El-Kafafi, S. (2020). The Role of Entrepreneurial Leadership in Higher Education in Recovering from COVID19. In: *5th EMI International Entrepreneurship and Social Sciences Congress Proceedings*. Gostivar: Dilkur Akademi.

El-Kafafi, S., Gular, M. O. (2016). Innovation in higher education institutes through the adoption of academic entrepreneurship. *ICL Journal*, 3(1), pp. 8–29.

Elliott, G. (2012). Higher education management and university culture. In: Bell, G., Warwick, J., Galbraith, P (eds.). *Higher Education Management and Operational Research*. Rotterdam: SensePublishers, pp. 49–63. DOI: 10.1007/978-94-6091-976-3_3

Elton, L. (2000). The UK research assessment exercise: Unintended consequences. *Higher Education Quarterly*, 54(3), pp. 274–283.

Elton, L. B. (1987). Warning signs. *Times Higher Education Supplement*, 11(9), p. 12.

Enders, J. (2006). The academic profession. In: Forest, J. J. F., Altbach, P. G. (eds.). *International Handbook of Higher Education*. Dordrecht: Springer, pp. 5–21.

Enebakk, V. (2007). The three Merton theses. *Journal of Classical Sociology*, 7(2), pp. 221–238.

Engel, L. et al. (2015). *The EAIE Barometer: Internationalisation in Europe*. Amsterdam: EAIE.

Entradas, M. (2015). Science and the public: The public understanding of science and its measurements. *Portuguese Journal of Social Science*, 14(1), pp. 71–85.

Erdogan, B., Bauer, T. N. (2015). Leader-member exchange theory. In: *The Oxford Handbook of Leader-Member Exchange*. Oxford: Oxford University Press, pp. 413–421. DOI: 10.1093/oxfordhb/9780199326174.013.0023

Erickson, M., Hanna, P., Walker, C. (2021). The UK higher education senior management survey: A statactivist response to managerialist governance. *Studies in Higher Education*, 46(11), pp. 2134–2151.

Eroshkin, S. Y. et al. (2017). Conceptual system in the modern information management. *Procedia Computer Science*, 103, pp. 609–612.

Etzkowitz, H. (2003). Innovation in innovation: The triple helix of university-industry-government relations. *Social Science Information*, 42(3), pp. 293–337.

Etzkowitz, H. (2016). The entrepreneurial university: Vision and metrics. *Industry and Higher Education*, 30(2), pp. 83–97.

Etzkowitz, H., Dzisah, J. (2007) Professors of practice and the entrepreneurial university. *Engevista*, 9(2), pp. 166–173.

Etzkowitz, H., Zhou, C. (2008). Introduction to special issue building the entrepreneurial university: a global perspective. *Science and Public Policy*, 35(9), pp. 627–635.

European Commission (2010). *Assessing Europe's University-Based Research*. Brussels: EC Publications Office. DOI: 10.2777/80193

Ezell Jr, O. A. (2002). Diploma Mills: Past, Present, and Future. *College and University*, 77(3), p. 39.

Faraasyatul'Alam, G., Supriyanto, A. (2021). Relation of good university governance with education management information system, excellent service, and student trust at the entrepreneur campus. In: *2021 7th International Conference on Education and Technology (ICET)*. Piscataway: IEEE, pp. 65–69.

Farkas, M. G. (2013). Building and sustaining a culture of assessment: Best practices for change leadership. *Reference Services Review*, 41(1), pp. 13–31.

Farooq, M. et al. (2017). Analysing the relationship between sustainable leadership, talent management and organization health as predictors of university transformation. *Journal of Positive Management*, 8(1), pp. 32–50.

Fassin, Y. (1991). Academic ethos versus business ethics. *International Journal of Technology Management*, 6(5-6), pp. 533–546.

Favaro, K. (2014). *Strategy or Culture: Which is More Important?*. Available from: https://www.strategy-business.com/blog/Strategy-or-Culture-Which-Is-More-Important [1 August 2021].

Fecher, B., Friesike, S. (2014). Open science: One term, five schools of thought. In: Bartling, S., Friesike, S. (eds.). *Opening Science*. Cham: Springer, pp. 17–47. 10.1007/978-3-319-00026-8_2

Federkeil, G. (2008). Rankings and quality assurance in higher education. *Higher Education in Europe*, 33(2-3), pp. 219–231.

Feenberg, A., Barney, D. eds. (2004). *Community in the Digital Age: Philosophy and Practice.* Lanham: Rowman & Littlefield Publishers.

Felin, T., Zenger, T. R., Tomsik, J. (2009). The knowledge economy: Emerging organizational forms, missing microfoundations, and key considerations for managing human capital. *Human Resource Management*, 48(4), pp. 555–570.

Fenton-O'Creevy, M., Knight, P., Margolis, J. (2006). A practice-centered approach to management education. In: Wankel, C., DeFillippi, R. (eds.). *New Visions of Graduate Management Education: Research in Management Education and Development, Vol. 5.* Greenwich: Information Age, pp. 103–123.

Fenwick, T. (2005). Ethical dilemmas of critical management education within class-rooms and beyond. *Management Learning*, 36(1), pp. 31–48.

Fernandez, F., Baker, D. P. (2017). Science production in the United States: An unexpected synergy between mass higher education and the super research university. In: Powell, J. J. W., Baker, D. P., Fernandez, F. (eds.). *The Century of Science.* Bingley: Emerald Publishing Limited, pp. 85–111. 10.1108/S1479-367920170000033006

Fernández-Cano, A. et al. (2018). Questioning the Shanghai ranking methodology as a tool for the evaluation of universities: An integrative review. *Scientometrics*, 116(3), pp. 2069–2083.

Festing, M., Maletzky, M. (2011). Cross-cultural leadership adjustment: A multilevel framework based on the theory of structuration. *Human Resource Management Review*, 21(3), pp. 186–200.

Fiedler, F. E. (1967). *A Theory of Leadership Effectiveness.* New York: McGraw-Hill.

Filip, A. (2012). Marketing theory applicability in higher education. *Procedia - Social and Behavioral Sciences*, 46, pp. 912–916.

Finardi, K. R., Guimaraes, F. F. (2020). Internationalization and the Covid-19 pan-demic: Challenges and opportunities for the Global South. *Journal of Education, Teaching and Social Studies*, 2(4), pp. 1–15.

Fleaca, E. (2017). Embedding digital teaching and learning practices in the modern-ization of higher education institutions. In: *Proceedings of 17th International Multidisciplinary Scientific GeoConference SGEM 2017.* Albena: SGEM, pp. 41–48.

Floros, J. D. (2015). Academic leadership through strategic planning – A Dean's per-spective. In: Sternberg, R. et al. (eds.). *Academic Leadership in Higher Education – From the Top Down and the Bottom Up.* Lanham: Rowman & Littlefield, pp. 161–168.

Fongwa, N. S., Marais, L. (2016). University, knowledge and regional development: Factors affecting knowledge transfer in a developing region. *Africa Education Review*, 13(3-4), pp. 191–210.

Ford, J. (2005). Examining leadership through critical feminist readings. *Journal of Health Organization and Management*, 19(3), pp. 236–251.

Fossatti, P. et al. (2020). University and the (UN) successfulness of the strategic management for innovation. *Educação em Revista*, 36(5), p. 1–21. 10.1590/0102-4698225188

Foucault, M. (1980). *Power/Knowledge: Selected Interviews and Other Writings 1972-1977.* New York: Pantheon.

Fowler, N., Lindahl, M., Sköld, D. (2015). The projectification of university research: A study of resistance and accommodation of projectmanagement tools & techniques. *International Journal of Managing Projects in Business*, 8(1), pp. 9–32. 10.1108/IJMPB-10-2013-0059

Frazzica, G., La Spina, A. (2019). Civic engagement, external impact and the third mission of universities. In: Pepe, V. (ed.), *Civic Engagement in Contemporary Italy.* Roma: Aracne Editrice, pp. 185–214.

Fuad, D. R. S. M., Musa, K., & Hashim, Z. (2022). Innovation culture in education: A systematic review of the literature. *Management in Education*, 36(3), pp. 135–149.

Fuqua, D. R., Newman, J. L. (2005). Integrating structural and behavioral leadership strategies. *Consulting Psychology Journal: Practice and Research*, 57(2), pp. 126–132.

Fuster, E. et al. (2019). The emerging role of university spin-off companies in developing regional entrepreneurial university ecosystems: The case of Andalusia. *Technological Forecasting and Social Change*, 141, pp. 219–231.

Gaiaschi, C. (2021). The academic profession in neoliberal times: A gendered view. *Professions and Professionalism*, 11(1), pp. 1–22. 10.7577/pp.3901

Gama, J. A. P. (2018). Intelligent educational dual architecture for university digital transformation. In: *Proceedings of the 2018 IEEE Frontiers in Education Conference (FIE)*. Piscataway: IEEE, pp. 1–9.

Gandhi, M. M. (2013). Autonomy and accountability in higher education: An Indian perspective. *IOSR Journal of Research & Method in Education*, 3(5), pp. 33–37.

Gao, J. H. H., Haworth, N. (2019). Stuck in the middle? Human resource management at the interface of academia and industry. *The International Journal of Human Resource Management*, 30(22), pp. 3081–3112.

García-Peñalvo, F. J. et al. (2021). Impact of the COVID-19 on Higher Education: an Experience-Based Approach. In: *Information Technology Trends for a Global and Interdisciplinary Research Community*. Hershey: IGI Global, pp. 1–18.

Gare, A. (2005). Democracy and education: Defending the Humboldtian university and the democratic nation-state as institutions of the radical enlightenment. *Concrescence: the Australasian Journal of Process Thought*, 6, pp. 3–27.

Gaus, O., Raith, M. G. (2016). Commercial transfer: A business model innovation for the entrepreneurial university. *Industry and Higher Education*, 30(3), pp. 183–201.

Ge, Z., Hu, Y. (2020). Innovative application of artificial intelligence (AI) in the management of higher education and teaching. *Journal of Physics: Conference Series*, 1533(3), 032089, pp. 1–5. 10.1088/1742-6596/1533/3/03208910.1088/1742-6596/1533/3/032089

Gedro, J. (2010). Lesbian presentations and representations of leadership, and the implications for HRD. *Journal of European Industrial Training*, 34(6), pp. 552–564.

Gehrke, S. (2014). The idea of the digital university: Ancient traditions, disruptive technologies and the battle for the soul of higher education by Frank Bryce McCluskey and Melanie Lynn Winter (review). *The Review of Higher Education*, 37(4), pp. 565–567. 10.1353/rhe.2014.0027

Geiger, R. L. (1986). *To Advance Knowledge: The Growth of the American Research University 1900-1940*. Oxford: Oxford University Press.

Geisler, E. (2007). A typology of knowledge management: Strategic groups and role behavior in organizations. *Journal of Knowledge Management*, 11(1), pp. 84–96.

Giannakis, M., Bullivant, N. (2016). The massification of higher education in the UK: Aspects of service quality. *Journal of Further and Higher Education*, 40(5), pp. 630–648.

Gibb, A., Haskins, G., Robertson, I. (2013). Leading the entrepreneurial university: Meeting the entrepreneurial development needs of higher education institutions. In: Altmann, A., Ebersberger, B. (eds.). *Universities in Change*. New York: Springer, pp. 9–45. 10.1007/978-1-4614-4590-6_2

Gibbs, P., Murphy, P. (2009). Implementation of ethical higher education marketing. *Tertiary Education and Management*, 15(4), pp. 341–354.

Gibson, N. (1993). Quality assurance through course validation and review. In: Roger, E. (ed.). *Quality Assurance for University Teaching*. Bristol: Open University Press, pp. 91–103.

Gieysztor, A. (1992). University buildings. In: de Ridder-Symoens, H. (ed.). *A History of the University in Europe. Volume I: Universities in the Middle Ages*. Cambridge: Cambridge University Press.

Gill, R. (2014). Academics, cultural workers and critical labour studies. *Journal of Cultural Economy*, 7(1), pp. 12–30.

Gilleard, C. (2017). The place of age in the digital revolution. In: Taipale, S., Wilska, T. A., Gilleard, C. (eds.). *Digital Technologies and Generational Identity*. London: Routledge, pp. 11–22. 10.4324/9781315398624

Giri, R., Chaudhuri, S. K. (2021). Ranking journals through the lens of active visibility. *Scientometrics*, 126(3), pp. 2189–2208.

Giroux, D., Karmis, D., Rouillard, C. (2015). Between the managerial and the democratic university: Governance structure and academic freedom as sites of political struggle. *Studies in Social Justice*, 9(2), pp. 142–158.

Giroux, H. A. (2001). *Theory and Resistance in Education: Towards a Pedagogy for the Opposition*. Connecticut: Greenwood Publishing Group.

Giroux, H. A. (2002). Neoliberalism, corporate culture, and the promise of higher education: The university as a democratic public sphere. *Harvard Educational Review*, 72(4), pp. 425–464.

Giroux, H. A., Myrsiades K. (2001). *Beyond the Corporate University: Culture and Pedagogy in the New Millennium*. Oxford: Rowman & Littlefield.

Gjerding, A. N. et al. (2006). Twenty practices of an entrepreneurial university. *Higher Education Management and Policy*, 18(3), pp. 1–28.

Gläser, J. et al. (2010). The limited use of research evaluation systems for managerial control in universities. In:Whitley, R., Gläser, J., Engwall, L. (eds.). *Reconfiguring Knowledge Production: Changing Authority Relationships in the Sciences and Their Consequences for Intellectual Innovation*. Oxford: Oxford University Press, pp. 149–183. 10.1093/acprof:oso/9780199590193.003.0005

Goddard, J., Kempton, L., Vallance, P. (2012). The civic university: connecting the global and the local. In: Capello, R., Olechnicka, A., Gorzelak, G. (eds.). *Universities, Cities and Regions*. London: Routledge, pp. 67–87.

Goldman, G. (2020). Using the critical management studies tenet of denaturalisation as a vehicle to decolonise the management discourse in South Africa. *African Journal of Business Ethics*, 14(1), pp. 42–61.

Goldstein, P. J. (2010). *Responding to Recession: IT Funding and Cost Management in Higher Education. Key Findings*. Boulder: EDUCAUSE.

González, A. G. (2006). Open science: Open source licenses in scientific research. *North Carolina Journal of Law & Technology*, 7(2), pp. 321–366.

Goodman, S. K. (1993). Information needs for management decision-making. *Information Management*, 27(4), pp. 12–23.

Google (2021). *Google Scholar*. Available from: scholar.google.com [8 August 2021].

Görason, B., Maharajh, R., Schmoch, U. (2009). New activities of universities in transfer and extension: multiple requirements and manifold solutions. *Science and Public Policy*, 36(2), pp. 157–164.

Gorbunova, N. V., Timirgaleeva, R. R., Khrulyova, A. A. (2021). Integrated model formation for the digital university development. *SHS Web of Conferences*, 113, pp. 1–9. 10.1051/shsconf/202111300024

Gorodilov, M., Chuchulina, E. (2018). Internalization of the University as a Factor in Improving the Quality of Education. *Managerial Challenges of the Contemporary Society Proceedings*, 11(2), 119.

Gourlay, L. (2020). *Posthumanism and the Digital University: Texts, Bodies and Materialities.* Bloomsbury Publishing.

Gómez, I. et al. (2009). Structure and research performance of Spanish universities. *Scientometrics*, 79(1), pp. 131–146.

Green, M. F. (2012). *Measuring and Assessing Internationalization.* Washington: NAFSA Association,of International Educators.

Green, M., McDade, S. (1994). *Investing in Higher Education: A Handbook of Leadership Development.* Phoenix: Oryx Press.

Griffiths, J. (2013). Dematerialization, pragmatism and the European copyright revolution. *Oxford Journal of Legal Studies*, 33(4), pp. 767–790.

Grosseck, G., Malița, L., Bunoiu, M. (2020). Higher education institutions towards digital transformation: the WUT case. In: Curaj, A., Deca, L., Pricopie, R. (eds.). *European Higher Education Area: Challenges for a New Decade.* Cham: Springer, pp. 565–581. 10.1007/978-3-030-56316-5_35

Groves, R. E. V., Pendlebury, M. W., Stiles, D. R. (1997). A critical appreciation of the uses for strategic management thinking, systems and techniques in British universities. *Financial Accountability & Management*, 13(4), pp. 293–312.

Grudzinskiy, A. O., Zakharova, L. N., Bureeva, N. N. (2016). Personal competences of succession pool of the entrepreneurial university. *University Management: Practice and Analysis*, 3, pp. 104–117.

Guenther, T. W., Schmidt, U. (2015). Adoption and use of management controls in higher education institutions. In: Welpe, I. et al. (eds.). *Incentives and Performance: Governance of Research Organizations.* Cham: Springer, pp. 361–378. 10.1007/978-3-319-09785-5_22

Guglietti, M. V. (2012). The university and a new definition of enlightenment. *TOPIA: Canadian Journal of Cultural Studies*, 1(28), pp. 306–311.

Gumport, P. J. et al. (1997). *Trends in United States Higher Education from Massification to Post Massification.* Stanford: National Center for Postsecondary Improvement, School of Education, Stanford University.

Gunn, B. (1995). The paradigm shift in university management. *International Journal of Educational Management*, 9, pp. 28–40.

Günther, W. A. et al. (2017). Debating big data: A literature review on realizing value from big data. *The Journal of Strategic Information Systems*, 26(3), pp. 191–209.

Guri-Rosenblit, S., (2006). The many ideas of the 'university' and their various manifestations. Available from: http://www.dsw.edu.pl/fileadmin/user_upload/seminars/Kropiwnicki_Guri_Rosenblit_Wiele_idei_university.doc

Guri-Rosenblit, S., Šebková S., Teichler U. (2007). Massification and diversity of higher education systems: interplay of complex dimensions. *Higher Education Policy*, 20(4), pp. 373–389.

Gurusamy, K., Srinivasaraghavan, N., Adikari, S. (2016). An integrated framework for design thinking and agile methods for digital transformation. In: Marcus, A. (ed.). *Design, User Experience, and Usability: Design Thinking and Methods: 5th International Conference of Design, User Experience, and Usability DUXU 2016.* Cham: Springer, pp. 34–42. 10.1007/978-3-319-40409-7_4

Guthey, E., Jackson, B. (2011). Cross-cultural leadership revisited. In: Bryman, A. et al. (eds.). *The SAGE Handbook of Leadership*. Los Angeles: SAGE Publications, pp. 165–178.

Habánik, J., Jambor, J. (2014). Implementation and certification of the quality management system at the university. In: *Proceedings of the Scientific Conference "Quality and Leading Innovation"*. Košice: Technical University of Košice. 10.12776/QALI.V1.#11

Habermas, J., Blazek, J. R. (1987). The idea of the university: Learning processes. *New German Critique*, 41, pp. 3–22.

Hackman, J. R. (1980). Work redesign and motivation. *Professional Psychology*, 11(3), pp. 445–455.

Hackman, J. R., Walton, R. E. (1985). *The Leadership of Groups in Organizations*. New Haven: School of Organization and Management, Yale University.

Hackman, J. R., Walton, R. E. (1986). Leading groups in organizations. In: Goodman, P. S. (ed.). *Designing Effective Work Groups*. San Francisco: Jossey-Bass, pp. 72–119.

Hai, W., Ye, Y. X. (2003). Study on efficiency evaluation of science technology and finance integration. *Policy-Making Reference*, 2, pp. 67–72.

Hallonsten, O. (2021). Stop evaluating science: a historical-sociological argument. *Social Science Information*, 60(1), pp. 7–26.

Hammer, M., Champy, J. (2009). *Reengineering the Corporation: Manifesto for Business Revolution*. New York: Zondervan.

Hamzehpour, F. et al. (2020). Regulating strategy of the development the field of research of Islamic Azad University using SWOT, SPACE and QSPM (study of branches of Tehran and Alborz provinces). *Journal of New Approaches in Educational Administration*, 11(43), pp. 93–126.

Han, S., Zhong, Z. (2015). Strategy maps in university management: A comparative study. *Educational Management Administration & Leadership*, 43(6), pp. 939–953.

Hannigan, J. B. (2007). *Leadership in Higher Education: An Investigation of Servant Leadership as a Predictor of College Performance*. Thesis (PhD), Capella University. Available from: https://www.servantleaderperformance.com/wp-content/uploads/2018/04/2008-Hannigan-Dissertation.pdf

Hardy, C. (1988). The rational approach to budget cuts: One university's experience. *Higher Education*, 17(2), pp. 151–173.

Harris, M. (2010). Interdisciplinary strategy and collaboration: A case study of American research universities. *Journal of Research Administration*, 41(1), pp. 22–34.

Harvey, L., Green, D. (1993). Defining quality. *Assessment & Evaluation in Higher Education*, 18(1), 9–34.

Harvey, S., Royal, M., Stout, D. (2003). Instructor's transformational leadership: University student attitudes and ratings. *Psychological Reports*, 92(2), pp. 395–402.

Hassan, R. (2017). The worldly space: The digital university in network time. *British Journal of Sociology of Education*, 38(1), pp. 72–82.

Hatten, M. L. (1982). Strategic management in not-for-profit organizations. *Strategic Management Journal*, 3(2), pp. 89–104.

Hauptman, A. M. (2006). Higher education finance: Trends and issues. In: Forest, J. J. F., Altbach, P. G. (eds.). *International Handbook of Higher Education*. Dordrecht: Springer, pp 243–280. 10.1007/978-1-4020-4012-2_6

Hava, H. T., Erturgut, R. (2010). An evaluation of education relations together with technology, employement and economic development components. *Procedia - Social and Behavioral Sciences*, 2(2), pp. 1771–1775.

Hawkins, A. G., Frohoff, K. M. (2010). Promoting the academy-the challenges of marketing higher education. *Research in Higher Education Journal*, 7, pp. 1–13.

Hayes, T. (2007). Delphi study of the future of marketing of higher education. *Journal of Business Research*, 60(9), pp. 927–931.

Hazelkorn, E. (2015). *Rankings and the Reshaping of Higher Education: The Battle for World-Class Excellence*. London: Palgrave Macmillan.

Hazemi, R., Hailes, S. eds. (2001). *The Digital University: Building a Learning Community*. London: Springer. 10.1007/978-1-4471-0167-3

Hazemi, R., Hailes, S., Wilbur, S. eds. (2012). *The Digital University: Reinventing the Academy*. London: Springer. 10.1007/978-1-4471-0625-8

Heckman, R., Crowston, K., Misiolek, N. (2007). A structurational perspective on leadership in virtual teams. In: Crowston, K., Sieber, S., Wynn, E. (eds). *Virtuality and Virtualization*. Boston: Springer, pp. 151–168. 10.1007/978-0-387-73025-7_12

Heim, I., Han, T., Ghobadian, A. (2018). Value co-creation in ICT services company: A case study of a cross-border acquisition. *Journal of East-West Business*, 24(4), pp. 319–338.

Held, J., Germelmann, C. C. (2018). Deception in consumer behavior research: A literature review on objective and perceived deception. *Projectics/Proyéctica/Projectique*, (3), pp. 119–145.

Helgesen, Ø. (2008). Marketing for higher education: A relationship marketing approach. *Journal of Marketing for Higher Education*, 18(1), pp. 50–78.

Helgesen, S. (1995). *The Web of Inclusion: A New Architecture for Building Great Organisations*. New York: Currency/Doubleday.

Hemsley-Brown, J., Oplatka, I. (2006). Universities in a competitive global marketplace: a systematic review of the literature on higher education marketing. *International Journal of Public Sector Management*, 19(4), pp. 316–338.

Henke, J. (2019). Third mission as an opportunity for professionalization in science management. *Publications*, 7(4), p. 62. 10.3390/publications7040062

Hensellek, S. (2020). Digital leadership: a framework for successful leadership in the digital age. *Journal of Media Management and Entrepreneurship*, 2(1), pp. 55–69.

Hides, M. T. et al. (2004). Implementation of EFQM excellence model self-assessment in the UK higher education sector-lessons learned from other sectors. *The TQM Magazine*, 16(3), pp. 194–201.

Hil, R., Thompsett, F., Lyons, K. (2022). Over the horizon: Is there an alternative to neoliberal university governance?. *Social Alternatives*, 41(1), pp. 63–69.

Hill, R. A. (1985). *Multicampus University Organizational Structure and Branch Campus Administrative Problems*. Thesis (PhD), The Florida State University.

Hinings, B., Gegenhuber, T., Greenwood, R. (2018). Digital innovation and transformation: an institutional perspective. *Information and Organization*, 28(1), 52–61.

Hirst, P., Thompson, G., Bromley, S. (2015). *Globalization in Question*. New York: John Wiley & Sons.

Hladchenko, M. (2015). Balanced Scorecard: A strategic management system of the higher education institution. *International Journal of Educational Management*, 29(2), pp. 167–176.

Hodgins, M., Mannix-McNamara, P. (2021). The Neoliberal University in Ireland: Institutional bullying by another name?. *Societies*, 11(2), p. 52. 10.3390/soc11020052

Hoecht, A. (2021). Trust, control, and responsibility in research–An accountability perspective. In: Gibbs, P., Maassen, P. (eds). *Trusting in Higher Education*. Cham: Springer, pp. 133–144. 10.1007/978-3-030-87037-9_9

Hogan, J., Lucke, T. (2006). Driving growth with new products: Common pricing traps to avoid. *Journal of Business Strategy*, 27(1), pp. 54–58.

Hogan, N. M., Sweeney, K. J. (2013). Social networking and scientific communication: A paradoxical return to Mertonian roots?. *Journal of the American Society for Information Science and Technology*, 64(3), pp. 644–646.

Hojjati, A. et al. (2018). Providing a talent management model for Shahed University Staff. *Iranian Journal of Educational Sociology*, 1(10), pp. 25–38.

Holmwood, J., Marcuello Servos, C. (2019). Challenges to public universities: digitalisation, commodification and precarity. *Social Epistemology*, 33(4), pp. 309–320.

Hong, M. (2020). A comparative study of the internationalization of higher education policy in Australia and China (2008-2015). *Studies in Higher Education*, 45(4), pp. 768–779.

Honu, Y. A. (2018). Shared governance: Opportunities and challenges. *Academy of Educational Leadership Journal*, 22(2), pp. 1–8.

Hopkins, S. (2015). Ghosts in the Machine: Incarcerated Students and the Digital University. *Australian Universities' Review*, 57(2), pp. 46–53.

Hosseini, M. A. (2021). Criticism and attachment in the Neoliberal University. In: Sridhar, A., Hosseini, M. A., Attridge, D. (eds.). *The Work of Reading*. Cham: Palgrave Macmillan, pp. 43–65. 10.1007/978-3-030-71139-9_3

House, R. J. (1976). A 1976 theory of charismatic leadership. *Working Paper Series [Faculty of Management Studies, University of Toronto]*, 76(06), pp. 1–34.

House, R. J., Wright, N. S., Aditya, R. N. (1997). Cross-cultural research on organizational leadership: A critical analysis and a proposed theory. In: Earley, P. C., Erez, M. (eds.). *New Perspectives on International Industrial/Organizational Psychology*. San Francisco: The New Lexington Press, pp. 535–625.

Howell, J. P. et al. (1990). Substitutes for leadership: Effective alternatives to ineffective leadership. *Organizational Dynamics*, 19(1), pp. 21–38.

Howells, J. R. et al. (2014). University management and organisational change: A dynamic institutional perspective. *Cambridge Journal of Regions, Economy and Society*, 7(2), pp. 251–270.

Huang, F. (2015). Building the world-class research universities: A case study of China. *Higher Education*, 70(2), pp. 203–215.

Huff, T. E. (2007). Some historical roots of the ethos of science. *Journal of Classical Sociology*, 7(2), pp. 193–210.

Hurd, F., Singh, S. (2020). 'Something has to change': A collaborative journey towards academic well-being through critical reflexive practice. *Management Learning*, 52(3), pp. 347–363. 10.1177/1350507620970723

Huxster, J. K. et al. (2018). Understanding 'understanding' in public understanding of science. *Public Understanding of Science*, 27(7), pp. 756–771.

Hvorecký, J. (2017). University leadership and role distribution. In: *2017 15th International Conference on Emerging eLearning Technologies and Applications (ICETA)*. Piscataway: IEEE, pp. 1–8.

Hyatt, S. A. (1969). *A Behavioral Study of Management and Leadership in Higher Education*. Thesis (PhD), The Ohio State University.

Ibragimovich, A. M. et al. (2022). On the need to implement innovative and digital technologies in universities. *International Journal of Culture and Modernity*, 13, pp. 110–114.

Ikpesu, O. C., Ken-Ine, O. G. (2019). Human resources management and job performance of non-academic staff in universities in rivers state. *International Journal of Education Development*, 25(2), pp. 1–11.

Iliashenko, O. et al. (2020). Formation of requirements for IT services of a research department at a digital university. *IOP Conference Series: Materials Science and Engineering*, 940(1), p. 1–11. 10.1088/1757-899X/940/1/012008

Inga, E. et al. (2021). Planning and strategic management of higher education considering the vision of Latin America. *Education Sciences*, 11(4), 188. 10.3390/educsci11040188

Innes, J., Booher, D. E. (1999). *Planning Institutions in the Network Society: Theory for Collaborative Planning*. Berkeley: University of California at Berkeley, Institute of Urban and Regional Development.

Ismail, A. R., Nguyen, B., Melewar, T. C. (2018). Impact of perceived social media marketing activities on brand and value consciousness: Roles of usage, materialism and conspicuous consumption. *International Journal of Internet Marketing and Advertising*, 12(3), pp. 233–254.

Iyer, P. et al. (2019). Market orientation, positioning strategy and brand performance. *Industrial Marketing Management*, 81, pp. 16–29.

Jaeger, J. et al. (2022). *An Epistemology for Democratic Citizen Science*. Preprint. 10.31219/osf.io/j62sb

Jafari, S. et al. (2018). A model for internationalization of universities in the fields of humanities and social science. *Journal of Higher Education Curriculum Studies*, 9(17), pp. 67–91.

Jameson, J. ed. (2019). *International Perspectives on Leadership in Higher Education: Critical Thinking for Global Challenges*. London: Routledge.

Jamshidi, L. et al. (2012). Developmental patterns of privatization in higher education: A comparative study. *Higher Education*, 64(6), pp. 789–803.

Jani, H. M. (2012). Modeling total quality management in higher education with case-based reasoning. *Journal of Next Generation Information Technology*, 3(3), p. 11.

Jankovič, P., Vukovič, G. (2006). Chief secretarial officer at a university-manager. *Ekonomska misao i praksa*, (1), pp. 113–124.

Jarrat, A. et al. (1985). *Jarratt Report: Report of Steering Committee for Efficiency Studies in Universities*. London: CVCP.

Jarvenpaa, S. L., Leidner, D. E. (1999). Communication and trust in global virtual teams. *Organization Science*, 10(6), pp. 791–815.

Jaschik, S., Lederman, D. eds. (2015). *The 2015 Inside Higher Ed Survey of Community College Presidents: A study by Gallup and Inside Higher Ed*. Washington: Inside Higher Ed. Available from: https://www.insidehighered.com/surveys [13 January 2016].

Javdani Gandomani, T., Ziaei Nafchi, M. (2016). Agile transition and adoption human-related challenges and issues. *Computers in Human Behavior*, 62(C), pp. 257–266.

Jenkins, R. (1982). Pierre Bourdieu and the reproduction of determinism. *Sociology*, 16(2), pp. 270–281.

Jensen, A., Thuesen, C., Geraldi, J. (2016). The projectification of everything: Projects as a human condition. *Project Management Journal*, 47(3), pp. 21–34.

Jessop, B. (2018). On academic capitalism. *Critical Policy Studies*, 12(1), pp. 104–109.

Jewitt, C. (2013). Multimodal methods for researching digital technologies. In: Price, S., Jewitt, C., Brown, B. (eds.). *The SAGE Handbook of Digital Technology Research*. Newbury Park: Sage Publications, pp. 250–265. 10.4135/9781446282229.n18

Jian, Y., Zhou, Z., Zhou, N. (2019). Brand cultural symbolism, brand authenticity, and consumer well-being: the moderating role of cultural involvement. *Journal of Product & Brand Management*, 28(4), pp. 529–539. 10.1108/JPBM-08-2018-1981

Johanson, J., Vahlne, J. E. (1993). Management of internationalization. In: Zan, L., Zambon, S., Pettigrew, A. M. (eds.). *Perspectives on Strategic Change*. Dordrecht: Springer, pp. 43–78. 10.1007/978-0-585-27290-0_2

Johnes, J., Taylor, J. (1989). *Performance Indicators in Higher Education*. Milton Keynes: Open University Press and the Society for Research into Higher Education.

Johnson J. M., Regets, M. C. (1998). International mobility of scientists and engineers to the united states - brain drain or brain circulation?. In: Johnson, J. M., Regets, M. C. (eds.). *SRS Issue Brief (NSF 98-316)*. Arlington: Division of Science Resources Studies, National Science Foundation.

Johnston, B., MacNeill, S., Smyth, K. (2018). *Conceptualising the Digital University: Digital Education and Learning*. Cham: Palgrave Macmillan, pp. 217–233. 10.1007/978-3-319-99160-3_11

Jones, C. (2013). The digital university: A concept in need of definition. In: Goodfellow, R., Lea, M. R. (eds.). *Literacy in the Digital University*. London: Routledge, pp. 176–186.

Jones, E. et al. (2021). Global social responsibility and the internationalisation of higher education for society. *Journal of Studies in International Education*, 25(4), pp. 330–347. 10.1177/10283153211031679

Jones, G. S. (2016). Utopian socialism reconsidered. In: Samuel, R. (ed.). *People's History and Socialist Theory*. London: Routledge, pp. 138–144.

Jones, S. et al. (2012). Distributed leadership: A collaborative framework for academics, executives and professionals in higher education. *Journal of Higher Education Policy and Management*, 34(1), pp. 67–78.

Jung, H., Kim, B. K. (2018). Determinant factors of university spin-off: The case of Korea. *The Journal of Technology Transfer*, 43(6), pp. 1631–1646.

Kalimullin, A. M., Dobrotvorskaya, S. G. (2016). Higher education marketing strategies based on factors impacting the enrollees' choice of a university and an academic program. *International Journal of Environmental and Science Education*, 11(13), pp. 6025–6040.

Kalimullin, A. M., Khodyreva, E., Koinova-Zoellner, J. (2016). Development of internal system of education quality assessment at a University. *International Journal of Environmental and Science Education*, 11(13), pp. 6002–6013.

Kalleberg, R. (2007). A reconstruction of the ethos of science. *Journal of Classical Sociology*, 7(2), pp. 137–160.

Kallio, T. J., Kallio, K. M., Blomberg, A. (2020). From professional bureaucracy to competitive bureaucracy-redefining universities' organization principles, performance measurement criteria, and reason for being. *Qualitative Research in Accounting & Management*, 17(1), pp. 82–108. 10.1108/QRAM-10-2019-0111

Kaminskyi, O. Y., Yereshko, J., Kyrychenko, S. O. (2018). Digital transformation of university education in Ukraine: Trajectories of Development in the conditions of new technological and economic order. *Information Technologies and Learning Tools*, 64(2), pp. 128–137. 10.33407/itlt.v64i2.2083

Kane, G. C. et al. (2019). How digital leadership is(n't) different. *MIT Sloan Management Review*, 60(3), pp. 34–39.

Kane, R., Sandretto, S., Heath, C. (2002). Telling half the story: A critical review of research on the teaching beliefs and practices of university academics. *Review of Educational Research*, 72(2), pp. 177–228.

Kaplan, G. E. (2006). Institutions of academic governance and institutional theory: A framework for further research. In: Smart, J. C. (ed.). *Higher Education: Handbook of Theory and Research*. Dordrecht: Springer, pp. 213–281. doi.org/10.1007/1-4020-4512-3_5

Karhapää, S. J., Savolainen, T. (2017). Management and governance change in a university organisation: A longitudinal study of changing discourses in the rector's speeches. In: Ndaba, Z., Thabang, M. (eds.). *Proceedings of the 5th International Conference on Management, Leadership and Governance ICMLG 2017.* Johannesburg: Academic Conferences International, pp. 200–207.

Karlsen, J. (2007). *The Regional Role of the University: A Study of Knowledge Creation in the Agora Between Agder University College and Regional Actors in Agder, Norway.* Thesis (PhD), Norwegian University of Science and Technology.

Karlsen, J. T., Larrea, M. (2019). Does a responsible university need a third mission? In: Sørensen, M. P. et al. (eds.). *The Responsible University: Exploring the Nordic Context and Beyond.* Cham, Palgrave Macmillan, pp. 173–199. 10.1007/978-3-030-25646-3_7

Karmoush, A. A., Theeb, I. A. K. (2013). Modern and contemporary trends in university management in colleges (change management as a model). *Journal of Education and Scientific Studies,* 1(1), pp. 1–35.

Karwowska, E., Leja, K. (2018). Is there any room for improvement for university social responsibility? Coopetition as a catalyst. *E-MENTOR,* (3), pp. 4–13.

Kasim, N. N. M., Khalid, F. (2016). Choosing the right learning management system (LMS) for the higher education institution context: A systematic review. *International Journal of Emerging Technologies in Learning,* 11(6), pp. 55–61.

Katsulis, Y. (2010). "Living like a king": Conspicuous consumption, virtual communities, and the social construction of paid sexual encounters by US sex tourists. *Men and Masculinities,* 13(2), pp. 210–230.

Kazmina, I. et al. (2020). Fourth industrial revolution-engineering innovations for labor productivity increasing. *Talent Development & Excellence,* 12(3), pp. 477–487.

Keeling, R. (2006). The Bologna Process and the Lisbon Research Agenda: The European Commission's expanding role in higher education discourse. *European Journal of Education,* 41(2), pp. 203–223.

Kehm, B. M. (2014). Global university rankings - Impacts and unintended side effects. *European Journal of Education,* 49(1), pp. 102–112.

Kenchakkanavar, A. Y. (2015). Facebook and Twitter for academic libraries in the Twenty First Century. *International Research: Journal of Library and Information Science,* 5(1), pp. 162–173.

Kenna, R., Mryglod, O., Berche, B. (2017). *A Scientists' View of Scientometrics: Not Everything That Counts Can be Counted.* arXiv preprint. arXiv:1703.10407. 10.48550/arXiv.1703.10407

Kerr, S., Jermier, J. M. (1978). Substitutes for leadership: Their meaning and measurement. *Organizational Behavior and Human Performance,* 22(3), pp. 375–403. 10.101 6/0030-5073(78)90023-5

Kesten, A. (2019). Analysis of the missions of higher education institutions within the scope of third mission understanding. *International Journal of Educational Methodology,* 5(3), pp. 387–400.

Kezar, A., Eckel, P. (2002). The effect of institutional culture on change strategies in higher education: Universal principles or culturally responsive concepts?. *The Journal of Higher Education,* 73(4), pp. 435–460.

Kezar, A., Eckel, P. (2004). Meeting today's governance challenges: A synthesis of the literature and examination of a future research agenda. *Journal of Higher Education,* 75(4), pp. 371–400.

Khademi Kolahlou, M. et al. (2019). A model for chief information officer's tasks in higher education institutions. *Journal of Management and Planning In Educational System*, 12(1), pp. 125–150.

Khalid, J. et al. (2018). Promising digital university: A pivotal need for higher education transformation. *International Journal of Management in Education*, 12(3), pp. 264–275.

Khamis, A., Kamarudin, N. K. K. B. (2014). Measuring job satisfaction among lecturers in public university using structural equation model. *Asian Journal of Science and Technology*, 5(11), pp. 705–712.

Khan, M. M., Rehman, Z. U., Dost, M. K. B. (2012). *Effects of Dynamics Persuading and Nurturing the Professional Learning Behavior of the University Students: A Knowledge Management Approach*. Singapore: National Library Singapore.

Khan, S. A., Islam, T., Husain, G. (2014). Artificial neural network based online sensor calibration and compensation. *International Journal of Computing*, 6(3), pp. 74–78.

Khatri, P., Dutta, S. (2020). Twists and turns in academic leadership during COVID-19 Pandemic. In: *International Conference on Global Economic Order in the Post-COVID-19 Era: Challenges, Opportunities and Strategies*. Delhi: Maharaja Agrasen University Publication, pp. 8–15.

Khomyakov, M. (2021). Should science be evaluated? *Social Science Information*, 60(3), pp. 308–317. 10.1177/05390184211022101

Khwaja, T. (2015). *The Language of Leadership a Feminist Poststructural Discourse Analysis of Inaugural Addresses by Presidents of High Profile Research Universities*. Thesis (PhD), The College of William and Mary.

Kim, C., Yang, K. H., Kim, J. (2008). A strategy for third-party logistics systems: A case analysis using the blue ocean strategy. *Omega*, 36(4), pp. 522–534.

Kim, S. Y., Kim, Y. (2018). The ethos of science and its correlates: An empirical analysis of scientists' endorsement of Mertonian norms. *Science, Technology and Society*, 23(1), pp. 1–24.

Kim, T. (2009). Transnational academic mobility, internationalization and inter-culturality in higher education. *Intercultural Education*, 20(5), pp. 395–405.

King, A. F. (2000). The changing face of accountability: Monitoring and assessing insti-tutional performance in higher education. *Journal of Higher Education*, 71(4), pp. 411–431.

King, R., Marginson, S., Naidoo, R. eds. (2011). *Handbook on Globalization and Higher Education*. Cheltenham: Edward Elgar Publishing.

Kinman, G., Jones, F. (2003). Running up and down escalator: Stressors and strains in UK academics. *Quality in Higher Education*, 9(1), pp. 21–38.

Kirby, D. A., Guerrero, M., Urbano, D. (2011). Making universities more en-trepreneurial: Development of a model. *Canadian Journal of Administrative Sciences*, 28(3), pp. 302–316.

Kirschner, P. A., Buckingham-Shum, S. J., Carr, C. S. eds. (2012). *Visualizing Argumentation: Software Tools for Collaborative and Educational Sense-Making*. London: Springer. 10.1007/978-1-4471-0037-9

Kiuppis, F., Waldow, F. (2008). 'Institute university' meets bologna process: The German system of higher education in transition. In: *Changing Universities in Europe and the Bologna Process: A Seven Country Study*. Roma: Aracne, pp. 73–99. 10.4399/97888548213545

Klofsten, M. et al. (2019). The entrepreneurial university as driver for economic growth and social change: Key strategic challenges. *Technological Forecasting and Social Change*, 141, pp. 149–158.

Knight, J. (2001). Monitoring the quality and progress of internationalization. *Journal of Studies in International Education*, 5(3), pp. 228–243.

Knight, J. (2003). Updating the definition of internationalization. *International Higher Education*, 33, pp. 2–3.

Knight, J., De Wit, H. (2018). Internationalization of higher education: Past and Future. *International Higher Education*, (95), pp. 2–4.

Knudsen, M. P., Frederiksen, M. H., Goduscheit, R. C. (2021). New forms of engagement in third mission activities: A multi-level university-centric approach. *Innovation*, 23(2), pp. 209–224.

Kobylarek, A. (2017). *The Polish Humboldtian University in the Face of Paradigmatic Change*. Cambridge: Cambridge Scholars Publishing.

Kodama, H., Watatani, K., Sengoku, S. (2013). Competency-based assessment of academic interdisciplinary research and implication to university management. *Research Evaluation*, 22(2), pp. 93–104.

Kohtamäki, M., Thorgren, S., Wincent, J. (2016). Organizational identity and behaviors in strategic networks. *Journal of Business & Industrial Marketing*, 31(1), pp. 36–46.

Kok, S. K. et al. (2010). The move towards managerialism: Perceptions of staff in 'traditional' and 'new' UK universities. *Tertiary Education and Management*, 16(2), pp. 99–113.

Kokkinakos, P. et al. (2016). Digital transformation: Is public sector following the enterprise 2.0 paradigm? In: *International Conference on Digital Transformation and Global Society*. Cham: Springer, pp. 96–105.

Kola, A., Leja, K. (2017). The third sector in the universities' third mission. In: Sulkowski, L. (ed.). *Management and Culture of the University*. Frankfurt am Main: Peter Lang, pp. 99–125.

Kønig, N., Børsen, T., Emmeche, C. (2017). The ethos of post-normal science. *Futures*, 91, pp. 12–24.

Konina, O. V., Tinkov, S. A., Tinkova, E. V. (2020). Management in higher education based on "smart technologies": Digital managerial staff vs. artificial intelligence. In: *Institute of Scientific Communications Conference*. Cham: Springer, pp. 1738–1745.

Kornelakis, A., Petrakaki, D. (2020). Embedding employability skills in UK higher education: between digitalization and marketization. *Industry and Higher Education*, 34(5), pp. 290–297.

Kortov, S. V. et al. (2019). Patent strategy as a key component of innovation development in universities. *Университетское управление: практика и анализ*, 23(5), pp. 85–96.

Kotarbiński, T. (2019). *Traktat o Dobrej Robocie*. Łódź: Wydawnictwo Uniwersytetu Łódzkiego.

Kotosz, B. G. et al. (2015). How to measure the local economic impact of universities? A methodological overview. *Regional Statistics*, 5(2), pp. 3–19.

Kozien, E., Kozien, A. (2017). Academic governance as a determinant of efficient management of a university in Poland-legal and comparative perspective. In: Potocan, V., Kalinic, P., Vuletic, A. (eds.). *Economic and Social Development: Book of Proceedings*. Varazdin: Varazdin Development and Entrepreneurship Agency, pp. 38–47.

Krachenberg, A. R. (1972). Bringing the concept of marketing to higher education. *The Journal of Higher Education*, 43(5), pp. 369–380.

Krause, M. et al. (2008). *The University Against Itself The NYU Strike and the Future of the Academic Workplace*. Philadelphia: Temple University Press.

Krehbiel, T. C. et al. (2017). Agile Manifesto for teaching and learning. *Journal of Effective Teaching*, 17(2), pp. 90–111.

Kretschmer, H. (1993). Measurement of social stratification: A contribution to the dispute on the Ortega hypothesis. *Scientometrics*, 26(1), pp. 97–113.

Krimsky, S. (1987).The new corporate identity of the American university. *Alternatives*, 14(2), pp. 20–29.

Kristensen, B. (1999). The entrepreneurial university as a learning university. *Higher Education in Europe*, 24(1), pp. 35–46.

Kristensen, K. H. (2016). *Winning Strategies for Internationalisation at Nordic Technical Universities*. Thesis (MS), University of Stavanger.

Kumar, A., Gill, B. S. (2012). Maintenance vs. reengineering software systems. *Global Journal of Computer Science and Technology*,11(23), pp. 59–64.

Kumar, P., Raju, N. V. S., Kumar, M. V. (2016). Quality of quality definitions: An analysis. *International Journal of Scientific Engineering and Technology*, 5(3), pp. 142–148.

Kwiek, M. (2001). The internationalization and globalization of higher education in central and eastern Europe. *Society for Research into Higher Education International News*, 47, pp. 3–5.

Kwiek, M. (2010). Finansowanie szkolnictwa wyższego w Polsce a transformacje finansowania publicznego szkolnictwa wyższego w Europie. *CPP Research Papers Series*, 16, pp. 1–54.

Kwiek, M. (2015a). The internationalization of research in Europe: A quantitative study of 11 national systems from a micro-level perspective. *Journal of Studies in International Education*, 19(4), pp. 341–359.

Kwiek, M. (2015b). Inequalities in scientific knowledge production: The role of the most productive scientists in 11 European countries. *Science and Higher Education*, 1(45), pp. 77–89.

Kwiek, M. (2016). From privatization (of the expansion era) to de-privatization (of the contraction era): A national counter-trend in a global context. In: Slaughter, S., Taylor, B. (eds.). *Higher Education, Stratification, and Workforce Development*. Cham: Springer, pp. 311–329. 10.1007/978-3-319-21512-9_16

Kwiek, M. (2018). *Changing European Academics: A Comparative Study of Social Stratification, Work Patterns and Research Productivity*. London: Routledge.

Kwiek, M., Antonowicz, D. (2015). The changing paths in academic careers in european universities: Minor steps and major milestones. In: Fumasoli, T., Goastellec, G., Kehm, B. (eds.). *Academic Work and Careers in Europe: Trends, Challenges, Perspectives*. Cham: Springer, pp. 41–68. 10.1007/978-3-319-10720-2_3

Laalo, H., Kinnari, H., Silvennoinen, H. (2019). Setting new standards for homo academicus: Entrepreneurial university graduates on the EU agenda. *European Education*, 51(2), pp. 93–110.

Labby, S. A. (2010). *The Relationship Among Principals' Emotional Intelligence Skills With Respect to School Accountability Ratings and Selected Demographic Factors*. Thesis (PhD), Sam Houston State University.

Lacković, N. (2020). Neoliberal higher education: Digital, innovative, relational, pictorial?. In: Lacković, N. (ed.). *Inquiry Graphics in Higher Education*. Cham: Palgrave Macmillan, pp. 25–43. 10.1007/978-3-030-39387-8_2

Lam, A. (2010). From 'ivory tower traditionalists' to 'entrepreneurial scientists'? Academic scientists in fuzzy university-industry boundaries. *Social Studies of Science*, 40(2), pp. 307–340.

Langbert, M., Fox, M. (2011). The compensation and benefits of private university presidents. *SSRN Electronic Journal*. Available from: https://ssrn.com/abstract= 2089641. 10.2139/ssrn.2089641

Lapsley, D., Chaloner, D. (2020). Post-truth and science identity: A virtue-based approach to science education. *Educational Psychologist*, 55(3), pp. 132–143.

Lapworth, S. (2004). Arresting decline in shared governance: Towards a flexible model for academic participation. *Higher Education Quarterly*, 58(4), pp. 299–314.

Laredo, P. (2007). Revisiting the third mission of universities: Toward a renewed categorization of university activities?. *Higher Education Policy*, 20(4), pp. 441–456.

Larson, C. E., LaFasto, F. M. J. (1989). *Teamwork: What Must Go Right/What Can Go Wrong*. Newbury Park: Sage Publications.

Larsson, A., Teigland, R. (2019). *Digital Transformation and Public Services: Societal Impacts in Sweden and Beyond*. London: Routledge. 10.4324/9780429319297

Lasi, H. et al. (2014). Industry 4.0. *Business & Information Systems Engineering*, 6(4), pp. 239–242.

Lassabe, L. (2021). An insider's guide to university administration. *The Journal of Faculty Development*, 35(1), pp. 82–83.

Latif, K. F., Marimon, F. (2019). Development and validation of servant leadership scale in Spanish higher education. *Leadership & Organization Development Journal*, 40(4), pp. 499–519.

Law, W. W. (2019). Conclusion: Issues and theoretical implications of politics, managerialism, and university governance in Hong Kong. In: Law, W. W. (ed.). *Politics, Managerialism, and University Governance*. Singapore: Springer, pp. 185–220. 10.1007/ 978-981-13-7303-9_9

Lawrence, S., Sharma, U. (2002). Commodification of education and academic labour- using the balanced scorecard in a university setting. *Critical Perspectives on Accounting*, 13(5-6), pp. 661–677.

Lebeau, Y., Cochrane, A. (2015). Rethinking the 'third mission': UK universities and regional engagement in challenging times. *European Journal of Higher Education*, 5(3), pp. 250–263.

Lee, J. (2008). Effects of leadership and leader-member exchange on innovativeness. *Journal of Managerial Psychology*, 23(6), pp. 670–687.

Lee, J. (2015). The false halo of internationalization. *International Higher Education*, 72, pp. 5–7.

Lee, J. (2020). Change in the digital age. In: Lee, J. *Accelerating Organisation Culture Change*. Bingley: Emerald Publishing Limited, pp. 1–22. 10.1108/9781789739657

Lee, M. H. (2017). Managerialism and the academic profession in Hong Kong. In: Postiglione, G., Jung, J. (eds.). *The Changing Academic Profession in Hong Kong*. Cham: Springer, pp. 201–213. / 10.1007/978-3-319-56791-4_11

Lee, M. N. (2016). Reforms of university governance and management in Asia: Effects on campus culture. In: Collins, C. S. et al. (eds.). *The Palgrave Handbook of Asia Pacific Higher Education*. New York: Palgrave Macmillan, pp. 261–277.

Lee, M., Park, H. W. (2012). Exploring the web visibility of world-class universities. *Scientometrics*, 90(1), pp. 201–218.

Lei, J. (2011). Taxonomy and typology: Two paradigms in overseas researches on classification of higher education institutions. *Tsinghua Journal of Education*, 32(2), pp. 110–124.

Leiden University, Centre for Science and Technology Studies (2017). *CWTS Leiden Ranking 2017*. Available from: www.leidenranking.com [3 June 2017].

Leja, K. (2010). University - the road to social responsibility. *Organisation and Management: A Quarterly Scientific Journal*, 4, pp. 43–57.

Lekka-Kowalik, A. (2021). Academic industrial science and its norms price. *Filozofia i Nauka*, 9(1), pp. 29–48.

Leontev, M. (2017). Impact of organizational culture, satisfaction of employees and students on the quality of education in University of Civil Engineering. *MATEC Web of Conferences*, 106, pp. 1–7. 10.1051/matecconf/201710609005

Levidow, L. (2002). Marketizing higher education: Neoliberal strategies and counter-strategies. *The Commoner*, 3, pp. 1–21.

Levine, A. (2018). Privatization in higher education. In: Levin, H. M. (ed.). *Privatizing Education*. London: Routledge, pp. 133–148.

Leys, J. M. (2000). *University Inc - the New World Order*. Paper presented at the Australasian Association for Institutional Research (AAIR) 11th International Conference, Sydney, 6 December 2000.

Li, J., Eryong, X. (2021). New directions toward internationalization of higher education in China during post-COVID 19: A systematic literature review. *Educational Philosophy and Theory*, 54(6), pp. 812–821. 10.1080/00131857.2021.1941866

Li, J., Yang, H. (2013). Towards a frame work of quality management for cooperative higher education. In: Huang, X. M. (ed.). *Proceedings of the 2013 the International Conference on Education Technology and Information System (ICETIS 2013)*. Zhengzhou: Atlantis Press. 10.2991/icetis-13.2013.251

Li, L. G., Liao, C. C. (2021). Globalization, neo-liberalism, and academic capitalism of higher education. *Psychology and Education Journal*, 58(4), pp. 2434–2443.

Lichtenberger, B. (2013).The roadmap from quality assurance in programmes and teaching towards quality development as a strategic instrument of university management. *Acta Universitatis Danubius: Communicatio*, 7(2), pp. 27–32.

Likert, R. (1967a). *New Patterns of Management*. New York: McGraw Hill.

Likert, R. (1967b). *The Human Organization: Its Management and Value*. New York: McGraw Hill.

Lim, H. T. (2018). Evaluation criteria for student-centered university education programs. *International Journal of Contents*, 14(3), pp. 69–74.

Lim, T. W. (2019). Digital disruptions and the workplace. In: Lim, T. W. *Industrial Revolution 4.0, Tech Giants, and Digitized Societies*. Singapore: Palgrave Macmillan, pp. 15–32. 10.1007/978-981-13-7470-8_13

Lin, P. L. (2019). Trends of internationalization in China's higher education: Opportunities and challenges. *US-China Education Review B*, 9(1), pp. 1–12.

Lindsay, B. (2021). The landscapes for comparative and international education. In: Lindsay, B. (ed.). *Comparative and International Education: Leading Perspectives from the Field*. Cham: Palgrave Macmillan, pp. 1–22. 10.1007/978-3-030-64290-7

Ling, P. (2005). Autonomy versus accountability: Measuring university teaching performance. In: *30th Annual Conference ATEE*. Amsterdam: Amsterdam Institute of Education, pp. 305–309.

Link, A. N., Scott, J. T. (2017). Opening the ivory tower's door: An analysis of the determinants of the formation of U.S. university spin-off companies. In: Audretsch, D. B., Link, A. N. (eds.). *Universities and the Entrepreneurial Ecosystem*. Cheltenham: Edward Elgar Publishing, pp. 37–43.

Linke, R. D., Australia Department of Employment, Education and Training, Performance Indicators Research Group (Australia). (1991). *Performance Indicators in Higher Education: Report of a Trial Evaluation Study*. Canberra: Australian Government Publishing Service.

Lis, M. (2021). Model of shaping relations between universities and enterprises under digital transformation. *Polish Journal of Management Studies*, 23(1), pp. 294–314. 10.1 7512/pjms.2021.23.1.18

Litten, L. H. (1980). Marketing higher education: Benefits and risks for the American academic system. *The Journal of Higher Education*, 51(1), pp. 40–59.

Liu, J., Gao, Y. (2022). Higher education internationalisation at the crossroads: Effects of the coronavirus pandemic. *Tertiary Education and Management*, 28(1), pp. 1–15.

Liu, L. et al. (2020). Global university president leadership characteristics and dynamics. *Studies in Higher Education*, 45(10), pp. 2036–2044.

Liu, N. C., Cheng, Y., & Liu, L. (2005). Academic ranking of world universities using scientometrics: a comment to the "Fatal Attraction". *Scientometrics*, 64(1), pp. 101–109.

Liu, X. K., Preston, D. S. (2021). The chief information officer: Impact on organizational forecasting outcomes. *Journal of the Association for Information Systems*, 22(4), pp. 968–1006. 10.17705/1jais.00686

Liu, Z. (2006). Thinking about the construction of "science of science" theory system: The report about the progress of "science of science" which based on scientometrics in China and foreign countries. *Studies in Science of Science*, 1, pp. 1–11.

Liu, Z. (2021). Research and practice of quality culture construction in universities. In: *IPEC2021: 2021 2nd Asia-Pacific Conference on Image Processing, Electronics and Computers*. New York: Association for Computing Machinery, pp. 1085–1088. 10.1145/3452446.3452727

Lizotte, M. (2021). If you do not deign to quantify, someone else will do it for you: In support of a balanced approach to the evaluation of science. *Social Science Information*, 60(3), pp. 363–371. 10.1177/05390184211021364

Lock, G., Lorenz, C. (2007). Revisiting the university front. *Studies in Philosophy and Education*, 26(5), pp. 405–418.

Lockett, A., Wright, M., Wild, A. (2013). The co-evolution of third stream activities in UK higher education. *Business History*, 55(2), pp. 236–258.

Loh, B. et al. (2003). Applying knowledge management in university research. In: Menkhoff, T., Evers, H. D., Chay, Y. W. (eds.). *Governing and Managing Knowledge in Asia*. Singapore: World Scientific Publishing, pp. 221–248. 10.1142/9789814289900_0011

Lomas, L. (1999). The culture and quality of higher education institutions: Examining the links. *Quality Assurance in Education*, 7(1), pp. 30–34.

Lombard, M., Gardenfors, P. (2017). Tracking the evolution of causal cognition in humans. *Journal of Anthropological Sciences*, 95, pp. 1–19.

London, H. B. (1978). *The Culture of a Community College*. New York: Praeger Publishers.

Lopdrup-Hjorth, T., Roelsgaard Obling, A. (2019). Monstrous rebirth: Re-instating the ethos of bureaucracy in public organization. *Organization*, 26(6), pp. 830–852.

Lord, R. G. (1977). Functional leadership behavior: Measurement and relation to social power and leadership perceptions. *Administrative Science Quarterly*, 22(1), pp. 114–133.

Losh, E. (2014). *The War on Learning: Gaining Ground in the Digital University*. Cambridge: MIT Press.

Lourens, R. (1990). University management: Tensions in a changing environment. *Journal of Tertiary Educational Administration*, 12(1), pp. 217–231.

Luke, A. (2010). Educating the other: Standpoint and theory in the 'Internationalization' of higher education. In: Unterhalter, E., Carpentier, V. (eds.). *Global Inequalities and Higher Education: Whose Interests Are We Serving?*. New York: Palgrave Macmillan, pp. 43–65. 10.1007/978-0-230-36507-0_2

Lundberg, H., Öberg, C. (2021). Digital university-SME interaction for business development. In: Ho, R. C., Nourallah, M. (eds.). *Impact of Globalization and Advanced Technologies on Online Business Models*. Hershey: IGI Global, pp. 55–71. 10.4 018/978-1-7998-7603-8

Luque-Martínez, T., Faraoni, N. (2020). Meta-ranking to position world universities. *Studies in Higher Education*, 45(4), pp. 819–883.

Lynch, K. (2006). Neo-liberalism and marketisation: The implications for higher education. *European Educational Research Journal*, 5(1), pp. 1–17.

Lynch, K. (2015). Control by numbers: New managerialism and ranking in higher education. *Critical Studies in Education*, 56(2), pp. 190–207.

Lynch, M. (2020). We have never been anti-science: Reflections on science wars and post-truth. *Engaging Science, Technology, and Society*, 6, pp. 49–57.

Lynn Jr, L. E., Heinrich, C. J., Hill, C. J. (2000). Studying governance and public management: Challenges and prospects. *Journal of Public Administration Research and Theory*, 10(2), pp. 233–262.

Maassen, P., Stensaker, B. (2019). From organised anarchy to de-coupled bureaucracy: The transformation of university organisation. *Higher Education Quarterly*, 73(4), pp. 456–468.

Macdonald, B. J., Young, K. E. (2018). Adorno and Marcuse at the barricades? Critical theory, scholar-activism, and the neoliberal university. *New Political Science*, 40(3), pp. 528–541.

Macfarlane, B. (1995). Business and management studies in higher education: The challenge of academic legitimacy. *International Journal of Educational Management*, 9(5), pp. 4–9. 10.1108/09513549510095059

Macfarlane, B. (2013). *Intellectual Leadership in Higher Education: Renewing the Role of the University Professor*. London: Routledge.

Macioł, S. et al. (2012). Employees on required competences and qualifications of university graduates: the research results. *E-Mentor*, 46(4), pp. 4–17.

MacNeill, S., Johnston, B. (2013). The digital university in the modern age: A proposed framework for strategic development. *Compass: Journal of Learning and Teaching*, 4(7), p. 1–5. 10.21100/compass.v4i7.79

MacNeill, S., Johnston, B., Smyth, K. (2020). Critical engagement for active participation: The digital university in an age of populism. *New Directions for Adult & Continuing Education*, 2020(165), pp. 115–127.

Madsen, D. Ø., Slåtten, K. (2017). The rise of HR analytics: a preliminary exploration. *Global Conference on Business and Finance Proceedings*, 12(1), pp. 148–159.

Magalhães, A. P. T. (2015). The medieval university and the ethos of knowledge: Franciscan friars, patristic tradition, and scholastic 'instruments'. *Acta Scientiarum: Education*, 37(3), pp. 237–245.

Maheshwari, S. K., Yadav, J. (2020). Leadership in the digital age: Emerging paradigms and challenges. *International Journal of Business and Globalisation*, 26(3), pp. 220–238.

Mahjoub, F. (2004). *Knowledge Management Processes: Introduction to Shift to a Digital University.* Paper presented at the 4th Annual Scientific Conference. Amman, Jordan: Zitouna University.

Mahony, P., Weiner, G. (2019). Neo-liberalism and the state of higher education in the UK. *Journal of Further and Higher Education,* 43(4), pp. 560–572.

Maier, W. (2018). Third mission of the university in the 21st century. *Редакційна колегія,* 19, pp. 19–32.

Mainardes, E. W., Alves, H., Raposo, M. (2011). The process of change in university management: From the "ivory tower" to entreprunialism. *Transylvanian Review of Administrative Sciences,* 7(33), pp. 124–149.

Mainardes, E. W., Alves, H., Raposo, M. (2012). A model for stakeholder classification and stakeholder relationships. *Management Decision,* 50(10), pp. 1861–1879. 10.1108/00251741211279648

Malar, D. A., Arvidsson, V., Holmstrom, J. (2019). Digital transformation in banking: Exploring value co-creation in online banking services in India. *Journal of Global Information Technology Management,* 22(1), pp. 7–24.

Mali, F. (2000). Obstacles in developing university, government and industry links. *Science & Technology Studies,* 13(1), pp. 31–49.

Malmberg, A., Serger, S. S. (2021) Innovation in higher education: Why, how and for whom?. In: Serger, S. S., Malmberg, A., Benner M. (eds.). *Renewing Higher Education: Academic Leadership in Times of Transformation.* Lund: Lund University, pp. 13–26.

Maltese, V. (2018). Digital transformation challenges for universities: Ensuring information consistency across digital services. *Cataloging & Classification Quarterly,* 56(7), pp. 592–606.

Mann, G. (2020). The models for the average number of applicants at Ivy League Schools. In: *Mathematics. 22nd Annual Student Research and Creativity Conference.* New York: SUNY Buffalo State.

Manuel, P. S. S. (2017). The digital university: Information security and transparency. *Journal of Information Systems & Operations Management,* 11(2), pp. 254–262.

Marginson, S. (2011). Higher education and public good. *Higher Education Quarterly,* 65(4), pp. 411–433.

Marginson, S. (2014). Higher education as a public good in a marketized East Asian environment. In: Yonezawa, A. et al. (eds.). *Emerging International Dimensions in East Asian Higher Education.* Dordrecht: Springer, pp. 15–33. 10.1007/978-94-017-8822-9

Marhl, M., Pausits, A. (2011). Third mission indicators for new ranking methodologies. *Evaluation in Higher Education,* 5(1), pp. 43–64.

Marin, L. (2021). *On The Possibility of a Digital University: Thinking and Mediatic Displacement at the University.* Springer Nature.

Marks, M. L., Mirvis, P. H. (2011). A framework for the human resources role in managing culture in mergers and acquisitions. *Human Resource Management,* 50(6), pp. 859–877.

Marquina, M., Centeno, C. P., Reznik, N. (2022). Academic power and institutional control of academia in Argentine public universities within the context of a managerial governance model. In: Sarrico, C. S., Rosa, M. J., Carvalho, T. (eds.). *Research Handbook on Academic Careers and Managing Academics.* Cheltenham: Edward Elgar Publishing, pp. 47–63.

Marshall, S., Adams, M., Cameron, A. (2000). In search of academic leadership. In: Richardson, L., Lidstone, J. (eds.). *Flexible Learning for a Flexible Society. Proceedings of ASET-HERDSA 2000 Conference.* Toowoomba: ASET and HERDSA, pp. 483–492.

Martini, R. et al. (2020). Good university governance and its implication on managerial performance. In: Tjahjono, A. et al. (eds.). *Proceedings of the First International Conference on Applied Science and Technology (iCAST 2018).* Zhengzhou: Atlantis Press, pp. 148–153.

Mascarenhas, C. et al. (2017). Entrepreneurial university: Towards a better understanding of past trends and future directions. *Journal of Enterprising Communities: People and Places in the Global Economy*, 11(3), pp. 316–338.

Matt, C., Hess, T., Benlian, A. (2014). Digital transformation strategies. *Business & Information Systems Engineering*, 57(5), pp. 339–343.

Matt, C., Hess, T., Benlian, A. (2015). Digital transformation strategies. *Business & Information Systems Engineering*, 57(5), pp. 339–343.

Maxwell, D., Norton, H., Wu, J. (2018). The data science opportunity: Crafting a holistic strategy. *Journal of Library Administration*, 58(2), pp. 111–127.

Maylor, H. et al. (2006). From projectification to programmification. *International Journal of Project Management*, 24(8), pp. 663–674.

Mazurek, G. (2019). *Digital Transformation: A Marketing Perspective.* Warsaw: PWN Scientific Publishers.

Mazza, C., Quattrone, P., Riccaboni, A. (2008). *European Universities in Transition: Issues, Models Cheltenham, UK and Cases.* Cheltenham: Edward Elgar Publishing.

McAfee, A. et al. (2012). Big data: The management revolution. *Harvard Business Review*, 90(10), pp. 60–68.

McCaffery, P. (2018). *The Higher Education Manager's Handbook: Effective Leadership and Management in Universities and Colleges.* London: Routledge.

McCluskey, F. B., Winter, M. L. (2012). *The Idea of the Digital University: Ancient Traditions, Disruptive Technologies and the Battle for the Soul of Higher Education.* Washington: Westphalia Press.

McCluskey, F. B., Winter, M. L. (2014). Academic freedom in the digital age. *On the Horizon*, 22(2), pp. 136–146.

Mcculloch, S. (2017). Hobson's choice: The effects of research evaluation on academics' writing practices in England. *Aslib Journal of Information Management*, 69(5), pp. 503–515.

McIntyre, L. (2018). *Post-truth.* Cambridge: MIT Press.

McKelvey, M., Holmén, M. eds. (2009). *Learning to Compete in European Universities. From Social Institution to Knowledge Business.* Cheltenham: Edward Elgar Publishing.

McLean, M. (2006). *Pedagogy and the University: Critical Theory and Practice.* London and New York: Bloomsbury Publishing.

McMaster, M., (2007). *Partnerships Between Administrative and Academic Managers: How Deans and Faculty Managers Work Together.* Melbourne: Association of Tertiary Education Management.

Mehralizadeh, Y. (2005). New reforms in the management of the university: transition from centralized to decentralized (university-based management) in Iran. *Higher Education Policy*, 18(1), pp. 67–82.

Mehralizadeh, Y., Shahi, S. (2004). University management and the dilemmas of strategic development planning: A case study. *SSRN Electronic Journal.* Available from https://ssrn.com/abstract=499987. 10.2139/ssrn.499987

Meier, F., Krücken, G. (2006). Turning the university into an organizational actor. In: Drori, G. S., Meyer, J. W., Hwang, H. (eds.). *Globalization and Organization: World Society and Organizational Change.* Oxford: Oxford University Press, pp. 241–257.

Melin, L. (1992). Internationalization as a Strategy Process. *Strategic Management Journal*, 13, pp. 99–118.

Mello, J. A. (2013). In support of others: An examination of psychological capital and job satisfaction in academic staff. *Journal of Academic Administration in Higher Education*, 9(2), pp. 1–9.

Merendino, A. (2018). Big data, big decisions: the impact of big data on board level decision-making. *Journal of Business Research*, 93, pp. 67–78.

Mergel, I. et al. (2018). Citizen-oriented digital transformation in the public sector. In: *DGO 2018. Proceedings of the 19th Annual International Conference on Digital Government Research: Governance in the Data Age.* New York: Association for Computing Machinery, pp. 1–3. 10.1145/3209281.3209294

Merton, R. K. (1996). *On Social Structure and Science.* Chicago: University of Chicago Press.

Metaxiotis, K., Psarras, J. (2003). Applying knowledge management in higher education: The creation of a learning organisation. *Journal of Information & Knowledge Management*, 2(4), pp. 353–359.

Metze, K. (2012). Impact of science-some critical reflections on its evaluation. *Journal of Unsolved Questions*, 2(2), pp. XV–XVII.

Meyer, H. D. (2002). The new managerialism in education management: Corporatization or organizational learning?. *Journal of Educational Administration*, 40(6), pp. 534–551.

Meyer, L. H. (2007). Collegial participation in university governance: A case study of institutional change. *Studies in Higher Education*, 32(2), pp. 225–235.

Meyer, M., Sporn, B. (2019). Leaving the ivory tower: Universities' third mission and the quest for legitimacy. In: Kövér, A., Franger, G. (eds.). *University and Society. Interdependencies and Exchange.* Cheltenham: Edward Elgar Publishing, pp. 39–57. 10.4337/9781788974714.00008

Meyer, M., Tang, P. (2007). Exploring the 'value' of academic patents: IP management practices in UK universities and their implications for Third-Stream indicators. *Scientometrics*, 70(2), pp. 415–440.

Michael, M. (1996). Ignoring science: Discourses of ignorance in the public understanding of science. In: Irwin, A., Wynne, B. (eds.). *Misunderstanding science: The public reconstruction of science and technology.* Cambridge: Cambridge University Press, pp. 107–125.

Middlehurst, R. (2004). Changing internal governance: A discussion of leadership roles and management structures in UK universities. *Higher Education Quarterly*, 58(4), pp. 258–279.

Middlehurst, R. (2008). Not enough science or not enough learning? Exploring the gaps between leadership theory and practice. *Higher Education Quarterly*, 62(4), pp. 322–339.

Mihardjo, L. W. W. et al. (2019a). Digital transformation: A transformational performance-based conceptual model through co-creation strategy and business model innovation in the Industry 4.0 in Indonesia. *International Journal of Economics and Business Research*, 18(3), pp. 369–386.

Mihardjo, L. W. W. et al. (2019b). Digital leadership role in developing business model innovation and customer experience orientation in industry 4.0. *Management Science Letters*, 9(11), pp. 1749–1762.

Mingers, J., Leydesdorff, L. (2015). A review of theory and practice in scientometrics. *European Journal of Operational Research*, 246(1), pp. 1–19.

Mintzberg, H., Lampel, J. (1999). Reflecting on the strategy process. *MIT Sloan Management Review*, 40(3), pp. 21–30.

Mintzberg, H., McHugh, A. (1985). Strategy formation in an adhocracy. *Administrative Science Quarterly*, 30(2), pp. 160–197. 10.2307/2393104

Miranda, F. J., Chamorro, A., Rubio, S. (2018). Re-thinking university spin-off: A critical literature review and a research agenda. *The Journal of Technology Transfer*, 43(4), pp. 1007–1038.

Mitchell, B. R. (2002). The relevance and impact of collaborative working for management in a digital university. In: Hazemi, R., Hailes, S. (eds.). *The Digital University: Building a Learning Community*. London: Springer, pp. 229–246. 10.1007/978-1-44 71-0167-3_16

Mitchell, S. D. (2008). Exporting causal knowledge in evolutionary and developmental biology. *Philosophy of Science*, 75(5), pp. 697–706.

Miyashita, S., Sengoku, S. (2021). Scientometrics for management of science: Collaboration and knowledge structures and complexities in an interdisciplinary research project. *Scientometrics*, 126(9), pp. 7419–7444.

Mlinar, A. (2013). John Henry Newman on University: Actuality of 160 Year Old Discourse. *Shynthesis Philosophica*, 28(1-2), pp. 131–148.

Mohamedbhai, G. (2014). Massification in higher education institutions in Africa: Causes, consequences and responses. *International Journal of African Higher Education*, 1(1), pp. 59–83. 10.6017/ijahe.v1i1.5644

Mohnot, H., Shaw, T. (2017). The study of academic leadership preparedness and leadership style in higher education. *International Journal of Education and Management Studies*, 7(3), pp. 408–416.

Mok, K. H. (2007). Questing for internationalization of universities in Asia: Critical reflections. *Journal of Studies in International Education*, 11(3-4), pp. 433–454.

Mok, K. H. et al. (2021). Impact of COVID-19 pandemic on international higher education and student mobility: Student perspectives from mainland China and Hong Kong. *International Journal of Educational Research*, 105. 10.1016/j.ijer.2020.101718

Mok, K. H., Marginson, S. (2021). Massification, diversification and internationalisation of higher education in China: Critical reflections of developments in the last two decades. *International Journal of Educational Development*, 84, 102405. 10.1016/j.ijedudev. 2021.102405

Mok, K. H., Montgomery, C. (2021). Remaking higher education for the post-COVID-19 era: critical reflections on marketization, internationalization and graduate employment. *Higher Education Quarterly*, 75(3), pp. 373–380.

Molas-Gallart, J. et al. (2002). *Measuring Third Stream Activities: Final Report to the Russell Group Of Universities*. Brighton: SPRU, University of Sussex.

Molas-Gallart, J., Castro-Martínez, E. (2007). Ambiguity and conflict in the development of 'Third Mission' indicators. *Research Evaluation*, 16(4), pp. 321–330.

Monaghan, C. H., Cervero, R. M. (2006). Impact of critical management studies courses on learners' attitudes and beliefs. *Human Resource Development International*, 9(3), pp. 379–396.

Montag, C., Elhai, J. D. (2019). A new agenda for personality psychology in the digital age?. *Personality and Individual Differences*, 147, pp. 128–134.

Montesinos, P. et al. (2008). Third mission ranking for world class universities: Beyond teaching and research. *Higher Education in Europe*, 33(2-3), pp. 259–271.

Moodie, G. C., Eustace R. (1974). *Power and Authority in British Universities*. London: Routledge. 10.4324/9780203802694

Mora, J. G. (2001). Governance and management in the new university. *Tertiary Education and Management*, 7(2), pp. 95–110.

Morais, R. (2019). Analysis of factors supporting SWOT in organizational strategic planning. *Strategie Manageriale*, 44(2), pp. 66–78.

Moreno, J. (2014). *The Economic and Social Value of Information in the Network Society*. Thesis (MA), ISCTE – Instituto Universitário de Lisboa.

Morrar, R., Arman, H., Mousa, S. (2017). The fourth industrial revolution (Industry 4.0): A social innovation perspective. *Technology Innovation Management Review*, 7(11), pp. 12–20.

Morrish, L. (2020). Academic freedom and the disciplinary regime in the neoliberal university. In: Dawes, S., Lenormand, M. (eds.). *Neoliberalism in Context*. Cham: Palgrave Macmillan, pp. 235–253. 10.1007/978-3-030-26017-0_13

Morrish, L., Sauntson, H. (2016). Performance management and the stifling of academic freedom and knowledge production. *Journal of Historical Sociology*, 29(1), pp. 42–64.

Mosteanu, N. R. (2020a). Using internet and edutech become a primary need rather than a luxury - the reality: A new skilled educational system-digital university campus. *International Journal of Engineering Science Technologies*, 4(6), pp. 1–9.

Mosteanu, N. R. (2020b). Digital university campus: change the education system approach to meet the 21st century needs. *European Journal of Human Resource Management Studies*, 4(4), pp. 79–93. 10.46827/ejhrms.v4i4.959

Mosteanu, N. R. (2021). Changing the higher education perspective under Covid-19 influence. *The International EFAL-IT BLOG Information Technology innovations in Economics, Finance, Accounting, and Law*, 2(1), p. 1.

Motala, E. (2015). Public scholarship, democracy and scholarly engagement. *Educational Research for Social Change*, 4(2), 22–34.

Motwani, J., Kumar, A. (1997). Te need for implementing total quality management in education. *International Journal of Educational Management*, 11(3), pp. 131–135.

Moula, M. G. (2021). A comprehensive study on effective administration of university leadership and limitations. *International Journal of Management and Humanities*, 5(7), pp. 49–53.

Moutinho, J. L., Heitor, M. (2007). Building human-centered systems in the network society. *Technological Forecasting and Social Change*, 74(1), pp. 100–109.

Mu, J., Tang, F., MacLachlan, D. L. (2010). Absorptive and disseminative capacity: Knowledge transfer in intra-organizational networks. *Expert Systems with Applications*, 37(1), pp. 31–38.

Muijs, D. (2011). Leadership and organisational performance: From research to prescription?. *International Journal of Educational Management*, 25(1), pp. 45–60.

Muktiyanto, A., Hermawan, A. A., Hadiwidjaja, R. D. (2020). The role of management control systems in the performance of higher education through good university governance. *International Journal of Trade and Global Markets*, 13(3), pp. 288–310.

Mumford, E. (1906). The origins of leadership. *American Journal of Sociology*, 12(2), pp. 216–240.

Münch, R. (2015). Science in the hands of strategic management: The metrification of scientific work and its impact on the evolution of knowledge. In: Welpe, I. et al. (eds.). *Incentives and Performance*. Cham: Springer, pp. 33–48. 10.1007/978-3-319-09785-5_3

Münch, R., Schäfer, L. O. (2014). Rankings, diversity and the power of renewal in science: a comparison between Germany, the UK and the US. *European Journal of Education*, 49(1), pp. 60–76.

Murphy, M. (2009). Bureaucracy and its limits: Accountability and rationality in higher education. *British Journal of Sociology of Education*, 30(6), pp. 683–695.

Musselin, C. (2021). University governance in meso and macro perspectives. *Annual Review of Sociology*, 47, pp. 305–325.

Mustafa, G. et al. (2022). Digitalization trends and organizational structure: bureaucracy, ambidexterity or post-bureaucracy?. *Eurasian Business Review*, February 2022, pp. 1–24. 10.1007/s40821-021-00196-8

Mutanov, G. et al. (2020). Applied research of data management in the education system for decision-making on the example of Al-Farabi Kazakh National University. *E3S Web of Conferences*, 159(99), pp. 1–12. 10.1051/e3sconf/202015909003

Nabaho, L. (2019). Shared governance in public universities in Uganda: Current concerns and directions for reform. *International Journal of African Higher Education*, 5(1), pp.45–65. 0.6017/ijahe.v5i1.10962

Nadiri, H. (2006). Strategic issue in higher education marketing: How university students' perceive higher education services. *The Asian Journal on Quality*, 7(2), pp. 125–140.

Najmi, K., Kadir, A. R., Kadir, M. I. A. (2018). Mediation effect of dynamic capability in the relationship between knowledge management and strategic leadership on organizational performance accountability. *International Journal of Law and Management*, 60, pp. 517–529.

Nambisan, S., Wright, M., Feldman, M. (2019). The digital transformation of innovation and entrepreneurship: Progress, challenges and key themes. *Research Policy*, 48(8), 103773. 10.1016/j.respol.2019.03.018

Neary, J., Osborne, M. (2018). University engagement in achieving sustainable development goals: a synthesis of case studies from the SUEUAA study. *Australian Journal of Adult Learning*, 58(3), pp. 336–364.

Nedeva, M. (2008). New tricks and old dogs? The 'third mission' and the re-production of the university. In: Epstein, D. et al. (eds.). *World Yearbook of Education 2008*. London: Routledge, pp. 105–123.

Nedeva, M., Boden, R. (2006). Changing science: The advent of neo-liberalism. *Prometheus*, 24(3), pp. 269–281.

Neilson, D. (2020). The democratic socialisation of knowledge: Integral to an alternative to the neoliberal model of development. In: Peters, M. A. et al. (eds.). *Knowledge Socialism*. Singapore: Springer, pp. 135–154. 10.1007/978-981-13-8126-3_8

Nelles, J., Vorley, T. (2010). From policy to practice: Engaging and embedding the third mission in contemporary universities. *International Journal of Sociology and Social Policy*, 30(7/8), pp. 341–353.

Neumann, M. (2021). Policy analysis: Patenting for the third mission. In: Neumann, M. (ed.). *Motives and Functions of Patenting in Public Basic Science*. Wiesbaden: Springer Gabler, pp. 109–135.

Newman, J. (2008). *The Idea of a University*. New Haven: Yale University Press.

Ngoc-Tan, N., Gregar, A. (2018). Impacts of knowledge management on innovations in higher education institutions: An empirical evidence from Vietnam. *Economics and Sociology*, 11(3), pp. 301–320. 10.14254/2071-789X.2018/11-3/18

Nguyen, D. (2018). The university in a world of digital technologies: tensions and challenges. *Australasian Marketing Journal*, 26(2), pp. 79–82.

Nicholas, D., Rowlands, I. eds. (2008). *Digital Consumers: Reshaping the Information Professions*. London: Facet Publishing.

Nicolescu, L. (2009). Applying marketing to higher education: Scope and limits. *Management & Marketing*, 4(2), pp. 35–44.

Nielsen, K. H. (2012). Sociological ambivalence in the commodification of academic research. *Science as Culture*, 21(3), pp. 405–408.

Niemelä, H. et al. (2014). Is an accreditation seal worth the effort? Observations of programme accreditations in Lappeenranta University of Technology, Finland. *Quality Assurance in Education*, 22(2), pp. 226–239. 10.1108/QAE-01-2013-0007

Nigsch, S., Schenker-Wicki, A. (2013). Shaping performance: do international accreditations and quality management really help? *Journal of Higher Education Policy and Management*, 35(6), pp. 668–681.

Ning, R., Lin, Z. (2007). Brief analysis of the human resources management in colleges and universities. *Journal of Hunan Institute of Engineering (Social Science Edition)*, 1, pp. 122–124.

NJ MED: New Jersey Minority Educational Development (2016). *Global Education Report 2016*. Available from: http://worldtop20.org/global-education-report-2016 [3 June 2017].

Nkomo, M. O. (1984). *Student Culture and Activism in Black South African Universities: The Roots of Resistance*. Westport: Greenwood Press.

Nordenbo, S. E. (2002). Bildung and the thinking of bildung. *Journal of Philosophy of Education*, 36(3), pp. 341–352.

North Central Association of Colleges and Schools (2000). *Academic Quality Improvement Project*. Chicago: Commission on Institutions of Higher Education, North Central Association of Colleges and Schools. Available from: http://www.aqip.org [20 September 2014].

NTU Ranking (2017). *NTU Rankings*. Available from: http://nturanking.lis.ntu.edu.tw/ [3 June 2017].

Nurhas, I. et al. (2021). Understanding the challenges of rapid digital transformation: The case of COVID-19 pandemic in higher education. *Behaviour & Information Technology*, ahead-of-print, pp. 1–17. 10.1080/0144929X.2021.1962977

Nybom, T. (2003). The Humboldt legacy: Reflections on the past, present, and future of the European university. *Higher Education Policy*, 16(2), pp. 141–159.

Nybom, T. (2012). The disintegration of higher education in Europe, 1970-2010: A post-Humboldtian essay. In: Rothblatt, S. (ed.). *Clark Kerr's World of Higher Education Reaches the 21st Century*. Dordrecht: Springer, pp. 163–181. 10.1007/978-94-007-4258-1_7

Oberer, B., Erkollar, A. (2018). Leadership 4.0: Digital leaders in the age of industry 4.0. *International Journal of Organizational Leadership*, 7(4), pp. 404–412.

Oestreicher-Singer, G., Zalmanson, L. (2012). Content or community? A digital business strategy for content providers in the social age. *MIS Quarterly*, 37(2), pp. 591–616. 10.2139/ssrn.1536768

O'Hanlon, N. (2002). Net knowledge: Performance of new college students on an Internet skills proficiency test. *The Internet and Higher Education*, 5(1), pp. 55–66.

Olk, P. (2020). Seeking ambidexterity in an increasingly turbulent environment: The case of the University of Denver's Daniels College of Business. *Journal of Management Inquiry*, 29(2), pp. 134–138.

Olsen, J. P. (2007). The institutional dynamics of the European University. In: Maassen, P., Olsen, J. (eds.). *University Dynamics and European Integration*. Dordrecht: Springer, pp. 25–54. 10.1007/978-1-4020-5971-1_2

Olsen, J. P., Maassen, P. (2007). European debates on the knowledge institution: The modernization of the university at the European level. In: Maassen, P., Olsen, J. (eds.). *University Dynamics and European Integration*. Dordrecht: Springer, pp. 3–22. 10.1007/978-1-4020-5971-1_1

Olson, K. W. (1973). The GI Bill and higher education: Success and surprise. *American Quarterly*, 25(5), pp. 596–610.

O'Mahony, K., Garavan, T. N. (2012). Implementing a quality management framework in a higher education organisation: A case study. *Quality Assurance in Education*, 20(2), pp. 184–200.

Omerzel, D. G. et al. (2011). Knowledge management and organisational culture in higher education institutions. *Journal for East European Management Studies*, 16(2), pp. 111–139.

O'Mullane, M. (2011). The university as 'organisation' in the context of leadership. In: O'Mullane, M. (ed.). *University Leadership*. London: Palgrave Macmillan, pp. 29–42. 10.1057/9780230346567_2

O'Neill O. (2005). Accountability, trust and professional practice. In: Ray, N. (ed.). *Architecture & its Ethical Dilemmas*. London: Taylor and Francis, pp. 77–88.

O'Neill, O. (2013). Intelligent accountability in education. *Oxford Review of Education*, 39(1), pp. 4–16.

Open Science Collaboration (2015). Estimating the reproducibility of psychological science. *Science*, 349(6251), pp. 943–951. 10.1126/science.aac4716

Ordorika, I., Lloyd M. (2015). International rankings and the contest for university hegemony. *Journal of Education Policy*, 30(3), pp. 385–405.

O'Reilly, D., Reed, M. (2011). The grit in the oyster: professionalism, managerialism and leaderism as discourses of UK public services modernization. *Organization Studies*, 32(8), pp. 1079–1101.

Örtenblad, A., Koris, R. (2014). Is the learning organization idea relevant to higher educational institutions? A literature review and a 'multi-stakeholder contingency approach'. *International Journal of Educational Management*, 28(2), pp. 173–214. 10.1108/IJEM-01-2013-0010

Orton, J. D., Weick, K. E. (1990). Loosely coupled systems: A reconceptualization. *Academy of Management Review*, 15(2), pp. 203–223.

Osland, J. S., Bird, A. (2000). Beyond sophisticated stereotyping: Cultural sensemaking in context. *Academy of Management Perspectives*, 14(1), pp. 65–77.

Östling, J. (2018). *Humboldt and the Modern German University: An Intellectual History*. Lund: Lund University Press.

Ota, H. (2018). Internationalization of higher education: Global trends and Japan's challenges. *Educational Studies in Japan*, 12, pp. 91–105.

Palgrave Macmillan, 2006. *World List of Universities & Other Institutions of Higher Education. Issue 25*. London: Palgrave Macmillan.

Paliulis, N. K., Labanauskis, R. (2015). Benchmarking as an Instrument for improvement of quality management in higher education. *Business, Management and Education*, 13(1), pp. 140–157. 10.3846/bme.2015.220

Palmqvist, M. (2009), *Shaping the Identity of the International Business School - Accreditation as the Road to Success?*. Umeå: Umeå School of Business.

Pan, Q., Yang, T. (2009). Characteristics of western medieval universities. *Modern University Education*, 1, p. 52–56.

Parakhina, V. et al. (2017). Strategic management in universities as a factor of their global competitiveness. *International Journal of Educational Management*, 31(1), pp. 62–75.

Park, J. H., Tran, T. B. H. (2018). Internal marketing, employee customer-oriented behaviors, and customer behavioral responses. *Psychology & Marketing*, 35(6), pp. 412–426.

Parker, L. D. (2002). It's been a pleasure doing business with you: A strategic analysis and critique of university change management. *Critical Perspectives on Accounting*, 13(5), pp. 603–619.

Parker, L. D. (2012). From privatised to hybrid corporatised higher education: A global financial management discourse. *Financial Accountability & Management*, 28(3), pp. 247–268.

Parker, M., Jary, D. (1995). The McUniversity: Organisation, management and academic subjectivity. *Organization*, 2(2), p. 319–338. 10.1177/135050849522013

Parrish, D. (2019). What's the story here? The effect of volatility on university leader sensemaking of undocumented student access. *The European Journal of Management Studies*, 24(2), pp. 53–78.

Parsons, T., Platt, G. M. (1973). *The American University*. Cambridge: Harvard University Press.

Parveen, S., Tariq, A. (2014). Leadership style, gender and job satisfaction: A situational leadership approach. *International Journal of Science and Research*, 3(12), pp. 1–6.

Pascall, G., Cox, R. (1993). *Women Returning to Higher Education*. Bristol: Open University Press.

Passeron, J. C., Bourdieu, P. (1970). *La Reproduction. Éléments Pour Une Théorie Du Système d'enseignement*. Paris: Les Éditions de Minuit.

Pearce, C. L. (2007). The future of leadership development: The importance of identity, multi-level approaches, self-leadership, physical fitness, shared leadership, networking, creativity, emotions, spirituality and on-boarding processes. *Human Resource Management Review*, 17(4), pp. 355–359.

Pechar, H. (2012). The decline of an academic oligarchy. The Bologna process and 'Humboldt's last warriors'. In: Curaj, A. et al. (eds.). *European Higher Education at the Crossroads*. Dordrecht: Springer, pp. 613–630. 10.1007/978-94-007-3937-6_33

Pedersen, O. (1997). *The First Universities: Studium Generale and the Origins of University Education in Europe*. Cambridge: Cambridge University Press.

Pekkola, E. et al. (2018). The sociology of professions and the study of academic profession. In: Pekkola, E. et al. (eds.). *Theoretical and Methodological Perspectives on Higher Education Management and Transformation: an advanced reader for PhD students*. Tampere: Tampere University Press, pp. 121–150.

Perakslis, C. (2017). Digital maturity: perceiving the digital-panopticon [last word]. *IEEE Technology and Society Magazine*, 36(4), p. 88.

Perkmann, M. et al. (2013). Academic engagement and commercialisation: A review of the literature on university-industry relations. *Research Policy*, 42(2), pp. 423–442.

Perriton, L., Reynolds, M. (2004). Critical management education from pedagogy of possibility to pedagogy of refusal?. *Management Learning*, 35(1), pp. 61–77.

Peters, M. A., Jandrić, P. (2018). Peer production and collective intelligence as the basis for the public digital university. *Educational Philosophy and Theory*, 50(13), pp. 1271–1284.

Peters, M. A., Liu, T. C., Ondercin, D. J. (2012). Managerialism and the neoliberal university: prospects for new forms of 'open management' in higher education. In: Peters, M. A., Liu, T. C., Ondercin, D. J. (eds.). *The Pedagogy of the Open Society*. Rotterdam: Brill Sense, pp. 91–104.

Peterson, M. W., Spencer, M. G. (1990). Understanding academic culture and climate. *New Directions for Institutional Research*, 68, pp. 3–18.

Peterson, T. O., Aikens, S. D. (2017). Examining the relationship between leader-member exchange (LMX) and objective performance within higher education: An exploratory empirical study. *Journal of Leadership Education*, 16(2), pp. 109–128.

Petrova, M., Popova, L., Dejniak, D. (2020). Children's University activities as implementation of the third mission of higher education institution. *Strategies for Policy in Science and Education*, 28(2), pp. 161–171.

Picciano, A. G. (2017). *Online Education Policy and Practice: the Past, Present, and Future of the Digital University*. New York: Routledge. 10.4324/9781315672328

Pickard, S. (2022). Massification, social reproduction, and social stratification. In: Côté, J. E., Pickard, S. (eds.). *Routledge Handbook of the Sociology of Higher Education*. London: Routledge, pp. 223–233.

Piercy, N. F. (1985). Company Internationalization: Active and reactive exporting. *European Journal of Marketing*, 3(15), pp. 26–40.

Pihie, Z. A. L., Sadeghi, A., Elias, H. (2011). Analysis of head of departments leadership styles: Implication for improving research university management practices. *Procedia - Social and Behavioral Sciences*, 29, pp. 1081–1090.

Pilbeam, C. (2008). Designing an entrepreneurial university in an institutional setting. *Higher Education Policy*, 21(3), pp. 393–404.

Pillania, R. K., Chang, J. (2009). Research note: Global innovation and knowledge scenario: The stars, followers and laggards. *International Journal of Technology and Globalisation*, 4(4), pp. 318–326.

Pinheiro, R., Stensaker, B. (2014). Designing the entrepreneurial university: The interpretation of a global idea. *Public Organization Review*, 14(4), pp. 497–516.

Polanyi, M. (1967). Sense-giving and sense-reading. *Philosophy*, 42(162), pp. 301–325.

Polo Peña, A. I., Frías Jamilena, D. M., Rodríguez Molina, M. Á. (2014). Value co-creation via information and communications technology. *The Service Industries Journal*, 34(13), 1043–1059.

Popescu, G. H. (2017). Organizational e-learning and knowledge management in higher education. *Journal of Self-Governance and Management Economics*, 5(1), 87–93.

Portnoff, A. Y., Soupizet, J. F. (2018). Artificial intelligence: Opportunities and risks. *Futuribles*, (5), pp. 5–26.

Posselt, T. et al. (2019). Opportunities and challenges of higher education institutions in Europe: An analysis from a business model perspective. *Higher Education Quarterly*, 73(1), pp. 100–115.

Pounder, J. S. (2001). "New leadership" and university organisational effectiveness: Exploring the relationship. *Leadership & Organization Development Journal*, 22(6), pp. 281–290.

Poutanen, M. et al. (2022). From democracy to managerialism: Foundation universities as the embodiment of Finnish university policies. *Journal of Education Policy*, 37(3), pp. 419–442.

Power, M. (1997). *The Audit Society*. Oxford: Oxford University Press.

Pramono, S. E. et al. (2018). Strategy to improve quality of higher education institution based on AUN-QA standard. *International Journal for Innovation Education and Research*, 6(9), pp. 141–152.

Proctor, C. (2021). The heart of academia: Medieval universities, textbooks, and the birth of academic libraries. *Library Philosophy and Practice*, 2021, pp. 1–14.

Profiroiu, M. C., Brişcariu, M. R. (2021). Universities as 'drivers' of local and regional development. *Transylvanian Review of Administrative Sciences*, 17(62), pp. 134–152.

Promsri, C. (2019). The developing model of digital leadership for a successful digital transformation. *GPH-International Journal of Business Management*, 2(8), pp. 1–8.

Provan, K. G., Kenis, P. (2008). Modes of network governance: Structure, management, and effectiveness. *Journal of Public Administration Research and Theory*, 18(2), pp. 229–252.

Pugh, R. et al. (2018). The entrepreneurial university and the region: What role for entrepreneurship departments?. *European Planning Studies*, 26(9), pp. 1835–1855.

Puriwat, W., Tripopsakul, S. (2021). Customer engagement with digital social responsibility in social media: A case study of COVID-19 situation in Thailand. *The Journal of Asian Finance, Economics, and Business*, 8(2), pp. 475–483.

Purwanto, A. J. (2016). Flexible organizational structure for learning organization: The case of Indonesia Open University (Universitas Terbuka). In: *Proceedings of the 3rd International Seminar and Conference on Learning Organization (isclo-15)*. Zhengzhou: Atlantis Press, pp. 43–47.

Quattrociocchi, B. et al. (2017). Technology and innovation for networks. *Journal of Organisational Transformation & Social Change*, 14(1), pp. 4–20.

Rabovsky, T. M. (2012). Accountability in higher education: Exploring impacts on state budgets and institutional spending patterns. *Journal of Public Administration Research and Theory*, 22(4), pp. 675–700.

Rachman, E. et al. (2017). Autonomy of private higher education management: A financial accountability perspective. *International Journal of Economic Research*, 14(11), pp. 1–11.

Raffaghelli, J. E. et al. (2016). Different views on digital scholarship: Separate worlds or cohesive research field?. *Research in Learning Technology*, 24, pp. 1–17. 10.3402/rlt.v24 .32036

Rahyasih, A. Y., Kurniady, D. A. (2017). The effectiveness of educational qualifications in organizational career development for education staff. In: Abdullah, A. G. et al. (eds.). *Ideas for 21st Century Education*. London: Routledge, pp. 267–270.

Rakonjac, I. et al. (2012). Sinergy of digital university and digital enterprise: Management of innovative activities. *Serbian Project Management Journal: Moving PM Competence Forward*, 2(1), pp. 46–61.

Ramachandran, S. D., Chong, S. C., Wong, K. Y. (2013). Knowledge management practices and enablers in public universities: A gap analysis. *Campus-Wide Information Systems*, 30(2), pp. 76–94. 10.1108/10650741311306273

Ramírez, Y., Tejada, Á. (2018). Corporate governance of universities: Improving transparency and accountability. *International Journal of Disclosure and Governance*, 15(1), pp. 29–39.

Ramírez, Y., Tejada, A. Manzaneque, M. (2016). The value of disclosing intellectual capital in Spanish universities: A new challenge of our days. *Journal of Organizational Change Management*, 29(2), pp. 176–198.

Ramos-Monge, E. L., Llinàs-Audet, X., Barrena-Martinez, J. (2017). Universities as corporate entities: The role of social responsibility in their strategic management. In: Emeagwali, O. L. (ed.). *Corporate Governance and Strategic Decision Making*. London: IntechOpen, pp. 199–215. 10.5772/intechopen.69931

Randall, L. M., Coakley, L. A. (2007). Applying adaptive leadership to successful change initiatives in academia. *Leadership & Organization Development Journal*, 8(4), pp. 325–335.

Rauhvargers, A. (2013). *Global University Rankings and Their Impact: Report II*. Brussels: European University Association.

Rauhvargers, A. (2014). Where are the global rankings leading us? An analysis of recent methodological changes and new developments. *European Journal of Education*, 49(1), pp. 29–44.

Razvan, Z., Dainora, G. (2009). Challenges and opportunities faced by entrepreneurial university: Some lessons from Romania and Lithuania. *Annals of the University of Oradea, Economic Science Series*, 18(4), pp. 874–876.

Redding, G. (2017). Critical thinking, university autonomy, and societal evolution: thoughts on a research agenda. *Centre for Global Higher Education Working Paper*, 11, pp. 1–24.

Reddy, S. K., Reinartz, W. (2017). Digital transformation and value creation: Sea change ahead. *Marketing Intelligence Review*, 9(1), pp. 10–17.

Rehman, U. U., Iqbal, A. (2020). Nexus of knowledge-oriented leadership, knowledge management, innovation and organizational performance in higher education. *Business Process Management Journal*, 26(6), pp. 1731–1758. 10.1108/BPMJ-07-2019-0274

Reichert, S. (2019). *The Role of Universities in Regional Innovation Ecosystems: EUA Study*. Brussels: European University Association.

Reiko, Y. (2001). University reform in the post-massification era in Japan: Analysis of government education policy for the 21st century. *Higher Education Policy*, 14(4), pp. 277–291.

Reindl, T., Reyna, R. (2011). *Complete to Compete: From Information to Action: Revamping Higher Education Accountability Systems*. Washington: NGA Center for Best Practices. Available from: https://files.eric.ed.gov/fulltext/ED522081.pdf [13 January 2016].

Reis, J. et al. (2018). Digital transformation: A literature review and guidelines for future research. In: Rocha, Á. et al. (eds.). *Trends and Advances in Information Systems and Technologies: World Conference on Information Systems and Technologies*. Cham: Springer, pp. 411–421.

Renaudie, M. (2018). French university management reforms: Critical perspectives from a legal point of view. *French Politics*, 16(1), pp. 96–116.

Revel, J. (2002). *Le Vocabulaire de Foucault*. Paris: Ellipses.

Rhoads, R. A. (2018). A critical analysis of the development of the US research university and emergence of the neoliberal entrepreneurial model. *Entrepreneurship Education*, 1(1), pp. 11–25.

Rhodes, C., Wright, C., Pullen, A. (2018). Changing the world? The politics of activism and impact in the neoliberal university. *Organization*, 25(1), pp. 139–147.

Rhodes, R. A. W. (1996). The new governance: Governing without government. *Political Studies*, 44(4), pp. 652–667.

Rhodes, R. A. W. (1997). *Understanding Governance: Policy Networks, Governance, Reflexivity and Accountability*. Philadelphia: Open University Press.

Richter, J. et al. (2020). Tempered radicalism and intersectionality: Scholar-activism in the neoliberal university. *Journal of Social Issues*, 76(4), pp. 1014–1035.

Ridley, D. (2017). Institutionalising critical pedagogy: Lessons from against and beyond the neo-liberal university. *Power and Education*, 9(1), pp. 65–81.

Ries, A., Trout, J. (1993). *The New Positioning: The Latest on the World's #1 Business Strategy*. New York: McGraw-Hill.

Rigby, D. K., Sutherland, J., Takeuchi, H. (2016). Embracing agile. *Harvard Business Review*, 94(5), pp. 40–50.

Risanty, R., Kesuma, S. A. (2019). The structure and the leadership: The actualization of good management of Indonesian University. *Jurnal Perspektif Pembiayaan dan Pembangunan Daerah*, 7(2), pp. 249–258.

Rodríguez, J., Osorio, J., Berriel, R. (1994). Contribution of the information technology/information systems to human resources management in the university. In: Barta, B. Z., Telem, M., Gev, Y. (eds.). *Information Technology in Educational Management: IFIP Conference on Information Technology in Educational Management*. Boston: Springer, pp. 139–144.

Rodríguez-Haro, F. et al. (2012). A summary of virtualization techniques. *Procedia Technology*, 3, pp. 267–272.

Roessler, I., Duong, S., Hachmeister, C. D. (2015). *Teaching, Research and More! Achievements of Universities of Applied Sciences with Regard to Society*. Guetersloh: Centrum für Hochschulentwicklung.

Rof, A., Bikfalvi, A., Marques, P. (2022a). Pandemic-accelerated digital transformation of a born digital higher education institution. *Educational Technology & Society*, 25(1), pp. 124–141.

Rof, A., Bikfalvi, A., Marques, P. (2022b). Born-digital universities. In: Kaplan, A. (ed.). *Digital Transformation and Disruption of Higher Education*. Cambridge: Cambridge University Press, pp. 237–300. 10.1017/9781108979146.024

Roger, E. (2014). *Quality Assurance for University Teaching*. London: Open University Press.

Rogers, P. L. (2001). Traditions to transformations: The forced evolution of higher education. *AACE Journal*, 9(1), pp. 47–60.

Roksa, J. (2008). Structuring access to higher education: The role of differentiation and privatization. *Research in Social Stratification and Mobility*, 26(1), pp. 57–75.

Roth, K. R., Ritter, Z. S. (2015). Diversity and the need for cross-cultural leadership and collaboration. In: Erbe, N. D., Normore, A. H. (eds.). *Cross-Cultural Collaboration and Leadership in Modern Organizations*. Hershey: IGI Global, pp. 196–215. 10.4018/978-1-4666-8376-1.ch012

Rothblatt, S. (1997). *The Modern University and Its Discontents: The Fate of Newman's Legacies in Britain and America*. Cambridge: Cambridge University Press.

Rothblatt, S., Wittrock, B. (1993). *The European and American University Since 1800: Historical and Sociological Essays*. Cambridge: Cambridge University Press.

Rourke, F., Brooks, G. E. (1966). *The Managerial Revolution in Higher Education*. Baltimore: The Johns Hopkins Press.

Rowlands, J. (2015). Turning collegial governance on its head: Symbolic violence, hegemony and the academic board. *British Journal of Sociology of Education*, 36(7), pp. 1017–1035.

Rowlands, J. (2017a). Strengthening academic governance into the future. In: Rowlands, J. (ed.). *Academic Governance in the Contemporary University*. Singapore: Springer, pp. 221–240. 10.1007/978-981-10-2688-1_12

Rowlands, J. (2017b). What is academic governance? In: Rowlands, J. (ed.). *Academic Governance in the Contemporary University*. Singapore: Springer, pp. 47–69. 10.1007/978-981-10-2688-1_3

Rowley, D. J., Sherman, H. (2003). The special challenges of academic leadership. *Management Decision*, 41(10), pp. 1058–1063.

Rowley, J. (2004). Partnering paradigms? Knowledge management and relationship marketing. *Industrial Management & Data Systems*, 104(2), pp. 149–157.

Rubens, A. et al. (2017). Universities' third mission and the entrepreneurial university and the challenges they bring to higher education institutions. *Journal of Enterprising Communities: People and Places in the Global Economy*, 11(3), pp. 354–372.

Rubins, I. (2007). Risks and rewards of academic capitalism and the effects of presidential leadership in the entrepreneurial university. *Perspectives in Public Affairs*, 4(4), pp. 3–18.

Ruoslahti, H. (2020). Complexity in project co-creation of knowledge for innovation. *Journal of Innovation & Knowledge*,5(4), pp. 228–235.

Russell, R. F. (2001). The role of values in servant leadership. *Leadership & Organization Development Journal*, 22(2), pp. 76–84.

Rutherford J. (2005) Cultural studies in the corporate university. *Cultural Studies*, 19(3), pp. 297–317. 10.1080/09502380500146899

Ruzic-Dimitrijevic, L., Dakic, J. (2014). The risk management in higher education institutions. *Online Journal of Applied Knowledge Management*, 2(1), pp. 137–152.

Ryan, J. F., Healy, R., Sullivan, J. (2012). Oh, won't you stay? Predictors of faculty intent to leave a public research university. *Higher Education*, 63(4), pp. 421–437.

Ryan, S. et al. (2013). *The Virtual University: The Internet and Resource-Based Learning*. London: Routledge.

Sabau, G. et al. (2009). Collaborative network for the development of an informational system in the SOA context for the university management. In: *2009 International Conference on Computer Technology and Development, Vol. I*. Piscataway: IEEE, pp. 307–311. 10.1109/ICCTD.2009.191

Sadchenko, O. et al. (2020). Marketing tools in stimulating innovative activity of enterprises. *International Journal of Management*, 11(6), pp. 241–251. 10.34218/IJM.11.6.2020.023

Safiullin, M. R., Akhmetshin, E. M. (2019). Digital transformation of a university as a factor of ensuring its competitiveness. *International Journal of Engineering and Advanced Technology*, 9(1), pp. 7387–7390.

Sagalyn, L. B. (2007). Public/private development: Lessons from history, research, and practice. *Journal of the American Planning Association*, 73(1), pp. 7–22.

Sahlin, K., Eriksson-Zetterquist, U. (2016). Collegiality in modern universities-the composition of governance ideals and practices. *Nordic Journal of Studies in Educational Policy*, 2016(2-3), pp. 1–10. 10.3402/nstep.v2.33640

Salicru, S. (2018). Storytelling as a leadership practice for sensemaking to drive change in times of turbulence and high velocity. *Journal of Leadership, Accountability & Ethics*, 15(2), pp. 130–140. 10.33423/jlae.v15i2.649

Salmi, J. (2016). Excellence strategies and the creation of world-class universities. In:Liu, N. C., Cheng, Y., Wang, Q. (eds.). *Matching Visibility and Performance: Global*

Perspectives on Higher Education. Rotterdam: SensePublishers, pp. 15–48. 10.1007/ 978-94-6300-773-3_2

Salminen, A. (2003). New public management and Finnish public sector organisations: The case of universities. In: Amaral, A., Meek, V. L., Larsen, I. M. (eds.). *The Higher Education Managerial Revolution?.* Dordrecht: Springer, pp. 55–69. 10.1007/978-94-010-0072-7_3

Samaniego, M., Deters, R. (2016). Management and internet of things. *Procedia Computer Science,* 94, pp. 137–143.

Sandhu, G. (2018). The role of academic libraries in the digital transformation of the universities. In: *2018 5th International Symposium on Emerging Trends and Technologies in Libraries and Information Services (ETTLIS).* Piscataway: IEEE, pp. 292–296. 10.1109/ ETTLIS.2018.8485258

Sandu, E. A. et al. (2014) Considerations on implementation of a social accountability management system model in higher education. *Procedia - Social and Behavioral Sciences,* 142, pp. 169–175.

Sangster, A., Stoner, G., Flood, B. (2020). Insights into accounting education in a COVID-19 world. *Accounting Education,* 29(5), pp. 431–562.

Sani, A. Y. (2021). University education as a public or private goods. *Journal of Educational Planning and Administration,* 6(3), pp. 56–66.

Santos, J. P., Caetano, A., Tavares, S. M. (2015). Is training leaders in functional leadership a useful tool for improving the performance of leadership functions and team effectiveness? *The Leadership Quarterly,* 26(3), pp. 470–484.

Sanyal, B. C., Johnstone, D. B. (2011). International trends in the public and private financing of higher education. *Prospects,* 41(1), pp. 157–175.

Saputra, N., Saputra, A. M. (2020). Transforming into digital organization by orchestrating culture: Leadership and competence in digital context. *GATR Global Journal of Business Social Sciences Review,* 8(4), pp. 208–216. 10.35609/gjbssr.2020.8.4(2)

Saravanamuthu, K., Filling, S. (2004). A critical response to managerialism in the Academy. *Critical Perspectives on Accounting,* 15(4), pp. 437–452.

Sarmadi, M. R. et al. (2017). Academic culture and its role in knowledge management in higher education system. *International Journal of Environmental and Science Education,* 12(5), pp. 1427–1434.

Sassower, R. (2022). The Neoliberal University and the common good. In: Cruickshank, J., Abbinnett, R. (eds.). *The Social Production of Knowledge in a Neoliberal Age: Debating the Challenges Facing Higher Education.* Lanham: Rowman & Littlefield Publishers.

Sata, R. (1989). Organizational learning-the key to management innovation. *Sloan Management Review,* 30(3), pp. 63–74.

Saule, K. et al. (2018). Development of the information and analytical system in the control of management of university scientific and educational activities. *Acta Polytechnica Hungarica,* 15(4), pp. 27–44.

Savoie, D. J. (1994). *Thatcher, Reagan, Mulroney: In Search of a New Bureaucracy.* Pittsburgh: University of Pittsburgh Press.

Sax, B. (2005). All that knowledge, and so what? Scholarship in the digital university. *On the Horizon,* 22(2), pp. 291–301.

Saxena, D. (2021). Big data for digital transformation of public services. In: Sandhu, K. (ed.). *Disruptive Technology and Digital Transformation for Business and Government.* Hershey: IGI Global, pp. 250–266. 10.4018/978-1-7998-8583-2.ch013

Scarlat, C. et al. (2012). Entrepreneurial vs. administrative management in not-for-profit organizations-public administration and universities. In: *Proceedings of the Management, Knowledge and Learning (MakeLearn) International Conference 2012*. Celje: International School for Social and Business Studies, pp. 671–682.

Schimank, U., Winnes, M. (2000). Beyond Humboldt? The relationship between teaching and research in European university systems. *Science and Public Policy*, 27(6), pp. 397–408.

Schlegelmilch, B. B., Penz, E. (2002). Knowledge management in marketing. *The Marketing Review*, 3(1), pp. 5–19.

Schmitz, A. et al. (2018). A systemic approach for universities in the knowledge-based society: a qualitative study. In: Ferreira, J. J. et al. (eds.). *Entrepreneurial Universities: Collaboration, Education and Policies*. Cheltenham: Edward Elgar Publishing, pp. 60–87.

Schoen, A. et al. (2006). *Strategic Management of University Research Activities: Methodological Guide*. PRIME Network Project 'Observatory of the European University (OEU)'. Available from: http://www.enid-europe.org/PRIME/documents/OEU_guide.pdf [14 November 2021].

Schofer, E., Meyer, J. W. (2005). The world-wide expansion of higher education in the twentieth century. *American Sociological Review*, 70, pp. 898–920.

Schofer, E., Ramirez, F. O., Meyer, J. W. (2021). The societal consequences of higher education. *Sociology of Education*, 94(1), pp. 1–19.

Scholtz, B., Kapeso, M. (2014). An m-learning framework for ERP systems in higher education. *Interactive Technology and Smart Education*, 11(4), pp.287–301.

Schulze-Cleven, T., Olson, J. R. (2017). Worlds of higher education transformed: Toward varieties of academic capitalism. *Higher Education*, 73(6), pp. 813–831.

Schuster, J. H. (1994). Emigration, internationalization, and "brain drain": Propensities among British academics. *Higher Education*, 28(4), pp. 437–452.

Scott P. (2007). Higher Education in Central and Eastern Europe. In: Forest, J.J. F., Altbach, P. G. (eds.). *International Handbook of Higher Education*. Dordrecht: Springer, pp. 423–441. 10.1007/978-1-4020-4012-2_21

Scott, J. C. (2006). The mission of the university: Medieval to postmodern transformations. *The Journal of Higher Education*, 77(1), pp. 1–39.

Scott, R. A. (2020). Leadership threats to shared governance in higher education. *AAUP Journal of Academic Freedom*, 11, pp. 1–17.

Sebastian, I. M. et al. (2020). How big old companies navigate digital transformation. In: Galliers, R. D., Leidner, D. E., Simeonova, B. (eds.). *Strategic Information Management*. London: Routledge, pp. 133–150. 10.4324/9780429286797

Secundo, G., Schiuma, G., Jones, P. (2019). Strategic knowledge management models and tools for entrepreneurial universities. *Management Decision*, 57(12), pp. 3217–3225. DOI: 10.1108/MD-12-2019-027

Sedziuviene, N., Vveinhardt, J. (2009). The paradigm of knowledge management in higher educational institutions. *Engineering Economics*, 65(5), pp. 79–90.

Sekerin, V. D. et al. (2018). Improving the quality of competence-oriented training of personnel at industrial enterprises. *Calitatea*, 19(165), pp. 68–72.

Selwyn, N., Henderson, M., Chao, S. H. (2018). 'You need a system': exploring the role of data in the administration of university students and courses. *Journal of Further and Higher Education*, 42(1), pp. 46–56.

Sendjaya, S., Sarros, J. C. (2002). Servant leadership: its origin, development, and application in organizations. *Journal of Leadership & Organizational Studies*, 9(2), pp. 57–64.

Seng, D. et al. (2018). Research on personalized recommendation of educational resources based on big data. *Educational Sciences: Theory & Practice*, 18(5), pp. 1948–1959. DOI: 10.12738/estp.2018.5.094

Serban, A. M., Luan, J. (2002). Overview of knowledge management. *New Directions for Institutional Research*, 2002(113), pp. 5–16.

Sergiovanni, T. J. (1987). The Theoretical Basis for Cultural Leadership. In: Sheive, L. T., Schoenheit, M. B. (eds.). *Leadership: Examining the Elusive*. Alexandria: Association for Supervision and Curriculum Development, pp. 120–133.

Shafiepoor, F., Atashac, M., Torabinahad, M. (2019). Making the scale of internationalization of universities. *Educational Administration Research*, 10(39), pp. 41–60.

Shahmandi, E. (2011). Competencies, roles and effective academic leadership in world class university. *International Journal of Business Administration*, 2(1), p. 44.

Shams, F. (2019). Managing academic identity tensions in a Canadian public university: the role of identity work in coping with managerialism. *Journal of Higher Education Policy and Management*, 41(6), pp. 619–632.

ShanghaiRanking Consultancy (2003). *2003 Academic Ranking of World Universities*. Available from: www.shanghairanking.com/rankings/arwu/2003 [3 June 2017].

Shannon, A. et al. (2008). Towards a model of the digital university: a generalized net model for producing course timetables. In: *2008 4th International IEEE Conference Intelligent Systems, Vol. 2*. Pistacaway: IEEE, pp. 16–25. DOI: 10.1109/IS.2008.4670542

Sharma, M. K., Jain, S. (2013). Leadership management: principles, models and theories. *Global Journal of Management and Business Studies*, 3(3), pp. 309–318.

Shattock, M. (1994). *The UGC and the Management of British Universities*. Buckingham: Society for Research into Higher Education and Open University Press.

Shattock, M. (2000). Strategic management in European universities in an age of increasing institutional self reliance. *Tertiary Education & Management*, 6(2), pp. 93–104.

Shattock, M. (2010a). The entrepreneurial university: an idea for its time. *London Review of Education*, 8(3), pp. 263–271.

Shattock, M. (2010b). *Managing Successful Universities*. 2nd ed. Maidenhead: Open University Press and McGraw-Hill Education.

Shattock, M., Temple, P. (2006). *Entrepreneurialism and the Knowledge Society: Some Conclusions From Cross National Studies*. Paper presented at the EAIR Forum, Rome 2006, pp. 1-2.

Shavit, Y. et al. (2022). Israel: Diversification, Expansion, and Inequality in Higher Education. In: Shavit, Y., Arum, R., Gamoran, A. (eds.). *Stratification in Higher Education: A Comparative Study*. Redwood City: Stanford University Press, pp. 39–62.

Shavit, Y., Blossfeld, H. P. (1993). *Persistent Inequality: Changing Educational AttainmentiIn Thirteen Countries*. New York: Avalon Publishing.

Shaw, M. J. et al. (2001). Knowledge management and data mining for marketing. *Decision Support Systems*, 31(1), pp. 127–137.

Sheail, P. (2018). Temporal flexibility in the digital university: full-time, part-time, flexitime. *Distance Education*, 39(4), pp. 462–479.

Shepherd, S. (2018). Managerialism: an ideal type. *Studies in Higher Education*, 43(9), pp. 1668–1678.

Shin, J. C. (2011). Organizational Effectiveness and University Rankings. In: Shin, J., Toutkoushian, R., Teichler, U. (eds.). *University Rankings: Theoretical Basis,*

Methodology and Impacts on Global Higher Education. Dordrecht: Springer, pp. 19–34. DOI: 10.1007/978-94-007-1116-7_2

Shin, J. C. (2014). The University as an Institution of Higher Learning: Evolution or Devolution? In: Shin, J., Teichler, U. (eds.). *The Future of the Post-Massified University at the Crossroads*. Cham: Springer, pp. 13–27. DOI: 10.1007/978-3-319-01523-1_2

Shin, J. C., Harman, G. (2009). New challenges for higher education: global and Asia-Pacific perspectives. *Asia Pacific Education Review*, 10(1), pp. 1–13.

Shore, C. (2008). Audit culture and illiberal governance universities and the politics of accountability. *Anthropological Theory*, 8(3), pp. 278–298.

Shore, C., Davidson, M. (2014). Beyond collusion and resistance: academic - management relations within the neoliberal university. *Learning and Teaching*, 7(1), pp. 12–28.

Shore, C., McLauchlan, L. (2012). 'Third mission' activities, commercialisation and academic entrepreneurs. *Social Anthropology*, 20(3), pp. 267–286.

Shrouf, F., Ordieres, J., Miragliotta, G. (2014). Smart factories in Industry 4.0: a review of the concept and of energy management approached in production based on the Internet of Things paradigm. In: *2014 IEEE International Conference on Industrial Engineering and Engineering Management*. Piscataway: IEEE, pp. 697–701.

Siala, H. (2013). Crowdsourcing project management to the 'open' community. *PM World Journal*, 10(2), pp. 1–17.

Sidrat, S., Frikha, M. A. (2018). Impact of the qualities of the manager and type of university on the development of the entrepreneurial university. *The Journal of High Technology Management Research*, 29(1), pp. 27–34.

Siekkinen, T., Pekkola, E., Carvalho, T. (2020). Change and continuity in the academic profession: Finnish universities as living labs. *Higher Education*, 79(3), pp. 533–551.

Sigahi, T. F. A. C., Saltorato, P. (2020). Academic capitalism: distinguishing without disjoining through classification schemes. *Higher Education*, 80(1), pp. 95–117.

Simon, H. A. (1960). *The New Science of Management Decision*. New York: Harper & Brothers. DOI: 10.1037/13978-000

Simonette, M., Magalhães, M., Spina, E. (2021). Digital Transformation of Academic Management: All the Tigers Come at Night. In: Burgos, D., Branch, J. W. (eds.). *Radical Solutions for Digital Transformation in Latin American Universities*. Singapore: Springer, pp. 77–92. DOI: 10.1007/978-981-16-3941-8_5

Sims Jr., H. P., Manz, Ch. C. (1996). *Company of Heroes: Unleashing the Power of Self-Leadership*. New York: John Wiley.

Sims, M. (2022). Academic leadership in a neoliberal managerial world: an auto-ethnography of my career. *Social Alternatives*, 41(1), pp. 70–75.

Sinclair, A. (1995). The chameleon of accountability: forms and discourses. *Accounting, Organizations and Society*, 20(2), pp. 219–237.

Singh, M. (2001). Re-inserting the 'public good' into higher education transformation. *KAGISANO Higher Education Discussion Series*, 1, pp. 8–18.

Sitnicki, M. (2018). Development of a model of digital research universities. *Baltic Journal of Economic Studies*, 4(1), pp. 311–318.

Slater, A., Moreton, R. (2007). Knowledge Management in Higher Education: A Case Study in a Large Modern UK University. In: Wojtkowski, W. et al. (eds.). *Advances in Information Systems Development*. Boston: Springer, pp. 371–382. DOI: 10.1007/978-0-387-70802-7_31

Slaughter, S., Rhoades, G. (2004). *Academic Capitalism and the New Economy*. Baltimore: The Johns Hopkins University Press.

Sloterdijk, P. (1987). *Critique of Cynical Reason*. Minneapolis: University of Minnesota Press.

Smagorinsky, P. et al. (2004). Praxis shock: making the transition from a student-centered university program to the corporate climate of schools. *English Education*, 36(3), pp. 214–245.

Smith, S. T. (2008). *Megatrends in Higher Education*. Thesis (PhD), University of North Texas.

Smyth, K., MacNeill, S., Johnston, B. (2015). Visioning the digital university-from institutional strategy to academic practice. *Educational Developments*, 16(2), pp. 13–17.

Sobral, S. R. et al. (2021). EU27 higher education institutions and COVID-19, year 2020. *International Journal of Environmental Research and Public Health*, 18(11), 5963, pp. 1–15. DOI: 10.3390/ijerph18115963

Söderhjelm, T. et al. (2018). Academic leadership: management of groups or leadership of teams? A multiple-case study on designing and implementing a team-based development programme for academic leadership. *Studies in Higher Education*, 43(2), pp. 201–216.

Soliman, F., Spooner, K. (2000). Strategies for implementing knowledge management: role of human resources management. *Journal of Knowledge Management*, 4(4), pp. 337–345.

Somers, P. et al. (2018). Academic capitalism and the entrepreneurial university: some perspectives from the Americas. *Roteiro*, 43(1), pp. 21–42.

Sørensen, M. P. et al. (2019). *The Responsible University: Exploring the Nordic Context and Beyond*. Cham: Palgrave Macmillan. DOI: 10.1007/978-3-030-25646-3

Sorkin, D. (1983). Wilhelm Von Humboldt: the theory and practice of self-formation (bildung), 1791-1810. *Journal of the History of Ideas*, 44(1), pp. 55–73. DOI: 10.2307/2709304

Sotirakou, T. (2004). Coping with conflict within the entrepreneurial university: threat or challenge for heads of departments in the UK higher education context. *International Review of Administrative Sciences*, 70(2), pp. 345–372.

Sperling, J. (1998). The American for-profit university: a model for the information economy. *Economic Affairs*, 18(3), pp. 11–16.

Sporn, B. (2001). Building adaptive universities: emerging organisational forms based on experiences of european and US universities. *Tertiary Education and Management*, 7(2), pp. 121–134. DOI: 10.1023/A:1011346201972

Sporn, B. (2007). Governance and Administration: Organizational and Structural Trends. In: Forest J. J. F., Altbach P. G. (eds.). *International Handbook of Higher Education*. Dordrecht: Springer, pp. 141–157. DOI: 10.1007/978-1-4020-4012-2_9

Stack, M. (2016). *Global University Rankings and the Mediatization of Higher Education*. London: Palgrave Macmillan. DOI: 10.1057/9781137475954

Stamps, D. (1998). The for-profit future of higher education. *Training*, 35(8), pp. 22–30.

Standing, G. (2011). *The Precariat: The New Dangerous Class*. London: Bloomsbury Academic.

Steenkamp, R. J. (2017). The exploration of university ethos-neoliberalism versus entrepreneurial wisdom. *Problems and Perspectives in Management*, 15(3), pp. 147–156.

Stehr, N. (1978). The ethos of science revisited. *Sociological Inquiry*, 48(3-4), pp. 172–196.

Steier, F. A. (2003). The changing nexus: tertiary education institutions, the marketplace and the state. *Higher Education Quarterly*, 57(2), pp. 158–180.

Stensaker, B., Vabø, A. (2013). Re-inventing shared governance: implications for organisational culture and institutional leadership. *Higher Education Quarterly*, 67(3), pp. 256–274.

Stensaker, B., Välimaa, J., Sarrico, C. (2012). *Managing Reform in Universities: The Dynamics of Culture, Identity and Organisational Change*. Basingstoke: Palgrave Macmillan.

Stephan, U., Pathak, S. (2016). Beyond cultural values? Cultural leadership ideals and entrepreneurship. *Journal of Business Venturing*, 31(5), pp. 505–523.

Stevens, R. E. et al. (2014). Differences in public and private university faculty perspectives of using collegiality in tenure and promotion decisions. *Global Education Journal*, 1, pp. 138–152.

Stiglitz, J. E. (2002). *Globalization and its Discontents*. New York: Norton.

Stogdill, R. (1974). *Handbook of Leadership: A Survey of Theory and Research*. New York: The Free Press.

Stogdill, R. M. (1950). Leadership, membership and organization. *Psychological Bulletin*, 47(1), pp. 1–14. DOI: 10.1037/h0053857

Storey, S. (1993). Total Quality Management Through BS 5750: A Case Study. In: Roger, E. (ed.). *Quality Assurance for University Teaching*. Bristol: The Society for Research into Higher Education and Open University Press, pp. 37–56.

Strathern, M. (2000). *Audit Cultures: Anthropological Studies in Accountability, Ethics, and the Academy*. London: Routledge.

Stringer, M., Finlay, C. (1993). Assuring Quality through Student Evaluation. In: Roger, E. (ed.). *Quality Assurance for University Teaching*. Bristol: The Society for Research into Higher Education and Open University Press, pp. 92–112.

Styron, R. A. (2015). Fostering innovation in higher education through entrepreneurial leadership. In: *Proceedings from The 13th International Conference on Education and Information Systems, Technologies and Applications: EISTA*.

Sulkowski, L. (2016b). Accountability of university: transition of public higher education. *Entrepreneurial Business and Economics Review*, 4(1), pp. 9–21.

Sulkowski, L., Dziedzic, J. (2020). Scientist organizational identity: the diversity of perspectives. *Journal of Intercultural Management*, 12(4), pp. 29–48.

Sulkowski, L., Fijałkowska, J., Dzimińska, M. (2019). Mergers in higher education institutions: a proposal of a novel conceptual model. *Managerial Finance*, 45(10/11), pp. 1469–1487. DOI: 10.1108/MF-01-2018-0048

Sulkowski, L., Seliga, R., Wozniak, A. (2019). Image and Brand Awareness in Universities in Consolidation Processes. In: Kantola, J., Nazir, S. (eds.). *Advances in Human Factors, Business Management and Leadership (AHFE 2019)*. Cham: Springer, pp. 608–615. DOI: 10.1007/978-3-030-20154-8_57

Sulkowski, L. (2009). Interpretative approach in management sciences. *Argumenta Oeconomica*, 2(23), pp. 127–149.

Sulkowski, L. (2016a). The Development of Post-academic Cultures in Higher Education Institutions. In: Teczke, J. (ed.). *State, Society and Business: Development of Contemporary Management*. Cracow and Saint Petersburg: International Management Fundation Publishing House, Cracow University of Economics, pp. 167–176.

Sulkowski, L. et al. (2020). Professionalization of university management in Poland. *Administratie si Management Public*, 35, pp. 167–183.

Sulkowski, L. (2022a). *Zarzadzanie Uniwersytetem Cyfrowym*. Warszawa: PWN.

Lenart-Gansiniec, R. Sulkowski L. (2022b). *Academic Crowdsourcing*. Routledge.

Sunalai, S., Beyerlein, M. (2015). Exploring knowledge management in higher education institutions: processes, influences, and outcomes. *Academy of Educational Leadership Journal*, 19(3), pp. 289–308.

Svensson, P., Klofsten, M., Etzkowitz, H. (2012). An entrepreneurial university strategy for renewing a declining industrial city: the Norrköping way. *European Planning Studies*, 20(4), pp. 505–525.

Svetlik, I., Stavrou-Costea, E. (2007). Connecting human resources management and knowledge management. *International Journal of Manpower*, 28(3/4), pp. 197–206.

Szelényi, K., Rhoads, R. A. (2013). Academic culture and citizenship in transitional societies: case studies from China and Hungary. *Higher Education*, 66(4), pp. 425–438.

Taberner, A. M. (2018). The marketisation of the English higher education sector and its impact on academic staff and the nature of their work. *International Journal of Organizational Analysis*, 26(1), pp. 129–152.

Tabrizi, B. et al. (2019). Digital transformation is not about technology. *Harvard Business Review*, 13(March), pp. 1–6.

Takagi, H. (2022). A Comparative Perspective between Japanese and Anglo-American Universities. In: Côté, J. E., Pickard, S. (eds.). *Routledge Handbook of the Sociology of Higher Education*. London: Routledge.

Tambotoh, J. J. et al. (2016). Software Quality Model for Internet of Things Governance. In: *2016 International Conference on Data and Software Engineering (ICoDSE)*. Piscataway: IEEE, pp. 1–6. DOI: 10.1109/ICODSE.2016.7936138

Tamtik, M. (2017). Who governs the internationalization of higher education? A comparative analysis of macro-regional policies in Canada and the European Union. *Comparative and International Education*, 46(1), pp. 1–15.

Tang, T. (2011). Marketing higher education across borders: a cross-cultural analysis of university websites in the US and China. *Chinese Journal of Communication*, 4(4), pp. 417–429.

Tao, Y. (2010). On the transformation and development trends of organizational structure in modern university. *Journal of Liaoning Educational Administration Institute*, 7, pp. 21–23.

Tarí, J. J. (2011). Research into quality management and social responsibility. *Journal of Business Ethics*, 102(4), pp. 623–638.

Tavernier, K. (1991). Strategic evaluation in university management. *Higher Education Management*, 3(3), pp. 257–268.

Taylor, A. (2017). Perspectives on the university as a business: the corporate management structure, neoliberalism and higher education. *Journal for Critical Education Policy Studies*, 15(1), pp. 108–135.

Taylor, J. (2010). The Management of Internationalization in Higher Education. In: Maringe, F., Foskett, N. (eds.). *Globalization and Internationalization in Higher Education: Theoretical, Strategic and Management Perspectives*. London: Bloomsbury Academic, pp. 97–108. DOI: 10.5040/9781350091122.ch-0007

Taylor, M. P. (2012). The entrepreneurial university in the twenty-first century. *London Review of Education*, 10(3), pp. 289–305.

Telli, S. G., Aydin, S. (2021). Digitalization of marketing education: new approaches for universities in the post-Covid-19 era. *Üniversite Araştırmaları Dergisi*, 4(1), pp. 61–74.

Terman, L. M. (1904). A preliminary study in the psychology and pedagogy of leadership. *The Pedagogical Seminary*, 11(4), pp. 413–483.

Thomas, P., Wilson, J., Leeds, O. (2013). Constructing 'the history of strategic management': a critical analysis of the academic discourse. *Business History*, 55(7), pp. 1119–1142.

Thompson, N., Franz, N. K. (2017). Decision points in academic leadership development as an engaged scholar: to lead or not to lead. *Journal of Higher Education Outreach and Engagement*, 9(2), pp. 78–80.

Thorn, K., Soo, M. (2006). *Latin American Universities and the Third Mission: Trends, Challenges and Policy Options*. Washington: World Bank. URI: http://hdl.handle.net/10986/9301.

Thornton, M. (2016). Public universities, managerialism and the value of higher education. *Prometheus*, 34(3-4), pp. 257–260. DOI: 10.1080/08109028.2017.1341676

Thorp, H., Goldstein, B. (2013). *Engines of Innovation: The Entrepreneurial University in the Twenty-First Century*. 2nd ed. Chapel Hill: University of North Carolina Press.

Tian, H. (2011). On strategies of operation and management of university brand. *Journal of Educational Science of Hunan Normal University*, 4, pp. 39–43.

Tian, J., Nakamori, Y., Wierzbicki, A. P. (2009). Knowledge management and knowledge creation in academia: a study based on surveys in a Japanese research university. *Journal of Knowledge Management*, 13, pp. 76–92.

Tian, Y., Xiang, D. (2008). On academic power development in early medieval universities. *Journal of Hunan University of Science & Technology (Social Science Edition)*, 4, pp. 211–247.

Tierney, W. G. (2004). Globalization and educational reform: the challenges ahead. *Journal of Hispanic Higher Education*, 3(1), pp. 5–20.

Tight, M. (2019a). The neoliberal turn in higher education. *Higher Education Quarterly*, 73(3), pp. 273-28.

Tight, M. (2019b). Mass higher education and massification. *Higher Education Policy*, 32(1), pp. 93–108.

Tihanyi, L., Graffin, S., George, G. (2014). Rethinking governance in management research. *Academy of Management Journal*, 57(6), pp. 1535–1543.

Tilak, J. B. G. (2008a). *Current Trends in Private Higher Education in Asia*. Paper presented at the Privatization in Higher Education Conference, Haifa, Samuel Neemen Institute, The Technion, 07 January 2008.

Tilak, J. B. G. (2008b). Higher education: a public good or a commodity for trade? Commitment to higher education or commitment of higher education to trade. *Prospects*, 38(4), pp. 449–466.

Tilak, J. B. G. (2016). Global rankings, world-class universities and dilemma in higher education policy in India. *Higher Education for the Future*, 3(2), pp. 126–143.

Times Higher Education (2021). *THE Impact Rankings 2021*. Available from https://www.timeshighereducation.com/rankings/impact/2021 [1 August 2021].

Titov, E., Tuulik, K. (2013). Management of higher education institution: quality management through value based management. *American International Journal of Contemporary Research*, 3(9), pp. 29–41.

Tomkins, C., Green, R. (1988). An experiment in the use of data envelopment analysis for evaluating the efficiency of UK university departments of accounting. *Financial Accountability & Management*, 4(2), pp. 147–164.

Toshmali, G. et al. (2020). Conceptualization of entrepreneurial university and pattern design of third generation university. *Iran Occupational Health*, 17(1), pp. 415–436.

Trakman, L. (2008). Modelling university governance. *Higher Education Quarterly*, 62(1-2), pp. 63–83.

Trapitsin, S. Y., Granichina, O. A., Granichin, O. N. (2017). Information and mathematical models for evaluation of the effectiveness and quality of the university. In:

2017 *International Conference "Quality Management, Transport and Information Security, Information Technologies" (IT&QM&IS)*. Piscataway: IEEE, pp. 287–291. DOI: 10.11 09/ITMQIS.2017.8085813

Trenkle, J. (2019). Survival in the Digital Age: A Framework for Formulating a Digital Transformation Strategy in SME. In: *Proceedings of the 19th International Conference on Electronic Business*. Newcastle upon Tyne: ICEB, pp. 428–442.

Trigg, A. B. (2001). Veblen, Bourdieu, and conspicuous consumption. *Journal of Economic Issues*, 35(1), pp. 99–115.

Trow, M. (2006). Reflections on the Transition from Elite to Mass to Universal Access: FOrms and Phases of Higher Education in Modern Societies Science WWII. In: Forest, J. J. F., Altbach, P. G. (eds.). *International Handbook of Higher Education*. Dordrecht: Springer, pp. 243–280. DOI: 10.1007/978-1-4020-4012-2_13

Trowler, P. ed. (2002). *Higher Education Policy and Institutional Change: Intentions and Outcomes in Turbulent Environments*. Buckingham: Open University Press and the Society for Research into Higher Education.

Tsay, V. et al. (2018). Peculiarities of the organizational changes in higher educational institutions. *Journal of Advanced Research in Law and Economics*, 9(1), pp. 323–332. DOI: 10.14505/jarle.v9.1(31).38

Tucker, B. P., Parker, L. D. (2019). The question of research relevance: a university management perspective. *Accounting, Auditing & Accountability Journal*, 33(6), pp. 1247–1275.

Tytherleigh, M. Y. et al. (2005). Occupational stress in UK higher education institutions: a comparative study of all staff categories. *Higher Education Research and Development*, 24(1), pp. 41–61. DOI: 10.1080/07294360520000318569

U.S. News & World Report L.P. (2017). *U.S. News & World Report*. Available from: www.usnews.com [3 June 2017].

Ubi, J. et al. (2012). *Data Mining the MNC Like Internal Co-Opetition Duality in a University Context*. arXiv preprint. arXiv:1208.5438.

Ulewicz, R. (2017). The role of stakeholders in quality assurance in higher education. *Human Resources Management & Ergonomics*, 11(1), pp. 93–107.

U-Multirank (2017). *World University Rankings U-Multirank*. Available from: www. umultirank.org [3 June 2017].

Unger, M., Polt, W. (2017). The knowledge triangle between research, education and innovation: a conceptual discussion. *Форсайт*, 11(2), pp. 10–26. DOI: 10.17323/25 00-2597.2017.2.10.26

Urdari, C., Farcas, T. V., Tiron-Tudor, A. (2017). Assessing the legitimacy of HEIs' contributions to society: the perspective of international rankings. *Sustainability Accounting, Management and Policy Journal*, 8(2), pp. 191–215.

Uzzi, B. (1996). The sources and consequences of embeddedness for the economic performance of organizations: the network effect. *American Sociological Review*, 61(4), pp. 674–698. DOI: 10.2307/2096399

Vaiman, V., Scullion, H., Collings, D. (2012). Talent management decision making. *Management Decision*, 50(5), pp. 925–941. DOI: 10.1108/00251741211227663

Valladares, L. (2021). Post-truth and education. *Science & Education*, ahead-of-print, pp. 1–27. DOI: 10.1007/s11191-021-00293-0

Vallé, H. A. C. et al. (2016). New Paradigms for University Management. In: Leitão, J., Alves, H. (eds.). *Entrepreneurial and Innovative Practices in Public Institutions*. Cham: Springer, pp. 19–39. DOI: 10.1007/978-3-319-32091-5_2 van Breukelen, W., Schyns, B., Le Blanc, P. (2006). Leader-member exchange theory and research: accomplishments and future challenges. *Leadership*, 2(3), pp. 295–316.

van Dalen, H. P. (2021). How the publish-or-perish principle divides a science: the case of economists. *Scientometrics*, 126(2), pp. 1675–1694.

Van de Walle, S., van Delft, R. (2014). Publishing in public administration: issues with defining, comparing and ranking the output of universities. *International Public Management Journal*, 18(1), pp. 87–107. DOI: 10.1080/10967494.2014.972482

Van der Meij, L., Schaveling, J., van Vugt, M. (2016). Basal testosterone, leadership and dominance: field study and meta-analysis. *Psychoneuroendocrinology*, 72, pp. 72–79. DOI: 10.1016/j.psyneuen.2016.06.005

Van der Sluis, M. E., Reezigt, G. J., Borghans, L. (2017). Implementing new public management in educational policy. *Educational Policy*, 31(3), pp. 303–329.

van der Wende, M. C. (2014). On Mergers and Missions: Implications for Institutional Governance and Government Steering. In: Wang, Q., Cheng, Y., Cai Liu, N. (eds.). *Global Outreach of World-Class Universities: How It is Affecting Higher Education Systems*. Shanghai: Sense Publishers, pp. 137–153.

van Dierendonck, D. (2011). Servant leadership: a review and synthesis. *Journal of Management*, 37(4), pp. 1228–1261.

van Dijk, J. A. (1999). The one-dimensional network society of Manuel Castells. *New Media & Society*, 1(1), pp. 127–138. DOI: 10.1177/1461444899001001015

van Laar, J. (2014). Higher Education in Forestry and the Way a PhD Track at Wageningen University Is Organised. In: Schmidt, P. et al. (eds.). *Bologna Cycles 1 to 3 and Higher Forest Education – Objectives and Reality. Proceedings of the SILVA Network Conference held at the Saint Petersburg State Forest Technical Academy, Saint Petersburg, Russian Federation, September 14th – September 16th, 2011*. Freiburg im Breisgau: University of Freiburg, pp. 28–37.

van Raan, A. (1997). Scientometrics: state-of-the-art. *Scientometrics*, 38(1), pp. 205–218.

van Vought, F. (1989). *Governmental Strategies and Innovation in Higher Education*. London: Jessica Kingsley Publishers.

van Winkel, M. A. et al. (2018). Identities of research-active academics in new universities: towards a complete academic profession cross-cutting different worlds of practice. *Journal of Further and Higher Education*, 42(4), pp. 539–555.

Varghese, N. V. (2015). Challenges of massification of higher education in India. *CPRHE Research Papers*, 1, pp. 1–52.

Vedder, P. (1994). Global measurement of the quality of education: a help to developing countries?. *International Review of Education*, 40(1), pp. 5–17.

Veer-Ramjeawon, P., Rowley, J. (2020). Embedding knowledge management in higher education institutions (HEIs): a comparison between two countries. *Studies in Higher Education*, 45(11), pp. 2324–2340.

Vefago, Y. B., Trierweiller, A. C., Barcellos de Paula, L. (2020). The third mission of universities: the entrepreneurial university. *Brazilian Journal of Operations & Production Management*, 17(4), pp. 1–9. DOI: 10.14488/BJOPM.2020.042

Veiga, A., Magalhaes, A., Amaral, A. (2015). From Collegial Governance to Boardism: Reconfiguring Governance in Higher Education. In: Huisman, J. et al. (eds.). *The Palgrave International Handbook of Higher Education Policy and Governance*. London: Palgrave Macmillan, pp. 398–416. DOI: 10.1007/978-1-137-45617-5_22

Velásquez, R. M. A., Lara, J. V. M. (2021). Knowledge management in two universities before and during the COVID-19 effect in Peru. *Technology in Society*, 64, 101479.DOI: 10.1016/j.techsoc.2020.101479

Velazquez, L. et al. (2006). Sustainable university: what can be the matter? *Journal of Cleaner Production*, 14(9-11), pp. 810–819.

Verdouw, C. N. et al. (2015). A control model for object virtualization in supply chain management. *Computers in Industry*, 68, pp. 116–131.

Vial, G. (2019). Understanding digital transformation: a review and a research agenda. *The Journal of Strategic Information Systems*, 28(2), pp. 118–144.

Vicente-Saez, R., Martinez-Fuentes, C. (2018). Open Science now: a systematic literature review for an integrated definition. *Journal of Business Research*, 88, pp. 428–436.

Vidal, J., Ferreira, C. (2020). Universities under pressure: the impact of international university rankings. *Journal of New Approaches in Educational Research*, 9(2), pp. 181–193.

Vidal, J., Ferreira, C., Vieira, M. J. (2017). Connecting universities and societies: types of activities and success factors. In: *XVIII Congreso Internacional de Investigación Educativa. Interdisciplinaridad y Transferencia*. Barcelona: AIDIPE, pp. 1011–1018.

Višňovský, E. (2019). The university as a philosophical problem. *Human Affairs*, 29(2), pp. 235–246.

Vlăsceanu, L., Grünberg, L., Pârlea, D. (2004). *Quality Assurance and Accreditation: A Glossary of Basic Terms and Definitions*. Bucharest: UNESCO-CEPES.

Vogel, A., Kaghan, W. N. (2001). Bureaucrats, brokers, and the entrepreneurial university. *Organization*, 8(2), pp. 358–364.

Volkova, V. N. et al. (2017). The Impact of NBIC-Technology Development on Engineering and Management Personnel Training. In: *2017 IEEE VI Forum Strategic Partnership of Universities and Enterprises of Hi-Tech Branches (Science. Education. Innovations), SPUE 2017*. Piscataway: IEEE, pp. 51–54. DOI: 10.1109/IVForum.2017.8246048

von Leipzig, T. et al. (2017). Initialising customer-oriented digital transformation in enterprises. *Procedia Manufacturing*, 8, pp. 517–524.

Vorley, T., Nelles, J. (2008). (Re)conceptualising the academy: institutional development of and beyond the third mission. *Higher Education Management and Policy*, 20(3), pp. 1–17.

Voss, R., Gruber, T., Szmigin, I. (2007). Service quality in higher education: the role of student expectations. *Journal of Business Research*, 60(9), pp. 949–959.

Waldmann, M. R., Hagmayer, Y. (2005). Seeing versus doing: two modes of accessing causal knowledge. *Journal of Experimental Psychology: Learning, Memory, and Cognition*, 31(2), pp. 216–227.

Wamsley, G. L. et al. (2020). A Legitimate Role for Bureaucracy in Democratic Governance. In: Wamsley, G. L. et al. (eds.). *The State of Public Bureaucracy*. London: Routledge, pp. 59–86.

Wan, C. (2011). Reforming higher education in Hong Kong towards post-massification: the first decade and challenges ahead. *Journal of Higher Education Policy and Management*, 33(2), pp. 115–129.

Wang, S. Y., Chang, L. (2019). Research on the influence of university organizational structure construction on social service capability. In: *Proceedings of the 2019 4th International Conference on Humanities Science and Society Development (ICHSSD 2019)*. Zhengzhou: Atlantis Press, pp. 527–530. DOI: 10.2991/ichssd-19.2019.106

Wang, Y. (2008). Internationalization in higher education in China: a practitioner's reflection. *Higher Education Policy*, 21(4), pp. 505–517.

Wang, Y. (2021). Educational management system of colleges and universities based on embedded system and artificial intelligence. *Microprocessors and Microsystems*, 82, 103884. DOI: 10.1016/j.micpro.2021.103884

Wang, Y., Liu, Q., Chen, R. (2021). Comparative study on the internal governance models of Chinese and European universities. *Asia Europe Journal*, 20(9), pp. 1–21. DOI: 10.1007/s10308-021-00636-0

Warrick, D. D. (1981). Leadership styles and their consequences. *Journal of Experiential Learning and Simulation*, 3(4), pp. 155–172.

Wasono, L. W., Furinto, A. (2018). The effect of digital leadership and innovation management for incumbent telecommunication company in the digital disruptive era. *International Journal of Engineering and Technology*, 7, pp. 125–130.

Watermeyer, R. (2019). *Competitive Accountability in Academic Life: The Struggle for Social Impact and Public Legitimacy*. Cheltenham: Edward Elgar Publishing.

Watermeyer, R., Lewis, J. (2018). Institutionalizing public engagement through research in UK universities: perceptions, predictions and paradoxes concerning the state of the art. *Studies in Higher Education*, 43(9), pp. 1612–1624.

Watson, T. J. (2001). Beyond managerism: negotiated narratives and critical management education in practice. *British Journal of Management*, 12(4), pp. 385–396.

Webb, A., McQuaid, R. W., Webster, C. W. R. (2021). Moving learning online and the COVID-19 pandemic: a university response. *World Journal of Science, Technology and Sustainable Development*, 18(1), pp. 1–19.

Weber, M. (1947). *The Theory of Social and Economic Organization*. New York: Free Press.

Webster, E., Mosoetsa, S. (2002). At the chalk face: managerialism and the changing academic workplace 1995-2001. *Transformation*, 48, pp. 59–82.

Weick, K. E. (1976). Educational organizations as loosely coupled systems. *Administrative Science Quarterly*, 21, pp. 1–19.

Weick, K. E. (1980). *Loosely Coupled Systems: A Thick Interpretation*. Unpublished manuscript. At: Graduate School of Business and Public Service, Cornell University.

Weingart, P. (2004). Impact of bibliometrics upon the science system: inadvertent consequences? *Scientometrics*, 62(1), pp. 117–131.

Welch, A. (2012). Academic Salaries, Massification and the Rise of an Underclass in Australia. In: Altbach, P. G. (ed.). *Paying the Professoriate: A Global Comparison of Compensation and Contracts*. London: Routledge, pp. 61–71.

Welch, L. S., Luostarinen, L. (1988). Internationalization: evolution of a concept. *Journal of General Management*, 14(2), pp. 34–55. DOI: 10.1177/030630708801400203

Welsh, H. A. (2010). Higher education in Germany: fragmented change amid paradigm shifts. *German Politics and Society*, 28(2), pp. 53–70.

Welsh, J., Dey, S. (2002). Quality measurement and quality assurance in higher education. *Quality Assurance in Education*, 10(1), pp. 17–25.

Wessels, L. (2020). *How South African Universities Can Contribute to Preparing the Future Workforce for the Fourth Industrial Revolution*. Thesis (PhD), Stellenbosch University.

Westerheijden, D. F. (2018). University governance in the United Kingdom, the Netherlands and Japan: autonomy and shared governance after new public management reforms. *Nagoya Journal of Higher Education*, 18, pp. 199–220.

Whorton Jr, J. W., Gibson, F. K., Dunn, D. D. (1986). The culture of university public service: a national survey of the perspectives of users and providers. *Public Administration Review*, 46(1), pp. 38–47.

Wiesel, F., Modell, S. (2014). From new public management to new public governance? Hybridization and implications for public sector consumerism. *Financial Accountability & Management*, 30(2), pp. 175–205.

Wikipedia Contributors (2017). *Simonyi professor for the public understanding of science.* Wikipedia. Available from: https://en.wikipedia.org/wiki/Simonyi_Professor_for_the_Public_Understanding_of_Science [3 June 2017].

Willett, B. P. (2012). Fostering leadership through organizational structure. *Journal of Case Studies in Education,* 4, pp. 1–9.

Williams, B. T. 2013. Control and the classroom in the digital university: the effect of course management systems on pedaogy. In: Goodfellow, R., Lea, M. R. (eds.). *Literacy in the Digital University: Critical Perspectives on Learning, Scholarship and Technology.* Abingdon: Routledge and Society for Research into Higher Education, pp. 173–184.

Williams, D. (2012). On the way to the entrepreneurial university: experience of Great Britain. *University Management: Practice and Analysis,* (6), pp. 51–58.

Willmott, H. (1995). Managing the academics: commodification and control in the development of university education in the UK. *Human Relations,* 48(9), pp. 993–1027.

Willmott, K. E., Wall, A. F. (2014). The entrepreneurial leadership turn in higher education. In: Eden, B. L., Fagan, J. C. (eds.). *Leadership in Academic Libraries Today: Connecting Theory to Practice.* Lanham: Rowman & Littlefield, pp. 163–184.

Wilson III, E. J. et al. (2004). Leadership in the digital age. *Encyclopedia of Leadership,* 4, pp. 858–861.

Wilson, D. D., Collier, D. A. (2000). An empirical investigation of the Malcolm Baldrige National Quality Award causal model. *Decision Sciences,* 31(2), pp. 361–383.

Winefield, A. H. et al. (2003). Occupational stress in Australian University Staff: results from a national survey. *International Journal of Stress Management,* 10(1), pp. 51–63. DOI: 10.1037/1072-5245.10.1.51

Wipawayangkool, K., Teng, J. T. (2016). Assessing tacit knowledge and sharing intention: a knowledge internalization perspective. *Knowledge and Process Management,* 23(3), pp. 194–206.

Wisdom, J. P. (2019). Approaching change in a challenging environment: Applying implementation science to academic administration. *The Psychologist-Manager Journal,* 22(3-4), pp. 133–153. DOI: 10.1037/mgr0000089

Wissema, J. G. (2009). *Towards the Third Generation University: Managing the University in Transition.* Cheltenham: Edward Elgar Publishing.

Wittrock, B. (1993). The Modern University: THe Three Transformations. In: Rothblatt, S., Wittrock, B. (eds.). (1993). *The European and American University Since 1800: Historical and Sociological Essays.* Cambridge: Cambridge University Press, pp. 303–362.

Wolter, A. (2007). From the Academic Republic to the Managerial University: The Implementation of New Governance Structures in German Higher Education. In: University of Tsukuba (ed.). *Reforms of Higher Education in Six Countries: Commonalities and Differences.* Tokyo: University of Tsukuba, pp. 111–132.

Wong, J. Y., Wan, T. H., Chen, H. C. (2018). The innovative grant of university-industry-research cooperation: a case study for Taiwan's technology development programs. *International Journal of Innovation Science,* 10(3), pp. 316–332. DOI: 10.1108/IJIS-01-2017-0004

Wongrassamee, S., Simmons, E. L., Gardiner, P. D. (2003). Performance measurement tools: the balanced scorecard and the EFQM excellence model. *Measuring Business Excellence,* 7(1), pp. 14–29.

Wrangham, R. W., Peterson, D. (1996). *Demonic Males: Apes and the Origins of Human Violence.* Houghton: Mifflin Harcourt.

Wu, T., Naidoo, V. (2016). The role of international marketing in higher education. In: Wu, T., Naidoo, V. (eds.). *International Marketing of Higher Education*. New York: Palgrave Macmillan, pp. 3–9. DOI: 10.1057/978-1-137-54291-5_1

Wu, W., & Zhou, Y. (2012). The third mission stalled? Universities in China's technological progress. *The Journal of Technology Transfer*, 37(6), pp. 812–827.

Wu, X. (2017). Research on college students' entrepreneurial model. In: *Proceedings of the 2017 2nd International Seminar on Education Innovation and Economic Management (SEIEM 2017)*. Zhengzhou: Atlantis Press, pp. 197–199. DOI: 10.2991/seiem-17. 2018.49

Xiaozhou, X. & Shan, X. (2012). The changing role of the academic: historical and comparative perspectives. In The Global University. New York: Palgrave Macmillan, pp. 153–173.

Xu, X. (2020). Performing under 'the baton of administrative power'? Chinese academics' responses to incentives for international publications. *Research Evaluation*, 29(1), pp. 87–99.

Xue, Y., & Zhu, C. (2022). Review of research on knowledge domains in university governance: Mapping literature in English and Chinese. *European Journal of Education*, 57(1), pp. 49–64.

Yahya, S., Goh, W. K. (2002). Managing human resources toward achieving knowledge management. *Journal of Knowledge Management*, 6(5), pp. 457–468.

Yang, H. et al. (2022). Design and implementation of university audit platform based on big data analysis. *Procedia Computer Science*, 202, pp. 115–121.

Yates, L. et al. (2017). New public management and the changing governance of universities. In: Yates, L. et al. (eds.). *Knowledge at the Crossroads?*. Singapore: Springer, pp. 59–75. DOI: 10.1007/978-981-10-2081-0_4

Yi, J., Oh, Y. K. (2021). Does brand type affect what consumers discuss? A comparison of attribute-based reviews of value and premium brands of an innovative product. *Internet Research: Electronic Networking Applications and Policy*, 32(2), pp. 606–619. DOI: 10.1108/INTR-08-2020-0478

Yielder J., Codling, A. (2004). Management and leadership in the contemporary university. *Journal of Higher Education Policy and Management*, 26(3), pp. 315–328.

Yielder, J., Codling, A. (2004). Management and leadership in the contemporary university. *Journal of Higher Education Policy and Management*, 26(3), pp. 315–328. DOI: 10.1080/1360080042000290177

Yoshikawa, T., Nippa, M., Chua, G. (2021). Global shift towards stakeholder-oriented corporate governance? Evidence from the scholarly literature and future research opportunities. *Multinational Business Review*, 29(3), pp. 321–347. DOI: 10.1108/ MBR-10-2020-0200

Yu, E. S., Mylopoulos, J. (1996). Using goals, rules and methods to support reasoning in business process reengineering. *Intelligent Systems in Accounting, Finance & Management*, 5(1), pp. 1–13.

Yu, J. (2021). Lost in lockdown? The impact of COVID-19 on Chinese international student mobility. *Journal of International Students*, 11(S2), pp. 1–18. DOI: 10.32674/ jis.v11iS2.3575

Yudianto, I. et al. (2021). The influence of good university governance and intellectual capital on university performance in Indonesia. *Academic Journal of Interdisciplinary Studies*, 10(1), p. 57. DOI: 10.36941/ajis-2021-0006

Zabrodska, K. et al. (2011). Bullying as intra-active process in neoliberal universities. *Qualitative Inquiry*, 17(8), pp. 709–719.

Zaharia, S. E., Gibert, E. (2005). The entrepreneurial university in the knowledge society. *Higher Education in Europe*, 30(1), pp. 31–40.

Zaitseva, E., Zapariy, V. (2016). The role of the university corporate culture in university management. In: Loster, T., Pavelka, T. (eds.). *10th International Days of Statistics and Economics*. Prague: Melandrium, pp. 2089–2095.

Zamani, A. (2021). Establishing and improving of tacit knowledge sharing network in higher education. *Journal of Studies in Library and Information Science*, 13(4). DOI: 10.22 055/slis.2021.34442.1773

Zapp, M., Lerch, J. C. (2020). Imagining the world: conceptions and determinants of internationalization in higher education curricula worldwide. *Sociology of Education*, 93(4), pp. 372–392.

Zeit Campus (2017). *CHE Ranking*. Available from: ranking.zeit.de/che/en [3 June 2017].

Zemsky, R. (2005). *On being market smart and mission centered*. Presentation at the International Seminar on University Management and Higher Education Policies: Trends, Issues and Prospects, Tokyo, September 19-20, 2005.

Zerem, E., Kunosić, S. (2021). Influence of development of scientometrics on the outlook and functioning of the science system in the world and in individual countries. *Special Editions ANUBiH CC*, 18, pp. 365–384. DOI: 10.5644/PI2021.200.18

Zhang, L., Wang, Y. (2010). Research on Transformation of University Organizational Structure Based on CE Theory. In: *2010 2nd International Conference on E-business and Information System Security*. Piscataway: IEEE, pp. 1–4. DOI: 10.1109/EBISS.2010. 5473741

Zhang, L., Yang, J. (2011). The fuzzy comprehensive evaluation of science and technological achievements with considered expert weight. *Science & Technology and Economy*, 4, pp. 1–5.

Zhang, Y., Song, L., Huang, W. (2016). Research on the college students' competition credit-assisted management system for practical universities. In: *Proceedings of the 6th International Conference on Electronic, Mechanical, Information and Management Society*. Zhengzhou: Atlantis Press, pp. 167–173. DOI: 10.2991/emim-16.2016.38

Zhang, Z. et al. (2018). *Framing alternative policies to achieve university mission: a case study of a Chinese regional university*. Paper presented at the 36th International System Dynamics Conference, Reykjavík, Iceland, 6-10 August 2018.

Zhao, F. (2003). Transforming quality in research supervision: a knowledge-management approach. *Quality in Higher Education*, 9(2), pp. 187–197.

Zhao, F., Chen, Z. F., Zhang, X. J. (2011). Reflect on academic human resources management in China's colleges and universities: based on the perspective of knowledge workers management. *Scientific Management Research*, 4, pp. 69–73.

Zhigang, Q. (2012). The legitimacy crisis of academic power and university organizational structure change. *Research in Educational Development*, 4, pp. 48–52.

Zhou, W. (2005). Establishing public higher education expenditures accountability and performance system of China. *Journal of Central University of Finance & Economics*, 8, pp. 12–16.

Ziman, J. (2002). *Real Science*. Cambridge: Cambridge University Press.

Zomer, A., Benneworth, P. (2011). The rise of the university's third mission. In: Enders, J., de Boer, H. F., Westerheijden D. F. (eds.). *Reform of Higher Education in Europe.* Rotterdam: SensePublishers, pp. 81–101. DOI: 10.1007/978-94-6091-555-0_6

Zumeta, W. M. (2011). What does it mean to be accountable? Dimensions and implications of higher education's public accountability. *The Review of Higher Education,* 35(1), pp. 131–148.

Zwick, D., Dholakia, N. (2004). Consumer subjectivity in the age of internet: the radical concept of marketing control through customer relationship management. *Information and Organization,* 14(3), pp. 211–236.

Index

Note: **Bold** page numbers refer to tables and *italic* page numbers refer to figures.